Robert Stam

Literature
through Film

Realism, Magic, and the Art of Adaptation

Blackwell
Publishing

© 2005 by Robert Stam

BLACKWELL PUBLISHING
350 Main Street, Malden, MA 02148–5020, USA
108 Cowley Road, Oxford OX4 1JF, UK
550 Swanston Street, Carlton, Victoria 3053, Australia

First published 2005 by Blackwell Publishing Ltd

Library of Congress Cataloging-in-Publication Data

Stam, Robert, 1941–
Literature through film : realism, magic, and the art of adaptation / Robert Stam.
p. cm.
Includes bibliographical references and index.
ISBN 1–4051–0287–X (hard. : alk. paper) — ISBN 1–4051–0288–8 (pbk. : alk. paper)
1. Film adaptations—History and criticism.   2. Motion pictures and literature.
I. Title.

PN1997.85.S76 2004
791.43'6 — dc22
2004011846

A catalogue record for this title is available from the British Library.

Set in 9.75/14pt Bell Gothic
by Graphicraft Ltd, Hong Kong
Printed and bound in the United Kingdom
by TJ International Ltd, Padstow, Cornwall

The publisher's policy is to use permanent paper from mills that operate a
sustainable forestry policy, and which has been manufactured from pulp
processed using acid-free and elementary chlorine-free practices. Furthermore,
the publisher ensures that the text paper and cover board used have met
acceptable environmental accreditation standards.

For further information on
Blackwell Publishing, visit our website:
http://www.blackwellpublishing.com

Literature Through Film

In memory of Edward Said

Contents

Contents

Illustrations

Illustrations

Preface

Literature Through Film: Realism, Magic, and the Art of Adaptation is part of a three-volume series devoted to literature and film, and, more specifically, to the history, theory, and practice of the filmic adaptations of novels. This first volume approaches the subject from the specific angle of the history of the novel. Arranged according to the chronology of the literary source texts rather than that of their filmic adaptations, *Literature Through Film* highlights key moments and trends in the history of the novel from *Don Quixote* and *Robinson Crusoe* to Nabokov's *Lolita* and Carpentier's *Concierto barroco*. All the novels are treated in their own terms, as novels, but also as seen **through** their various filmic adaptations. In each case, I stress the historical importance of the novel, its central narrative and aesthetic strategies, and its verbal texture, before moving to the "re-readings" of these same novels as "performed" by film. In sum, I provide an historicized overview of privileged moments in the development of the novel, but as refracted and "rewritten" in the form of cinematic adaptations.

The second volume, *Literature and Film: A Guide to the Theory and Practice of Film Adaptation* (co-edited with Alessandra Raengo), consists of a wide range of essays, virtually all previously unpublished, covering a wide spectrum of subjects and problematics. My introductory essay on "The Theory and Practice of Adaptation" is followed by a wide variety of essays concerning single novels/adaptations, essays that both illustrate and problematize the methodologies.

The third book in the series, entitled *A Companion to Literature and Film* (also co-edited with Alessandra Raengo), complements the first two volumes by exploring the broader question of the interface between the literary and the filmic. More specifically, the *Companion* features theoretical and analytical essays, again previously unpublished, concerning such issues as: (1) **the narratology of adaptation**; (2) **adaptation in the oeuvre of single directors** (for example, Alfred Hitchcock); (3) **hidden intertextualities** (for example, the unacknowledged presence of *Les Liaisons dangereuses* in the work of Eric Rohmer; and (4) **thematic/ generic essays** on such topics as apocalyptic fiction/film, cross-cultural adaptation, the Hollywood novel/film, *noir* novels and films, the Bible as cultural object in popular cinema. The *Companion* moves the discussion beyond adaptation per se into broader questions of transtextuality and intermediality.

Although the essays in the two edited collections do not conform to any a priori theory or model, they all share a reflexive awareness of key orienting questions or "problematics." In diverse ways, they mingle the methods of literary theory, semiotics, narratology, cultural studies, and media theory. The totality of the essays will move adaptation discourse forward, through a tour de force of sophisticatedly literate (and cine-literate) readings, performed so as to reconfigure the field of literature/film studies. Cumulatively, the work is highly international, covering novels/films from England, the United States, France, Italy, Germany, Spain, Ireland, Russia, China, India, Egypt, Senegal, Cuba, Brazil, Argentina, Mexico, and Venezuela. The work represented in all three volumes points the way, it is hoped, toward a richly theorized and complexly contextualized and transformalist approach to adaptation. While paying homage to the classics of world literature, the work will also highlight the contemporary relevance of adaptation studies in the age of the Internet.

Acknowledgments

Literature Through Film: Realism, Magic, and the Art of Adaptation is primarily composed of newly minted material. The book does, however, at times revisit issues that I have previously considered, although they are now seen in a different light. Most notably, some of the material on *Don Quixote, Tom Jones, Contempt,* and *Last Year at Marienbad* was first "essayed" in my book *Reflexivity in Film and Literature: From Don Quixote to Jean-Luc Godard* (New York: Columbia University Press, 1989). Yet my optic there was completely different, since that book focused on the issue of reflexivity, while *Literature Through Film* focuses on the issue of adaptation. In my past writing, I have also repeatedly returned to the subject of Mário de Andrade's 1928 novel *Macunaíma* and the 1969 film adaptation based on that book; it appears in *Reflexivity in Film and Literature*, in *Subversive Pleasures: Bakhtin, Cultural Criticism, and Film* (Baltimore, MD: The Johns Hopkins University Press, 1989), and in *Tropical Multiculturalism: A Comparative History of Race in Brazilian Cinema and Culture* (Durham, NC: Duke University Press, 1997). Each time, I have changed the discussion in the light of the larger topic; here it forms part of a larger discussion of adaptation and "magic realism." (Perhaps I return so obsessively to *Macunaíma* in the hope that renewed interest will lead to a new translation of that brilliant novel and a new distribution of the equally brilliant adaptation.)

Since this book emerges from three decades of teaching and writing about film and literature, there is no way I can acknowledge all those who have helped or supported or influenced me. Indeed, to name any names at all is to risk offending the many I have left out. While my intellectual debts should be obvious from the notes to each chapter, I do want to recall just a few names among many supportive friends and colleagues: Bertrand Augst, Robert Alter, and Walnice Galvao were all helpful in the first phases of my career. Thanks also go to Ella Shohat (my constant interlocutor and critical reader), to my colleagues in New York and elsewhere (many of whom are included in the anthology volumes in this series), and to the academic audiences to whom I have presented various versions of these materials: at the University of São Paulo, Brazil; the Federal University in Rio (Niteroi); the University of California at Santa Cruz; the Udine Conference on Silent Cinema; and the University of Delhi (the 2004 Conference on Literature, Culture, Film).

I also want to pay homage to all the wonderful literarily inclined colleagues here at NYU: Diana Taylor, Mary Louise Pratt, Kamau Brathwaite, Renato Rosaldo, Andrew Ross, Howard Besser, Ed Guerrero, Anna McCarthy, Zhen Zhang, Toby Miller, Faye Ginsburg, George Yudice, Manthia Diawara, Ana Dopico, Patrick Deer, Gabriela Basterra, Mary Schmidt-Campell, Randy Martin, Silvia Molloy, Michael Dash, and Awam Amkpa; and elsewhere: Caren Kaplan, Eric Smoodin, Richard Pena, Randal Johnson, James Naremore, Joao Luiz Vieira, and Ismail Xavier. I would also like to thank the research assistants who helped me with the project: Alonso Quinteros, Juan Monroy, Cecilia Sayad, and Karen Wang. Finally, I would like to express my gratitude to the lively and insightful students in my long-running "Film/Novel" course in the Cinema Studies Department at NYU.

I would also like to thank the wonderful people at Blackwell Publishing. I have by now published six books with Blackwell, and I could not be more satisfied with the process. To Andrew McNeillie: thank you for the warm dialogue and the Jap Stam soccer shirt. To Jayne Fargnoli: thank you for your graciousness and intelligence and sensitive readings of the manuscript. Thanks as well to Annie Lenth, Ken Provencher, and Sue Ashton.

To anyone who has had the privilege of knowing Edward Said, as I have, or only of reading his work, there is no need whatsoever to explain why this book would be dedicated to him. As Ana Dopico put it at a memorial commemoration: "Now it is up to the rest of us."

The author and publisher gratefully acknowledge the permission granted to reproduce the copyright material in this book:

Figure 1.1 Kozintsev's *Don Quixote* (1957), produced by Lenfilm Studio, distributed by Artkino Pictures Inc. / Top 1 Video; picture reproduced courtesy of the British Film Institute.

Acknowledgments

Figure 1.2 Francisco Reigueira in Orson Welles's *Don Quixote*, produced by El Silencio Producciones, distributed by Jacinto Santos Parras; picture reproduced courtesy of Juan Amalbert.

Figure 1.3 Welles as Welles in *Don Quixote*, produced by El Silencio Producciones, distributed by Jacinto Santos Parras; picture reproduced courtesy of Juan Amalbert.

Figure 2.1 Crusoe (Costinha) and Friday (Grande Otelo) in *As aventuras de Robinson Crusoe* (1978), produced by J. B. Tanko Filmes, distributed by UCB; picture reproduced courtesy of Cinemateca de São Paulo.

Figure 2.2 The biracial idyll: Buñuel's *Adventures of Robinson Crusoe* (1954), produced by OLMEC / Producciones Tepeyac / Ultramar Films, distributed by United Artists; picture reproduced courtesy of United Artists.

Figure 2.3 Peter O'Toole and Richard Roundtree in *Man Friday* (1975), produced by ABC Entertainment / Incorporated Television Company (UK) / Keep Films, distributed by AVCO Embassy Pictures; picture reproduced courtesy of AVCO Embassy.

Figure 2.4 Deschamel's *Crusoe* (1989), produced and distributed by Island Pictures; picture reproduced courtesy of Island Pictures.

Figure 3.1 Sex and food in Richardson's *Tom Jones* (1963), produced by Woodfall Film Productions, distributed by Lopert Pictures Corporation / Samuel Goldwyn Company / United Artists; picture reproduced courtesy of Photofest: Nation Screen Service Corporation.

Figure 3.2 Lady Booby (Ann-Margret) and Joseph (Peter Firth) in *Joseph Andrews* (1977), produced by Woodfall Film Productions, distributed by Paramount Pictures / United Artists Corporation Ltd; picture reproduced courtesy of Paramount Pictures and Photofest.

Figure 3.3 Magical effects in *Posthumous Memoirs of Bras Cubas* (2001), produced by Cinemate Material Cinematográfico / Cinematográfica Brasileira / Instituto Português da Arte Cinematográfica e Audiovisual (IPACA) / Lusa Filmes / PIC-TV / Secretaria de Estado da Cultura (SEC) / Superfilmes; picture reproduced courtesy of André Klotzel.

Figure 4.1 Valentine Tessier as Emma in Renoir's *Madame Bovary* (1934), produced by Nouvelle Société des Films (NSF), distributed by John S. Tapernoux / La Compagnie Indépendante de Distribution (CID); picture reproduced courtesy of Photofest.

Acknowledgments

Figure 4.2 Emma as star in Minnelli's *Madame Bovary* (1949), produced and distributed by Metro-Goldwyn-Mayer (MGM); picture reproduced courtesy of Photofest.

Figure 4.3 Chabrol's *Madame Bovary* (1991), produced by CED Productions / Club des Investissments / Conseil General de L'Eure / Conseil Regional de Haute-Normandie / France 3 Cinéma / MK2 Productions, distributed by Samuel Goldwyn Company; picture reproduced courtesy of the British Film Institute / Arrow Film.

Figure 4.4 Leonor Silviera as Ema in Manoel de Oliveira's *Vale Abraão* (1997), produced by Gémini Films / Light Night / Madragoa Filmes, distributed by Artificial Eye; picture reproduced courtesy of Photofest.

Figure 5.1 Henry Czerny in Walkow's *Notes from Underground* (1995), produced by Renegade Films Inc. / Walkow-Gruber Pictures; picture reproduced courtesy of Photofest.

Figure 5.2 Sergio and his mirror in *Memories of Underdevelopment* (1968), produced by Cuban State Film / Instituto Cubano del Arte e Industrias Cinematográficos (ICAIC), distributed by Tricontinental; picture reproduced courtesy of Photofest.

Figure 5.3 Sergio as voyeur in *Memories of Underdevelopment* (1968), produced by Cuban State Film / Instituto Cubano del Arte e Industrias Cinematográficos (ICAIC), distributed by Tricontinental; picture reproduced courtesy of Photofest.

Figure 5.4 Humbert (James Mason) as voyeur in Kubrick's *Lolita* (1962), produced by Anya / Harris-Kubrick Productions / Seven Arts Productions / Transwood, distributed by Metro-Goldwyn-Mayer (MGM); picture reproduced courtesy of Seven Arts / Photofest.

Figure 5.5 Jeremy Irons and Dominique Swain in Lyne's *Lolita* (1997), produced by Guild / Pathé, distributed by Showtime Networks Inc. / Vidmark Entertainment; picture reproduced courtesy of the British Film Institute.

Figure 5.6 Macabeia (Marcelia Cartaxo) in *Hour of the Star* (1984), produced by Kino International Corp. / Raíz Produções Cinematográficas; picture reproduced courtesy of Suzana Amaral.

Figure 6.1 The ghostlike dance in *Last Year at Marienbad* (1961), produced by Argos Films / Cineriz / Cinétel / Como / Cormoran Films / Les Films Tamara / Precitel / Silver Films / Société Nouvelle des Films / Terra Film, distributed by Astor Pictures Corporation / Fox Lorber.

Figure 6.2 Polysemy and memory in *Hiroshima mon amour* (1959), produced by Argos Films / Como / Daiei Studios / Pathé Entertainment, distributed by Cocinor / Zenith International.

Figure 6.3 Paul, Prokosch, and Lang in *Contempt* (1963), produced by Compagnia Cinematografica Champion / Les Films Concordia / Rome Paris Films, distributed by Embassy Home Entertainment / Embassy Pictures Corporation / Strand Releasing; picture reproduced courtesy of the British Film Institute.

Figure 6.4 Camille's ironic invitation: Bardot and Piccoli in *Contempt* (1963), produced by Compagnia Cinematografica Champion / Les Films Concordia / Rome Paris Films, distributed by Embassy Home Entertainment / Embassy Pictures Corporation / Strand Releasing; picture reproduced courtesy of the British Film Institute.

Figure 7.1 Glauber Rocha's *Terra em transe* (1967), produced by Mapa Filmes, distributed by Difilm / Facets Multimedia Distribution / Globo Vídeo / New Yorker Films; picture reproduced courtesy of Cine World.

Figure 7.2 Nelson Pereira dos Santos's *How Tasty Was My Little Frenchman* (1971), produced by Condor Filmes / L.C. Produes Cinematograficas, distributed by New Yorker Films.

Figure 7.3 Grande Otelo in *Macunaíma* (1968), produced by Condor Filmes / Films do Serra / Grupu, distributed by New Line Cinema.

Figure 7.4 The birth of the hero in *Macunaíma* (1968), produced by Condor Filmes / Films do Serra / Grupu, distributed by New Line Cinema.

Figure 7.5 The about-to-be-transformed Macunaíma in *Macunaíma* (1968), produced by Condor Filmes / Films do Serra / Grupu, distributed by New Line Cinema.

Figure 7.6 Irene Papas as the matriarch in *Erendira* (1983), produced by Atlas Saskia Film / Austra / Cinequanon / Films A2 / Les Films de Triangles / Ministère de la Culture de la Republique Françalse, distributed by Miramax Films.

Figure 7.7 Musical performance in Paul Leduc's *Barroco* (1988), produced by Instituto Cubano del Arte e Industrias Cinematográficos (ICAIC) / Sociedad Estatal Quinto Centenario / Ópalo Films, distributed by International Film Circuit; picture reproduced courtesy of the British Film Institute.

Every effort has been made to trace copyright holders and to obtain their permission for the use of copyright material. The publisher apologizes for any errors or omissions in the above list and would be grateful if notified of any corrections that should be incorporated in future reprints or editions of this book.

Introduction

Literature Through Film: Realism, Magic, and the Art of Adaptation presents the history of literature through film. The book, which might have been entitled *Literary Classics in the Cinema*, provides an historicized account of key moments in the history of the novel, both in literary terms and as refracted through the prism of adaptation. Since it would obviously be a "Quixotic" task to cover the entire history of the novel since Cervantes, I focus on crucial "moments," tendencies, and trends. Most of the novels analyzed here are "key" in the sense of being "classics" which generated a vast progeny of literary and filmic "descendants." Both *Don Quixote* and *Robinson Crusoe*, for example, initiate opposing lineages within the novel, and both have been rewritten and filmed countless times. *Don Quixote* is the source text for the parodic, intertextual, and "magical" tradition of novels such as *Tom Jones* and *Tristram Shandy*, which flaunt their own artifice and technique. Defoe's *Robinson Crusoe*, meanwhile, is a seminal source text for the tradition of the mimetic novel supposedly based on "real life" and written in such a way as to generate a strong impression of factual reality.

Flaubert's *Madame Bovary*, meanwhile, counterpoints **both** traditions, the realist and the Cervantic/reflexive. It too was vastly influential, both in terms of its themes – provincial boredom, sexual desire, disillusionment – and its techniques – the free indirect style, the use of the imperfect, the deployment of pastiche. *Notes from Underground*, similarly, initiated a long line of novels deploying problematic and self-demystifying narrators, a line which leads to Sartre's *La*

Nausée, Ellison's *Invisible Man*, Nabokov's *Lolita*, and Lispector's *Hour of the Star*.

Each chapter of *Literature Through Film* sketches out a literary trend – Cervantic parody, Defoe-style realism (and the attempts to "write back" against it), Fieldingesque reflexivity, Flaubertian perspectivalism, Dostoevskian polyphony, New Wave experimentation, Márquezian "magic realism" – before exploring the cinematic ramifications of that trend. At the end of each chapter, I suggest the relevance of these novels for contemporary life and culture. The chapter on *Don Quixote* ends with observations on the Cervantic aspects of postmodernism; the chapter on *Robinson Crusoe* with commentary on *Castaway* and the "reality game show" *Survivor*. The chapter on *Madame Bovary* leads us to Woody Allen's *The Purple Rose of Cairo*. The chapter on *Notes from Underground* reveals the subterranean kinship between Dostoevsky's tormented narrators and present-day stand-up comedians. My hope is not only to address literature and film scholars, but also to bring literature to life for media-saturated students not necessarily versed in the literary canon, both by bringing in contemporary media and through reflections on the novels' (and the films') present-day actuality.

All art has been nourished by the tension between magic and realism, reflexivity and illusionism. All artistic representations can pass themselves off as "reality" or straightforwardly admit their status as representation. Illusionistic realism presents its characters as real people, its sequence of words as substantiated fact. Reflexive and magical texts, on the other hand, call attention to their own factitiousness as textual constructs, whether through a magical hyperbolization of improbabilities or through the minimalist, reflexive emptying out of realism. *Don Quixote*, in this sense, orchestrates both magic and realism and in this sense anticipates "magic realism." Indeed, for René Girard, "all the ideas of the western novel are present in germ in *Don Quixote*."[1] Since we will return frequently to *Don Quixote* as a seminal matrix for magical reflexivity, this book might have been called, to paraphrase Ortega y Gasset, a "meditation on the *Quixote*," or, better, a meditation on both the "Quixotic" and the "Cervantic." Many of the novels central to the European tradition – Stendhal's *Le Rouge et le noir* (The Red and the Black), Balzac's *Les Illusions perdues* (Lost Illusions), Flaubert's *Madame Bovary*, Proust's *A la recherche du temps perdu* (Remembrance of Things Past) – chart a Cervantic trajectory of disenchantment in which the illusions fostered by adolescent reading are systematically undone by experience in the real world. But this kind of Quixotism is just as available to the cinema as it is to literature. If *The Sorrows of Young Werther* inspired a wave of suicides all over Europe, films too have often inspired imitative behavior. Indeed, countless films, for example *Play It Again Sam* and *Reservoir Dogs*, explore this Cervantic theme of characters/spectators trying to emulate their filmic heroes.

Beyond "Fidelity"

Although *Literature Through Film* is organized diachronically, according to the chronology of the **literary** rather than the filmic texts, certain synchronic themes will emerge in relation to all the texts discussed. And although this is not the place for a systematic theory – something I attempt in my essay "The Theory and Practice of Adaptation" in the companion volume, *Literature and Film* – I can briefly sketch out my understanding of some of the crucial categories operative throughout the text.

The overall "argument" of *Literature Through Film* will weave together a number of threads: the critique of "fidelity" discourse, the multicultural nature of artistic intertextuality, the problematic nature of illusionism, the wealth of "magical" and reflexive alternatives to conventional realism, and the crucial importance both of medium specificity – film as film – and of the migratory, crossover elements shared between film and other media.

The traditional language of criticism of filmic adaptation of novels, as I have argued elsewhere,[2] has often been extremely judgmental, proliferating in terms that imply that film has performed a disservice to literature. Terms such as "infidelity," "betrayal," "deformation," "violation," "vulgarization," "bastardization," and "desecration" proliferate, with each word carrying its specific charge of opprobrium. Despite the variety of the accusations, their drift seems always to be the same – the book was better.

The notion of "fidelity" does, admittedly, contain its grain of truth. When we say an adaptation has been "unfaithful" to the original, the very violence of the term gives expression to the intense disappointment we feel when a film adaptation fails to capture what we see as the fundamental narrative, thematic, and aesthetic features of its literary source. The notion of fidelity gains its persuasive force from our sense that (a) some adaptations **do** fail to "realize" what we most appreciated in the source novels; (b) some adaptations **are** indeed better than others; and (c) some adaptations miss at least some of the salient features of their sources. But the mediocrity of some adaptations, and the partial persuasiveness of "fidelity," should not lead us to endorse fidelity as a methodological principle. Indeed, it is questionable whether strict fidelity is even **possible**. An adaptation is **automatically** different and original due to the change of medium. The shift from a single-track verbal medium such as the novel to a multitrack medium like film, which can play not only with words (written and spoken) but also with music, sound effects, and moving photographic images, explains the unlikelihood, and I would suggest even the **undesirability**, of literal fidelity.

Literature Through Film simply assumes rather than articulates the many theoretical developments that have undermined the substratal premises on which the fidelity doctrine has historically been based. Structuralist and poststructuralist developments cast suspicion on ideas of purity and essence and origin, and thus indirectly impacted on the discussion of adaptation. The intertextuality theory of Kristeva, rooted in Bakhtinian "dialogism," stressed the endless permutation of textual traces rather than the "fidelity" of a later text to an earlier one, and thus facilitated a less judgmental approach. The Bakhtinian proto-poststructuralist conception of the author as the orchestrator of pre-existing discourses, meanwhile, along with Foucault's downgrading of the author in favor of a "pervasive anonymity of discourse," opened the way to a "discursive" and non-originary approach to all arts. Bakhtin's attitude toward the literary author as living on "inter-individual territory" suggests a revised attitude toward artistic "originality." The artistic utterance is always what Bakhtin calls a "hybrid construction" mingling one's own word with the other's word. Bakhtin's words about literature as a "hybrid construction" applies even more obviously to a **collaborative** medium like film. Complete originality, as a consequence, is neither possible nor even desirable. And if "originality" in literature is downplayed, the "offense" in "betraying" that originality, for example through an "unfaithful" adaptation, is that much the less.

If "fidelity" is an inadequate trope, what tropes might be more appropriate? Adaptation theory has available a rich constellation of terms and tropes – translation, actualization, reading, critique, dialogization, cannibalization, transmutation, transfiguration, incarnation, transmogrification, transcoding, performance, signifying, rewriting, detournement – all of which shed light on a different dimension of adaptation. The trope of adaptation as a "reading" of the source novel, one which is inevitably partial, personal, conjunctural, for example, suggests that just as any literary text can generate an infinity of readings, so any novel can generate any number of adaptations. An adaptation is thus less a resuscitation of an originary word than a turn in an ongoing dialogical process. Intertextual dialogism, then, helps us transcend the aporias of "fidelity."

Building on Bakhtin's "dialogism" and Kristeva's "intertextuality," Gérard Genette in *Palimpsestes* (1982)[3] proposes the more inclusive term "transtextuality" to refer to "all that which puts one text in relation, whether manifest or secret, with other texts," ultimately positing five types. Genette's fifth type, "hypertextuality," seems especially productive in terms of adaptation. The term refers to the relation between one text, which Genette calls "hypertext," to an anterior text or "hypotext," which the former transforms, modifies, elaborates, or extends. In literature, *The Aeneid*'s hypotexts include *The Odyssey* and *The Iliad*, while the hypotexts of Joyce's *Ulysses* include *The Odyssey* and *Hamlet*. Filmic adaptations, in this sense, are hypertexts spun from pre-existing hypotexts which have been transformed by operations of selection, amplification, concretization, and actualization. The diverse filmic adaptations of *Les Liaisons dangereuses* (Vadim, Frears, Forman), for example, constitute variant hypertextual "readings" triggered by the same hypotext. Indeed, the diverse prior adaptations taken together can form a larger, cumulative hypotext available to the filmmaker who comes relatively "late" in the series.

By adopting a broad intertextual as opposed to a narrow, judgmental approach, we have still not abandoned all notions of judgment and evaluation. But our discussion will be less moralistic, less implicated in unacknowledged hierarchies. We can still speak of successful or unsuccessful adaptations, but this time oriented not by inchoate notions of "fidelity" but rather by attention to specific dialogical responses, to "readings" and "critiques" and "interpretations" and "rewritings" of source novels, in analyses which always take into account the inevitable gaps and transformations in the passage across very different media and materials of expression. Filmic adaptations get caught up in the ongoing whirl of intertextual reference and transformation, of texts generating other texts in an endless process of recycling, transformation, and transmutation, with no clear point of origin. Rather than take an evaluative approach, then, I will focus here on the twists and turns of intertextual dialogism.

The Question of Genre

Adaptation theory inevitably inherits antecedent questions regarding intertexuality and genre. Etymologically drawn from the Latin *genus* ("kind"), "genre" criticism began, at least in the "West,"[4] as the classification of the diverse kinds of literary texts and the evolution of literary forms. Aristotle, for example, distinguished between the medium of representation, the objects represented, and the mode of presentation, resulting in the familiar triad of epic, drama, and lyric. The film world inherited this ancient habit of arranging art works into "types," some drawn from literature (comedy, tragedy, melodrama), while others were more specifically visual and cinematic: "views," "actualities," "tableaux," "travelogues," "animated cartoons." Filmic adaptations of novels invariably superimpose a double set of generic conventions, one drawn from the generic intertext of the source novel itself, and the other consisting of those genres engaged by the translating medium of film. The art of filmic adaptation partially consists in choosing **which** generic conventions are transposable into the new medium, and **which** need to be discarded, supplemented, transcoded, or replaced. The novel *Tom Jones*, as we shall see (chapter 3), draws on epic poetry, the Cervantic novel, pastoral, and so forth, while the filmic adaptation by Tony Richardson draws not only on those literary genres but also on specifically filmic genres such as silent period burlesque film and cinema verité.

Filmic genre, like literary genre before it, is permeable to historical and social tensions. The entire course of Western literature, Erich Auerbach argues in *Mimesis*, has worked to erode the elitist "separation of styles" inherent in the Greek tragic model, with its clear hierarchies of tragedy over comedy and nobility over **demos**.[5] A realism rooted in the ethos of egalitarian Judaism slowly democratizes literature. The Judaic notion of "all souls equal before God" gradually comes to accord the dignity of a noble style to ever "lower" classes of people. Genres come equipped, in this sense, with class connotations and social evaluations. In literature, the novel, rooted in the common-sense world of bourgeois facticity, challenges the romance, often linked to aristocratic notions of courtliness and chivalry. Art revitalizes itself by drawing on the strategies of previously marginalized forms and genres, canonizing what had earlier been reviled.

Throughout, we will be concerned with these interlinked issues of social and aesthetic hierarchies, of generic as well as societal stratifications. Does a novel or its adaptation push society toward a more egalitarian condition by critiquing social inequities based on axes of stratification such as race, gender, class, and sexuality, or does it simply assume (or even glorify) these inequities and hierarchies as natural and God-given? Which social group is represented in a novel/film? Who are the subjects and who are the objects of representation? Which group enjoys social or aesthetic privilege? In what language and style is the representation framed, and what are the social connotations of those styles and languages?

In historical and generic terms, both novel and film have consistently cannibalized antecedent genres and media. The novel began by orchestrating a polyphonic diversity of materials – courtly fictions, travel literature, religious allegory, jestbooks – into a new narrative form, repeatedly plundering or annexing neighboring arts, creating new hybrids like poetic novels, dramatic novels, epistolary novels, and so forth. The cinema subsequently brought this cannibalization to its paroxysm. As a rich, sensorially composite language, the cinema as a medium is open to all kinds of literary and pictorial energies and symbolism, to all collective representations, to all ideological currents, to all aesthetic trends, and to the infinite play of influences within cinema, within the other arts, and within culture generally. The intertextuality of cinema, further-more, is multitrack. The image track "inherits" the history of painting and the visual arts, while the sound track "inherits" the entire history of music, dialogue, and sound experimentation. Adaptation, in this sense, consists of amplifying the source text through these multiple intertexts.

---------------- Literary Realism and Magic ----------------

Another thread in the overall argument of *Literature Through Film: Realism, Magic, and the Art of Adaptation* has to do with the perennial question of artistic "realism." An uncommonly contested and elastic term, "realism" comes heavily laden with millennial encrustations from antecedent debates in phil-osophy and literature. While ultimately rooted in the classical Greek conception of *mimesis* (imitation), the concept of realism gains programmatic significance only in the nineteenth century, when it comes to denote a movement in the figura-tive and narrative arts dedicated to the observation and accurate representation of the contemporary world. A neologism coined by French art critics, realism was originally linked to an oppositional attitude toward romantic and neo-classical models in fiction and painting. The Realist novels of writers such as Balzac, Stendhal, Flaubert, George Eliot, and Eça de Queiroz brought intensely individualized, seriously conceived characters into typical contemporary social situations. Underlying the realist impulse was an implicit teleology of social democ-ratization favoring the artistic emergence of "more extensive and socially infer-ior human groups to the position of subject matter for problematic-existential representation."[6] Literary critics distinguished between this deep, democratiz-ing realism, and a shallow, reductionistic, and obsessively veristic "naturalism" – realized most famously in the novels of Emile Zola – which modeled its human representations on the biological sciences.

Each of the texts discussed in this book can be analyzed in terms of its vary-ing coefficients of magic, reflexivity, and realism: the parodic anti-illusionism of *Don Quixote*, the documentary-realist approach of *Robinson Crusoe*, the perspectival realism of *Madame Bovary*, the subjective realism of *Hiroshima mon amour*, the reflexive modernism of *Contempt*, the "magical realism" of

Erendira and *Barroco*. Throughout the book, I will return to the productive tensions between the reflexive, parodic tradition going back to *Don Quixote*, on the one hand, and the "realistic" tradition going back to *Robinson Crusoe*, on the other. At the same time, we are still being rather provincial and Eurocentric when we posit only **two basic** traditions. Critics like Arthur Heiserman (*The Novel before the Novel*) and Margaret Anne Doody (*The True Story of the Novel*) argue that the novel did not begin in the Renaissance but rather "has a continuous history of about two thousand years."[7]

Some critics reject the critical tradition, invoked earlier, which demonizes romance, often codified as female, archaic, superstitious, and suspectly "magical," while defining the novel as the very quintessence of European modernity. Anglocentric critics overemphasize the novel's links to Protestantism and capitalism. Critics like Ian Watt privilege the eighteenth century, precisely the zenith of strength for the **English** novel, eliding other national traditions and other possible narrativizations.[8] A wide variety of critics have in common a teleological, almost Hegelian, approach which stresses the "progressive" supercession of the vestiges of the past. Within this exterminationist narrative, "archaic" and "medieval" forms like epic and romance inevitably give way to modern forms like the novel, the courtly aristocracy inevitably gives way to the middle class, and "oriental" magic inevitably gives way to "Western" science. Despite his pan-European cosmopolitanism, even a figure like Auerbach still sees "Western" literature as moving inexorably toward a single telos of realism. The general teleological view dismisses ancient novels such as *The Golden Ass* as somehow not really novels, even though they were "prose fictions of a certain length."[9]

Canonical Eurocentric criticism tends to plot artistic history, like history in general, "north by northwest," in a trajectory that leads from the Bible and *The Odyssey* to literary realism and artistic modernism. But can those two foundational texts, the Bible and *The Odyssey*, be seen as "Western?" The Bible was rooted in Africa, Palestine, Mesopotamia, and the Mediterranean, and classical Greek culture was deeply impacted by Semitic and Egyptian and Ethiopian cultures.

If one defines the novel, simply and directly, as "prose fiction of a certain length," then the genre goes much farther back even than *Don Quixote* to the great novelists of antiquity such as the Egyptians, the Arabs, the Persians, the Indians, and the Syrians. While the Eurocentric diffusionist narrative emplots the history of the novel as emerging from Europe and then "spreading" to Africa and Asia, it would be just as logical to see the novel as emerging outside of Europe and then spreading to Europe. According to Margaret Doody, the novel was the product of combinatory "contact between Southern Europe, Western

Asia, and Northern Africa."[10] The novel is thus rooted in the history of the multiracial, multilingual Mediterranean basin. The canon, pace Harold Bloom, is not exclusively "Western." Papyrus fragments of novels have suggested that novel reading was popular among Egyptians in the second century AD. Nor is it an accident that the title of Heliodorus' *Aithiopika*, the longest of the surviving Greek novels, means "**Ethiopian** Story" (my emphasis). A Renaissance Italian writer like Boccaccio found it normal to draw on the Eastern repertoire of the *Fables of Bidpai* and *Sindbad the Philosopher*. (Even Disney draws on Aladdin and *The Thousand and One Nights*.) Writers like Cervantes and Fielding were quite aware of and influenced by such texts. As Doody puts it, "Whoever has read *Pamela* or *Tom Jones* is in contact with Heliodorus, Longus, Amadis, Petronius" and we too are in contact with them when we "read authors of the nineteenth or twentieth century [such as Salman Rushdie] who have read other authors who read those works."[11]

There is "more in heaven and earth," then, than is dreamed of within the provincial canons of Western verism. The valorization of realism is often linked to the idea that magic and the fantastic have been superseded by Enlightenment Reason. A linear, "progressive" view of such matters sees humanity as "moving beyond" such archaic and irrational forms; the world moves inexorably forward on a global, unidirectional course. Magic and romance become devalued as anachronistic vestiges or prior modes of consciousness to be "surmounted" by the more evolved and rational forms of Enlightened Modernity. Fantasy and magic, within this view, are vestiges of a past better left behind. But these archaic forms are never completely buried. Rather, their specters haunt, or better animate, the entire history of modern fiction, whether in the marvelous and the romance present in *Don Quixote*, or in the romantic longings of Emma Bovary, or in Underground Man's bitter rejection of science and enlightenment, or in Magical Realism's affirmation of the archaic and the fantastic as aspects of the "quotidian surreal" of contemporary Latin America.

Artistic modernism, too, was traditionally defined in contradistinction to realism as the dominant norm in representation. But outside the West, realism was rarely dominant; modernist reflexivity as a reaction against realism, therefore, could scarcely wield the same power of scandal and provocation. Modernism, in this sense, can be seen as in some ways a rather provincial, local rebellion. Vast regions of the world, and long periods of artistic history, have shown little allegiance to or even interest in realism. In India, a two-thousand-year tradition of narrative circles back to the classical Sanskrit drama and epic, which tell the myths of Hindu culture through an aesthetic based less on coherent character and linear plot than on the subtle modulations of mood and feeling (*rasa*).

Realism as norm can be seen as provincial even within Europe. In *Rabelais and his World*, Bakhtin speaks of the "carnivalesque" as a counterhegemonic tradition with a history that runs from Greek Dionysian festivals and the Roman saturnalia through the grotesque realism of the medieval "carnivalesque" on through Shakespeare and Cervantes and finally to Jarry and Surrealism.[12] As theorized by Bakhtin, carnival embraces an anticlassical aesthetic that rejects formal harmony and unity in favor of the asymmetrical, the heterogeneous, the oxymoronic, the miscegenated.

--------------------- **Magic and Realism in the Cinema** ---------------------

In relation to cinema, the issue of "realism" has always been present, whether posited as ideal or as an object of opprobrium. The very names of many filmic movements ring the changes on the theme of realism: the "**sur**realism" of Buñuel and Dali, the "poetic realism" of Carné/Prevert, the "neo-realism" of Rossellini and de Sica, the "subjective realism" of Antonioni, the "*sur-realismo*" (South-Realism) of Glauber Rocha, the "bourgeois realism" denounced by *Cahiers du Cinéma* critics in their Marxist–Leninist phase. Several broad tendencies co-exist within the spectrum of definitions of cinematic realism. The most orthodox definitions of realism make claims about verisimilitude, the putative adequation of a fiction to the brute facticity of the world. These definitions often become linked, in the work of Bazin and Kracauer for example, to the supposedly "objective" nature of the cinematic apparatus, with its indexical, photo-chemical link to real pro-filmic objects. Other definitions stress the differential aspirations of film movement to mould a **relatively** more truthful representation, seen as a corrective to the falsity of antecedent cinematic styles or protocols of representation. This corrective can be stylistic – as in the French New Wave attack on the artificiality of the "tradition of quality" – or social – Italian Neo-realism aiming to show postwar Italy its true face – or both at once – Brazilian Cinema Novo revolutionizing both the social thematics and the cinematic procedures of antecedent Brazilian cinema.

Still other definitions stress the conventionality of realism, seeing realism as linked to a text's degree of conformity to widely disseminated cultural models of "believable stories" and "coherent characters." In this sense, plausibility and verisimilitude are shaped by **generic** codes. The crusty, conservative father who resists his show-crazed daughter's entrance into show-business, in a backstage musical, can "realistically" be expected to applaud her on-stage apotheosis at the end of the film. Psychoanalytically inclined definitions of cinematic realism, meanwhile, touch on spectatorial belief, a realism of subjective response, rooted less in mimetic accuracy than in spectatorial credence. A purely formalist definition of "realism" emphasizes the conventional nature of all fictional constructions, seeing realism as nothing more than a constellation of stylistic devices, a set of conventions that, at a given moment in the history of an art, manage, through the fine-tuning of illusionistic technique, to crystallize a strong **feeling** of authenticity. For Gilles Deleuze, finally, realism no longer refers to a mimetic, analogical adequation between sign and referent, but rather to the sensate feel of time, to the intuition of lived duration, the mobile slidings of Bergsonian *durée*. Realism, it is important to add, is culturally relative; for Salman Rushdie, Bollywood (Bombay) musicals make Hollywood musicals look like neo-Realist "kitchen-sink" documents in comparison.[13] Filmic realism is also historically conditioned. Generations of filmgoers found black-and-white more "realistic," for example, even though "reality" itself comes in color. The key point here is that realism is itself a discourse, an artful fabrication, one that creates and reshapes what it speaks.

An important question for all adaptations is that of film's relation to modernism, and how it differs from that of literature. This question bears on the specific spatio-temporality of film, and especially on "continuity" as the very kernel of the dominant style. Hollywood and its counterparts around the world invented a way of telling stories through a specifically cinematic organization of time and space. The dominant model devised what became the aesthetic cornerstone of dominant cinema: the reconstitution of a fictional world characterized by internal coherence and by the appearance of continuity. This continuity was achieved by an etiquette for introducing new scenes (a choreographed progression from establishing shot to medium shot to close shot); conventional devices for evoking the passage of time (dissolves, iris effects); conventional techniques for rendering imperceptible the transition from shot to shot (the 30-degree rule, cutting on movement, position and movement matches, "inserts" and "cutaways" to cover up discontinuities); and devices for implying subjectivity (point of view editing, reaction shots, eyeline matches). The conventional Hollywood aesthetic promoted the ideal not only of coherent, cause–effect, linear plots revolving around "major conflicts" but also of motivated, believable characters. A specific spatio-temporal decorum deployed this whole panoply of devices in order to convey a feeling of seamless continuity. In fact, of course, the processes of film production are highly discontinuous; a single scene conveying a few consecutive minutes in the story is often shot over a period of days or even months. Yet the normative aesthetic requires that films do everything to "cover over" such discontinuities, in the name of "continuity" and narrative flow.

Another key word in these discussions is the word "reflexivity." Etymologically derived from the Latin **reflexio/reflectere** ("bend back upon"), the term was first borrowed from philosophy and psychology, where it referred to the mind's capacity to be both subject and object to itself within the cognitive process. We find reflexivity, in this sense, in some of the most celebrated dictums of philosophy, such as Socrates' grammatically and philosophically reflexive "Know Thyself" and Descartes's **cogito ergo sum**, where the skeptical observation of consciousness, consciousness watching itself consciousing, as it were, becomes key to epistemology. Kant, similarly, championed the idea of reflexive philosophical judgment, while some social theorists have called for "reflexive sociology." Indeed, artistic reflexivity comes in many forms: methodological self-consciousness, meta-theoretical reflection, the *mise-en-abyme* of reflections ad infinitum, the breaking of frames, the relativization of cultural standpoint. Recently, critics have called attention to certain pitfalls within reflexivity theory. Film theory of the 1970s too often saw reflexivity as a political panacea, while missing the progressive potential of realism. At times, reflexivity becomes a form of narcissism or a show of self-confessional virtues: "I'm reflexive but you're not!," an ambiguity satirically anticipated, as we shall see, by Dostoevsky in his *Notes from Underground*.

Within the arts, reflexivity in the psychological/philosophical sense is extended to apply to the capacity for self-reflection of any medium or language or text. In the broadest sense, artistic reflexivity refers to the process by which texts, whether literary or filmic, foreground their own production (for example, Balzac's *Les Illusions perdues* or Truffaut's *La Nuit Américaine*), their authorship (Proust's *Remembrance of Things Past*, Fellini's *8½*), their textual procedures (the modernist novels of John Fowles, the films of Michael Snow), their intertextual influences (Cervantes or Mel Brooks), or their reception (*Madame Bovary*, or *The Purple Rose of Cairo*). By calling attention to artistic mediation, reflexive texts subvert the assumption that art can be a transparent medium of communication, a window on the world, a mirror promenading down a highway.

As I have argued elsewhere, reflexivity is not limited to what is often mistakenly labeled the "Western" tradition.[14] Reflexivity exists wherever language-using human beings "talk about talk." For Henry Louis Gates in *The Signifying Monkey*, the Yoruba trickster figure Eshu-Elegbara is a figure for the deconstructive "signifying of Afro-diasporic art."[15] Reflexivity is not limited to erudite, literary, or academic traditions; it can be found in popular songs, rap video, stand-up comedy, and TV commercials. Nor can we regard reflexivity and realism as necessarily antithetical terms. A film like Godard's *Contempt*, as we shall see, is at once reflexive and realist, in the sense that it illuminates the everyday lived social realities, while also reminding the readers/spectators of the constructed nature of the film's mimesis. Realism and reflexivity are not strictly opposed polarities but rather interpenetrating tendencies or poles of attraction quite capable of coexisting within the same text.

The cinema has been associated from the beginning both with realism **and** with the magical and the oneiric. In his call for a "shamanic cinema," filmmaker/theorist Raul Ruiz traces the origins of the cinema back to a series of "magical" events: "a caveman's hand pressed against a lightly colored surface . . . simulators (half-transparent demons of the air, described by Hermes Trimegistus); shadows, pre and post-Platonic; the Golem . . . Robertson's Fantascope; the magic butterflies at Coney Island. All prefigure the movies."[16]

Just as the tradition of the novel bifurcates into the parodic *Don Quixote* and the mimetic *Robinson Crusoe* traditions, so the cinema, at the time of its birth, divides into the realism of the "views" and "actualities" of Lumière, on the one hand, and the magical sketches of Meliès on the other. Yet Godard, a half-century later, reversed the dichotomy by suggesting that Lumière filmed like an impressionist painter, while Meliès documented the future by sending his characters to the Moon.[17]

Meliès discovered that editing made possible magical substitutions and transformations, thus leaving a rich inheritance which allowed the cinema to reshape the coordinates of time and space. Orson Welles is thus the heir of Meliès when he portrays himself as magician in *F for Fake*. The cinema conjugates the realistic and the fantastical. It deploys both the realism of what theoreticians call "monstration" – objective and without "human intervention," as Bazin famously claimed – and the "magic" of montage and superimposition, allowing film to perform impossible temporal transformations and spatial overlays. The cinema can also convey the persuasive magic of dreams. From Munsterberg to Metz, film theorists have noted not only the capacity of film to represent dreams, but also its analogies **with** dream in terms of its operating procedures, its metonymic and metaphoric fusions and displacements. Films, in sum, are potentially "magical realist;" they can make dreams realistic and reality dreamlike, giving fantasy what Shakespeare called a "local habitation and a name."

As a technology of representation, the cinema is ideally equipped to magically multiply times and spaces; it has the capacity to mingle very diverse temporalities and spatialities; a fiction film, for example, is produced in one constellation of times and spaces, it represents still another (diegetic) constellation of times and places, and is received in still another time and space (theater, home, classroom). Film's textual conjunction of sound and image means not only that each track presents two kinds of time, but also that these two forms of time mutually inflect one another in a form of synchresis. Atemporal static shots can be inscribed with temporality through music, for example.[18] The panoply of cinematic techniques further multiplies these already multiple times and spaces. Superimposition redoubles time and space, as do montage and multiple frames within the image. Those who argue that film inherently lacks the "flexibility" of the novel forget these protean possibilities.

The beginnings of cinema coincided with the zenith of the veristic project as expressed in the realist novel, in the naturalist play (where theatrical producers like Antoine would place real meat in staged butcher shops), and in obsessively mimetic exhibitions. The artistic modernism which flourished in the early decades of the twentieth century, and which became institutionalized as "high modernism" after World War II, promoted an anti-realist, non-representational art characterized by abstraction, fragmentation, and aggression. Although the technological razzle-dazzle of the cinema makes it seem superficially modern, its dominant aesthetic inherited the mimetic aspirations of nineteenth-century literary realism. Dominant forms of cinema were thus "modern" in their technological and industrial up-to-dateness, but not modernist in their aesthetic drift. Unsurprisingly, the most bitter disappointments, on the part of literate readers, have had to do with adaptations of **modernist** novels like those of Joyce and Woolf and Proust, precisely because in such cases the aesthetic gap between source and adaptation seems most startling, less because of cinema's inherent flaws but rather because of the option for a pre-modernist aesthetic.

Yet this narrative too can sometimes encode a modernist fairy tale of progress, a melioristic emplotment whereby realism yields to reflexivity as art's ultimate telos. The dichotomy between realist cinema and modernist novel, moreover, can easily be overdrawn. Many realisms are modernist. When Hitchcock collaborates with Salvador Dali on the dream sequence in *Spellbound* is he still **pre**modernist? And when Buñuel makes films within the Mexican industry, conversely, does he remain the avant-gardist of *Chien Andalou* and *L'Age d'or*?[19] The cinema has often been modernist (and postmodernist); the problem is that its modernism did not usually take the form of adaptations. Much of Alain Resnais's work can be seen as a cinematic prolongation of Proust's work in the novel, yet Resnais never **adapted** *A la recherche du temps perdu*. Glauber Rocha incarnated Latin American "magic realism" in *Terra em transe*, yet he never **adapted** Márquez or Carpentier. Limiting the discussion to actually existing adaptations, in this sense, results in a falsely diminished sense of the modernist **potential** of the cinema. My own assumption, in contrast, is that the cinema's variegated chronotopic capacities enable it to transpose and enrich absolutely **any** aesthetic, whether realist or anti-realist, illusionist or self-reflexive.

Multicultural Dialogism

The palimpsestic multi-trace nature of art, I will assume throughout this text, operates both within and across cultures. Another intermittent theme will be the multicultural dialogue between Europe and its others, a dialogue which is not of recent date. Although a Eurocentric narrative constructs an artificial wall of separation between European and non-European culture, in fact Europe itself is a synthesis of many cultures, Western and non-Western. The "West," then, is itself a collective heritage, an omnivorous *mélange* of cultures; it did not simply absorb non-European influences, as Jan Pietersie points out, "it was constituted by them."[20] In light of these constitutive and mutually imbricated differences, *Literature Through Film* adopts a multi-perspectival or polycentric approach to film and literature. Spanish critic Ortega y Gasset anticipated this idea in 1924 in *Las Atlantidas*, where he foresaw a future decentering of Europe and an expanding of horizons:

> In the past twenty years, the horizons of history have been expanded enormously – so much that Europe's old pupil, accustomed to the circumference of her traditional horizon, of which she was the center, cannot manage now to fit within one perspective the huge territories suddenly added. If up to the present "universal history" has suffered from an excessive concentration on a single gravitational point, toward which all processes of human existence converged – the European point of view – at least for one generation, a polycentric universal history will be elaborated, the totality of the horizon will be obtained by a simple juxtaposition of partial horizons, with heterogeneous radii, which, held as a bunch, will yield a panorama of human destinies similar to a cubist painting.[21]

While I do not see this opening of horizons as a recent development (it can be traced back to the Renaissance and even earlier), I do endorse Ortega's notion of a polycentric literary history. My approach here will be multicultural and anti-Eurocentric not so much in terms of the corpus of texts – most of the texts treated are European or "Eurotropic" classics – but rather in terms of seeing the texts themselves as multicultural, whether through manifest presences or through structuring absences.

Adaptation theory is what Bakhtinian translinguistics would call an "historically situated utterance." And just as one cannot separate the history of adaptation theory from the history of the arts and of artistic discourse, one can also not separate it from history *tout court*, defined by Jameson as "that which hurts" but also as that which inspires. In the long view, the history of literature, like that of film, must be seen in the light of large-scale historical events like colonialism, the process by which the European powers reached positions of economic, military, political and cultural hegemony in much of Asia, Africa, and the Americas. While nations had often annexed adjacent territories, what was new in European colonialism was its planetary reach, its affiliation with global institutional power, and its imperative mode, its attempted submission of the world to a single "universal" regime of truth and power. This process reached its apogee at the beginning of the twentieth century, when the earth surface controlled by European powers rose from 67 percent (in 1884) to 84.4 percent (in 1914), a situation that began to be reversed only with the disintegration of the European colonial empires after World War II.[22] The literary tradition explored here runs from *Don Quixote*, written just a century or so after conquistadors like Columbus and Cortez invaded the Americas, to the magic realism of *Erendira* and *Barroco*, written centuries later, but still bearing the scars of conquest and slavery in the Americas. The entire tradition is inevitably marked by colonialism and imperialism. In this sense, the book is consonant with Edward Said's call in *Culture and Imperialism* for a "contrapuntal approach which stresses the overlapping and intertwined histories of Europe and its 'others.' "[23]

The various European empires embodied themselves and projected their power through texts, not only through political treatises, diaries, edicts, administrative records, letters, but also through novels and, later, films. Usually, Europeans novels simply took for granted the reach and power of empire. Novels like Jane Austen's *Mansfield Park* (1814) revolve around issues of both property (ownership) and propriety (right behavior), in a situation where property was rooted in the colonies. The Mansfield Park estate, in this sense, is sustained by Sir Thomas Bertram's sugar plantations in Antigua, where slavery was practiced until the 1830s. The recent adaptation of *Mansfield Park*, by calling attention to Sir Thomas's dependence on slavery, re-envisions the novel through the anti-colonial grid provided by Fanon, Said, and others.[24] In Thackeray's *Vanity Fair* the empire is presented as a source of profits, while in Virginia Woolf's *Mrs Dalloway* (1925) the empire is described as wielding its "truncheon" over "thought and religion; drink; dress; manners; marriage too." Postcolonial and multicultural critics have begun to "desegregate" and "transnationalize" criticism, exploring the ways that the character of Huck Finn was shaped by a black prototype, for example, or the ways that Melville's Pequod, in *Moby Dick*, forms a multicultural microcosm, or the ways that *Benito Cereno*'s story of a slave mutiny reflects on the politics of race in nineteenth-century America. While these multicultural elements have always been present, the advent of postcolonial critique has endowed them with renewed interpretative significance.

If the beginnings of the European novel (*Robinson Crusoe*) coincided with the early era of colonial conquest and transatlantic slavery, the beginnings of the cinema coincided with the imperial paroxysm of European domination. The most prolific film-producing countries of the silent period – England, France, the US, Germany – also "happened" to be among the leading imperialist countries, in whose clear interest it was to laud the colonial enterprise. The cinema combined narrative and spectacle to tell the story of colonialism from the colonizer's perspective. Of all the celebrated "coincidences" – of the beginnings of cinema with the beginnings of psychoanalysis, with the rise of nationalism, with the emergence of consumerism – it is this coincidence with imperialism that has been least studied. This book, I hope, indirectly addresses this omission.

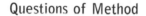

Questions of Method

Since it is impossible to say everything about the films and novels examined here, especially in a book which hopes to cover centuries of literary and cinematic development in a wide range of countries (Spain, England, France, Russia, the United States, Brazil, Cuba, Argentina, India, Portugal), there must of necessity be a principle of selection and framing. One principle of selection has to do with my own fields of competence. Formed in the field of comparative literature, I have respected the principle of treating only texts written in languages that I can read in the original, i.e. English, French, Portuguese and Spanish (the Russian of *Notes from Underground* here forms the exception).

But in another sense my chosen principle of pertinence is largely aesthetic. I am concerned principally with the stylistic and narrative challenges that a range of novels offers to the filmic adapter. I therefore offer detailed exegeses of specific passages in the novels or of specific sequences in the film adaptations, using close comparative analysis as a way of foregrounding the differing modes of representation. My emphasis is generally on style and voice and narrational

Introduction

technique. When discussing *Don Quixote* I do not speak of the novel's representation of the history of Spain, but rather of Cervantes' narrative and textual strategies: interpolated tales, the insertion of literary criticism, systematic digression, and so forth. At the same time, this privileging of the aesthetic does not mean that the analysis will be asocial or apolitical or ahistorical. Aesthetic questions, for me, are intricately bound up with social questions concerning social stratification and the distribution of power. A formalist approach, which Edward Said in *Culture and Imperialism* compares to "describing a road without its setting in the landscape,"[25] is clearly inadequate. What interests me, in this sense, is the historicity of forms themselves, the ways that stylistic choices in terms of genre, voice, point of view resonate with what translinguistics calls "social evaluations," the ways that violations of aesthetic norms resonate with the undermining of social norms.

Given that methodological preamble, it remains only to sketch out the overall movement of *Literature Through Film*. Following this conceptual introduction, chapter 1, "A Cervantic Prelude: From *Don Quixote* to Postmodernism," installs the themes of both realism and magic by discussing the novel *Don Quixote* along with its filmic adaptations, notably those by Orson Welles and Gregory Kozintsev, before moving on to the Cervantic aspects of postmodernism.

Chapter 2, "Colonial and Postcolonial Classics: From *Robinson Crusoe* to *Survivor*," focuses on the documentary, "just the facts" realism of Defoe's seminal novel *The Adventures of Robinson Crusoe*. After delineating the crucial historical importance of Defoe's novel, I explore just a few of the scores of adaptations based on *Crusoe*, focusing especially on Buñuel's *Robinson Crusoe*, Jack Gold's *Man Friday*, and Caleb Deschamel's *Crusoe*. A leitmotif here will be the anti-colonialist "writing back" trend in literature.

Chapter 3, "The Self-conscious Novel: From Henry Fielding to David Eggers," returns to the Cervantic tradition of the self-conscious novel. While *Robinson Crusoe* suppresses its own intertextual sources in the name of verisimilitude, the "self-conscious" novels written "in the manner" of Cervantes call attention to their own intertextuality. Here I will focus on two novels by Henry Fielding (*Joseph Andrews* and *Tom Jones*) and one by Machado de Assis (*Posthumous Memoirs of Bras Cubas*). I will conclude by addressing the reflexive aspects of both the contemporary novel (Dave Eggers's *A Heartbreaking Work of Staggering Genius*) and the contemporary mass media.

Chapter 4, "The Proto-cinematic Novel: Metamorphoses of *Madame Bovary*," brings us to the classic nineteenth-century realist novel, which provided not only countless stories for adaptation but also helped shape the dominant aesthetic paradigm within the cinema. Here I will focus on Flaubert's *Madame Bovary*, which counterpoints and synthesizes the two traditions explored in the previous chapters, to wit the documentary-mimetic (Defoe) and the reflexive-parodic (Cervantic) traditions. After demonstrating the "proto-impressionist" and "proto-cinematic" aspects of Flaubert's novel, I will focus on its various adaptations, notably on those directed by Jean Renoir (1934), Vincente Minnelli (1949), Claude Chabrol (1991), Ketan Mehta (1992), and Manoel de Oliveira (1997). I will conclude with a discussion of some of the "Flaubertian" work of Woody Allen.

Chapter 5, "Underground Man and Neurotic Narrators: From Dostoevsky to Nabokov," negotiates the transition from the nineteenth-century mimetic novel into modernist narratives, particularly those deploying unreliable first-person narrators. After a discussion of the seminal importance of Dostoevsky's "polyphonic" writing, and an analysis of *Notes from Underground* and two of its adaptations, I focus on a series of adaptations of modernist novels, all influenced by Dostoevsky, featuring neurotic, unreliable, self-discrediting narrators: Tomas Gutierrez Alea's adaptation of Edmundo Desnoes' *Memories of Underdevelopment*; the two adaptations of Nabokov's *Lolita* (by Stanley Kubrick and Adrian Lynne); and Suzana Amaral's adaptation of Clarice Lispector's *The Hour of the Star*.

Chapter 6 focuses on "Modernism, Adaptation, and the French New Wave." After some initial observations about the practice of adaptation by the New Wave, and about the theoretical quarrels about adaptation in the pages of *Cahiers*, I focus on the experimental novel/film in France, and especially the cine-roman, devoting special attention to *Hiroshima mon amour* and *Last Year at Marienbad*. The cine-romans forge a completely new modality of film/novel relation, where the notion of "adaptation" becomes even more problematic than usual, where novelist and filmmaker work on a basis of equality and even symbiosis, while also respecting the specificity of each medium. It is within this frame that I will offer an in-depth analysis of Godard's adaptation of Alberto Moravia's novel *Contempt*, before concluding with some comments about the Cervantic and "Quixotic" aspects of the French New Wave in general.

The final chapter brings issues of realism and magic full circle by focusing on the Latin American "boom" and "magic realism." While Godard in *Contempt* problematizes realism by reflexively foregrounding the formal mechanics of illusionism and by "emptying out" narrative, the "magical realist" approach interrogates realism by moving in the opposite direction, by spinning out a delirious profusion of improbable tales. If one form of reflexivity is "infra-realist," the other approach might be called "supra-realist." After sketching out the historical background of magic realism, I offer an in-depth analysis of a relatively unknown precursor of "magic realism," Mário de Andrade's brilliant modernist novel *Macunaíma* (1928) – for me the unsung "mother" of all magic realist novels – and of its equally brilliant cinematic "translation" by Joaquim Pedro de Andrade in 1968. Then I will turn to the filmic adaptations based on the work of Gabriel Garcia Márquez (*An Old Man with Enormous Wings, Erendira*) and Alejo Carpentier (*Barroco*).

Overall, *Literature Through Film* offers a history of the novelistic tradition via its filmic re-envisionings, stressing the complex energetic and synergistic shifts involved in trans-media migration. Rather than follow a single model, my analytical approach will be flexible, "adapted," as it were, to the specific qualities of **each** film and novel. Deploying simultaneously literary theory, media theory, and (multi)cultural studies, I will deploy multiple grids – a kind of methodological cubism – in order to illuminate the relations between novel and film in what is, I hope, a rich, complex, and multidimensional fashion.

--- Notes ---

1 René Girard, *Deceit, Desire and the Novel* (Baltimore, MD: The Johns Hopkins University Press, 1961), p. 52.

2 See Robert Stam, "Beyond Fidelity: The Dialogics of Adaptation," in James Naremore (ed.), *Film Adaptation* (New Brunswick, NJ: Rutgers University Press, 2000). See also "Introduction: The Theory and Practice of Adaptation," in Robert Stam and Alessandra Raengo (eds), *Literature and Film: A Guide to the Theory and Practice of Film Adaptation* (Oxford: Blackwell, 2005), pp. 1–52.

3 Gérard Genette, *Palimpsestes: La littérature au second degré* (Paris: Seuil, 1982).

4 I place the "West" in quotation marks here because classical Greece is often constructed as the point of origin of an idealized West, when in fact classical Greece was an amalgam of African, Semitic, and (what later became known as) European cultures. See Robert Stam and Ella Shohat, *Unthinking Eurocentrism: Multiculturalism and the Media* (London: Routledge, 1994).

5 Erich Auerbach, *Mimesis: The Representation of Reality in Western Literature* (Princeton, NJ: Princeton University Press, 1953).

6 Ibid., p. 491.

7 Arthur Heiserman, *The Novel before the Novel: Essays and Discussions about the Beginnings of Prose Fiction in the West* (Chicago: University of Chicago Press, 1977); Margaret Anne Doody, *The True Story of the Novel* (New Brunswick, NJ: Rutgers University Press, 1996), p. 1.

8 See Ian Watt, *The Rise of the Novel: Studies in Defoe, Richardson, and Fielding* (Harmondsworth: Penguin, 1963).

9 We are reminded of debates in film history whereby a teleological view, which scorned early silent films as "primitive" gropings toward the dominant continuity style which

came later, gave way to a less teleological approach, which saw silent films not as exemplars of failed modernity but rather as proleptic instances of an alternative aesthetic.

10 Doody, *True Story of the Novel*, p. 18.

11 Ibid., p. 198.

12 Mikhail Bakhtin, *Rabelais and his World*, trans. Helene Iswolsky (Cambridge, MA: MIT Press, 1968).

13 Salman Rushdie, *The Wizard of Oz* (London: British Film Institute, 1992), p. 9.

14 See Robert Stam, *Reflexivity in Film and Literature* (New York: Columbia University Press, 1992), and Stam and Shohat, *Unthinking Eurocentrism*.

15 See Henry Louis Gates, Jr, *The Signifying Monkey* (New York: Oxford University Press, 1988).

16 See Raul Ruiz, *Poetics of Cinema* (Paris: Editions Dis Voir, 1995), p. 73.

17 Ruiz once planned to resolve the contradiction in the form of a film, which would have concerned a putative competition between Georges Meliès and the Lumière Brothers to produce a version of Verne's *Around the World in 80 Days* for screening at the 1900 World Exhibition in Paris. The Lumières would spend eighty days traveling around the world with their camera, while Meliès would recreate the trip in his Paris studio. Hesitant about which project to back, the promoters go directly to Jules Verne, who tolerantly supports both kinds of adaptation. See Ruiz, *Poetics of Cinema*, p. 74.

18 See Michel Chion, *Audio-vision: Sound on Screen* (New York: Columbia University Press, 1994), especially the first chapter "Projections of Sound on Image."

19 For more on Hitchcock as modernist, see my "Hitchcock and Buñuel" essay in Walter Raubicheck and Walter Srebnick (eds), *Hitchcock's Rereleased Films* (Detroit: Wayne State University Press, 1991).

20 Jan Pietersie, "Unpacking the West: How European is Europe?," unpublished paper made available to me by the author.

21 *Las Atlantidas* (Madrid 1924), p. 31, quoted in Roberto Gonzalez Echevarria, *Alejo Carpentier: The Pilgrim at Home* (Austin: University of Texas Press, 1990), p. 117.

22 See H. Magdoff, *Imperialism: From the Colonial Age to the Present* (New York: Monthly Review Press, 1978), p. 108.

23 Edward Said, *Culture and Imperialism* (New York: Knopf, 1993), p. xx. For more on a "contrapuntal" approach, see my *Subversive Pleasures: Bakhtin, Film, and Cultural Criticism* (Baltimore, MD: The Johns Hopkins University Presss, 1989).

24 See Tim Watson, "Improvements and Reparations at Mansfield Park," in Stam and Raengo (eds), *Literature and Film*, ch. 1.

25 Said, *Culture and Imperialism*, p. 105.

Chapter 1

A Cervantic Prelude: From *Don Quixote* to Postmodernism

Literary critics have spoken, in connection with *Don Quixote*, of a "self-conscious" genre in the novel, a tradition which has historically often been slighted or condemned. In his *Partial Magic: The Novel as a Self-conscious Genre*, Robert Alter defines the self-conscious novel as:

> one in which from beginning to end, through the style, the handling of narrative viewpoint, the names and words imposed on the characters, the patterning of the narration, the nature of the characters and what befalls them, there is a consistent effort to convey to us a sense of the fictional world as an authorial construct set up against a background of literary tradition and convention.[1]

Alter disengages an ongoing tradition of self-consciousness going back to Cervantes, continuing with Fielding and Sterne in England and Diderot in France, and undergoing a veritable Renaissance in the twentieth century with writers such as Gide, Queneau, Borges, Nabokov, Pyncheon, and Fowles. The works of all these novelists form "the other great tradition," where novels systematically flaunt their own condition of artifice, reflexively engaging their own procedures and techniques.

Self-conscious fictions à la Cervantes defiantly call attention to their own artifice and operations, refusing a transparent, self-effacing language that opens quietly onto the world. When Cervantes interrupts the story of Don Quixote's battle with the Biscayan, in what is perhaps the most famous freeze-frame of literary history, leaving them both with swords upraised, on the grounds that his source went no farther, only to resume his account upon discovering a parchment depicting the very same battle, he is consciously destroying the illusion created by his story. When Fielding in *Tom Jones* halts the flow of his narrative to expatiate on the novelist's craft, he reminds us of the artifice involved in writing a novel. By seeing themselves not as nature's slaves but as fiction's masters, self-conscious artists cast doubt on the central assumption of mimetic art: the notion of an antecedent reality on which the artistic text is supposedly modeled. Unlike the self-effacing artist of Stephen Dedalus, who, "like the God or creation, remains within or behind or beyond or above his handiwork, invisible," the self-conscious artist, with a differing sense of supernatural decorum, is fond of making comic epiphanies in the created universe. The god of anti-illusionist art is not an immanent pantheistic deity but an Olympian, making noisy intrusion into fictive events. We are torn away from the events and the characters and made aware of the pen, or brush, or camera that has created the fictive figures.

Since the stuff of self-conscious art is the tradition itself – to be alluded to, played with, outdone, or exorcized – parody has often been of crucial importance. The very idea of parody implies some self-evident truths about the artistic process. The first is that the artist does not imitate nature but rather other texts. One paints, or writes, or makes films because one has seen paintings, read novels, or attended films. Art, in this sense, is not a window on the world but rather an intertextual dialogue between artists. The intertextual references may be explicit or implicit, conscious or unconscious, direct and local or broad and diffuse. These truths apply with equal self-evidence to the cinema. Directors make films in a certain genre, or "in the manner of" a certain director, or according to a set of generic conventions. Whether artists call attention to these intertextual influences or obscure them, the intertext is always present.

Cervantes' *Don Quixote* constitutes a generative matrix and *locus classicus* of reflexive parody. As is well known, *Don Quixote* concerns the adventures of a mad geriatric **hidalgo**, a lover of chivalric literature, who sets forth to realize the literary ideal of the wandering knight or **caballero andante**. The plot needs no summarizing here, since even people who have never read the novel are familiar with the character, whether through pop productions like *Man of La Mancha* or simply through adjectives like "Quixotic" or expressions like "tilting at windmills." Indeed, *Don Quixote* is one of those texts that have been universally disseminated without, in most cases, actually having been read.

Don Quixote has left a long trail of prestigious commentary. Polyperspectival in its own terms, the novel has itself been read perspectivally, in that its protagonist has been made to incarnate everything from the nobility of defending lost causes to the blind folly of pursuing an *idée fixe*. Critics have argued for centuries about whether Don Quixote was crazy or lucid, just as they have argued about whether Hamlet, who appeared on stage just four years before *Don Quixote* was published, was mad or just putting on an "antic disposition." The entire history of modern literature can be seen as a footnote to *Don Quixote*. Its influence extends over such diverse writers as Dickens, Melville, Goethe, Flaubert, Twain, Turgenev, Borges, Machado de Assis and Alejo Carpentier. Over the centuries, the novel itself seems to have metamorphosed in genre, from being read as a burlesque travesty to being admired as a respected classic. For Hegel, Quixote encapsulated the dilemmas of metaphysics, while for Marx he incarnated false consciousness. For Dostoevsky, this "saddest of all books" provided the human model for his own "Idiot." For Miguel de Unamuno, this "saddest story ever written" inspired his own "tragic sense of life." In his novel *The Wheel*, Jensen portrays Quixote as representing the energy and adventure of America, now out of place in tired, enervated Europe. For Ernst Bloch, Quixote was Christ-like in his noble, derided purity.[2]

But for Vladimir Nabokov, who has unceremoniously dismissed many of history's greatest writers, Cervantes' novel forms an "encyclopedia of cruelty," one of the "most bitter and barbarous books ever penned." In this "symphony of mental and physical pain," the physical cruelty of the first part competes with the mental cruelty of the second part, where the novelist takes pleasure in humiliating his character with ritual beatings and ingenious tortures.[3] For the romantics, in contrast, Quixote represented the transmogrifying power of the imagination, the alchemical capacity to turn quotidian dross into artistic gold. But for René Girard, the romantics are themselves Quixotic; they idealize Quixote's egomania, prettifying a personage who in real life would be experienced as an obnoxious fool.[4]

For Girard, "all the ideas of the Western novel are present in germ in *Don Quixote*."[5] The nineteenth-century French realist novelists, as we shall see in chapter 2, both created Quixotic characters and deployed Cervantic techniques. They took as their own what Harry Levin calls the "literary technique of systematic disillusionment,"[6] the theme pithily evoked in Balzac's infinitely suggestive title: *Lost Illusions*. According to this scenario, a book-inspired protagonist undergoes excruciating adventures only to end up, like Quixote on his deathbed, renouncing romance (in all the senses of that word). As a paradigm of "triangular desire," Don Quixote himself had "surrendered to Amadis the individual's fundamental prerogative: he no longer chooses the objects of his own desire."[7] Much as contemporary adolescents model themselves on pop stars, Don Quixote models himself on his literary heroes. In the world of *Don Quixote*, characters draw swords over hermeneutics, rather like present-day movie fans who fight over the value and meaning of movies, sometimes experiencing emotional rupture over their sharply differing responses.

As a cultural artifact, *Don Quixote* emerges from a complex, multicultural and multilingual Mediterranean world, and from a Spain shaped for centuries by three religious civilizations: Catholic, Muslim, and Jewish. It is often forgotten that the Jews and Muslims of Iberia lived in symbiotic closeness, while the Catholics were the enemies of both groups. The *reconquista*, the expulsion of the Muslims, and the Inquisition against both Muslims and Jews did not instantly erase the Muslim and Jewish presence in Spain. In *Don Quixote*, the narrator has a Castilian-speaking "Morisco" (i.e. a Muslim forced to convert to Christianity) translate a parchment book in Arabic, and he mentions that a translator for "a more ancient language" (i.e. Hebrew) also would not be hard to find. Cervantes thus suggests that his own art comes out of various "oriental" sources – from the Bible, from Arabic stories – from which the Spanish learned the art of novelizing. (Cervantes also wrote many plays on Turkish and Islamic and Arab themes: *The Dungeons of Algiers, The Grand Sultana, Life in Istanbul,* and *The Death of Selim*.)

Both Jews and Muslims were victimized by the Inquisition. Anti-semitism as well as anti-Muslimism played an important role in European literature. The French **chansons de geste** which fed into the chivalric tradition, for example, revolved around the defense of the Christian empire against the Moors. (Cervantes himself lost the use of his left hand at the Battle of Lepanto, and was imprisoned for five years in Algiers.) Yet some scholars have suggested that Cervantes himself was from a **marrano** or **cristiano nuevo** background, i.e. from a Jewish family forced to convert by the Spanish Inquisition. When Sancho proclaims himself the "mortal enemy of the Jews," Don Quixote, *marrano*-like, says nothing. Cervantes' status as a descendant of **marranos** would help explain Cervantes' quietly skeptical view of the events he recounts.

Cervantes' novel is also indirectly related to the other key event of 1492: Columbus's voyages to the "New World." Spain in Cervantes' time was haunted by diverse internal and external "others:" Jews, Muslims, Africans, and the indigenous people then being colonized by their conquistadores. Repeatedly, *Don Quixote* echoes with the rumors of such world-historical events as the Crusades, the *reconquista*, the Inquisition, and the conquest of the Americas. It is the execrable behavior of **Moorish** puppets, significantly, that triggers Don Quixote's intervention in Master Pedro's puppet show. When Quixote transforms windmills into pernicious giants, similarly, his language recalls the *reconquista* and the Inquisition: "I intend to do battle with them and slay them. With their spoils we shall begin to be rich, for this is a righteous war and the removal of so foul a brood from off the face of the earth is a service God will bless" (VIII, 98). The innumerable references in *Don Quixote* to the "accursed religion of Mohammed" make us forget that pre-Inquisition Spain was characterized by the relatively peaceful coexistence of the three "religions of the book," and especially between Islam and Judaism. Cervantes gives vivid expression, in sum, to the Spain that was at once the master of empire, the oppressor of Muslims and Jews (although Cervantes does not speak in the language of "oppression"), and at the same time a culturally miscegenated country still marked by the traces of its expelled ethnicities.

Although critics have usually emphasized the comicity of Quixote's alchemical imaginings, that comicity is sometimes spoken in an exterminationist language redolent of the *reconquista* (and the Inquisition) in Spain, and of the *conquista* in the Americas. The European conquest of the Americas was, on one level, a bookish enterprise, a clash of intertexts, shaped not only by Roman imperial law and literature of the Christian crusade, but also by Marco Polo's *Travels*, by romances of chivalry and Renaissance epic poems. Alejo Carpentier points out that Hernan Cortes and his colleagues, on arriving in Mexico, repeatedly cited the same chivalric romances mocked by Cervantes to evoke the wonders of the (misnamed) "New World." "God gave us good luck in war," writes Cortes, "as he did to the knight Roldan."[8] Just two years after the appearance of the First Part of *Don Quixote*, Quixote, Sancho, and even Rocinante, were appearing as processional figures within Spanish festivals in the Americas.[9] The Conquest itself, furthermore, can be seen as Quixotic, not only in the sense of idealizing violence through what Joseph Conrad, centuries later, would call a "redeeming idea," but also in the sense of being thoroughly imbued by a "bookish" imaginary. The "New" World was seen through the lenses and prisms and legends provided by the Old: Atlantis, Eldorado, the Amazons, the Fountain of Youth, and The Seven Cities of Cibola. "America" was both a real place on a map and a fantasy "mapped" on to a tabula rasa through an intertextual imaginary. European intruders, formed by readings from the Scriptures, Herodotus, Marco Polo and about King Arthur and chivalric romances, encountered indigenous peoples who also tried to account for the invaders through their own pre-existing myths and intertexts, invoking the long-prophesied return of a divinity or hero (Quetzalcoatl in Mexico, Wiraqoch in the Andes) or the emergence of a great shaman (in the Tupi-Guarani cultural region). While the Europeans tried to force the native peoples into a pre-set Biblical schema – for example, as the "lost tribe" of Israel – the native peoples counterposed their own texts and beliefs to those professed in the Christian Scriptures.

One wonders, then, and here I am being admittedly speculative, if Cervantes was not on some level mocking the Quixotic aspects of conquest discourse, which transformed grisly massacres into heroic exploits. Anti-semites and racists and conquistadores, Don Quixote-like, also transformed what they saw; their imaginations turned ordinary Jewish human beings into "devils" and "enchanters," turned the pacific indigenous peoples of the Americas into "cannibals." Columbus encountered an already-named, Taino-populated island, but misrecognized it as "Asia" and renamed it "San Salvador." (We will return to these transatlantic exchanges from a different angle when we discuss the "marvelous American real" in chapter 7.)

My point is not that Cervantes was a multiculturalist *avant la lettre*, but rather that a multicultural approach can illuminate *Don Quixote*. In chapter 29 of *Don Quixote*, for example, Sancho Panza fantasizes about inheriting a kingdom in "the land of the blacks." Instantly, his imagination runs to taking a boatload of them and selling them for hard cash in Spain. Here Sancho Panza, like Robinson Crusoe a century later, becomes, if only in his imagination, the *petit blanc*, the poor white who prospers thanks to colonial exploitation. Cervantes' cameo surrogate in the book, similarly, a soldier named like Cervantes himself "Saavedra," remarks that, during his imprisonment in Algiers, the Moors never flogged him or subjected him to a harsh word, an indirect criticism perhaps of the widespread image of a cruel and "accursed" race. Even the ironic tribute to his "source," Cid Hamete Benengeli, can be seen as a homage not only to Arab storytelling traditions, but also to a tradition of "courtly love" which, according to Denis de Rougemont, was very much indebted to Arabic love poetry.[10] Don Quixote's love for Dulcinea, we recall, was also courtly and Platonic; in the many years that he loved her he saw her only three or four times, and then without speaking to her.

The presence of parodic reflexivity in *Don Quixote* does not imply an absence of social realism. Spain in the seventeenth century was the scene of intense ideological battles over class and culture, and Cervantes, *picaro*-like, was himself familiar with all the class positions, from jail to the royal palace. In chapter 6, Cervantes becomes a sociologist *avant la lettre*: he has Quixote describe the social world of Spain as consisting of four classes: (1) the humble who become great; (2) the great who remain great; (3) the great who become humble; and (4) the humble who remain humble. Later, he describes two superimposed pyramids: "those that trace their descent from princes and monarchs, whom time has gradually reduced to a point, like a pyramid upside down; others that derive their origin from common folk and ascend step by step until they arrive at being great lords" (XXI, 207). Don Quixote implicitly describes himself as among "those who were and are no longer" and Sancho as among those "who are but once were not." We could not have a more apt description of the destabilized social world typical of the novel, conjugating social movement downward (Quixote's) with social movement upward (Sancho's).

Parodies like *Don Quixote* construct themselves on the destruction of literary or cinematic codes. The historical function of novels like *Don Quixote*, for Fredric Jameson, is to perform the secular "decoding" of "preexisting inherited traditional or sacred narrative paradigms."[11] Cervantes' comic epic shows a contemporary world refractory to epic/chivalric values, where such values can **only be** comic. Indeed, Cervantes was completely explicit about his destructive project: he wrote in order to destroy the chivalric romance, then the most popular genre of his time. Indeed, he names his satiric targets in the novel itself. The scene where Quixote's niece burns his romances becomes an excuse to name the objects of parody in the book: *Amadis de Gaula*, *Lisuarte de Grecia*, *Cirongilio de Tracia*, *Felixmarte de Hircania*. Cervantes mocks the chivalric romances for their sexual exploitativeness, their predictability, and their ludicrous irreality. He mocks not only their themes, but also their techniques – the pretense of being "translations" from Arabic or Greek, the claptrap of prologues, the penchant for abruptly interrupting stories in the middle, and so forth – even as he uses them himself.

Cervantes also criticizes the romances on Spanish nationalist grounds. Quixote, in this sense, constitutes the antithesis of the conventions of the chivalric tradition. The heroes of chivalric romances are invariably from elsewhere – Quixote's hero Amadis of Gaul, as his name implies, is from France, while King Arthur is from England. The heroes are never from Spain. Rather than being from a romanticized elsewhere, Quixote comes from one of the poorest and driest regions of Spain. Rather than being young and rich and handsome, Quixote is old, poor, decrepit, and probably impotent, whence, perhaps, his preference for an ideal, unconsummated love. He is as clumsy in action as he is elegant in language. Wherever Quixote extends his helping hand, as Ernst Bloch puts it, "he knocks something over."[12] Sancho Panza too is a degraded version of the sidekick figure from the chivalric novels; rather than an admiring apprentice figure, he is motivated by hunger, greed, and ambition, and is baffled, rather than impressed, by his master.

In *Don Quixote*, the parodic principle applies even to Cervantes' own book, since Part II parodies and comments on Part I. But parody is the genre that combines critique and affection, and Cervantes' project is not purely destructive. The parody itself prolongs the devices that it denounces. Cervantes was writing at a time when most readers had **read** the chivalric romances, which is no longer the case. Yet one of the paradoxes, as Daniel Eisenberg points out, is that even though Cervantes destroyed the chivalric romance genre, it is only thanks to him that nowadays people read the romances at all.[13]

While realistic novels hide their artifice in the name of truth, novels in the Cervantic tradition flaunt their artifice in the name of another truth – that of art itself. While realistic novels dissimulate their rootedness in the imitation of other texts, claiming to imitate only nature, Cervantic texts proudly display their own imitative strategies by crowding the novel with quotations, stories, and poems, constantly molding a bookish universe inundated with manuscripts, printed matter, and illustrations. Indeed, the prologue of *Don Quixote* reflects a kind of "citation envy." Although "Cervantes" claims that he is "too slack and indolent to go in search of authors to say for me what I myself can say without them," his "friend" convinces him that self-respecting books should be "crammed with sentences from Aristotle and Plato and the whole mob of philosophers as to astound their readers and win for their authors a reputation for scholarship and eloquence" (p. 42).[14] On the advice of the same friend, he scribbles a few laudatory poems recommending the book, rather like contemporary authors who pen their own blurbs for their friends to sign.

Despite Cervantes' claim to "speak for himself," he does not claim originality. Rather, he proudly bases his story on a found manuscript by a Moorish author, Cid Hamete Benengeli, whom he admires as a fountain of truth and yet at the same time condemns as the descendant of a "nation of liars." In fact, the source text is doubly unreliable, in itself and because its translation cannot be trusted. Cervantes also problematizes the act of writing itself. He takes the readers into his confidence and asks for their collaboration. The prologue, he confesses, was even harder to compose than the story itself: "Many times I picked up my pen to write it, and many times I put it down, not knowing what to write" (p. 42). In this sense, *Don Quixote* inaugurates that strain of the novel (and later film) which foregrounds the process of creation itself, all those novels (like Gide's *Faux monnayeurs* or John Fowles's *The French Lieutenant's Woman*) or those films (like Fellini's *8½* or Woody Allen's *Stardust Memories*) that foreground the labor pains of the creative process. At the same time, by including criticism of his own novel – for example, Carrasco tells the Don that some readers have criticized the inserted novellas – *Don Quixote* anticipates another strain of texts: those that incorporate the criticisms that have been made, or might be made, of the texts themselves.

The author's claim to "truth," in *Don Quixote*, is troubled from the outset. Even the protagonist's name is unstable:

> It is said his surname was Quixada, or Quesada (for in this there is some difference among the authors who have written upon this subject), though by probable conjectures it maybe gathered that he was called Quixana. But this is of little import to our story; let it suffice that in relating it we do not swerve a jot from the truth. (p. 23)

Thus, Don Quixote as a character is born under the sign of semantic and historiographic instability. The message is double: fictioners speak the truth and nothing but the truth, yet they also engage multiple perspectives and opinions about that truth. At the same time, this alleged multi-perspectivalism constitutes one of the standard confidence tricks of fiction: the idea that there are multiple perspectives on an object or character confers, through a kind of holographic projection, an illusory ontological solidity on the object in question. The indisputable "fact" of the multiple points of view implies that there must be **something** being regarded from those multiple points of view.

Urged on by what Girard calls "mimetic desire," Don Quixote imitates his hero Amadis of Gaul.[15] His madness is triggered by what Ernst Bloch calls the "spontaneous combustion of accumulated reading matter."[16] Quixote suffers from the "Alonso Quijano syndrome," defined by Juan Bonilla as the pathological tendency to "prolong identification with literary characters beyond the strict duration of the reading."[17] Although Cervantes condemns chivalric literature, he never condemns reading; in fact, he was himself a fanatic reader, reportedly reading even bits of torn paper lying in the street.[18] A core "readerly" analogy subliminally informs *Don Quixote*. Don Quixote reads and interprets reality just as readers interpret the books they read, spectators interpret the films they see, and filmmakers interpret the novels they adapt. Don Quixote's transformation of windmills into giants is no more marvelous and magical than the miracle of reading itself, which transforms barren symbols, bare arbitrary scribbles on a page or a parchment, into landscapes and characters and narratives and emotions. Quixote himself, Foucault suggests, is "himself like a sign, a long, thin graphism, a letter that has just escaped from the open pages of a book."[19]

Cervantes was writing after Gutenberg and the invention of the printing press, which was introduced into Spain in 1472, roughly a century before Cervantes wrote the first part of *Don Quixote*. Cervantes wrote, in other words, in a world that was beginning to be inundated by books to an extent never seen before, so that readers en masse **could** imitate literary heroes. In no way obscured, this mimetic imitation-of-reading theme stares out at us from the very surface of *Don Quixote*, emphatically "theorized," as it were, by Don Quixote himself. The phrases "imitation of" and "likeness of" proliferate, as when Don Quixote spends the night thinking of his Lady Dulcinea "in imitation of Marcela's lovers" (XII, 128). Or again, when Don Quixote transforms Dulcinea in his fantasy "into the likeness of that princess of whom he had read in his books" (XVI, 157). So many of the events in *Don Quixote* are triggered by art: the Don looking for, or better creating, bookish adventures, or the Duke and the Duchess entertaining themselves by staging Don Quixote's fantasies.

At times, "mimicry" comes close to mockery, as when others make fun of Don Quixote "in a mimicking manner." Explaining to Sancho the need to imitate his literary hero, Don Quixote argues:

> when any painter wishes to win renown in his art, he endeavors to copy the originals of the most illustrious painters he knows, and this rule holds good for all the crafts and callings of any importance . . . And so what he who would win the name of prudent and patient must do, and does, is to imitate Ulysses, in whose person and labors Homer depicts for us a lively picture of a patient and long-suffering man, just as Virgil shows in the person of Aeneas the virtue of a dutiful son and the wisdom of a brave and expert captain. They do not portray them or describe them as they were but as they should have been, to give example by their virtues to the men to come after them . . . In this way Amadis was the North Star . . . and all of us who fight under the banner of love and chivalry ought to imitate his example. (XXV, 241)

Here Cervantes plays on the multiple meanings of the word "mimesis." Derived from the Greek root *mimos*, "mimesis" (imitation) has variously evoked the act of portraying a likeness, the imitation of another person, the presenting of the self, the theatrical staging of an action, the identification of one person with another, or the imitation of another art work.[20] *Don Quixote* engages all of these meanings. Quixote the character imitates literary characters, just as Cervantes the author imitates his literary models and antecedents. Before deciding how to act, Don Quixote reflects on how his literary heroes would have acted in his place. At times he hesitates about which literary hero he should direct his mimetic energies toward: Orlando in his "outrageous frenzies" or Amadis in his "melancholy moods?"

Cervantes weaves a novel by needling romance, pitting the veracity of the novel against the mendacity of the romance. Cervantes' battered hidalgo attempts to act out the idealistic imperatives of chivalric literature, imperatives which were always improbable but which were now even more implausible in a no-longer feudal Spain. For Karl Marx, Don Quixote paid for the error of believing that knight-errantry was compatible with all economic forms of society. As Don Quixote maps literary patterns onto real experience, he tries to "match" every situation with some literary precedent. Since there is no textual precedent for monetary payment in his sacred texts, he refuses to pay Sancho for his services. Asked to pay expenses, Quixote answers that he had "never read in the stories of knights-errant that they ever carried money with them" (p. 69). Since Homer never mentions Agamemnon's salary or Nestor's pension, and since romance never mentions the **per diems** and tax deductions of Amadis of Gaul, Don Quixote dismisses such questions as beneath his dignity.

The self-conscious novel like *Don Quixote* has its deep roots in the millennial tradition of antique fictions like *The Odyssey*, *The Golden Ass*, and Heliodorus' *Aithiopika*. In fact, Cervantes' last novel *Persiles y Sigismunda*, by Cervantes' own admission, attempts to "compete with Heliodorus." Thus the modern novel begins as a parodic summa, mocking in turn epic, pastoral, romance, comedy, and devotional literature. *Don Quixote* is what Bakhtin calls "pluri-stylistic," a collage of literary fragments, ballads, poems, proverbs, histories, and pastiches. The self-conscious novel, in this sense, has strong affinities with what Northrop Frye calls the "anatomy," and what both Frye and Bakhtin call the "Menippea," a strand of fiction given to constant digressions, comic erudition, and the **mes-alliance** of genres.[21] The great anatomists are those on whom no genre is lost. Exploiting the widest possible range of sources, from Sancho Panza's earthy proverbs to the Don's celestial fights, anatomists like Cervantes take "high" and "low" materials and tease them into art, seducing "minor" genres into brilliance. The jarring clash between the Don's lofty language and Sancho's "lower" and more earthy speech, for example, brings high ideals down into the earthly realm, into the world of what Bakhtin called the "lower bodily stratum."

Many critics have commented on the carnivalesque aspects of *Don Quixote*. Bakhtin pointed to Sancho, with his *panza* (belly), and his appetite, as a typical carnival figure. In Bakhtinian terms, the Quixote/Sancho pair represent the odd couple, the oxymoronic duo which hybridizes the lofty and the grotesque. For Auerbach, they recall the contrasting pairs of comedy: the tall, gaunt, thin man and the short, fat one, the clever man and his stupid companion, the Laurel and Hardy yoking/joking of contrasts.[22] Yet the dynamic of the book, as many critics have noted, is to work toward convergence: the Quixotization of Sancho and the Sanchification of Don Quixote.[23] In *Deceit, Desire, and the Novel*, Girard mocks the "romantic" critics who reduce the dialogue of *Don Quixote* to one between Don Quixote the **idealist** and Sancho Panza the **realist**, overlooking the subterranean affinities between the two characters, forgetting the ways in which Sancho, for example, absorbs and mimics Don Quixote's desires.[24] Sancho Panza, too, leaves his family and friends for the sake of a dream, to the point that Don Quixote, in a rare moment of lucidity, tells Sancho to "drop these fooleries." It is the Don, Sancho's "mediator," after all, who sets Sancho to dreaming of islands and governorships.

Although illiterate, Sancho, too, is also a potential artist. His linguistic creativity exemplifies Bakhtin's critique of the Formalist hierarchy which posits poetic speech as superior to practical speech; the "practical" Sancho is also poetic.[25] The speech of both characters "embeds" various strata of discourse. While Don Quixote's speech "embeds" Platonic ideas of beauty, courtly love, chivalric romance, and the *dolce stil novo*, Sancho's discourse embeds popular slang and speech genres, the proverbial wisdom of the already said. His speech consists in stringing proverbs together in comic (and often contradictory) profusion: "Who buys and lies, his purse will rue the price; what's more, naked I was born, and naked am I now . . . Many expect flitches of bacon when there's not even a hook to hang them on" (XXV, 240). But in later episodes, Sancho emulates the Don's language, just as the Don, in imitation of Sancho, waxes colloquial and proverbial. The entire novel is informed by this process of reciprocal chameleonism, operative on both a characterological and a linguistic/discursive register.

It is therefore simplistic to adopt a "progressive" narrative whereby *Don Quixote* simply "buries" romance and thus announces a triumphal entry into Modernity. Within the conventionalist triumphalist narrative, as Doody puts it, the "Novel replaces the Romance as Reason replaces Superstition, and as the Model-T Ford replaces the horse and carriage."[26] But romance itself had an element of realism, since castles, knights and equestrian heroes really **were** part of the medieval landscape. And Nabokov points out that a country gentleman might have mistaken windmills for giants, since they were a cutting-edge technological innovation in seventeenth-century Spain.[27] The point in *Don Quixote* is the dialectic between the two modes, between the romantic and the novelistic, between fantasy and the reality principle, the utopian and the dystopian, even though the various poles occasionally change places.

The paradox about *Don Quixote*, Harry Levin points out, is that it casts a spell while dispelling an illusion: "By disenchanting his readers, he could cast a spell of his own."[28] Cervantes is simultaneously the smart demystifier and the "sage enchanter" hidden "behind" the Spanish narrator and presumed author Cid Hamete Benengeli. This simultaneous joy in both mystification and demystification reflects some truths about the process both of art's creation and of its consumption. Within the artist a struggle takes place between the will to create an illusion and the conscious decision to interrogate or even destroy that illusion. The lucidity of the illusionist, the puppeteer, or the filmmaker does battle with the desire to create a believable and lifelike image. For the reader or spectator, meanwhile, all the reflexive and distancing devices in the world do not necessarily preclude affective participation. Although the character Don Quixote is on one level a purely textual artifact, on another level this imaginary artifact has served for centuries as a magnet for readerly identification. How many people, over the centuries, have described themselves as "a little bit like Don Quixote?"

Don Quixote proliferates in what Bakhtin calls, in relation to the Menippea, "threshold encounters," impossible meetings between literary characters. A sonnet included in the prologue, for example, is sent by one literary character, Amadis of Gaul, to another, Don Quixote de la Mancha. At one point, Don Quixote converses with Don Alvaro Tarfe, a character from a spurious continuation of the Cervantes novel, inducing what Robert Alter calls the "ontological vertigo" provoked by a "fictional character from a 'true' fictional chronicle confronting a fictional character from a false one in order to establish beyond doubt his own exclusive authenticity."[29] At another point, Cervantes has his protagonist walk into a Barcelona printing shop where he observes the processes of proofreading, typesetting, and revision and is lectured on the economics of the publishing industry. Cervantes thus focuses attention on the concrete procedures by which all books, including his own, were produced. After meeting one of the characters from Avellaneda's spurious Second Volume of *Don Quixote*, the equally fictitious character Don Quixote (in chapter 72) has a notary draw up a document stating that the real Don Quixote and Sancho Panza are not the ones referred to in Avellaneda's book, thus leading to what Alter calls a "Copernican revolution in the practice and theory of mimesis."[30]

One especially suggestive episode involves Master Pedro and his puppet show. Just as the book as a whole offers a critique of a certain kind of readership, here Cervantes becomes a kind of theoretician of "spectatorship." In the episode, the protagonist, in an outburst of knightly rage, brings Master Pedro's puppet show to an abrupt halt by venting his fury on hapless puppets, which he presumes to be real Moors attacking a real Maiden, while Master Pedro protests that all the characters are only pasteboard figures. In this allegory of spectatorship, an artistic representation is brought to a halt by the naïve intervention of a personage who confounds reality with spectacle. As Robert Alter points out, the novelist unmasks the contingent precariousness of the illusion generated by the play-world of art. Through his proxy protagonist, Cervantes breaks off the purely verbal puppet show which is *Don Quixote* itself, suspending the narrative and reminding us of its papier-mâché factitiousness.[31]

Master Pedro's puppet show provides an unwitting model of anti-illusionistic theater, an anticipatory storehouse of Brechtian "alienation effects." Cervantes begins his account with a quotation from *The Aeneid* – "Here Tyrians and Trojans, all were silent" – which evokes Aeneas telling the Troy story to Dido and the assembled listeners. The allusion reminds us of the perennial fascination of tales and the excited anticipation, the "growing silent" which usually precedes the beginning of spectacle, whether it be puppet show, play, or film. The narrative structure of the episode, as Robert Alter has pointed out, is paradigmatic of the narrative structure of *Don Quixote* as a whole: a multiple regress of imitations calling attention to their own status as imitations.[32] Master Pedro's assistant, rather like a literary **benshi**, the silent-era explicators of films, narrates the action while Master Pedro manipulates the puppets. He cites the sources of his purportedly "true" story, in imitation of Cervantes himself with his facetious concern about the sources of *Don Quixote*. In tones reminiscent of Prospero in Shakespeare's *The Tempest*, the assistant acknowledges the poverty of the means of representation ("Turn your eyes, gentlemen, to that tower, which you must imagine to be one of the towers of the alcazar of Saragossa"), much in the manner of Brechtian theater, with its minimal sets and exposed construction. The assistant presents the characters ("that character who appears over there . . . is the Emperor Charlemagne") and calls attention to certain incidents and gestures ("Take notice, gentlemen, how the emperor . . . ," "See, too, that stately Moor . . .") much like certain of Brecht's mediating characters, such as Wong in *The Good Woman of Sctzuan*, who serve the same function.

In the puppet show episode, Cervantes ridicules Don Quixote's penchant for taking the representational fictions of art as fit objects for passionate identification. It is the desire to rescue papier-mâché maidens from fictional distresses that triggers Don Quixote's intervention in the puppet show. Many of the self-conscious novelists who come in Cervantes' wake try to make their readers critically aware of the pitfalls of taking a naïvely erotic stance toward their fictions. Anti-illusionistic art reminds us of our own eroticized complicity in artistic illusion. All fiction places us in the realm of half-belief, of "*je sais, mais quand même*," where we believe even while we doubt. No one, presumably, accepts the naïve illusions of trompe l'oeil. The **impression** of reality does not generally become the **illusion** of reality. No sane person tries to swim in cinematic oceans or converse with statues, and not even the most ardent cinephile literally confuses Elizabeth Taylor with an Egyptian queen. No spectator at a play, Samuel Johnson pointed out, really forgets that he is seated in a theater. Yet fiction requires the kind of complicitous contract that Don Quixote suggests to Sancho Panza when Sancho presumes to overreach him in the description of an adventure: "Sancho, if you want me to believe what you saw in the sky, I wish you to accept my account of what I saw in the cave of Montesinos. I say no more." It is precisely

A Cervantic Prelude

Chapter 1

this pact of reciprocal deception that anti-illusionists refuse to obscure, even while they take advantage of it in order to spin out new fictions.

Don Quixote on the Screen

Don Quixote has, from the very beginning, been caught up in the irresistible logic of sequels and adaptations. The "original" book underwent many mutations. The first part started as a short story, and then got padded with additional stories and materials and a new character, Sancho Panza. The second part of the novel, written years after the first part, was itself a kind of sequel. In Part II Cervantes takes into account some of the commentaries made about Part I. He admits that he included too many interpolated tales, but deflects the blame toward his Arab source. (Don Quixote himself also complains about Benengeli.) Indeed, Don Quixote encounters, in the second part, other characters reading a novel that claims to be "the Second part of *Don Quixote*," by a certain "Avellaneda," which is nothing less than a literary rip-off of the Cervantes novel. Like a novelist denouncing an unfaithful film adaptation based on his work, Cervantes denounces the theft of his characters. (Although Barthes and Foucault could announce, over three centuries later, the "death of the author," flesh-and-blood authors demand respect, citation, and their royalty checks.) In a sense, then, *Don Quixote* itself thematizes the issue of adaptation, for example by bringing up story sources as relayed by different media. When Cervantes cuts off the battle between Don Quixote and the Biscayan because his **verbal source** has run out, but then continues the story when he discovers a **visual source** in the form of an illustration, he has already invoked a kind of "adaptation."

Cervantes' "hijo" (son) *Don Quixote* has itself generated many **hijos** and **nietos**. Even the subsequent translations of the novel, some of them consciously dishonest, along with the novel's many illustrated versions and painterly renditions by figures ranging from Gustave Doré and Honoré Daumier to Picasso and Dali, can be seen as "adaptations."[33] *Don Quixote* has furnished the theme for poets and dramatists, composers, orchestrators, cartoonists, painters, sculptors, and weavers of tapestries. Within six months of the novel's first appearance in print, E. C. Riley points out, we find the "visual materializations" in the form of processional figures and carnival personae. There are also the innumerable literary and theatrical and operatic rewritings of *Don Quixote*: Chesterton's *The Return of Don Quixote*, Miguel de Unamuno's *Vida de Don Quixote y Sancho*, Borges' *Pierre Menard*, Kathy Acker's *Don Quixote*, the opera *Don Quixote*, the musical *Man of La Mancha* and so forth. The post-text of *Quixote*, in the wider sense, would include Kafka's parable "The Truth about Sancho Panza," where Sancho turns into the character who has absorbed all the chivalric romances and Don Quixote into his imagined demon, thus transforming Cervantes' novel into what Harold Bloom calls "one long and rather bitter Jewish joke."[34] There have also been adaptations "at one remove," as it were. Graham Greene's novel *Monsignor Quixote* rewrites *Don Quixote* as a story of a provincial Spanish clergyman who goes to Madrid with a sectarian communist as his Sancho Panza. (Alec Guinness starred as Don Quixote in a made-for-television version in 1988.)

Cervantes' novel has also been adapted directly for the screen. I can only begin to address here the vast (and never-ending) production drawn from the Cervantes novel. A 1997 Spanish Film Festival, entitled "Cervantes in Images," offered no less than thirty-four films – features, shorts, documentaries, animated cartoons – inspired by *Don Quixote* and other Cervantic texts, and that is assuredly but a tiny proportion of the total. The list of adaptations would have to include at least the following: the 1903 silent French version; the 1908 silent Spanish version; the 1909 Emile Cohl animation; the 1915 American Edward Dillon version; the 1923 UK Maurice Elvey version; the 1926 Danish Lau Lauritzen version; the 1933 G. W. Pabst version; the 1934 animated cartoon by Ub Iwerks; the 1947 Spanish Rafael Gil version; the Orson Welles version initiated in 1955; the 1956 Israeli Nathan Axelrod version; the 1957 Russian Kozintsev version; the 1959 TV play *I, Don Quixote* (the theatrical source of *Man of La Mancha*); the 1962 Finnish version; the 1962 (Spanish) Vicente Escriva version; the 1963 Carlo Rim version; the 1965 Russian (Yevgeni Karelov) *Deti Don-Kikhota* also known as *Quixote's Children*; the 1972 (Mexican) Roberto Gavaldon version; the 1972 musical *Man of La Mancha*; the 1973 Nureyev version of the Ballet; the 1988 Korean *Asphaltwiui Don Quixote* ("Quixote on Asphalt"); the 1989 Korean version *Naesalang Don Quixote*; the 1990 Alfonso Alvarez surreal short *Quixote Dreams*; the 1991 experimental video *The Cyberkinetic Dream of Don Quixote*; the 1992 Spanish Television version by Manuel Gutierrez Aragon; the 1996 (Russian/Bulgarian) version *Don Kikhot Vozratchatetsya* ("Don Quixote is Coming Back"); and the 2000 TNT Peter Yates version. Nor has this intertextual stream dried up. Currently there is talk of a Disney version slated for 2004 and a Phoenix Pictures project to feature John Cleese as Don Quixote and Robin Williams as Sancho.

Here I will discuss just a tiny sampling from this hypertextual cornucopia. Most adaptations of *Don Quixote* have been somewhat pedestrian costume dramas, as if the adapters were overwhelmed, even paralyzed, by the auratic prestige of an original that has generated so many copies. Thus most adaptations of the novel simply place an actor, of a certain age, dressed in heavy, often rusty, knightly armor, riding on horseback alongside a portly Sancho Panza, of a certain grossness, mounted on his donkey. The adaptations then have the archetypical duo meander across whatever landscape has been chosen to stand in for the seventeenth-century Spanish countryside. Most of the adaptations include the well-known episodes – the windmills, the flock of sheep, the helmet – but edit out all presumably "uncinematic" materials – literary criticism, interpolated tales, and *mise-en-abyme* techniques. Some of the recent adaptations of *Don Quixote*, for example the TNT television version (2000) directed by Peter Yates and starring John Lithgow (Quixote), Bob Hoskins (Sancho Panza), Isabella Rossellini (the Duchess), and Vanessa Williams (Dulcinea), exploit special effects. Ripply images and strange superimpositions communicate the distorted nature of Quixote's vision which turns windmills into giants. At one point, the Yates film has Quixote charge onto the stage of a troupe of traveling players to save a damsel in distress – an obvious transposition of the Master Pedro puppet-show episode. But his insanity is integrated into the spectacle; he joins the cast and accepts a round of applause. The interpretation of Cervantes' protagonist, in this as in most of the adaptations, tends to be locked into the doxa of conventional post-romantic interpretation: Don Quixote the noble defender of lost causes, Don Quixote the hero of the imagination, Don Quixote the deluded knight, foiled always by Sancho Panza the earthbound realist. Few adaptations have tried to create a new gloss not only on Cervantes' themes but also on his artistic processes and procedures: the inclusion of literary criticism as an integral part of creation, the multimedia effect of the juxtaposition of representations, and so forth.

There are occasional exceptions to this rule, however, cases where directors make imaginative leaps of interpretation, and such adaptations will provide my focus here. One of the most prestigious filmmakers to take on *Don Quixote* was the Russian Gregory Kozintsev. The director's artistic roots were to be found in the experimental Soviet avant-garde of the 1920s, but over the years Stalinist censors obliged him to make many compromises. For Kozintsev, who also adapted *Hamlet* and *King Lear*, the adaptation of literary classics became a way of mollifying the authorities while still retaining a certain "edge." Kozintsev filmed *Don Quixote* in 1957, just a year after Khrushchev's anti-Stalinist speech to the Twentieth Congress of the Soviet Communist Party. The story is filmed against the backdrop of a harsh Crimean landscape, which becomes a kind of character in the film. Nicolai Cherkasov stars as Don Quixote, Yuri Tolubeyev as Sancho Panza, and I. Kasianova as Dulcinea.

Figure 1.1   Kozintsev's *Don Quixote* (1957), produced by Lenfilm Studio

A Cervantic Prelude

Chapter 1

Kozintsev's version of *Don Quixote* highlights both the novel's comic and burlesque features as well as its tragic and philosophical aspects. Just as Kozintsev had stressed the class dimension in his adaptation of *King Lear* – where Shakespeare's king begins to understand the "poor naked wretches" of the world only as he is himself shorn of his regal privileges – so too his *Don Quixote* stresses class conflict and ideology. Don Quixote, wearing a rusty suit of armor and a tin plate on his head, crusades for justice on behalf of the poor and down-trodden. The film especially denounces the cruelty of the aristocrats who torture Don Quixote with their malevolent pranks. The aristocratic Altisadora, for example, pretends to be in love with Quixote, but then laughs at him for thinking she could fall in love with a "broken, old stick" like Quixote. For a Russian audience, the aristocrats presumably triggered memory of the time of the Czars. Kozintsev also introduces a note of anti-clerical critique by having Sancho note that the sexton is not ringing the church bells to call the faithful to prayer, but rather to inform his mistress in a nearby village of the hour of his arrival.

The character of Don Quixote, meanwhile, is socially ambivalent. On the one hand, despite his **hidalgo** status, he confronts the powerful in order to rescue the oppressed, although he also never stops being enamored of nobility. But he really does succor the weak and defenseless; inherent in his notion of knight-errantry is a democratic principle of fair play and equality. The Dulcinea of the film admires Quixote because "he beats up people, irrespective of rank." (Sancho too, in the end, catches the contagion of Quixote's passion for justice; he too becomes a righter of wrongs.) But as someone who imposes his rigid chivalric dogmas and who declares war on anyone who does not share them, Kozintsev's Quixote might also be seen as a veiled critique of the contradictions of Stalinism. Quixote's impotent fundamentalism is ultimately less dangerous than that of the masters of Soviet power, of course, but as someone who sees himself as "ahead" of the benumbed and passively obedient masses, Quixote does seem to incarnate the commandeering ideology of the "vanguard party." His egalitarian projects result only in suffering. He rescues the child abused by his master, for example, but the "rescue" only leads to more beatings, to the point that the child asks Quixote not to rescue him any more.

Unlike the novel, and unlike many other adaptations of *Don Quixote*, Kozintsev's *Quixote* has no narrator. Instead, we have a surrogate narrator (and addressee) in the form of a group of Quixote's relatives and friends and neighbors. As a dramatized, intradiegetic, collective narrator, a kind of village chorus, they tell us about Quixote's exploits. Here Kozintsev picks up on a concern in the novel itself, since Don Quixote asks Sancho what people are saying about him in the village, to which Sancho has to reply that "the common people look upon your Grace as an utter madman" (Part II, chapter 2). It is this village chorus that worries over Quixote's madness – "He's reading those romances again!" – and who report that Quixote mistook a flock of sheep for an army of giants. Perhaps as a concession to the then regnant aesthetic of "socialist realism," the village chorus provides a kind of default baseline of reality for the fiction. With deliberate anachronism, they call Quixote's language of sorcerers and potions and enchantments "out of date:" after all, they say, "we're in the year 1605!"

One of the special "finds" of Kozintsev's *Don Quixote* is to transform the peasant Aldonza Lorenzo, the woman who triggers Don Quixote's fantasies, into a major figure. At the beginning of the film, just after Alonso Quijano has decided to become a knight-errant, Kozintsev stages a conversation between Don Quixote and Aldonza Lorenzo, where she expresses jealousy of Dulcinea as the ideal figure who Quixote has molded out of the raw materials of her body. Kozintsev thus humanizes Aldonza Lorenzo as someone who wants to be worthy of the imaginary Dulcinea that Quixote has created. Indeed, as Juan Bonilla points out, spectators of the film might even speculate that everything they are about to see is a fiction invented not by Quixote but by Aldonza, whose mind has been addled by the reading of chivalric romances and who has turned the pale and decrepit Alonso Quijano into a powerful knight who can restore her legitimate status as a noblewoman. This reading would give us, as Bonilla puts it, "a peasant who dreams of becoming a noblewoman thanks to the madness of a hidalgo who pretends to be a knight, while a hidalgo becomes a knight thanks to the fantasies of a peasant who needs him in order to be recognized as a noblewoman."[35] Aldonza is thus "Quixotized;" she absorbs his fevered imagination. Or is it the other way around?

For Bakhtin, Cervantes wrote within the carnivalesque Menippean tradition. Apart from the many festival-like scenes in the film – for example, the circus-like dance sequence at the inn – this carnivalesque element is also evidenced in the first appearance of Sancho Panza. The film emphasizes what Bakhtin would call the "protuberances" of Sancho's body, in this case his enormous buttocks.[36] Kozintsev also captures the dialogical, polyperspectival nature of the novel. Repeatedly, Don Quixote and Sancho Panza give rival, contrapuntal interpretations of what they see. Where Sancho sees an aristocratic carriage, Quixote sees a "devil's chariot." In such judgments, Quixote is often technically wrong, but poetically correct; it is indeed a carriage, but the aristocrats inside it are in fact virtual devils. His admired Aldonza/Dulcinea is a peasant, technically, but she also has beauty and spiritual nobility, so Quixote is not wrong to see her as noble. The discourses of both Don Quixote and Sancho Panza thus undergo what Bakhtin would call "mutual relativization."

An emphasis on class cruelty emerges in Kozintsev's treatment of the episode, from Part II, involving Quixote and Sancho's visit to the Dukes' palace. The aristocrats in this sequence are aware of Don Quixote because they have already read about his adventures in Part I. Converting the palace into a theater, they mount a huge spectacle with the sole purpose of tricking Don Quixote into thinking that the illusory spectacle is real life. Here it is difficult to tell who is more mad, the initially tricked Quixote, or those who invest such excessive energies in tricking him. (Quixote's ideal, mental knights drawn from romances behave much more humanely than the "real-life" aristocrats.) Kozintsev emphasizes the perverted cruelty of the "dupers," and the naïve dignity of the duped. The "enchantment" consists in pretending to take literally Don Quixote's own pretensions that he is a knight-errant. The aristocrats act out Quixote's own fantasies. At the end of the episode, the buried, presumably dead Altisidora rises from the grave to applaud the spectacle, at which point Quixote finally recognizes the fiction for what it is. We become painfully aware of the gravity of the spiritual defeat of Quixote; having lost his dreams, he no longer has any reason to live. Yet as he lays dying, we see on his eyelids the superimposed image of the silhouetted Quixote and Sancho, looking like armed phantoms, wandering off into an infinite plain, presumably ready to do battle again for the Don's ideals. Although Don Quixote had told Sancho about the many **books** that would be written about them, he neglected to mention the many films, such as Kozintsev's, which would be made about their exploits.

Two adaptations of *Don Quixote* rewrite the Quixote story by emphasizing Dulcinea. Vicente Escriva's *Dulcinea* (1962), explores the Cervantes novel from the perspective of the Aldonza character who scarcely exists in the novel except as Quixote's delirious fantasy of feminine perfection. In the film, Dulcinea is, like the original Dulcinea, a peasant, but this time she is a peasant who absorbs and then carries on Don Quixote's ideals, ultimately dying for her convictions. Made during the twilight of the Franco dictatorship, much as the Kozintsev version was made during the twilight of Stalinism, the Escriva version turns both the Don and Dulcinea into victims of the Inquisition, thus resuscitating what had been merely a tacit subtext in the original. Don Quixote is presented as Christ-like – a characteristic noted by many literary critics – and Dulcinea is his disciple. Yet the *mise-en-scène* pushes Don Quixote into the background, as Dulcinea moves to the foreground. In a gendered rewriting of the novel, Dulcinea is less interested in military valor and prowess than her hero and prototype. While the novel's Don Quixote receives blows only because he has already given them, the

Christ-like Dulcinea receives them unprovoked. It is implied that Dulcinea and Quixote are victims of the Franco-like authorities. As Andrea Cervatiuc points out, the film's Dulcinea ultimately becomes a martyr in the Joan of Arc tradition, while the portrayal of the cruel authorities mocks the cynical idealizations of Franquista propaganda.[37] Cervantes' ironic picaresque is here transformed into hagiography as political allegory.

The Radio-TV Espanola short, *A Myth Called Dulcinea*, directed by Juan Guerrero Zamora, meanwhile, portrays Quixote's love object as a prostitute who treats the enamored Don most cruelly. While her friends try to persuade her to accept Quixote, she sarcastically rejects the Platonic love he celebrates. When her friends dress her up as a "Lady," Quixote ironically sees through the artifice; sorcerers, he complains, have masked the true Dulcinea, turning her into a whore. In a scene reminiscent of the **vade retro** sequence in Buñuel's *Simon of the Desert*, Quixote tells the over-made-up devil woman to "get thee behind me." The film ends with a Dulcinea of sad countenance in the foreground, regretful that she has not accepted Quixote's love, as Quixote and his squire wander off toward the setting sun.

Roberto Gavaldon's *Don Quijote cabalga de nuevo* (roughly "Don Quixote Rides Again," 1972) also takes the Cervantes novel as a point of departure for a new creation, this time from a Mexican point of view. The "de nuevo" in the title alerts the spectator that this adaptation will be impertinent and disrespectful. Indeed, the film's opening intertitles beg personal forgiveness from Miguel de Cervantes himself. The Gavaldon adaptation, as Andrea Cervatiuc points out, builds on a specifically Mexican intertext, to wit the tradition of seeing *Don Quixote* through a juridical lens, emphasizing Quixote himself as an advocate or legal purist. But here Quixote is the accused, while Sancho Panza becomes a means for satirizing legal discourse. Sancho's political platform, meanwhile, forms a parody not of Franco but rather of the official "revolutionary" discourse of Mexico's PRI (Institutional Revolutionary Party). Political allusions also inform the Channel 4 TV film *Rocinante* (1987). Set in mid-1980s' England, and more specifically during the aftermath of the 1984–5 miners' strike, the film has a Quixotic character named Bill who embarks on a dreamlike odyssey around England, taking photographs of anything that interests him.

The Spanish Television version by Manuel Gutierrez Aragon is much more thorough than most, since its serial five-part film form allows for a more comprehensive version. The film spends a good deal of time establishing the character of Don Quixote as an obsessive reader **before** his launching out into the land of adventures. A veteran of Cervantes adaptations – he had already made very free adaptations of *Novelas ejemplares* – Aragon departs from the romantic view of Quixote as the idealistic dreamer of impossible dreams in order to stress the more classical view that he is mad, and that some of his beatings are well deserved. The casting of Fernando Rey as Quixote also brings with it a number of intertextual echoes. First, Rey had already played two other characters from *Don Quixote* – Sanson Carrasco in the 1947 Rafael Gil version, and Sancho Panza in the 1963 Carlo Rim version. He also brings with him the memory of the Quixotic characters that he had played in Buñuel films, most notably Don Jaime in *Viridiana* and Mathieu in *That Obscure Object of Desire*.

The Realistic Magic of Orson Welles

One of the most intriguing adaptations of *Don Quixote* is the partially finished and never commercially released version by Orson Welles. Arguably one of the most "Cervantic" of directors, Welles was one of the most versatile practitioners of the art of adaptation in diverse media – radio, film, television – having adapted not only Shakespeare's plays (*Othello*, *Macbeth*, *The Merchant of Venice*, the Henry plays in *Chimes at Midnight*) but also such varied works of fiction as Tarkington's *The Magnificent Andersons*, Conrad's *Heart of Darkness*, Kafka's *The Trial*, Isak Dienson's *The Immortal Story*, Eric Ambler's *Journey into Fear*, Whit Masterson's *Badge of Evil*, and Melville's *Moby Dick*.[38] The more important point, however, is that Welles was a believer in **unfaithful** adaptations. Why adapt a work, he frequently said, if you're not going to change it? Even Welles's most famous media stunt, the Mercury Theater's Hallowe'en "War of the Worlds" CBS broadcast, was an "unfaithful version" of the H. G. Wells science-fiction novel, one which relocated the story from Victorian England's future to Depression Era New York City. Welles's broadcast alarmed listeners, who took it as real, precisely because it was **not** set in Victorian England, and because Welles innovatively mingled the codes of radio reporting with the fabulous idea of a Martian onslaught. (For more on Welles and H. G. Wells, see the essay by Julian Cornell in *A Companion to Literature and Film*.)[39]

Welles was not only a "Renaissance Man" – in the sense of being a multi-talented artist who staged plays, wrote novels, scripted radio programs, and directed films – but also a "Man of the Renaissance," in that his aesthetic enthusiasms were rooted in the carnivalesque exuberance of Shakespeare and Cervantes. In a case of elective artistic affinities, Welles represents a latter-day high-tech prolongation of the Menippean, carnivalesque, and Cervantic tradition. Welles's Rabelaisian spirit and "excessive" body reminds us in its gigantism of Bakhtin's account of carnival and Rabelais in *Rabelais and his World*. Welles's body is cut to the measure of Falstaff (whom Welles portrayed in *Chimes at Midnight*), the most grossly irreverent of Shakespeare's protagonists. The Welles body is reminiscent of Bacchus, or of the fat lords of misrule, called Rei Momos, who launch the carnival celebrations in Brazil, and that Welles himself registered in *It's All True*, much as he registers carnival celebrations and the running of the bulls in Pamplona in his *Don Quixote*. It is no accident that Welles's *Don Quixote* shows the Dionysian director himself accepting an award from the "Sherry Wine Association."

Welles had always been a breaker of rules, a rebel figure who placed himself in opposition to dominant theatrical and cinematic practice. And here we have another sense in which Welles can be compared to Cervantes. The Spanish author, as we have seen, wrote **against** a tradition – chivalric romance – while creating for the reader the same pleasures generated by the tradition being attacked. Welles in a sense also filmed against a tradition, to wit the dominant Hollywood tradition. Hollywood entertainments, in this sense, can be seen as the twentieth-century equivalent of the facile and improbable pleasures of chivalric romance. (Harrison Ford and Mel Gibson and Samuel Jackson now play the contemporary Amadises who rescue damsels and slay dragons.) Yet Welles never forgot the need for spectatorial pleasure. His goal was to make complex, multi-leveled, critical films which were nevertheless hugely entertaining, in a manner reminiscent of a Shakespeare or a Cervantes.

Like Cervantes himself, Welles represents the zenith of **both** realism, on the one hand – we recall his fastidious concern with accuracy in the symptomatically titled *It's All True*, or the deep-space *mise-en-scène* praised for its realism by André Bazin – **and** reflexivity and magic, on the other. Indeed, Welles was a practiced magician, as he demonstrated not only in *F for Fake* but also in numerous television performances. Indeed, one might say that Welles is the magician behind his films, much as Cervantes was ultimately the "sorcerer" lurking behind the "enchantments" of *Don Quixote*. Welles's oeuvre as a whole creates a dialectic between two poles: the "true" and the "real" of *It's All True* and the "fake" and the "magical" of *F for Fake*.

Welles began shooting *Don Quixote* as a CBS-TV drama in 1955. The drama was refused by a CBS executive, but Welles continued with the film, and was reportedly still working on it on the eve of his death in 1985. Shot in Spain, Italy, Morocco, and Mexico, the film was to feature Francisco Reigueira as Don Quixote, Akim Tamiroff as Sancho Panza, and Patty McCormak as Dulcinea. The film was so slow in arriving that Welles joked that he planned to entitle it after the question so often asked of him: *When Will You Ever Finish Your Don*

Quixote? The film was only posthumously assembled, culled from reams of footage and an hour of Orson Welles's recorded voice reading the voice-over narration and the lines of the two main characters. The search for the footage was itself a chivalric quest, since it was compiled by Spanish film distributor Patxi Irigoyen after an 18-month search across two continents. The material was finally fashioned by Spanish director Jesus Franco into a 116-minute 35 mm film, culled from over 300,000 feet of footage. Irigoyen was convinced that he had all the material **except** a scene in which Don Quixote attacks the movie screen. Yet at one point Italian film editor Mauro Bonnani asked for a halt in the première of the Irigoyen/Franco version because the film did not include 20,000 meters of footage in his possession. The more or less completed film was presented at the 1992 Expo in Seville under the title *Don Quixote by Orson Welles.* Just as Cervantes' *Don Quixote* was beset by debates about the relations between its two parts, so Welles's adaptation was the trampoline for posthumous debates about how Welles, as opposed to Jesus Franco, would have edited the film. (Jesus Franco himself said that he had used only a tiny proportion of the footage that Welles had filmed.)

Figure 1.2 Francisco Reigueira in Orson Welles's *Don Quixote*, produced by El Silencio Producciones

Welles's experience in filming *Don Quixote* in some ways homologized Cervantes' experience in writing *Don Quixote*. As Welles himself put it, "The same thing happened to me that had happened to Cervantes; just as he started to write a short story and ended up writing a novel, I started with a short TV project and ended up with a feature film."[40] The theme of the lure of the ideal and the brute resistance of the real, so central to the Cervantes novel, was in this case played out on the plane of film production, in the form of well-laid plans being rudely laid to rest by the financial and practical contingencies of independent production. Cervantes' interrupted textual narrative became in the Welles case the constantly interrupted narrative of the production itself, constantly beset by shortages of funds and the untimely death of key performers. Like most novels, but unlike most films, *Don Quixote* was self-financed. As Welles himself pointed out, publishers, unlike producers, do not usually force a novelist to finish a book if the author wants to take a break."[41] Just as Cervantes referred to *Don Quixote* as his **hijo** (son), Welles referred to his adaptation as **il mio bambino**. And just as Cervantes never stopped tinkering with *Don Quixote* – indeed, he only finished it because it was beginning to be plagiarized – Welles continued playing with and re-editing the materials of *Don Quixote* until the very eve of his death.

Welles's project was itself Quixotic, in that it pursued the impossible dream of adapting an extremely prestigious work of fiction on a shoestring budget. Welles called *Don Quixote* a "home movie," and his low-budget approach homologizes, as it were, Quixote's own genteel poverty and low-budget adventurism. The shoot itself was an improbable adventure. Welles's improvisational approach, with a minimal crew of six people, resembled that of an underground film. Welles did lighting and second camera, his wife Oja Kodar worked as continuity person, the driver carried the lamps, and so forth. Welles described the process as follows:

> it was made without cuts, without even a narrative trajectory, without even a synopsis. Every morning, the actors, the crew and I would meet in front of the hotel. Then we'd set off and invent the film in the street, like Mack Sennett ... The story, the little events, everything is improvised. It's made of things we found in the moment, in the flash of a thought, but only after rehearsing Cervantes for four weeks. Because we rehearsed all the scenes from Cervantes as if we were going to perform them ... Then we went into the street and performed not Cervantes, but an improvisation supported by these rehearsals, by the memory of the characters.[42]

Here filmmaking itself becomes a form of knight-errantry, a picaresque series of on-the-road improvisations.

A Cervantic Prelude

Chapter 1

Welles treats the filming of *Don Quixote* not as a "faithful" costume drama but rather as a transposition and actualization of the novel. In this sense, the film recalls Welles's innovative practices in the theater, for example his audacious modern-dress version of *Julius Caesar*, which compared the politics of ancient Rome to contemporary fascism, or his all-black "Voodoo *Macbeth*," performed in Harlem in 1936, which used African musicians and relocated the play in the revolutionary Haiti of the "Black Jacobins."

Welles does not only update the story of *Don Quixote*, he also emulates and updates Cervantes' narrative techniques. Unlike most adapters of *Don Quixote*, Welles does not eliminate the self-reflexive touches. Picking up on a technique developed in Part II of the novel, he repeatedly has people say: "Look! There's Don Quixote and Sancho Panza. We read a book about them." Working "in the manner of Cervantes," Welles also self-reflexively thematizes the obstacles and hazards and trade secrets of film production, just as Cervantes had spoken in *Don Quixote* of the mechanical processes of printing and publishing. While Cervantes stressed the anachronistic nature of Don Quixote's worldview, rooted as it was in medieval values and in an outmoded forms of literature, Welles in the film also deploys anachronism as a structuring device. Sancho is amazed to discover the "box full of news," i.e. a TV monitor. But at the end of the film, Quixote reconciles himself with "progress," proclaiming that he sees nothing wrong with human beings going to the moon; what bothers him is the transformation of human beings into machines. The moon is still associated with poetry and dreams, but the earth has become dominated by mechanical apparatus. Welles transposes the notion of anachronism. He originally wanted to send Quixote to the moon, but since astronauts had actually gone to the moon, Welles gave up a sequence that would no longer have had the charm of the fantastic.

Welles pointed out in interviews that the anachronisms in *Don Quixote* had lost their efficacy because "the differences between the sixteenth and the fourteenth centuries are not very clear in our minds . . . [therefore] I've simply translated this anachronism into modern terms."[43] As a result, Welles shows Quixote in medieval armor walking alongside Spaniards in contemporary dress, knights on horseback next to drivers in cars, the presence of television, and so forth. A newsreel speaks of NASA and missiles. If Quixote's swords and armor were already anachronistic in the age of gunpowder, Welles's film implies, they are astronomically more anachronistic in the world of NASA and space missions. Indeed, Sancho Panza lacks the vocabulary to even name the new technologies. For him, a radio is a "singing box." After glimpsing Welles's Don Quixote on a TV monitor, Sancho asks passers-by, as his hands outline the shape of a TV set, whether they have seen his master "in a small box."

Welles's treatment of anachronism betrays a certain amount of ambivalence. While ridiculing Quixote's blindness, Welles seems to sympathize with his veritable rage against mechanistic modernity. In his *Vida de Don Quixote y Sancho*, the Spanish philosopher Miguel de Unamuno had argued that Quixote was not deluded in seeing windmills as monsters. Although windmills later became an object of nostalgia, in Cervantes' time they exemplified a new form of high-tech modernity which revolutionized the social landscape. As producers of energy, windmills anticipated locomotives, turbines, steam engines, automobiles, and missiles, expressive of all the ambiguity of the "dialectics of enlightenment."

According to Juan Cobos, Welles's original project was entitled "Here comes Don Quixote; a Spanish Panorama," and was intended just as much as an introduction to Spain as an adaptation of Cervantes' novel. Welles wrote the following introduction to the project:

> This is not a film **about** Don Quixote. It is a film about Spain. A very personal vision of the country and its people through the regard of a producer-director, presented by himself as if he were playing host to a group of friends and guests.
>
> Orson Welles will appear throughout the film as himself, speaking to the public in direct and intimate terms. He will be a guide, the narrator, and master of ceremonies.[44]

In this sense, the Quixote film forms part of a Wellesian tradition which began with another personally narrated and ultimately unfinished film, *It's All True* (made in 1992), meant to be a "very personal vision" of Brazil much as *Don Quixote* was a personal vision of Spain.

The Welles version of *Don Quixote* revels in the language and style of the novel. Welles is among the few who seems to have grasped the novel's fundamental **modernity**, here updated through a jazzistic montage and a stylized *mise-en-scène* deploying Welles's usual baroque, oblique-angled style. Welles is strictly "faithful" to the letter of the text, especially insofar as Don Quixote's dialogue is concerned, yet he recontextualizes the words through surprising images. Don Quixote's encounter with an "infernal machine," for example, is rendered as a highway meeting between Quixote and a woman astride a Lambretta motorbike. Perhaps remembering the crucial role of radio in his initial formation as an artist, Welles recorded his commentaries first, then dubbed the voices, and had his editor follow the verbal rhythms set down by the recordings. Like Cervantes, who makes a cameo appearance in *Don Quixote*, Welles too appears in the fiction: he is both heard as a narrating voice and seen as a character going by his own name and as the filmmaker that he is, in the film itself. We hear Welles's directorial cues, and see him filming, with lightweight equipment, from a moving automobile. The novel's references to "enchantments" are here rendered as the "magic" of cinema.

While Welles's *Don Quixote* is marred by the posthumous editing and by the monotony of the studio-sound of the dubbed voices, it is nevertheless possible at least to glimpse the exhilarating aesthetic possibilities the film opens up. First of all, the film audaciously mingles a wide gamut of storytelling procedures. Unlike most adapters of *Don Quixote*, Welles does not see the novel merely as a source of story episodes, but also as a series of cues for very diversified narrational techniques. First, we have Welles as voice-over narrator speaking in his own voice. As narrator, Welles describes the film as an affectionate introduction to Spain. He also offers his own theories about Don Quixote. The "knight of the sad countenance," he tells us, "was not a madman but a gentleman," who moves us because, in words that could apply equally to Welles himself at Don Quixote's age, he has "so much heart, and so little means." Sancho Panza, meanwhile, is "marvelous even in his stupidity." His friendship with Don Quixote as registered by Cervantes "has survived" – and here we find a veiled reference to Spanish dictator Generalissimo Franco – "various tyrannical regimes." By offering a commentary on the novel and its characters, Welles emulates, as it were, Cervantes' own metafictional technique of including literary criticism in the work.

Welles's second narrational strategy involves the relaying of the exact words of the novel itself, whether directly through dialogue, or indirectly through narrative voice-over, or through summary, as in the following: "The author of this work remembers that he preferred to pass over the following events in silence as he fears that he will not be believed. Nevertheless, the author says he recorded everything just as it happened." Although the words are Cervantes' own, in a filmic context they become an ironic allusion to the veristic claims made for film as a medium, i.e. claims that film represents reality "just as it is" due to the objectivity of the camera.

A third narrational technique involves a kind of "threshold encounter" between the off-screen narrator and the on-screen character. When Welles as off-screen narrator expresses an opinion, for example, Sancho as on-screen character dialogues with him (and with us as spectators), telling us that "He's right too!" The narrator's grateful "Thank you, Sancho" is then followed by Sancho's polite "You're welcome."

A fourth narrational device involves soliloquy, as when Sancho's interior monologues are "overheard" by the spectator. We are reminded of Welles's Shakespeare adaptations, where close-to-camera soliloquy forms a frequent technique.

Figure 1.3 Welles as Welles in *Don Quixote*, produced by El Silencio
Producciones

Or at times the film offers something close to interior monologue, as when we overhear Sancho's thoughts, acoustically up-close, but visually distant.

Welles's adaptation, like the novel, is relentlessly reflexive, much in the "manner of Cervantes." Not only do we see Welles in the act of filming, but we also hear reports that the character Don Quixote has attacked the movie screen, much as his literary prototype attacked Master Pedro's puppets. (Unfortunately, the footage staging this key passage seems to have been lost.) Sancho's job as an extra on the Welles film-within-the-film becomes the pretext for calling attention to the actual processes of making films. As Sancho follows his donkey off the road, he is repeatedly warned by the director to stay "in frame." When the scene is finished, we hear production jargon such as "Cut" and "That's a wrap." Sancho promises his wife that the film will make him rich and famous. Sancho's mediatic "fifteen minutes of fame" come to replace the islands and governorships which formed the promised booty in the novel, a perfect correlative in an age where celebrity often seems more desirable than property or position. And just as Cervantes, in the second part of *Don Quixote*, has other characters recognize the Don and Sancho because they had already read about them, so Welles has other characters speak of having seen them, whether in person or on television.

In Welles's *Don Quixote*, film's "automatic difference" reveals the feats that only film can perform. We discern this special quality in Welles's renderings of many of the anthological passages from the novel. In the sequence based on Don Quixote's battle with a flock of sheep – imagined to be an enemy army – Welles places the camera at ground level. We see Don Quixote, lying on his back, as the sheep jump laterally over his flattened body. Sancho Panza, meanwhile, runs toward the camera from the deep background space, rushing to rescue his fallen master. Throughout the film, Welles exploits the specific resources of the cinema. He plays with scale and focal length, so that the spatial relationships and the relative scales between Don Quixote and Sancho Panza are in constant mutation. High angles make both characters disappear, as if camouflaged, into the arid landscape, or solarized backlighting renders Quixote as an abstract silhouette, reminiscent of the stringy lines of Picasso's famous drawing.

Only a film can show, rather than merely describe, the plastic beauty of windmills. Cervantes spoke poetically of the "big wings" of the windmills, but only a film can literally mobilize the Cubist multiplication of perspectives on a windmill, as Welles does, so that the blades of the windmill slice toward the camera, or "wipe" the frame, or cut up the landscape by being placed in the foreground. Such are the potential "gains" in the translation from novel to film. And while the Cervantes novel features very little physical description, cinema's "excess" physicality can also give us the **actual** landscapes (or more accurately their imagistic simulacrum) and the beautifully striated skies of Spain (and of the other Mediterranean countries where Welles filmed). And while Cervantes can verbally describe Sancho Panza looking at the moon through a telescope, only a film such as Welles's can give us a point-of-view shot showing what Sancho sees as he looks through a telescope. Film also provides the material and visual contextualization of abstract ideas. Welles deploys angle and *mise-en-scène*, for example, to contrast the Don's idealism and the squire's down-to-earthness; while low angles idealize and heroicize Don Quixote, high angles place Sancho Panza against an earthly backdrop, since he is "of the earth, earthly." Parallel montage contrasts Quixote's lofty encomiums to Dulcinea's beauty, set on mountain-tops, with Sancho's skeptical reflections as he searches for her in rural settings crowded with pigs, cows, and farm girls.

Welles also captures the multi-perspectival feeling of the novel. His rendering of the combat with the windmills, for example, alternates the perspective of Quixote, imagining giants, and the perspective of the skeptical Sancho Panza who sees only windmills. But Welles does not use special effects to achieve this result; he deploys only *mise-en-scène* and framing to mold two contrasting perspectives. Just as Cervantes alluded to the historical events of his time, Welles laces the film with critical comments on contemporary issues. Welles even manages to throw barbs both at General Franco – an off-screen voice denounces "obscurantism, oppression, and tyranny" – and at the entertainment industry. A street salesman tries to sell Sancho "the moon for two pesetas," i.e. a look through a telescope taken as the equivalent of the moon itself.

Welles also practices the Cervantic technique of **mise-en-abyme**, of representations embedded in other representations. The film proliferates in shots of statues, coats of arms, etchings, and other representations of Don Quixote. A newsreel in the film refers to "Orson Welles's adaptation of Cervantes' well-known novel." Just as Cervantes' novel was multi-generic and pluri-stylistic, Welles's film too mingles staged episodes and documentary materials, for example mini-documentaries about Spanish cities and festivals. Correlating genre with character, Welles links Don Quixote to the fiction film, and Sancho Panza to the documentary, as if the two major modalities of filmmaking formed generic correlatives to Quixote's romanesque fantasies and Sancho's novelistic realism. At times, Welles places his fictional characters in the middle of documentary footage, much as Cervantes mingled fictional and "real" characters. Sancho Panza is included in footage of the "running of the bulls" in Pamplona, where we also see Henry Fonda as a camera-wielding tourist. Many sequences consist of documentary-like successions of still shots of photogenic windmills, historical monuments, steel-and-glass buildings, and so forth. Sancho Panza's quest for Dulcinea triggers documentary shots of the Spanish provinces. A newsreel, reminiscent of the parodic "March of Time" newsreel that opens *Citizen Kane*, shows Welles being interviewed by Spanish television, alongside reports on US Navy missiles, NASA and the space race. Welles, who later became known for his Charles Masson wine commercials on TV, even receives a sherry wine prize for his connoisseurship. Here Welles brings us close to the media-saturated reflexive world of postmodern representation.[45]

--------------------- From *Don Quixote* to Postmodernism ---------------------

Although it might seem a stretch to link Cervantes to postmodernism, in a sense the novel *Don Quixote* anticipated virtually all of the contemporary reflexive devices characteristic of both modernism and postmodernism: the cameo appearance by the author; the metacritical commentary on fiction itself; the recycling of pre-existing materials; the direct address to the reader/spectator; the penchant for interruption and "breaks;" the foregrounding of readership (and spectatorship); the inclusion of interpolated materials; polyperspectivalism; the combinatory collage aesthetics; the mutual relativization of genre; the blurring of boundaries between the fictive and the real; and *mise-en-abyme* technique. Cervantes' practice of juxtaposing various types of media representations, for example the placing of the original manuscript by Cid Hamete Benengeli, in Arabic, alongside lifelike pictures representing scenes from that novel (Don Quixote and the Biscayan), makes him a proleptic practitioner of what would now be called "multimedia" or "hypertext." At the same time, the very fact that we can see Cervantes as postmodern suggests that the term itself is somewhat inflated and ahistorical; what postmodern discourse presents as "new and exciting" is in fact not new at all.

Nor is aesthetic postmodernism new in the cinema. Long before postmodernism, a venerable tradition in the cinema explored the same frame-breaking, puppet-smashing theme developed in the Master Pedro's puppet-show passage in *Don Quixote*, through scenes where cinematic representation is brought to a halt by the naïve intervention of a personage who confounds reality with filmic spectacle. In E. S. Porter's *Uncle Josh at the Picture Show* (1902), the country bumpkin title character goes to the movies and sees a farmer taking advantage of a woman. Josh rolls up his sleeves and angrily rushes toward the projected image, felling the screen and revealing the rear projector and the projectionist. Godard's Jarryesque *Les Carabiniers* (1963) cites and revises the Porter film by having the film's obtuse protagonist, ironically named Michelangelo, try to caress the screen image of a naked woman in a bathtub, succeeding only in pulling down the screen.[46] (Woody Allen's *The Purple Rose of Cairo*, as we shall see in chapter 4, reverses the movement by having the characters leave the screen to join the spectators.)

In the broadest sense, the post-text "adaptations" of *Quixote* include the audio-cassette "adaptation" readings of the novel, the 1985 Nick Kershaw pop song "Don Quixote what do you say . . . are we shouting at windmills like you?" and even the Don Quixote Restaurant and the Dulcinea Ballroom at the Hotel Cervantes in Torremolinos, Spain. The post-text also includes the 1960s' cartoon that shows Quixote in his underwear, on a donkey, and Sancho in armor on Rocinante, anachronistically predicting: "You realize, don't you, that this will change all of Western literature."[47] Don Quixote has even been symbolically launched into space to defend a new damsel in distress – Mother Earth. In an article entitled "Don Quixote against the Asteroids," *Le Monde* (October 18,

2002) informs us that the European Space Agency is considering a number of projects articulating possible defenses against asteroids. One of the projects foresees two spaceships: one, named "Don Quixote," is to crash into an incoming asteroid, while the other, named "Sancho Panza," will observe what occurs before, during, and after impact. As in the original novel, this space odyssey "adaptation" has Quixote receive most of the blows, while Sancho just stands by and watches.

In literary terms, *Don Quixote* has been "postmodernized," not only by Borges in *Pierre Menard* but also by Kathy Acker in her 1986 novel *Don Quixote*. Published in the same year as the English translation of Lyotard's essay on postmodernism, the Acker "adaptation" is divided into three parts: "The Beginning of Night," "Other Texts," and "The End of the Night." Don Quixote is now a woman, but a dead one, who narrates the story. (We will encounter both the "dead narrator" and "the mute character" again in subsequent chapters). The subtitle of the Second Section goes as follows: "Being dead, Don Quixote could no longer speak, being born into and part of a male world, she had no speech of her own. All she could do was read male texts which weren't hers."[48]

The book opens as Don Quixote – Acker does not feminize the name into **Dona** Quixote – is about to have an abortion, at which time she conceives the improbable goal of loving another person and thus righting "every manner of political, social and individual wrong" (p. 9). For this Don Quixote, "having an abortion is a method of becoming a knight and saving the world" (p. 11). But the portrayal of the abortion also spoofs Quixotic/chivalric language so that the mundane act of urination becomes a "formidable adventure:"

> This was the manner in which she pissed. "For women, Oh woman who is all woman who is my beauty, give me strength and vigor. Turn the eyes of the strength and wonderfulness of all women upon this one female, this female who's trying . . . this female who's locked up in the hospital and thus must pass through so formidable an adventure." (p. 12)

Acker also spoofs Cervantes' chapter titles ("How Don Quixote cured the infection left-over from her abortion so she could keep having adventures"), his interpolated tales ("The Selling of Lulu") and his metacritical disquisitions ("Intrusion of a Badly Written Section"). Like the Latin American "magic realists," Acker takes Quixote to the Americas: "Don Quixote in America, the Land of Freedom." By using cut-'n'-mix hypertextual strategies, Acker interbreeds various texts. Emulating Cervantes' own practice of citation, she has her

A Cervantic Prelude

Chapter 1

characters discuss the work of Deleuze, Lacan, Derrida, and Foucault, while also evoking the Derridean critique of origins by claiming that the Arabs "do not believe in "originality.""[49] Acker further carnivalizes the Cervantic text by inserting obscene materials from the Marquis de Sade, while citing anti-porn feminist Andrea Dworkin, alongside Ronald Reagan, as "evil enchanters" with whom Quixote must do battle (p. 102).

Acker's Quixote is, above all, a reader, although a skeptical one. And here we remember that Quixote himself, rather like a contemporary adolescent addicted to video games or to Internet surfing, buried himself in his books so that his "brain dried up and he lost his wits." Living his literary life 150 years after the invention of the printing press, Don Quixote exemplifies the power of books to create an alluring realer-than-real world. The perennial desire to live out a fantasy drawn from fictional worlds takes on new proportions in the world of the new media. The computer, as Janet H. Murray points out, can now provide a cyber location for places we long to visit:

A few clicks on the World Wide Web and we are instantly in one of the feudal fiefdoms of the "current Middle Ages" set up by the Society for Creative Anachronism . . . Unlike Don Quixote's books, digital media take us to a place where we can act out our fantasies. With a telnet connection or a CD-Rom drive, we can kill our own dragons . . . putting on a VR helmet or standing before a megascreen, we can do it all in 3-D. For the modern Don Quixote, the windmills have been pre-programmed to turn into knights.[50]

Just as Cervantes has Don Quixote and Sancho Panza meet people who have read about them, mingling readers and fictional characters in an impossibly hybrid space, characters on world wide web serials answer public fan mail and invite fans to post their own opinions on common bulletin boards.

As the cinema in its long-heralded specificity now seems to be dissolving into the larger bit-stream of the audiovisual media, be they photographic, electronic, or cybernetic, the cinema must now compete, as purveyor of fictions, with television, video games, computers, and virtual reality. These new media open up "immersive" possibilities far beyond those enjoyed (and suffered) by Don Quixote. A new blockbuster cinema, made possible by huge budgets, sound innovations, and digital technologies, favors a "sound and light show" cinema of sensation. "Concert films" immerse the spectator "in" the image. Sensation predominates over narrative, and sound over image, while verisimilitude is no longer a goal but only the technology-dependent production of vertiginous, prosthetic delirium. No longer the deluded master of the image, the spectator becomes the inhabitant of (and interlocutor with) the image. And Don Quixote himself has now wandered into this digital world. A laser-generated cartoon game called *Super Don Quixote* is advertised as showing "a would-be windmill-tilter [guiding] the Don past hazards new, fending off giants or skipping from rock to rock to avoid being swept off in a flood."[51]

Cervantes meets the postmodern again in the recent abortive attempt by Terry Gilliam, one of the founders of the eminently postmodern group Monty Python and director of *Brazil*, to make a revisionist version of *Don Quixote*. Like Orson Welles, Terry Gilliam had been trying for years to adapt the Cervantes novel. Gilliam had a $35 million budget to make an adaptation, to be entitled *The Man Who Killed Don Quixote*, in a transparent allusion to *The Man Who Shot Liberty Valance*. It was to feature Jean Rochefort as Don Quixote, Vanessa Paradis as Dulcinea, and Johnny Depp as a modern advertising genius who, while shooting a commercial, gets magically transported back into Cervantes' seventeenth century, where Don Quixote mistakes him for Sancho Panza. But the film production itself became a tragic-comic epic, as Gilliam took the kinds of body-blows to which the Don himself had been subjected. After seven weeks of pre-production in Spain, the whole project was undone by catastrophic floods, disabling illnesses (Jean Rochefort's prostate infection), translation problems, and the anachronistic roar of jets taking off from a nearby NATO base. Finally, the insurance company, the contemporary equivalent of Cervantes' obscure and demonic forces, called a halt to the enterprise. It was as if, as Gilliam himself pointed out, a "Quixotic" project was undone by modern-day "sorcerers." The journalistic accounts of the disaster, meanwhile, inevitably spoke of "tilting at windmills" and "pursuing the impossible dream." An "unmaking of" documentary, *Lost in La Mancha*, records the film's "trajectory of disenchantment," summed up in Gilliam's anti-climactic phrase: "Lights, camera, and inaction." (Like the Don himself, Gilliam plans to continue despite the blows.)

On reflection, it makes perfect sense that one of the founders of *Monty Python* would adapt *Don Quixote*. Artists like Gilliam are, in a sense, the Cervantic **picaros** of our own time, much as *Don Quixote* was the *Monty Python* of its time. Apart from Gilliam's own delusional foibles – the delirious budget of *The Adventures of Baron Munchausen*, his quixotic struggles with powerful producers – the title itself, with its allusion to the Western, reminds us that the Western genre is the contemporary equivalent of the chivalric fictions mocked by Cervantes. And *Monty Python* too has always been highly Cervantic. Comic epic, for example, has been a *Monty Python* staple. *Monty Python and the Holy Grail* invoked the same archive of materials referenced by chivalric literature and *Don Quixote* – the legends revolving around Arthur and the Knights of the Round Table. *The Life of Brian* constitutes mock hagiography, where an ordinary man is mistaken for the Messiah. But apart from theme, *Monty Python* is stylistically Cervantic by being parodic, multigeneric, reflexive, and digressive (partly because it is the product of six very different people writing disconnected scenes). And what could be more Cervantically polyperspectival than the unforgettable debate, on one of the *Monty Python* TV shows, that opposed the Sancho-like realist Mr Praline, convinced that the parrot is dead – given the visual evidence of its falling to the ground, lack of perceptible respiration, being nailed to its perch, and so forth – against the Quixotic shopkeeper, who cites the bird's strength and his affection for fjords as clear evidence that it is alive.

If *Don Quixote* evokes the advent of both modernity as an epoch and of modernism as an artistic tendency, the contemporary reincarnations of Cervantic reflexivity evoke the hyper-real world of media politics, the incessant self-consciousness of contemporary television programming, and the postmodern novel. Umberto Eco's *The Name of the Rose*, for example, calls up the category on which *Don Quixote* was based – comic epic – in that the plot revolves around a monk's censorship (and burning) of the lost volume of Aristotle's *Poetics*, the one having to do with comedy rather than tragedy. At the same time, reflexivity evokes the referentless world of the simulacrum, where all of life is always already caught up in mass-mediated representations. Postmodernism also implies an altered approach to parody. In the mid-1980s, Fredric Jameson suggested that the modern and modernist uses of a critical, hard-edged parody – rooted, as we have seen, in traditions going back to Cervantes and beyond – had given way to the postmodern practice of pastiche as expressive of the cultural logic of late capitalism. John Docker, in *Postmodernism and Popular Culture*,[52] on the other hand, saw parody as the all-pervasive genre in contemporary mass culture. In this context, we find the "postmodern reflexivity" of commercial television, which is often reflexive and self-referential. TV shows like *The David Letterman Show* and *Beavis and Butthead* and *The Daily Show* are relentlessly reflexive, usually within a pervasively ironic stance which looks with distaste at any position-taking. Young people today are as likely to learn about the news from the Jon Stewart parody *Daily Show* as from the "real" news, which given the nature of "serious" news is probably just as well. Many of the distancing procedures characterized as reflexive in Cervantes or Welles or Godard now typify MTV and many television shows. Pastiche, as the most typical aesthetic expression of postmodernism, constitutes a blank, neutral practice of mimicry, without any satiric agenda or sense of alternatives, nor, for that matter, any mystique of "originality" beyond the ironic orchestration of dead styles, whence the centrality of "intertextuality" and what Jameson calls the "random cannibalization of all the styles of the past."[53] While Cervantic parody exposed social reality through the critique of fictions, postmodern television exposes nothing but its own devices.

Strategies of parodic and reflexive allusion that go back at least as far as Cervantes are therefore central to postmodern popular culture in both its liberatory and regressive forms. The interrelated worlds of rap and hip-hop show a fondness for direct address within a cut-'n'-mix "sampling" aesthetic. The postmodernist, as Gilbert Adair put it in a title, "always rings twice." Thus commercials for Diet Coke feature long-deceased Hollywood actors, updating and commercializing the Kuleshov experiments in montage. The music video for Madonna's *Material Girl*, meanwhile, encodes *Gentlemen Prefer Blondes*, even though some of Madonna's contemporary fans might not be aware of the fact. TV shows like *Northern Exposure, The Simpsons, The Critic, Beavis and Butthead, Twin Peaks, The Osbornes*, are endlessly reflexive and self-referential. The titles of postmodern films themselves pay homage to this strategy of recycling (*Pulp Fiction, True Romance*).

René Girard offers another way of looking at this same phenomenon. For Girard, the European novel, and the history of culture more generally, show a coherent trajectory; they progressively reveal the ever more bitter fruits of mimetic desire, beginning with Cervantes and finally exploding in the work of Dostoevsky, where the mediator is seen as loved and hated, as simultaneously admired model and despised obstacle. According to Girard, the victims of metaphysical desire (like the protagonist of *The Talented Mr Ripley*) seek to appropriate their mediator's being by imitating them. Cervantes thus anticipates the fandom phenomenon: Don Quixote wants to be a star like Amadis, and Sancho too wants his "fifteen minutes of fame." This same love/hate amalgam is imaged in films like *Stardust Memories* and *The King of Comedy*, where "fans" torment and even kill the stars (Selena, John Lennon) that they presumably love.

Cervantes, as Alter put it in a humanist language, was the first of many artists "to see in the mere fictionality of fictions the key to the predicament of a whole culture, and to use this awareness centrally in creating new fictions of their own."[54] Postmodern culture also stresses the "fictionality of fictions," otherwise known as the "precession of simulacra," but in a quite different mode and key. Yet at their best, the contemporary arts and media also write, in their fashion, in "the manner of" but also "differently from" Cervantes. And, on occasion, they manage to do what Cervantes did — to lay bare the devices of art while also exposing the mechanisms of society.

1 Robert Alter, *Partial Magic: The Novel as a Self-conscious Genre* (Berkeley, CA: University of California Press, 1975), p. xi.

2 See Ernst Bloch, *The Principle of Hope*, vol. III, trans. Neville Plaice, Stephen Plaice, and Paul Knight (Cambridge, MA: MIT Press, 1986), p. 1048.

3 See Vladimir Nabokov, *Lectures on Don Quixote* (New York: Harcourt, Brace, Jovanovich, 1983).

4 Some dictators, like Augusto Pinochet, banned *Don Quixote* because it seemed a plea for freedom and an attack on established authority.

5 René Girard, *Deceit, Desire, and the Novel: Self and Other in Literary Structure*, trans. Yvonne Freccero (Baltimore, MD: The Johns Hopkins University Press, 1961), p. 52.

6 Harry Levin, *The Gates of Horn: A Study of Five French Novelists* (New York: Oxford University Press, 1963), p. 48.

7 Girard, *Deceit, Desire, and the Novel*, p. 1.

8 Cited in Ramon Chao, *Conversaciones con Alejo Carpentier* (Madrid: Alianza Editorial, 1985), p. 165.

9 See F. Rodriguez Marin, "Don Quixote en America," *Estudios Cervantinos* (Madrid: Atlas, 1947), pp. 592–3.

10 See Denis de Rougemont, *Love in the Western World*, trans. Montgomery Belgion (Princeton, NJ: Princeton University Press, 1983).

11 Fredric Jameson, *The Political Unconscious* (Ithaca, NY: Cornell University Press, 1981), p. 152.

12 Bloch, *Principle of Hope*, vol. III, p. 1035.

13 See Daniel Eisenberg, *Cervantes y Don Quixote* (Barcelona: Montesinos, 1993). p. 92.

14 All references are to *Don Quixote*, trans. Walter Starkie (New York: Signet, 1987).

15 Girard, *Deceit, Desire, and the Novel*.

16 Bloch, *Principle of Hope*, vol. III, p. 1036.

17 Quoted in José Luis Garcia Martin, *Nuevas visiones del Quixote* (Oviedo: Collecciones Nobel, 1999), p. 14.

18 See Alberto Manguel, *A History of Reading* (London: Penguin, 1996), p. 8.

19 Michel Foucault, *The Order of Things: An Archaeology of the Human Sciences* (in French *Les Mots et les choses*) (New York: Random House, 1970), p. 46.

20 For a comprehensive survey of the uses of the concept of mimesis, see Gunter Gebauer and Christoph Wulf, *Mimesis: Culture, Art, Society*, trans. Don Reneau (Berkeley, CA: University of California Press, 1992).

21 See Northrop Frye, *Anatomy of Criticism* (Princeton, NJ: Princeton University Press, 1957); and Mikhail M. Bakhtin, *Problems of Dostoevsky's Poetics*, trans. Caryl Emerson (Minneapolis, MN: University of Minnesota Press, 1984).

22   Erich Auerbach, *Mimesis: The Representation of Reality in Western Literature*, trans. Willard Trask (Princeton, NJ: Princeton University Press, 1953).

23   Salvador de Madariaga develops this theme in his *Guia del lector del "Quixote," Ensaio Psicologico* (Madrid: Espasa-Calpe, 1926).

24   Girard, *Deceit, Desire, and the Novel*.

25   See M. M. Bakhtin and P. N. Medvedev, *The Formal Method in Literary Scholarship* (Cambridge, MA: Harvard University Press, 1985).

26   Margaret Anne Doody, *The True Story of the Novel* (New Brunswick, NJ: Rutgers University Press, 1996), p. 3.

27   See Nabokov, *Lectures on Don Quixote*, p. xvi.

28   Levin, *The Gates of Horn*, p. 43.

29   Alter, *Partial Magic*, p. 6.

30   Ibid., p. 8.

31   Ibid.

32   Ibid.

33   Nabokov speaks of "the army of Don Quixotes engendered in the cesspools or hothouses of dishonest or conscientious translation." See Nabokov, *Lectures on Don Quixote*, p. 112.

34   See Harold Bloom, *The Western Canon* (New York: Harcourt Brace, 1994), p. 129.

35   See Juan Bonilla, "El Quixote de Kozintsev," in Martin, *Nuevas visiones del Quixote*, p. 55 (my translation).

36   For an analysis of the carnivalesque elements in the film, see Barbara Leaming, *Grigori Kozintsev* (Boston: Twayne Publishers, 1980), pp. 77–93.

37   See Andrea Cervatiuc, "El punto de vista en las adaptaciones filmicas de Don Quijote," unpublished masters thesis in the Department of French, Italian, and Spanish at the University of Calgary, Alberta, 1999.

38   I am very much indebted to Juan Amalbert, the owner and restorer of the Welles film, who generously provided me with a videotape of the film.

39   Julian Cornell, "All's Wells that Ends Wells: Apocalypse and Empire in *The War of the Worlds*," in Robert Stam and Alessandra Raengo (eds), *A Companion to Literature and Film* (Oxford: Blackwell, 2004).

40   Quoted in Youssef Ishaghpour, *Orson Welles cineaste: une camera invisible*, vol. III (Paris: Editions de la Difference, 2001), p. 824 (my translation).

41   Ibid., p. 823.

42   See Mark W. Estrin (ed.), *Orson Welles: Interviews* (Jackson: University of Mississippi Press, 2002), p. 38.

43   Ibid., p. 37.

44   Cited in Cervatiuc, "El punto," p. 69.

45   I would like to thank Gabriela Basterra, my colleague at New York University, for our lively discussion while screening Welles's *Don Quixote*.

46   I explore these Master Pedro-like sequences in more detail in my *Reflexivity in Film and Literature* (New York: Columbia University Press, 1992).

47 Cited in E. C. Riley, "*Don Quixote*: From Text to Icon" (http://www2h-net.msu.edu/-cervantes/csa/articw88/riley/htm), p. 4.

48 Page 39. All references are to Kathy Acker, *Don Quixote* (New York: Grove Press, 1986).

49 For an extended discussion of Acker's *Don Quixote*, see Nicola Pitchford's on-line essay "Flogging a Dead Language: Identity Politics, Sex, and the Freak Reader in Acker's *Don Quixote*" (http://www.iath.virginia.edu/pmc/text-only/issue.900/11).

50 See Janet H. Murray, *Hamlet on the Holodeck* (Cambridge, MA: MIT Press, 1997), p. 98.

51 Quoted in Riley, "*Don Quixote*: From Text to Icon."

52 John Docker, *Postmodernism and Popular Culture: A Cultural History* (New York: Columbia University Press, 1994).

53 Fredric Jameson, *Postmodernism, or the Cultural Logic of Late Capitalism* (Durham, NC: Duke University Press, 1991), p. 65.

54 Alter, *Partial Magic*, p. 3.

Chapter 1

Chapter 2

Colonial and Postcolonial Classics: From *Robinson Crusoe* to *Survivor*

French critic Marthe Robert argues that both *Don Quixote* and *Robinson Crusoe* can be seen as the first "modern" novels, but in different senses of the word "modern." *Robinson Crusoe*, she argues, is the first "modern" novel in the sense of reflecting the social dynamism and vision of the bourgeois commercial class which emerges from the English revolution. *Don Quixote*, meanwhile, is the first "modern" novel in the very different sense of initiating a self-conscious literature which makes its own doubts and reflections the very subject of its narrative. Although Marthe Robert does not mention it, the two senses of "modern" conform, **grosso modo**, to the distinction between "modernity" as an historical epoch — i.e. the shift from the feudal to the modern, individualist, incipiently capitalist ethos — and "moder**nism**" as an artistic style or dominant, one characterized by epistemological skepticism, stylistic reflexivity, and the rejection of illusionism. Neither novelistic tradition has a monopoly on "reality" and truth. While some writers opt for an oxymoronic "realist illusion," other writers, no less prestigious, emphasize the fictive character of their creations. Marthe puts the question as follows: "Either the story reveals itself as such, disclosing even in its storytelling the conventions that it has chosen to obey; or the story surrounds itself with all the appearances of life, and in this case, naturally, it goes out of its way not to call attention to its desire to create an illusion."[1] In sum, the two traditions represent two ways of "lying," two different ways of exploiting (or confronting) readerly credulity.

Despite its indisputable importance, *Robinson Crusoe* was not in any way the first novel. It was preceded by *Don Quixote* and by centuries of prose fictions going back to antiquity. But if *Don Quixote* hides its sincerity under the guise of irony, *Robinson Crusoe* hides its mendacity by masquerading as "sincere." And while Cervantes' hero seeks out adventure "in imitation of" literary heroes, Defoe's hero wants to be an original, a successful innovator who imitates no one, even though Defoe himself was imitating sensationalist travel literature. He lights out for adventure against paternal prohibitions, as if performing the act of departure for the first time. A corollary contrast between the two books has to do with narrative voice. While Cervantes uses dialogue, interpolated tales, and quotations to dialogically multiply voices, *Robinson Crusoe* tends to incorporate others' voices into a single voice. While *Don Quixote*, in a kind of epistemological cubism, stages a mutual relativization of perspectives, *Robinson Crusoe* stresses a more or less homogeneous point of view. While *Don* Quixote gives voice to Don Quixote's déclassé, hidalgo ethos, *Robinson* Crusoe expresses an upwardly mobile, parvenu world. And while *Don Quixote* is flamboyantly multigeneric, *Robinson Crusoe* represses the traces of other genres. While *Don Quixote* works through comic distance, *Crusoe* operates in terms of pathos and identification. The contrasting deployment of chapter titles in the two texts exemplifies this difference. While the titles of *Don Quixote* are comically minimalist or mockingly self-aggrandizing – "In which is told what therein shall be seen;" and "Which treats of what the reader shall see or the listener hear" – the titles of *Robinson Crusoe* are straightforward and concrete: "I Furnish Myself with Many Things;" "I Make Myself a Canoe."

On the other hand, we should not overdraw the contrast between *Don Quixote* and *Robinson Crusoe*. The two novels share a number of salient features: the uncertain status of the text due to its self-generating "sequels;" the pretenses of "editing" or "translating;" the picaresque motif of travel; the bookish references (chivalric romances in Cervantes, the Bible in Defoe); the oxymoronic duo (fat/thin; black/white); the friendly master–servant relationship; the feudal rituals of naming ("Friday" and "Sancho Panza"); the presence of social mobility; the shared relation to epic (comic and aristocratic in Cervantes' case; serious and middle class in Defoe's); and even their anomalous status as classics deemed suitable for children, despite the casual cruelty that informs both books. The two novels share even their referencing of the prejudices of the time: Sancho declares himself "the mortal enemy of the Jews" and the "accursed race" of Muslims, and Crusoe speaks of "cannibals" and "savages." Surprisingly, both novels are arguably marked as well by Arabic narrative traditions, explicitly referenced in *Don Quixote* and more subterranean in *Crusoe* (Samar Attar argues that *Crusoe* draws on two Arabic models popular in translation in Defoe's time: Ibn Tufayl's *Havy Ibn Yaqsan* and Sinbad the Sailor from *Arabian Nights*).[2]

If not the first novel, *Robinson Crusoe* does nonetheless constitute one of the seminal source texts of a specific European tradition – that of the mimetic novel based on "real life" and written so as to generate a strong impression of reality. Defoe's zero-degree style provided the model for one strain in the novel, one favoring a business-like "reportorial" prose rooted in the world of middle-class facticity. The word "reportorial" is here more than metaphoric, since 20 years of journalistic practice gave Defoe an acute sense of how to entertain readers through engagingly plausible stories fleshed out with persuasive descriptive details. *Robinson Crusoe* forms part of an oxymoronic genre: the realistic fictional autobiography. The title page offers the first "factual lie:" it tells us that Crusoe's narrative was "written by himself," i.e. by Crusoe. In a puritanical age, which saw fiction as the "work of the devil," an unsigned preface assures readers that "the editor" – another lie – "believes the thing to be a just history of fact; neither is there any appearance of fiction in it." Interestingly, *Robinson Crusoe* itself inadvertently provides an image which encapsulates this concept of realism as hiding all "appearance of fiction," in the form of Crusoe's island dwelling. Crusoe's home – a camouflaged fortification not recognizable as a "habitation" from the outside, designed so that strangers might not detect any appearance of human habitation on the island – can be read as a metaphor for Defoe's own stylistic option of realism, which, like Crusoe's home, is also a construct built with great effort, but one camouflaged as "natural" and organic.

All works of art inevitably get caught up in the ongoing whirl of dialogical transformation, of texts generating other texts in an interminable circuit of recycling and transformation. But this same process **already** informed the source novel itself, whose very status is unstable. Defoe wrote the book in three parts: *Robinson Crusoe* (1719); *The Farther Adventures* (1719); and the *Serious Reflections* (1720), yet only Part One has been granted canonical status as **the** version of the novel. The principle of the "sequel" was thus already built into the earliest version of the novel. Despite Defoe's claim of basing his text solely on real life, moreover, his "realistic" novel is itself an artifact rooted in various intertexts: the Bible, homiletic tracts, journalistic writing about castaways, and sensationalist travel literature, just to mention a few. The original title – *The Life and Strange Surprising Adventures of Robinson Crusoe of York, Mariner: Who Lived Eight and Twenty Years all alone in an uninhabited Island on the Coast of America, near the mouth of the Great River of Oroonoque; Having been cast on Shore by Shipwreck, wherein all the Men perished but himself, With an Account how he was at last as strangely deliver'd by Pirates. Written* *by himself* – perhaps gives a more vivid sense of the book's affiliation with the travel genre. And here Defoe was not "faithful" to his real-life model. The prototype for Defoe's character was Alexander Selkirk, an Englishman who spent four years on a Pacific island ("Juan Fernandez") near Chile. But while Selkirk was something of an agnostic and a womanizer, Crusoe is a pious dissenter and puritan. And while Selkirk was put ashore at his own request, Crusoe was shipwrecked. Ignoring the facts concerning Selkirk, Defoe has Crusoe spend 28 years on the island, this time located not in the Pacific but in the Caribbean near the mouth of the Orinoco river. Most importantly, the real-life Selkirk never met **anyone** on **his** island, while Crusoe's encounter with Friday forms the very kernel of the story. In terms of adaptation theory, one is led to ask: if Defoe was not "faithful" to his sources, i.e. to the journalistic accounts concerning his prototype Selkirk, why should a film adaptation be "faithful" to a novel which claims to be "faithful" to fact but which is actually a fabrication? Why prosecute the demand for "fidelity" only at the point along the larger trajectory where the novel turns into a film?

Clearly one of the most influential novels ever written, *The Adventures of Robinson Crusoe* was hardly the first long piece of prose fiction, but it was perhaps the first piece of prose fiction intended to create the illusion of reality. Anterior novels such as *Don Quixote* had explicitly drawn their plots from previous fictions, while *Robinson Crusoe* claims to be presenting new and "novel" incidents freshly fished from the ponds of life. At the same time, *Crusoe*'s "realism" can just as easily be seen as the sheerest fantasy, the product of a middle-class Englishman's daydreams of adventure and social ascension. The "magical" *Don Quixote*, conversely, can just as easily be seen as a realistic portrait of seventeenth-century Spain.

It was certainly not the quality of the writing that generated *Crusoe*'s primordial role within the history of the novel. For Coleridge, the very mediocrity of the style flattered readers by implying that they could have written it as well. More than just a novel, *Crusoe* provided an archetype for the West, a quintessential culture hero like Faust or Don Juan.[3] At this point in history, the character Crusoe has become thoroughly intertwined with the long trail of prestigious commentary about him. For French Enlightenment philosopher Jean-Jacques Rousseau, *Crusoe* provided a pedagogical model of "natural education" for his pupil Emile. Rousseau's idea of Crusoe as the embodiment of the love of nature was clearly an idealization, since Defoe's Crusoe is actually less concerned with loving nature than with dominating and profiting from it. For Karl Marx, in contrast, Crusoe incarnated *Homo economicus* and the labor theory of value, but in strangely asocial and anti-communal form, since Crusoe produces not for others but for himself alone. But it is the Irishman James Joyce (in 1912) who most foreshadows contemporary attitudes toward Crusoe. Anticipating Benedict Anderson's concept of "imagined communities,"[4] Joyce sees *Crusoe* as the expression of a "truly national spirit." In an appreciation perhaps colored by anti-colonial resentment against the British, Joyce sees the book as a "prophecy of the empire:"

> The true symbol of the British empire is Robinson Crusoe . . . He is the true proto-type of the British colonist, as Friday (the trusty savage who arrives on an unlucky day) is the symbol of the subject races. The whole Anglo-Saxon spirit is in Crusoe: the manly independence, the unconscious cruelty; the persistence; the slow yet efficient intelligence; the sexual apathy; the practical well-balanced religiousness; the calculating taciturnity. Whoever reads this simple, moving book in the light of subsequent history cannot help but fall under its prophetic spell.[5]

The very fact that Joyce sees Friday's encounter with Crusoe as an unlucky day, I would suggest, betokens Joyce's identification with the colonized and the enslaved.

Diverse elements feed into the culture-hero status of Crusoe. First, Crusoe's life and experience recapitulate human evolution and "progress" as conceptualized by the Western mind. Crusoe on his island moves from being a hunter and gatherer through being an agriculturalist to being a colonial entrepreneur. Second, Crusoe initiates what might be called the "Oedipal paradigm" within the novel, the structure by which the novelistic hero (usually a man) leaves the familiar and the familial, the known and the comfortable, for a world of risk and danger, ultimately against the conservative prohibitions of paternal law. Crusoe's father warns him against giving up the comfortable "middle station" – i.e. the stable middle-class life – for the chimera of wealth and adventure. Crusoe's shipwreck momentarily seems to bear out the clairvoyance of the father's warnings and the "punishment" for what Crusoe himself calls his "original sin" – the violation of the patriarchal taboo. Yet the wealth and success granted Crusoe at the end of the novel confirm the strategic rightness of his original defiance of paternal prohibition.

Third, to switch from a psychoanalytic to a social register, Crusoe incarnates the social mobility dreamed of by many middle-class readers of the time. While the novel as genre might often be reactionary in its specific ideological choices, *Crusoe* shows the ways in which the novel has historically been linked to social dynamism and mobility, and to the simultaneous construction and destruction which Marx saw as typical of capitalism. Crusoe's self-shaping parvenu status as a character in this sense corresponds to the parvenu, *arriviste* status of the novel genre itself.[6] (Once the novel as a genre "arrived," so to speak, it became film's turn to become the parvenu.)

Fourth, *Crusoe* incarnates the religious-cultural discourse of work not as curse (the biblical "sweat of your brow") but as salvation, a kind of spiritual therapy. *Crusoe* embodies, in short, the Protestant work ethic, as well as the Calvinist theory of the "invisible hand," the process by which God presumably guides wealth into the hands of an "elect" of hardworking believers, much as a novel's "Providential" author or narrator might rig the plot to reward the "good" characters and punish the "bad."

Fifth, Crusoe's story forms a Christian allegory of a particular type, that of the Protestant individual's personal dialogue with God, nourished by constant reading of the Bible within the framework of the "priesthood of every believer." Crusoe's Christianity is, however, highly selective and opportunistic, with little place for charity, for example, or for "doing unto others as you would have them do unto you" or "we are all members of one another." Crusoe would not be enthusiastic about the resolve of the early Christians to "have all things in common," or about Christ's admonition to "take all that thou hast and give to the poor." In the novel, Crusoe is the constant beneficiary of **unreciprocated** solidarity; he constantly takes from others while giving little in return. As Ian Watt points out, Crusoe believes only in a cost-free, bottom-line "always deferred" charity, often delegated to others.[7] He sells Xuri, the Moor who had saved his life, to a ship captain, for example, but on condition that the captain free Xuri later if he becomes Christian. Thus charity involves no real sacrifice on Crusoe's part. Nor does his personal experience of enslavement induce empathy for the enslaved.

Crusoe is a multifaceted "hero." As Derek Walcott puts it, he is simultaneously Adam (as the first inhabitant of a second paradise), Columbus (in having discovered a new world), and God (in his power of naming and creating and in ruling the world he has made).[8] Often seen as a children's book, designed to initiate young people into ethical ideals such as hard work, thrift, perseverance and independence, the novel is also a "child's book" in another sense. *Robinson Crusoe* acts out the infantile "logic" of what Freud called the "family romance," i.e. the mechanism by which the childish imagination conjures up mythic "solutions" to the crises emerging from the Oedipal situation. The family romance emerges during the passage between an early period when dependent children idealize their parents, seen as near divine and providential beings, to a period of disillusionment, when they perceive that their parents are neither unique nor perfect, and therefore conjure up alternative parents, richer, nobler, and more loving than their own. The Oedipal situation generates infantile "tellers of stories" who imagine themselves as foundlings or bastards, to pick up Marthe Robert's terms, anyone but the legitimate offspring of their now delegitimized actually existing parents.

Crusoe's discourse betrays infantile dreams of omnipotence, a gigantesque will to power. He calls himself "king" of the island, and revels in the lack of rivals: "I was lord of the whole manor; or if I pleased I could call my self king or emperor over the whole country . . . There were no rivals; I had no competitor, none to dispute sovereignty or command with me."[9] Or again: "I was absolute lord and law-giver; they all ow'd their lives to me" (p. 190). The insular Crusoe pursues an ideal of total self-sufficiency; he not only lives on an island, but he believes, **pace** John Donne, that "man is an island." He practices a veritable cult of solitude, experienced as almost voluptuous. In Crusoe's world of solip-sistic self-absorption, every potential interlocutor is a threat to his autonomy. Indeed, one might posit an isomorphism between the **character** Crusoe's denial of human relationality and the **author** Defoe's denial of **literary** relationality. The denial of interdependency in human relations goes hand in hand with the denial of intertextuality in literary relations. The character's rebellion against the father, in this sense, homologizes the author's anxious rebellion against any responsibility to **literary** fathers (and sisters and brothers).

According to the conventional view, Crusoe incarnates practical courage, do-it-yourself ingenuity, perseverance, the spirit of "if at first you don't succeed, try, try again." But this view of Crusoe "edits out" other features such as his ledger book mentality, his proprietary attitude, his instrumental view of others in a world where all fellow-feeling is drowned in what Marx called the "icy waters of selfish calculation." Crusoe's real love is not for others but for his own pos-sessions. One of the most rapturous passages in the novel, symptomatically, has to do not with human intercourse but rather with Crusoe's discovery of the "jackpot" of material goods found on the wrecked ship.

Crusoe embodies possessive individualism in its most extreme form: a virtu-ally complete denial of the potential claims of others on the monadic self. Crusoe himself reflects that "life in general is, or ought to be, but one universal act of solitude." In *Serious Reflections*, Defoe describes human beings as "alone in the midst of crowds" and indifferent to others: "What are the sorrows of other men to us, and what their joy? . . . It is for ourselves we enjoy, and for ourselves we suffer."[10] While Crusoe displays an almost erotic pleasure in the accumula-tion of wealth, he expresses little emotion about his relations with human beings. This lack of comradely feeling goes hand in hand with a panoptical paranoia, which gives him an agonizing sense of being always on the lookout, while also constantly being watched. Rather like a postlapsarian Adam, Crusoe is deathly afraid of anyone (God?) seeing him in his bare-forked nakedness, yet as master of the gaze, he enjoys observing the "naked savages" from a protected, unseen vantage point. Like the voyeuristic spectator constructed by 1970s' psycho-analytic film theory, Crusoe is eager to see without being seen, to be in the position of what Mary Louise Pratt calls the "monarch of all [he] surveys."[11]

Crusoe is also profoundly puritanical and body-phobic. After decades on a tropical island, Crusoe still cannot "go quite naked . . . or abide the thought of it." Sex for Crusoe is a dangerously irrational and disruptive force within his common-sense world of pragmatic pursuits. In Reichean terms, Crusoe girds him-self in "psychic armor;" he conceives of his body, like his home, as a fortress. His fear is of penetration and engulfment. He walls himself up both literally and figuratively, shoring up the furniture of his own solitude. He spends three and a half months building the wall, and cannot feel secure until it is finished. In constant search of the chimera of the pristinely isolate self, Crusoe is the antithesis of the dialogical self imagined by Bakhtin, for whom solitude is "theoretically impossible," since we learn everything, including language, from the other.

A barely contained hysteria boils beneath the bottom-line "realism" of *Robinson Crusoe*. What is interesting is not Defoe's claim to factual realism, but rather the tensions operating within this realism. Despite the narrator's claims of documentary realism, the narrator is unreliable. Defoe's narrative clings obses-sively to "fact," yet the facts disintegrate under pressure. The "realist" Crusoe is prone to hallucinatory imaginings, constantly surprised by uncanny doubles, demonized alter egos. His very narration is unstable. Defoe gives us four vary-ing accounts of Crusoe's first day on the island, each significantly different in detail. An assertiveness about fact masks ontological insecurity and severe internal self-doubt. As Defoe himself puts it in *Serious Reflections*: "Everything revolves in our minds by innumerable circular motions, all centering in ourselves."[12]

Crusoe's historically and socially shaped desire, like that of Defoe, who spent his life begging for favor from the wealthy, was to live like the English nobil-ity. Like many of his real-life peers, Crusoe achieves this goal by taking advan-tage of the opportunities opened up by colonial expansion. Crusoe's fantasy, basically, is to get rich and to enjoy the services of a compliant slave. Friday is not usually called a "slave" of course, only "servant," but in fact he fulfills all the functions of the slave. Indeed, in Defoe's period, "slave" and "servant" were sometimes functionally equivalent, synonymous terms. (Indeed, not all slaves were black; some were white convicts or debtors who were sent to New World plantations against their will.)

In his desire to corral potentially complex relationships into binding "contracts," Crusoe very much anticipates the Enlightenment values of Rousseau's "social contract." At the same time, the novel inadvertently illustrates the claim, on the part of critics of the Enlightenment, that what was a "social contract" for white Europeans, was an "anti-social contract" for non-Europeans such as Africans and native Americans. The "social contract" was also implicitly a "racial contract;" the liberties encoded as the "Bill of Rights" and "the Rights of Man" were not meant to apply to non-European peoples. Crusoe presumably has the right to enslave Friday because Friday is in his debt, since Crusoe has saved Friday's life. Yet this "law" of enslavement and gratitude is racially differentiated. When Crusoe saves Spaniards, he does not turn them into slaves or make them call him "master."

Crusoe's "social contract" is also a "sexual contract." Crusoe's environment is a homosocial one of all-male merchant ships and brief "bondings" with men like Xuri. Crusoe's island, as has often been pointed out, lacks the fundamental component of the desert island fantasy: the woman. There is also no gainsaying Crusoe's misogyny. Crusoe devotes only two sentences to his marriage: "In the meantime, I in part settled myself here; for first of all I married, and that not either to my disadvantage or dissatisfaction, and had three children, two sons and one daughter. But my wife dying . . ." (p. 240). Thus Crusoe marries in one sentence and "kills off" his (unnamed) wife in a subordinate, concessive clause. The narrator/protagonist seems eager to get his wife into the preterit and out of his life.[13] She is ultimately less a character than a function, the means by which he gains three children, that is, heirs to his fortune.

At the same time, a clear homoerotic subtext animates the novel. While Crusoe's wife merits no physical description at all, Friday is granted a long, affectionate, even caressing account.

> He was a comely, handsome fellow, perfectly well made, with straight strong limbs, not too large, tall and well-shaped, and, as I reckon, about twenty-six years of age. He had a very good countenance, not a fierce and surly aspect, but seemed to have something very manly in his face, and yet he had all the sweetness and softness of an European . . . (p. 162)

The relation between Crusoe and Friday is described as idyllic, free from "passions, sullenness or designs." Their "perfectly and completely happy" relationship combines the best of friend-to-friend and father-to-son relations: "his very affections were ty'd to me, like those of a Child to a Father." In colonial adventure tales like *Robinson Crusoe*, the truly important relationships tend to be between

Colonial and Postcolonial Classics

Chapter 2

men, and colonial writing proliferates in scenes of male bonding between doubled, self-mirroring individuals. Indeed, critics like Leslie Fiedler have traced
the origins of the biracial buddy novel (Huck and Jim in *Huckleberry Finn*, Ishmael
and Queequeg in *Moby Dick*) – and I would add the biracial buddy film (Danny
Glover and Mel Gibson in the *Lethal Weapon* series) – to the cross-racial idyll
of Crusoe and Friday.[14] Both catalyst and receptacle for Crusoe's projections,
Friday is the object of colonial desire, both figuratively in terms of his labor
and literally in terms of his body.

Defoe uses diacritical markers to clarify Friday's status as an indigenous Indian
rather than African – "his hair was long and black, not curled like wool . . . his
nose small, not flat like the Negroes" – perhaps in order to avoid triggering any
inconvenient associations with slavery, which would have placed the island idyll
within another, less savory paradigm. Yet despite Defoe's attempts to distance
Friday from blackness and Africa, any number of filmic adaptations (not to mention illustrated versions) of *Robinson Crusoe* have intuitively turned Friday back
into an African and a black man, thus restoring precisely what Defoe himself
had gone to such pains to repress. (The cover of an abridged children's version
published in Brazil, for example, shows a gratefully genuflecting and very black
Friday pledging obeisance to a blond Crusoe, an image with clear implications
for contemporary racial politics in Brazil.)

The colonialist ideology of *Robinson Crusoe* was also rooted in Defoe's
autobiography. As a journalist, Defoe enthusiastically supported colonization in
South America. Crusoe's choice of Brazil as a place to do business is not surprising, since Brazilian sugar was one of the world's most profitable industries
in Defoe's time and was basically run by foreigners of relatively low social extraction. Crusoe, we often forget, becomes wealthy thanks to the slave trade and
specifically through the production of sugar in Bahia. In Defoe's capitalist utopia,
Crusoe's Brazilian investments are administered with complete honesty by his
trustees, in no way endangered by his absence of 28 years. Crusoe's voyages, as
Peter Hulme points out, recapitulate the history of colonialism: the encounter
with Islam, slavery in Africa, the transatlantic slave trade.[15] Crusoe participates
directly in the lucrative triangular commerce which sent manufactured goods
from Europe to Africa, slaves from Africa to the Americas, and raw materials
from the Americas to Europe, where the same cycle repeated itself in a triple
movement which generated profits at every stage, reinforcing European domination both of Africa and of the Americas.

As colonial explorer, Crusoe demiurgically molds a whole civilization. Although
Friday is variously described as servant, slave, and companion, Crusoe's relationship to Friday is ultimately a colonial relationship, one marked by linguistic,

religious, and economic subordination. Crusoe names "his" islander Friday in memory of the day he presumably saved the native's life. (Friday, we recall, is the day God created Adam, further reinforcing the analogy between the overweening Crusoe and Almighty God.) Crusoe simply assumes the right to name Friday; he never asks Friday his given name in Friday's language. The names themselves reflect asymmetrical power: Crusoe names himself not "Crusoe" but "Master," i.e. not as a person with a name given by his parents but rather as an abstract function of positional superiority, in a relation where he is the structurally superordinate member. Here slavery gains medieval, feudal overtones. Indeed, Friday performs a gesture – obeisance – drawn from the repertoire of feudal subservience: "at length he came close to me, and then he kneeled down again, kissed the ground, and laid his head upon the ground, and taking me by the foot, set my foot upon his head; this, it seems, was in token of swearing to be my slave forever" (p. 161). In accord with the colonial model, Crusoe imposes his language (English), his religion (Christianity), while relegating Friday to what amounts to slave labor, which is prettified by the book to look like cheerful collaboration.

Profoundly paranoid, Crusoe fantasizes horrors on every side. He encapsulates in himself the diverse fears inventoried in Jean Delameau's *La Peur et l'occident*, imagining himself surrounded by devils, beasts, and savages – three entities strongly linked in the colonial imagination. When he first sees the fabled footprint (which is **not** Friday's) his first reaction is not one of joy at the prospect of human companionship, but rather one of fear, mingled with glee at the prospect of "getting [himself] a servant." (Crusoe himself wonders about his own bizarre response.) Crusoe is obsessed with cannibals, and he predictably encounters what he had so vividly fantasized. Here the novel gives inadvertent evidence of the European's phantasmatic relation to the cannibal. Defoe, it is important to remember, is making all of this up; his prototype Selkirk never encountered **anyone** on his island, much less cannibals. The appeal to cannibalism also reveals the novel's generic affiliation with the sensationalist travel genre, in which writers try to outdo rival texts through ever-more-outlandish revelations. Although Friday explains that his group only cannibalizes during war, Crusoe is obsessed with the possibility of being cannibalized even in peacetime. At times Crusoe regards Friday as a dietary cannibal, i.e. someone who eats out of a craving for human flesh. Yet if that is true, one wonders, how can Crusoe be so relaxed with Friday? If Friday has a "hankering" for human flesh, should not Crusoe be frightened whenever meal time comes around?

Although Crusoe's voice is ideologically saturated and tendentiously monological, the text is vacillating and contradictory in its account of cannibalism.

At times, Crusoe excites himself into self-righteous, quasi-genocidal rage over native cannibalism, yet elsewhere he censures the cruelty of the Spanish, who slaughtered Indians without any justification. Whatever the horrific practices of the natives toward one another, Crusoe reflects at one point, at least they have done him no harm. Here the text might be reflecting the contradictions of Defoe's intertextual sources, which mingled racist travel literature with what French Historian Frank Lestringant has called the "Huguenot corpus," i.e. a series of sixteenth-century texts about Brazilian Indians by French Protestants like Jean de Lery and Abbé Thevet, texts which mingle hostility to Spanish Catholics — seen as the true cannibals, devourers of God in the form of the transubstantiated host/Eucharist — with a surprising sympathy for the cannibalistic Tupinambá, who only devoured their dead enemies as an act of symbolic appropriation.[16]

Indeed, cannibalism has been the object of animated debate during five centuries of colonialism. More than a century before *Robinson Crusoe*, the French philosopher Montaigne, in an essay (*Des cannibales*), very much inflected by the Huguenot corpus, excoriated the hypocrisy of Europeans, who were horrified by the Tupinambá practice of eating dead men, yet who approved the tearing apart of live men. The ritual cannibalism of the Tupinambá, for Montaigne, was less barbaric than the practices of Europeans, who tortured their fellows because of narrow doctrinal differences, all in the name of a religion of love. Some scholars, such as R. Arens, doubt that cannibalism ever existed, or at least point to the conspicuous lack of direct eye-witness evidence for such practices.[17] Others believe that it did exist but only as a ritual in warfare, a way of symbolically appropriating the fighting spirit of the enemy. (The Brazilian modernists, as we shall see in chapter 7, turned cannibalism into an anti-colonialist trope.)

The ideological role of cannibalism in the Defoe novel is, ultimately, to **differentiate** Crusoe the European from the others. As Crusoe puts the point himself: "I gave God thanks that ... I was **distinguished** from such creatures as these" (my emphasis). The point is (dia)critical: Europe constructs its own sense of cultural superiority on the backs of otherized natives. Crusoe's portrayal of barbarous native peoples leaves aside the fact that there were highly developed indigenous civilizations in the Americas, such as those of the Aztecs, the Incas, and the Mayas.[18] Absurdly, Defoe has Crusoe teach Friday to eat the flesh of animals, as if the idea of eating animal meat instead of human flesh had never occurred to him or his tribe. Peter Hulme points out that Crusoe "teaches" Friday two skills that Europeans in fact learned from the natives: how to barbecue and how to use a canoe, both of which are designated by words, according to Hulme, of Arawak extraction.[19]

Robinson Crusoe, like every work of art, is Janus-faced: it points both to an anterior intertext and to a kind of "post-text." In this sense, *Robinson Crusoe* generated an extraordinarily rich and variegated "afterlife" or "post-text." Indeed, Pierre Macheray calls Defoe an "*auteur d'anticipation*," whose importance derives from supplying a text which virtually begged to be rewritten, an idea which resonates with Derrida's idea that the copy creates the prestige of the original.[20] Michel Tournier compares the dissemination of copies of Defoe's novel around the world to "seeds" spread by the wind, generating new works wherever they fell.[21] Some of the Crusoe post-text was generated by Defoe himself when he tried to capitalize on the success of *Crusoe* with two hasty sequels: *The Farther Adventures of Robinson Crusoe*, published only four months after the initial volume, and *The Serious Reflections of Robinson Crusoe*, published a year later.

Few books have had such a vast and international progeny. In France, the literary exemplars of the "post-textual" imitations of *Robinson Crusoe* were called "Robinsonades." Already in 1805, less than a century after the publication of the Defoe novel, a German encyclopedia (*Bibliotek der Robinsone*) offered a comprehensive guide to all the works inspired by *Robinson Crusoe*. In England, hundreds of Crusoe imitations were published, resulting in such books as Agnes Strickland's *The Rival Crusoes* (1826) and J. M. Ballantine's *The Coral Island* (1858). More broadly, the seminal power of *Robinson Crusoe* was expressed in what one might call a Robinsonian diaspora of formulaic imagery: islands, shipwreck, treasure, solitude, cannibalism. In the French novel by Jean-Richard Bloch, *Le Robinson juif* (1925), a Jewish Robinson goes not to the New World but rather to the old – Palestine. Jules Vernes, for his part, parodied *Crusoe* in his *L'Ecole des Robinsons*, where everything occurs more or less as in the original novel, except that Crusoe discovers in the end that "his" island had already been purchased by an American millionaire for the purpose of the edification of his children.

The *Crusoe* post-text also ramifies into the world of film. Beginning with the Georges Meliès *Les Aventures de Robinson Crusoe* in 1902, there have been scores of feature adaptations. A partial list would include: the American *Robinson Crusoe* in 1916; *Miss Robinson Crusoe* (1917); the Brian Foy version *Robinson Crusoe* in 1924; *Little Robinson Crusoe* in the same year; the Walter Lantz version in 1925; the UK M. A. Wetherell version in 1927; the American Frank Moser version in 1933; the Walter Lantz cartoon in 1935; the Russian Alexander

Andrivevsky version in 1946; the Buñuel version in 1954; the French TV series in 1965; the Dutch *Een Nederlanse Robinson Crusoe* (A Dutch Crusoe) in 1969; the Mexican *Robinson Crusoe* in 1969; the British TV version in 1974; the MTV version in 1974; the (inevitable) porn version *The Erotic Adventures of Robinson Crusoe* in 1975; the Italian version in 1977; the Brazilian version (*As aventuras de Robinson Crusoe*) featuring Grande Otelo in 1978; the French TV series in 1980; the 1990 French cartoon version *Robinson et compagnie*; and the George Miller/Rod Hardy version featuring Pierce Brosnan in 1996. There have also been shorts, features, and serials **indirectly** linked to the Defoe novel: *Male and Female* (1919); *The Isle of Lost Ships* (1923, remake 1929); *Mysterious Island* (1929); *Mickey Mouse: The Castaways* (1931); *The Lost Jungle* (1934); *Mickey Mouse: Mickey's Man Friday* (1935); *Robinson Crusoe on Mystery Island* (1936); *The Beachcomber* (1938); *The Blue Lagoon* (1948); *Enchanted Island* (1958); *Lost Lagoon* (1958); *In Search of the Castaways* (1962); *Gulliver's Travels Beyond the Moon* (1966); *Rescue from Gilligan's Island* (1978); *Mountain Family Robinson* (1979); *The Blue Lagoon* (1980); and *Castaway* (2000).

Figure 2.1 Crusoe (Costinha) and Friday (Grande Otelo) in *As aventuras de Robinson Crusoe* (1978), produced by J. B. Tanko Filmes

This long pageant of adaptations rings the changes on the basic themes of *Robinson Crusoe*, generating a series of adaptive permutations of the source text. The 1919 film *Miss Crusoe* performs a variation in gender, an interesting twist since the novel, against the grain of the "desert island" genre, scarcely mentions women at all. *Little Robinson Crusoe* (1924), within the logic of *Crusoe-as-children's-book*, lowers the age of the protagonist, having a winged Jackie Coogan coming to the island to be worshiped by the credulous natives. *Mr Robinson Crusoe* (1932) keeps the Crusoe character but supplies him with a feminine companion, called not "Friday" but "Saturday." *Swiss Family Robinson* (1940) permutates the number and social status of the characters; Crusoe's lonely solitude becomes the marooning of an entire family. The Laurel and Hardy film *Robinson Crusoeland* (1950) performs a shift in genre, from colonial adventure story into slapstick comedy. In *Lieutenant Robinson Crusoe*, the transformation is both professional and zoological, as Defoe's protagonist becomes the sailor played by Dick van Dyke, and as Crusoe's parrot is replaced by a chimpanzee. *Robinson Crusoe on Mars* (1964), finally, turns the novel into science fiction: the "pioneer" on earth becomes the pioneer in space. This transformation betrays a certain historical logic, since space travel has conventionally been compared to pioneering on "new frontiers." Here Crusoe, i.e. astronaut Christopher "Kit" Draper, rescues Friday from alien slavers. The slaver has become an abolitionist.

Given the almost three centuries separating *Robinson Crusoe* from its film adaptations, some latter-day versions, not surprisingly, submit the novel to intense ideological critique. Indeed, the colonialist and misogynistic premises of the source novel turn "infidelity" into a kind of political obligation. Here I will address a number of socially critical rewritings and adaptations of *Robinson Crusoe*. The first is Buñuel's 1954 Mexican-American co-production. Although Buñuel made 18 adaptations (out of 32 features), one is struck by what seems a clear social and stylistic mismatch between director and novelist. While the other novels that Buñuel adapted all make a modicum of auteurist sense – *La Femme et le pantin* (adapted in *That Obscure Object of Desire*) would logically attract Buñuel through its love and pathos theme (and Andalusian setting), *Wuthering Heights* through its l'amour fou, *Nazarin* for its anti-clericalism, and so forth – *Robinson Crusoe* does not dovetail with any of Buñuel's favorite themes, although a few Buñuel films (*Exterminating Angel*, *La Mort en ce jardin*) do treat shipwreck-like situations. Indeed, the contrasts between the two artists are many and deep. While Defoe incarnated the new forces of bourgeois individualism, Buñuel, whose childhood and adolescence came straight out of what he himself called "the Middle Ages," was simultaneously linked both to the pre-bourgeois world of the medieval carnivalesque and to the anti-bourgeois world of artistic modernism and the avant-garde.[22] In aesthetic, social, and even biographical terms, Defoe, the "realist" and middle-class *arriviste*, seems at the antipodes of Buñuel, the genteel hidalgo and paradigmatic surrealist.

While Defoe would seem to have the imagination of a puritanical accountant, Buñuel is anti-moralistic, anti-clerical, and anti-bourgeois. While Defoe is nar-ratologically linear, Buñuel is given to Cervantic zigzags and absurdist digressions. While Defoe is ponderously "sincere" and straightforward, Buñuel is slyly ironic. Buñuel's literary affinities, furthermore, would not logically be with the middle-class realism of Defoe but rather with what literary critics like Bakhtin and Northrop Frye variously call the Menippea or the "anatomy," i.e. the exuberantly self-deconstructing and pluristylistic tradition which culminates in Rabelais and Cervantes. Think, for example, of the carnivalesque pilgrimage of *La Voie lactée* or the systematically digressive storytelling of *The Discreet Charm of the Bourgeoisie*, or the coitus-interruptus structure of both *Chien Andalou* and *That Obscure Object of Desire*. Defoe's concern for law and legal contracts is foiled by Buñuel's anarchistic assault on social and aesthetic decorum. Crusoe's pragmatic and materially motivated marriage in the novel could not be more antithetical to the exaltation of **l'amour fou** typical of Buñuel's *L'Age d'or*. Defoe the Protestant has little to do with Buñuel the lapsed Catholic, and Defoe's (and Crusoe's) colonialism hardly accords with the anti-colonialist stance of surrealists like Buñuel.

In adapting *Robinson Crusoe* in Mexico, Buñuel inherited a draft of a script from Hugo Butler, a blacklisted Hollywood screenwriter who used the pseudonym Philip Roll. (The film was made during the MacCarthy period when Mexico became a refuge for many blacklisted filmmakers.) The international co-production required a principal actor with quasi-star status, whence the choice of Daniel O' Herlihy as Crusoe. Jaime Fernandez, who plays Friday, was the younger brother of the famous Mexican director Emilio Fernandez (also known as "el indio"). Despite his authorship, Buñuel subsequently distanced himself from the film, claiming that he had had no control over the music and that he had never even seen the finished film. And, indeed, the film's emphatic, even bombastic use of music contrasts with Buñuel's general preference, in his fiction films, for only diegetic (as opposed to commentative) music. The Buñuel adaptation of *Crusoe* is in some ways disappointingly conventional, much less audacious and irreverent than many of his other adaptations such as *Tristana* and *That Obscure Object of Desire*. Buñuel follows the basic storyline of the voyages, shipwreck, Crusoe's solitude, the encounter with Friday, the arrival of the mutineers, and the departure from the island. He condenses the novel's events, however, since in the novel Friday appears only two-thirds of the way into the story, while in the film Friday appears somewhat earlier. In terms of point of view, Buñuel retains the centrality of Crusoe, and the film's intermittent voice-over narration approximates the first-person autobiographical memoir format of the book.

Buñuel's adaptation does make an important structural change, however. In the novel, the father's admonitions against going beyond the "middle station" are placed at the very beginning, thus endowing the entire story with an oedipal thrust: the son's revolt against paternal prohibitions. Although Crusoe's ship-wreck and his other travails would seem to bear out his father's warning, as we suggested earlier, Crusoe's ultimate success, thanks to which he becomes rich beyond his wildest dreams, discredits the paternal taboo. In the Buñuel film, the paternal prohibitions come later. On one level, then, they would seem to have **less** importance. But at the same time they take on a different semiotic-narrative form, to wit an oneiric form, and thus have a **more** intense and bodily impact. Shot in the typical Buñuelian dream-style of his Mexican period, the film shows Crusoe's father scrubbing a pig (the carnivalesque animal *par excellence*) as he sternly lectures Crusoe. Dressed in the typical hat of the puritans, the father is portrayed as cold and heartless. Like the dream in Buñuel's *Los olvidados*, the dream in *Crusoe* has to do with the parental denial of sustenance. Pedro in the earlier film is robbed by Jaibo of the meat proffered by his mother, while here the father himself refuses his son the basic source of life: water.

The film portrays the son's oedipal revolt in more violent terms than those of the book: Crusoe runs at his father with an ax. The father's skull is then seen floating in the very water previously refused the son. At the same time, father and son are linked through performance, since the same actor (O'Herlihy) plays **both** father and son – a simultaneous condensation and displacement that reminds us of Freud's dictum that we are ourselves always at the center of our dreams. Through the postsynchronization, the rebellious son also comes to occupy the place of the oppressive patriarch who is only the temporary and provisional object of his rebellion.

Although somewhat conventional, the Buñuel adaptation is not completely un-critical of the novel, although the critique takes a rather surprising form. In line with Buñuel's observation that he hated the novel but liked the character, the film critiques the novel by **improving** the character, by making him **less** of a colonialist and racist. (Other critical adaptations of *Crusoe*, as we shall see, move in exactly the opposite direction.) It is as if Buñuel could only tolerate Defoe's hero by refashioning him as a typically Buñuelian idealist. Thus the Buñuel film reconfigures Marthe Robert's dichotomy – Cervantes **versus** Defoe – by reading Defoe, as it were, **through** Cervantes. As a result, Buñuel's Crusoe becomes more Quixotic, and thus more sympathetic.

Colonial and Postcolonial Classics

Chapter 2

Buñuel also upgrades Crusoe in what might be called "ecological" terms. Defoe's Crusoe, as we have seen, has a purely instrumental, exploitative, even predatory attitude toward nature; for him, land is essentially real estate. Buñuel, in contrast, turns Crusoe into a pastoral lover of nature and animals who dialogues cheerfully with dogs, cats, parrots, and insects. One shot shows Crusoe carrying a kid on his shoulder, evoking a Christ-like shepherd. At another point, Crusoe helps a chick out of its eggshell. While the novel's Crusoe shows no sensitivity whatsoever to sentient nature or natural beauty, the film's cinematography, by Alex Philips, immerses the spectator in vegetative exuberance, highlighting the lush beauty of the tropical landscape and Crusoe's pleasure in it. Here again we encounter the "automatic difference" which separates filmic from literary realism. While Defoe, writing in London, without any pro-filmic model, simply describes in words a tropical landscape he had not seen, Buñuel, thanks to the filmic apparatus with its indexical link to the visual world, "recaribbeanizes" the novel by bringing us those Caribbean landscapes in all their chromatic plenitude. What is mere inventory and bare bones description in the novel becomes in the film actual tropical landscapes in all their visual splendor.

Buñuel also makes Defoe's hero more gregarious and sociable. In the novel, Crusoe prefers a solitude undisturbed by potential competitors. Buñuel's Crusoe, in contrast, adores human company; in his solitude, in a scene not taken from the novel, he hallucinates a cohort of remembered drinking companions. But the film's "improvement" of Crusoe operates especially in relation to the Crusoe/ Friday relationship. On one level, Buñuel critiques the colonial master/slave relationship; the opening voice-over narration mentions Crusoe's involvement in the slave trade, superimposed on shots of a map of what would later be called "the black Atlantic." On the other hand, Buñuel serves up a utopian vision of transracial camaraderie. Crusoe evolves from what Buñuel himself called "a typically Anglo-Saxon sense of superiority" toward a feeling of reciprocity and brotherhood. Crusoe and Friday hunt together, smoke pipes together, and cut each other's hair in what seems like a conjugal idyll. The end of the film, however, undermines this idyll by returning us to established patterns of social hierarchy. On the way back to England, Crusoe becomes the gentleman, and Friday his glorified valet. The open ending, however, induces us to wonder whether their "friendship" will ever survive "civilization."

Buñuel's adaptation is disappointingly acquiescent in the racist and imperialist conventions that undergird Defoe's novel. Although surrealists like Buñuel were staunchly anti-colonialist – they excoriated the French colonization of North Africa and denounced the Paris colonial exposition of 1931, for example – and although Buñuel produced a powerful filmic indictment of anti-black racism (*La*

Figure 2.2 The biracial idyll: Buñuel's *Adventures of Robinson Crusoe* (1954), produced by OLMEC / Producciones Tepeyac / Ultramar Films

Joven) just six years after *Robinson Crusoe*, his film here lapses into many of the colonialist *topoi* typical of dominant cinema. Thus the film features stereotypical drums evoking "restless natives," along with the stereotypical blackface convention that paints the actor Jaime Fernandez black. More gravely, Buñuel on some levels seems to accept without irony Defoe's sensationalist charge of native cannibalism. At the same time, however, Buñuel does critique Crusoe's genocidal rage at what Crusoe calls the native's "ghastly entertainment," while Crusoe himself later starts to question his own self-righteousness. He has no right to kill the natives, Crusoe speculates in a voice-over, since the cannibals had done **him** no injury. At one point, the film briefly frames cannibalism within a cultural relativist perspective which emphasizes **European** evils. Asked by Friday whether whites also eat people, Buñuel's Crusoe replies bitterly: "no, they just murder them," an echo of Montaigne's relativist argument in *Des cannibales*.

Buñuel also provides some critical glimpses of Crusoe the colonialist. When Friday sneaks into Crusoe's fortress, motivated by his curiosity about Crusoe's living conditions, Crusoe reacts with disproportionate anger and suspicion. At the same time, an important structural change in the architectonics of the text further "improves" Defoe's protagonist. The novel is plotted as a pilgrim's progress toward both salvation and wealth, the two going together according to the Protestant "invisible-hand" schema, whereby Providence subtly guides wealth, as if by remote divine control, into the hands of the "elect." But Crusoe's discovery that he has access to the ship's "loot" — a trigger for exaltation in the novel — becomes in the Buñuel film a catalyst for melancholy ruminations on the ephemeral nature of wealth. Contemplating some gold coins, Crusoe ponders their uselessness for him. While the novel emplots a quest, at once spiritual and financial, the Buñuel film has Crusoe's spirituality zigzag from crisis to crisis, with no clear teleology or providential design. Careening between exaltation and despair, Buñuel's Crusoe at times seems manic-depressive, with the nadir marked by the terrible dream about his father, the inane echoing of the 23rd Psalm against the cliffs (reminiscent of the echoes of the Malabar Caves in E. M. Forster's *Passage to India*) and the extinguishing of the torch into the sea. These sequences make nature seem indifferent to human beings, lacking in all moral or supernatural purpose, a portrayal which resonates with the existentialist motifs that dominated the intellectual atmosphere in the period when the film was made.

Buñuel puts his personal stamp on the film through intermittent Buñuelean "moments:" the surreal dream about the father, the fetishistic dress blowing in the wind, Friday's experiment with transvestism, the homages to Buñuel's adored insects, the Magritte-like shot of an older Crusoe contemplating himself in the mirror as a beardless younger man. Buñuel also leaves the spectator with a number of his typical enigmas, many of them involving his beloved animals: the litter of a cat with no visible father, the mysterious dog barking as Friday and Crusoe leave the island. Buñuel also throws the usual satiric barbs at established religion. Using the classical device of the naïf, Buñuel radicalizes Defoe's own reflections by having Friday pose challenging questions about Christian theology, questions that leave Crusoe dumbfounded and inarticulate: "If God let man sin," Friday asks astutely, "why God mad when man sin?" and "If God more powerful than devil, why God no kill devil?" (Friday's words echo the Marquis de Sade's "words of the dying man to the priest.") The note of absurdity is further amplified by Buñuel's visual play on the cross and a scarecrow frame. (In a 1930 preface to a surrealist exposition, poet Louis Aragon had spoken of turning the cross into a scarecrow.) Here a materialist undercutting of religious metaphysics suggests that Christian religiosity is ultimately rooted in irrational terrors.

Any text that has been around for as long as *Robinson Crusoe* will have inevitably undergone an interminable process of re-evaluation, carrying with it an accretive history of commentary and critique. It is as if the novel, after entering a new space of transfigured ideologies and grids, were "waiting" to be read "against the grain." In a formulation rich in implication for adaptation, Bakhtin suggested that "every age reaccentuates in its own way the works of [the] past."[23] In the colonial and postcolonial eras, literature and film have often "written back" against empire, often in the form of critical rewriting of key texts from the European novelistic tradition. Jean Rhys's *The Wide Sargasso Sea* (1966) retells Charlotte Brontë's *Jane Eyre* as the story of Bertha Mason, Mr Rochester's first wife (and the by-now celebrated "madwoman in the attic" of feminist criticism), leading us to reassess the racialized presentation of Bertha as a "creole savage." Rhys, herself the daughter of a Creole mother from Dominica, writes against Brontë's racist construction of the Caribbean woman, although other critics, such as Gayatri Spivak, have found imperial overtones in the Rhys book as well.[24] Interestingly, critics treat literary "adaptations" of *Robinson Crusoe* like *Foe* not as failed "unfaithful" copies of their source text, but as artistic creations in their own right, while film critics often disparage filmic adaptations – which might also be seen as "rewritings" – as "betrayals" of the original.

In the case of *Robinson Crusoe*, we see this revisionist process in novels such as Michel Tournier's *Vendredi, ou les limbes du Pacifique* and in J. M. Coetzee's *Foe*, as well as in poems such as Derek Walcott's *Castaway* or plays like the same author's *Pantomime*, all of which reread *Crusoe* through contemporary critical grids. Going against the grain of Defoe's puritanical novel, Tournier resexualizes Crusoe, endowing him with a protean, animistic, priapic sexuality, rather like the colonist who deflowers and impregnates "virgin land." But in Tournier the pan-eroticism of *"sexualité solaire"* takes on mystical overtones. Instead of Defoe's *Homo economicus*, as Lorna Milne suggests, we are given *Homo ludens*, in a world sanctified by play.[25] At the end of the novel, Crusoe decides to remain on the island, but he is surprised when Friday leaves on the rescue ship *Whitebird*, a conclusion which questions the interracial idyll of the source novel. In narratological terms, meanwhile, Tournier reinvisions the novel through anachronistically modernist artistic procedures, such as le style indirect libre, which were not available to novelists in Defoe's time.

The Derek Walcott *Castaway* poems, finally, bring Crusoe back to the Caribbean of Walcott's birth. A number of critics have noted a shift in allegiance, in

Walcott's work, since in his early verse Walcott saw *Robinson Crusoe* as "our first book, our profane *Genesis*." But if in his earlier work Walcott identified with Crusoe, in his later verse he identifies, ambivalently, with Friday. In *Pantomime*, Crusoe and Friday exchange roles.[26] Walcott sees "black, little girls in pink" in the Caribbean as forming part of "Friday's progeny/The brood of Crusoe's slave." The missionary's "Word" to the "savages," for Walcott:

> alters us
> into good Fridays who recite His praise
> parroting our master's
> style and voice, we make his language ours,
> converted cannibals
> we learn with them to eat the flesh of Christ.

Here Walcott describes a form of colonial mimicry which is not terribly subversive, and which includes mimicry of the Eucharist as cannibalism.

Coetzee's rewriting of *Crusoe*, entitled simply *Foe* (1986), meanwhile, consists of four parts, only the first of which really constitutes a new version of *Robinson Crusoe*. The rest consists in the new narrator's (Susan Barton) attempts to get Foe to write **her** story. Here Susan Barton is a woman shipwrecked with Crusoe, a woman character whom Defoe (here "Foe") has presumably "written out" of **his** story. In the Coetzee version, Crusoe is redubbed "Cruso." The slight, almost imperceptible shift from "Crusoe" to "Cruso" suggests a variation on Derrida's *différence*, the change in spelling that is seen graphically but not heard phonetically. Unlike the narrator of *Robinson Crusoe*, Barton is self-conscious about genre (she refers to "readers reared on travelers' tales"), precise about the flora and fauna of the island, and skeptical about the existence of cannibals ("I am not persuaded, despite Cruso's fears, that there are cannibals in those oceans"), and unsure of the nature of truth ("So in the end I did not know what was truth, what was lies, and what was mere rambling.")[27]

Coetzee "contaminates" his novel with intertextual echoes of other Defoe texts such as *Moll Flanders*. Crusoe too is changed; here he is incommunicative and senile, and he dies a third of the way into the book. Even more importantly, he does not keep a journal, so that Susan has to speak for both Cruso and Friday. She also speaks about Cruso to Foe himself. Just as there is a power struggle between Susan and Cruso on the island, there is a power struggle between the narrator and Foe as author-in-the-text, so that the novel becomes a polyphonic battle royal between "real author 1 (Coetzee)," real author 2 (Defoe), fictive author in the text (Foe), and the narrator, Susan Barton. In a narratological equivalent of a feminist insurrection, Susan Barton tries to usurp first the role of protagonist from Cruso, and then the role of writer from Foe.

Even more silenced than Cruso is Friday, whose tongue has been cut out by slavers and who cannot even tell the story of his mutilation. Throughout the novel, Susan speculates about the real meaning of Friday's missing tongue. Friday becomes a cipher; he cannot represent himself; as Marx said of the peasantry, he "must be represented by others." Although Coetzee is writing before the advent of postcolonial discourse in the academy, Friday is in some sense the "sub-altern who cannot speak," as if the author (and his narrator) were afraid to commit what Foucault called the "indignity of speaking for others." According to Barton, the true story cannot be heard until Friday gains voice: "Friday has no command of words and therefore no defense against being re-shaped day by day in conformity with the desires of others. I say he is a cannibal and he becomes a cannibal" (pp. 121–2). The Coetzee version does not "give voice" to Friday; rather it hyperbolizes Friday's abject, tongue-less and voiceless status. Unlike Shakespeare's Caliban, this Friday is unable even to use the master's language to curse him with it. Indeed, Coetzee's Friday seems to mingle the traits of Caliban (without the rebelliousness) and those of the Kaspar-Hauser-like "wild children" of Europe. "While he works I teach him the names of things. I hold up a spoon and say "Spoon, Friday" and give the spoon into his hand" (p. 57). Indeed, the passages where Susan tries to teach Friday speech are eerily reminiscent of the scientist Itard teaching the untutored "wild child" Victor in Truffaut's *L'Enfant sauvage*:

> On the slate I drew a house with a door and windows and a chimney, and beneath it wrote the letters h-o-u-s. "This is the picture," I said, pointing to the picture, "and this the word." I made the sounds of the word **house** one by one, pointing to the letters as I made them, and then took Friday's finger and guided it over the letters as I spoke the word, and finally gave the pencil into his hand and guided him to write h-o-u-s beneath the h-o-u-s I had written. Then I wiped the slate clean, so that there was no picture left save the picture in Friday's mind, and guided his hand in forming the word a third and fourth time . . . (p. 145).

Although Friday remains mute, Susan Barton never stops talking to him. And although he has trouble knowing what a spoon is, he is assumed to be able to understand Susan's words about narrational technique:

"This is a book, Friday," I say. "In it is a story written by the renowned Mr Foe. You do not know the gentleman, but at this very moment he is engaged in writing another story, which is your story, and your master's, and mine. Mr Foe has not met you, but he knows of you, from what I have told him, using words. This is part of the magic of words. (p. 58)

In the end, Friday does achieve a kind of writerly voice. The eighteenth-century part of the narrative concludes with Friday donning Foe's robes and wigs and usurping Foe's place at the writer's table, but all he can do is use his quill to produce smudged versions of the letter "o." We are reminded of the carnivalesque inversions of Genet's *The Maids* or *The Blacks*, where the oppressed mockingly wear the attire of the elite, but here the oppressed figure does not achieve expressive subjecthood.

In the final paragraph of the novel, Friday opens his mouth and gives birth to an inchoate stream of expression which "passes through the cabin, through the wreck; washing the cliffs and shores of the island, it runs northward and southward to the ends of the earth. Soft and cold, dark and unending, it beats against my eyelids, against the skin of my face" (p. 157). In *Foe*, the world of Robinson Crusoe meets the world of Gabriel Garcia Márquez, mediated by reminiscences of Shakespeare's (equally Carribean) *Tempest*. While Defoe's own style is verist and self-effacing, Coetzee's style is reflexive and magical; Susan reflects on the arbitrariness of Foe's narration and on the processes of producing fiction; the realist tradition becomes "contaminated" by its opposite number. *Foe* is the Crusoe story written **after** magic realism, after Derrida and Lyotard and postmodernism. Challenging Defoe not only in terms of character and plot but also in terms of narrational technique, *Foe* represents what might be called the "Cervantification" and "Márquezification," as it were, of *Robinson Crusoe*.

Filmic adaptations have also "written back" against empire and Robinson Crusoe. Jack Gold's adaptation of *Robinson Crusoe*, entitled *Man Friday* (1975), in this sense forms part of the same revisionist tradition we find in *Foe*. The film "writes back" against Defoe and empire, taking a much more irreverent and anti-canonical stance toward the Defoe source novel. It answers, as it were, Susan Barton's call to "give Friday voice." In still another intertextual turn of the screw, *Man Friday* is based not directly on the Defoe novel but rather on a 1972 play by Adrian Mitchell. Through a series of semiotic transmutations, novel becomes play becomes film. (At the end of the Mitchell play, Crusoe asks to return to Friday's island, but Friday is worried that Crusoe might corrupt the tribe, at which point the audience is invited to vote on the outcome.)

The differences between the Buñuel and the Gold versions of *Robinson Crusoe* have to do, in part, with differences in the ideological-cultural "dominant" of the distinct periods of production of the two films. While Buñuel was adapting *Crusoe* at a time when some in the "West" were just beginning to be conscious of the wave of decolonization and the dissolution of European empires, when anti-colonialist independence movements had not yet achieved their full momentum, Jack Gold worked in the 1970s, after the formal demise of colonialism in most of the world. In this sense, *Man Friday* can be seen as a "postcolonial" film. At the same time, Gold is working in the wake of the international "counter-cultural" movement; Friday's real tribe is "Woodstock nation." Within the counter-cultural ethos, Crusoe loses his heroic stature, as Defoe's puritanical fable-cum-colonial-romance mutates into a counter-cultural anti-colonialist allegory. Like most adaptations of the novel, *Man Friday* sees the Crusoe/Friday relationship as at the very core of the fiction. But the title signals a major shift in perspective: here the colonized is a **Man**, not the "**boy**" of colonialist discourse, and the focalizing agent is Friday, not Crusoe. Now it is Friday who "sees" (point of view, ocularization), "knows" (focalization), and tells (narration). Now **Crusoe** is observed from the outside, while Friday is seen, in narratological terms at least, from the inside.

This shift in attitude operates from the outset. The film opens with a shot of a whirling globe materializing out of chaos, underlined by a musical score whose bombastic overtones recall *Thus Spoke Zarathustra*. The quavering, "Shakespearean" voice of Peter O'Toole reads from the Genesis account of creation. What is conventionally called a "voice-of-God" (off-screen) narration is here particularly appropriate since Crusoe not only speaks of God but also regards himself as God-like. What we took to be an off-screen voice then gives way to on-screen synchronous sound; the formerly acousmatic voice is now matched with a human image – that of a ragged figure sitting on a log on a tropical beach. "Man," Crusoe reads from the Scriptures, "was created in the image of God." But since the "image of God" presented here is of a rather ridiculous man, we are prodded toward two possible (theologically incorrect) inferences: (1) either God himself is somewhat ridiculous, since Crusoe is made in God's image; or (2) man is not in fact made in the image of God. Crusoe then reads the biblical passage which exhorts man to "have dominion over every living thing on the face of the earth," while muttering his own overconfident gloss: "Yes, I think that's possible." The sarcastic idea of Crusoe personally taking on the formidable project of "dominating every living thing" resonates not only with the film's ecological theme but also with what the film sees as Crusoe's megalomaniacal personality. And by placing the sacred words of Scripture in the mouth of a prattling codger, the film points not only to the absurdity but also to the disastrous ecological consequences of this idea of dominion over "every living thing."

When Crusoe subsequently comes upon the fabled footprint in the sand, the camera zooms in to the footprint, followed by a close shot of Crusoe's horrified expression. As the music becomes more agitated, flames emerge from the footprint, giving way to Crusoe's hallucinatory mirage-like image of a black man, dressed in a grass skirt and "warrior" regalia, brandishing a spear and stomping in what appears to be a hostile attitude. (The image is that of the classical Hollywood "spear-chucker" extra, as if the eighteenth-century Crusoe had anachronistically absorbed the racist stereotypes of Hollywood safari films.) The comic impact of the scene derives from the disproportion between the signifier – a mere footprint – and the overwhelming horrible signification which the thunder-struck Crusoe attributes to it. The image of the single man stamping his foot then segues to a scene of an entire village stamping happily in a communal dance. In other words, the film offers benign images as a corrective to Crusoe's paranoid vision, a vision left unquestioned in the novel, where Crusoe controls the discourse. With the appearance of the communal celebration, the film reframes the narrative by switching to Friday's version of the same events. The village chief says: "If it hurts you or pleases you, if it hurts us or pleases us, it is time for you to tell your story." Thus the story is officially designated not as individual property but rather as belonging to the whole community. (Interestingly, when Friday speaks with his "tribe" he speaks normative, correct English, while with Crusoe his English is more fractured and hesitant.)

We then move to Crusoe's encounter with Friday and other natives. After being washed up on shore by a storm, the natives affectionately and ritualistically devour their fellows who died by drowning. Coming upon the funerary feast, Crusoe gets caught up in a murderous rage. When the natives make friendly, welcoming gestures of invitation to share in their banquet, a repulsed Crusoe murders them. He murders, moreover, "in the name of God the Father" – he slays one of the men – "the Son" – he slays another – and the "Holy Spirit" – a third is dispatched. The invocation of the Holy Trinity is superimposed on a religiously sanctioned triple murder; the recitation of the liturgy is punctuated by lethal gunfire. *Man Friday* suggests that Crusoe's claim to have saved Friday's life is a mystification; in fact, he simply did not **kill** Friday as he did the others. The only danger from which Crusoe saved Friday was the danger presented by Crusoe himself. At the same time, the film critically revisions the typical colonial massacre scenes of colonialist Hollywood films, in which Europeans mow down hundreds of natives. In the Hollywood racist vision, European "quality" –

here largely the effect of the possession of firearms — triumphs over native "quantity."

The white European/American in colonialist films, including the American Western, is often portrayed as surrounded, menaced, figured within what Tom Engelhardt calls an "imagery of encirclement."[28] In response to this perceived threat, the European has the right to exercise righteous, regenerative violence.[29] In the novel, this colonial will-to-power is clearly marked, and not only toward the "native." Crusoe tells the English captain as well that all of the mutinous crew now belong to Crusoe, and that they will live or die depending on their behavior toward him. God-like, the European colonialist wields power over life itself. *Man Friday* changes all this dramatically.

Friday's fellow tribesmen are no longer the cardboard cannibals of the Defoe novel; they are individualized, they have names, and they exercise precise occupations, such as storyteller or craftsman. (Interestingly, the characterizations valorize them as artists, unlike the novel, whose puritanical ethos exudes deep suspicion of the arts, despite the novel's clear status as art.) In *Man Friday*, Crusoe's fears are repeatedly exposed as irrational, the product of paranoia. The cannibals, furthermore, are decent and generous, while Crusoe is a murderer. The film performs a transvaluation of some of the conventional signs of the "other." While cannibalism is still a theme, it is now portrayed as a loving ingestion of one's dead relatives and companions into the transindividual tribal body.

Man Friday shifts the perspective to Friday; the colonial narrative is "interrupted" by another point of view. *Man Friday* mocks Crusoe for his contractual mentality, his national chauvinism, and his puritanical phobias. In a paradigmatic sequence, Crusoe tries to explain the laws of ownership, but Friday cannot understand why any one would be so deranged as to believe in **individual** property. Friday tells his community about Crusoe's strange, fetishistic worship of private property. "Do you mean to tell me," asks the chief, "that this Crusoe fellow comes from a tribe of people who go around saying that 'this is mine' and 'this is yours?' " The community greets the very concept with gales of incredulous laughter. (Here the film unfortunately reverts to a "positive" stereotype about indigenous peoples, imagined as having a golden age innocence of "mine and thine," when in fact it is usually **land** that indigenous people hold in common, not personal objects and possessions such as clothing.)

Such sequences offer a glimpse of the instability of colonial forms of emulation and "mimicry." Crusoe is surprised that Friday is such a fast learner, amazed that he can recite the names of all the body parts in English even faster than he can, rather like those Brazilian slave-masters, often illiterate, who were surprised to discover that their Hausa slaves were literate in Arabic. When Crusoe

Figure 2.3 Peter O'Toole and Richard Roundtree in *Man Friday* (1975); produced by ABC Entertainment / Incorporated Television Company (UK) / Keep Films

tries to teach Friday his own name, similarly, pointing to himself as "Master" and Friday as "Friday," Friday thinks that whoever points the finger at himself is "Master," as if it meant "I" and "Friday" meant "you." The deployment of what linguists call "shifters," i.e. words whose meaning depends on who is articulating them and from what position, takes on an anti-colonial dimension. The misunderstanding gives us a glimpse of the instabilities within colonial mimicry, the potentially "shifting" positions of colonizer and colonized. Friday, who has never been enslaved, who comes from a community where equality is the norm, and who is just beginning to learn what it means to be a slave, cannot "master" the concept of mastery itself. Unable to imagine that someone as ridiculous as Crusoe could ever think himself superior, he assumes Crusoe is just playing a silly game, while Crusoe takes the game in deadly earnest.

Man Friday thus overturns a number of colonialist hierarchies: Crusoe claims to be rational, yet he is ultimately revealed to be **irr**ational, even hysterical, while Friday maintains a calm reasonableness throughout. Although Crusoe treats Friday as if he were a child, in fact Crusoe is the childish one. Friday becomes a lucid, broken-English Montaigne, the native exegete of cultural relativism, who "talks back" to empire. In words that echo Caliban's dialogue with Prospero in *The Tempest*, Friday reminds Crusoe: "I taught you to dance and sing." When Crusoe reneges on his promise to sell his house to Friday, Friday takes Crusoe's gun. As Friday tires of his role as teacher and entertainer, we begin to get a glimpse of a possible, more rebellious Friday.

Prodded by Friday's Socratic provocations, Crusoe comes to humanist, egalitarian insight. While Crusoe thinks he is teaching Friday, in fact Friday is teaching **him**. Friday shows Crusoe how **not** to take himself seriously, how to play and enjoy. For Crusoe, a footrace is a competitive ordeal, for Friday it is a dance of gazelle-like grace. (Here again, unfortunately, the film comes close to the stereotype of "natural athletic talent.") Friday embodies the corrosive power of laughter, while Crusoe is ultimately a sad and joyless man. When Friday mocks England as a cold country sadly lacking in bananas and breadfruit, Crusoe responds sternly that "There's nothing funny about England." The film casts derision on what Norbert Elias calls the "civilizing process," the sphinctered world of etiquette and decorum. More important, the film shows Friday humanizing Crusoe, not only for the sake of his own survival but also for Crusoe's sake. At the same time, this view of Crusoe in some ways constitutes reverse paternalism, an exercise in white narcissism. Friday becomes the "ebony saint," the therapist and healer who ministers to the unhappy consciousness of the white man.

The film also draws out the novel's homoerotic subtext. As I noted earlier, Defoe's Crusoe seems less erotically energized by his wife, whom he marries and "kills off" with dispatch, than by Friday, whom he caressingly describes as "handsome" and "well-shaped." In *Man Friday* Crusoe alternates paternalistic domination of Friday with (unconscious) erotic attraction to him. When Friday comes across Crusoe guiltily flagellating himself over an erotic dream, Friday fails to see the problem. "Couldn't she do it well?" he asks innocently. He refuses to believe that God could be angry at Crusoe for having such a wonderful dream. And as for Crusoe's need for erotic succor, Friday reassures him: "Master," he tells Crusoe, "I am here to satisfy you if you need it. I am a loving man." Friday's generous offer triggers a biblically tinged outburst from Crusoe: "Friday, man shalt **not** love man!" In a clear case of homoerotic panic, Crusoe's fears of homosexual attraction lead him to rampant paranoia, to the bemusement of Friday, who does not share his phobias and inhibitions. The parrot then squawks: "I love you," implying not only that Crusoe **does** need love, but also hinting at another taboo – zoophilia – man shall not love animal! Indeed, the film hints at links between diverse pathologies: between the need to dominate self and the need to dominate others; between sexual repression and political repression; between the various ways in which fear of the irrational becomes itself an irrational fear.

Man Friday also mocks Crusoe's social *arrivisme*. Picking up cues in the novel, the film portrays Crusoe's home as a kind of medieval fortress, disproportionately protective in relation to the presumed threat. Crusoe's self-made mechanical ladder recalls a medieval drawbridge, thus ridiculing Crusoe's aristocratic pretensions of living like a feudal lord. The film also resignifies some of the conventional signs and symbols of Britishness: Crusoe, wearing his rags, salutes the Union Jack, while "Rule Britannia" plays on the sound track. In the end, the film mocks narrow patriotism in favor of comic demonstrations of cultural relativism. On frequent occasions, Friday, Socrates-like, deploys the maieutic principle to lead Crusoe to see the absurd implications of his original premises. When Crusoe praises England's cold climate and reserves of coal as evidence of English superiority, Friday argues the advantages of the Tropics. His island's warm climate renders coal superfluous; it is therefore superior to England. Man Friday's corrosive questions, however puerile in appearance, remind us of Henry Louis Gates's suggestion, in *Figures in Black*, that blacks (and one might add native peoples in the Americas) were the first "deconstructionists" because they deconstructed, from the vantage point of oppression and alterity, Europe's narcissistic claims about its civilizing mission.[30]

I am not arguing, I hasten to add, that *Man Friday* is a "great" film in either aesthetic or political terms. Its critique is, in many ways, "skin-deep." Despite the film's critique of European colonialism and Anglo-Christian puritanism, in the end it has Friday embody the ideal Christian, who patiently and lovingly tries to educate his errant master. While the revised title signals an apparent shift in focalization from master to slave, Friday's subjectivity ultimately serves a white counter-cultural utopia of festive and erotic community. The "natives" here are no longer "restless;" they are peaceful, communal, festive. Indeed, their collective life offers the endless *jouissance* of the perpetual party. But leaving Friday in a cultural and historical vacuum, the film does not dare to imagine Friday's life before Crusoe. We are not even told Friday's real name. We have little sense of his language, society, or even his anger at dispossession; in sum, we never learn who Friday is. The film critiques Eurocentrism, then, but remains Eurocentric in its incapacity to imagine Friday. While Cesaire in his version of Shakepeare's *Tempest* could reimagine Shakespeare's Caliban as "Caliban X," now seen from an anti-colonial perspective, *Man Friday* remains confined to an asymmetrical allegory in which one character is historically fleshed out, if only because the audience already **knows** Crusoe and his ethos, while the other is a counter-cultural token of innate philosophical wisdom and sensuous negritude. Although conventional binaries have been wittily questioned, at times they are merely reversed rather than complicated or addressed in depth. Rather than the usual decorative masses, the natives are seen sympathetically, albeit still very stereotypically. Friday's community offers the image of an alternative society, one animated by communitarian values, echoing with irreverent banter, raucous laughter, and expressive music and dance.

But what is most promising in the film is its way of linking narratological procedures to ideological issues through a recurring contrapuntal shift between Crusoe's perspective and Fridays's. To be more precise, the film shuttles between two perspectives: (1) the film's usually sarcastic, but also occasionally sympathetic, version of Crusoe's perspective (a distanced, satiric version of what Defoe presents in the book); and (2) the film's generally sympathetic version of the perspective of Friday and his community, who become a kind of (anti) Greek chorus commenting on the action. In narratological terms, the film recasts the point of view of the novel, operating a kind of transvocalization, a shift in voice. The largely single-voiced narrative of the novel ramifies into the double or even triple-voiced narrative of the film, in which the voice of Crusoe, Friday, and the narration itself compete for our adherence. In the novel, Crusoe gathers up unto himself the powers of author, narrator, and self-expressive character. But in *Man Friday*, those powers are undermined. Crusoe, the conquering hero, the omnipotent master of all he surveys, is exposed as a ridiculous, pompous figure. The film makes us aware of Crusoe's own blindspots, his grotesquerie. Inverting the "imagery of encirclement," here the native becomes the subject (and not the object) of fear.

It remains for us to examine a few final "rewritings" of the Crusoe story, most of which push the novel in a slightly more progressive direction. Caleb Deschamel's film *Crusoe* (1989) – ironically a product of "Island" Pictures – moves the Crusoe story forward by a century into colonial Virginia, where Crusoe (Aidan Quinn) begins as a slave-trader, only later shipwrecked on a remote island like his namesake. The film opens with a black fugitive fleeing slave-catchers, hiding in the muck of a swamp, as a subtitle informs us: "Tidewater, Virginia, 1808." A white man, whom we subsequently learn to be the Crusoe of the title, leads the chase. The film's sympathy for the runaway is shown not only through point-of-view shots from the fugitive's perspective, but also through the dissonantly ominous music which evokes, at that point in the narrative, the fugitive's fear as he runs from yelping search dogs and whinnying horses.

The film then segues to the auction block, where Crusoe has placed the captive on sale. Exchanging glances with the captive, Crusoe mutters to his associate that "I don't think he likes me." The slave's hostile reaction contrasts with what the Defoe novel had idealized as Friday's "spontaneous" fondness for Crusoe. The auction scene emphasizes slavery as a commercial and financial institution, something downplayed in the Defoe novel. In *Crusoe*, slaves are clearly treated as commodities, and terms like "first sale" and "resale" are bandied about. At the auction block, slavers bid over a "strong buck" and a "healthy female, with a musical voice." Some captured blacks, speaking African languages, laugh boisterously, and although we do not know exactly at whose expense, we suspect that the laughter might be directed at Crusoe and other whites.

Crusoe then petitions a slave-trader, with the historically resonant name of "Mather" — evoking both "Master" and the Puritan divine "Cotton Mather" — for the command of a transatlantic slave ship. Crusoe takes the ship in the direction of Africa, thus inverting the geographical trajectory of the novel, which moved from England to Africa to the Americas. The result of this revectored directionality is a loss of innocence for Crusoe; he is established from the outset as a slaver rather than as an innocent adventurer who "falls into" slaving by accident. Although the ship's pastor whitewashes their project as one of carrying "Christ's spirit to Africa," the film mocks this euphemization of injustice. The film brings back to the surface the inherent violence of racialized slavery. During the storm sequence, Crusoe shows complete indifference as other sailors and passengers drown, thus casting particularly harsh light on the selfish individualism that dominates the book. With the storm and the shipwreck, we catch up, as it were, with the other adaptations, which had tended to rush almost immediately to the shipwreck and the island. In contrast with *Man Friday*, Crusoe is presented here as relatively "normal," capable of self-mockery and laughter at the absurdity of his situation. As he watches his ship go under the waves, he evokes an imaginary auction – "Going, going, gone." Prior to the arrival of a companion, the film turns into a man–dog buddy film, with constant crosscutting between Crusoe and his dog, who becomes Crusoe's interlocutor, filling the actantial slot later fulfilled by the film's Friday figure. At the same time, the film gestures toward the classical depiction of Crusoe, showing his ingenuity, for example, by having him construct a kind of conveyor belt for the merchandise he recovers from the ship.

A change in narrational strategy differentiates *Crusoe* both from the book and from other versions of *Robinson Crusoe*. While the Buñuel version of *Robinson Crusoe* moves from retroactive voice-over narration (drawn from Crusoe's account) into direct dialogue, the Deschamel version eliminates the voice-over and the journals altogether. The actions are set in the present, and many sequences have no dialogue at all. (There are no conversations about Christian theology, for example.) Spectators, as a result, are thrown back on their own resources.

The net result, and this is a shared feature with many of the contemporary rewritings of *Crusoe*, is to undermine Crusoe's power as narrator. Still, Crusoe is clearly the focalizing character; we still see through his eyes and hear through his ears. At the same time, the film is precariously balanced, in generic terms, between comedy – evoked through Quinn's acting style and some quasi-farcical episodes – and what might be called the historical horror genre, evoked by the ominous music and the use of off-screen sound to suggest a sense of a horrifying threat.

As in the novel, Crusoe observes "natives" – some in ritual blackface, others in whiteface – through a telescope, and, as in the novel, he sees them participating in savage rituals such as slitting the throats of prisoners and draining their blood. Unfortunately, these scenes, which basically reproduce the spirit of the novel, have the effect of undermining the social critique implicit in the earlier sequences. Retroactively, the practices of slavery, which shocked us in the opening sequence, become more palatable through invidious comparison. "So is that the way," a character asks, "they treated each other in Africa?" Slavery, if only in retrospect, is subliminally implied to be a punishment for the natives' barbarous practices. Since Africans were already enslaving and abusing each other, the spectator might conclude, it was not so terrible to enslave them. Here the film simply reproduces the rescue *topos* of colonialist discourse: the peoples conquered by European colonial powers were always already at each other's throats, and Europe did Africans a favor by imposing a superior, more humane and peaceful, civilization.

Crusoe rescues one of the prisoners and names him "Lucky" (rather than Friday) because, as Crusoe points out, he's "lucky to be alive," and because he's "lucky to have [Crusoe] as a master." Furthermore, he adds, "I have no one to sell you to." Thus the slavery subtext, which Defoe tends to downplay and prettify, gurgles back up to the surface. Like all the other filmic Crusoes, this Crusoe too tries to initiate Lucky into the "civilizing process." Crusoe uses his gun to prod "Lucky" to wipe his face with a napkin after eating. But in an inversion reminiscent of *Man Friday*, the slave ends up taming the master. Each time Crusoe hits him to discipline him, Lucky strikes back more forcefully. When Crusoe insists on the English word, Lucky sticks with his native language; rather than simply say "meat," he teaches Crusoe "jellah." When Lucky escapes from Crusoe's chains at night, Crusoe pursues him, in a sequence that echoes the slave-catching of the overture sequence. On locating him, Crusoe tries to shoot Lucky but runs out of ammunition – Crusoe disarmed is a paltry figure – at which point the two wrestle in quicksand-like mud. In a scene heavy with symbolism, both men become mud-colored, their epidermic difference neutralized; now they are just two human beings clinging to life. As Lucky manages to escape the mud and Crusoe

Figure 2.4   Deschamel's *Crusoe* (1989), produced by Island Pictures

is about to sink below the surface and suffocate, Lucky, in what seems to be an allegory of human interdependence (reminiscent of *The Defiant Ones*), leans on a branch to lower it, thus offering Crusoe an escape route. The man Crusoe had tried to kill ends up saving his life. In the Defoe novel, Crusoe's "saving" of Friday's life provided the rationale for enslavement, but here, in a clear narrative inversion, Crusoe's very life has come to depend on the "native." Gradually, their relationship evolves toward greater reciprocity — they construct a raft together, for example — but without ever becoming the interracial idyll portrayed in both the Buñuel version and in *Man Friday*. In one scene, they each sing in their native languages, trying to drown out the other. But later we realize that Lucky has learned the words (or at least the sounds) of Crusoe's favorite ditty "One Man and his Dog." Lucky continues to wear his native dress and body ornaments, but the shared music hints at the possibility of a more equal, syncretic, intercultural dialogue.

Subsequently, Europeans come and take Lucky captive, in a scene reminiscent, again, of the slave-catching of the overture sequence. Infiltrating their ship, Crusoe learns that European "scientists" hope to exhibit Lucky as a "cannibal." They invite Crusoe to lecture about Lucky as an exotic specimen of primitiveness, but that very night, Crusoe frees Lucky, who sails away to freedom. The slave-catcher of the opening sequence has become the slave-freer of the final sequence. Crusoe's personal trajectory thus recapitulates that of the British empire, which moved from practicing slavery to trying to abolish it. Rather than save Crusoe by making him more gregarious and humane (à la Buñuel) or mock him as a babbling colonialist (à la *Man Friday*), *Crusoe* redeems him by making him an abolitionist.

The Rod Hardy/George Miller version of *Robinson Crusoe* (1996) starring Pierce Brosnan, finally, also makes token gestures toward a shallow political correctness. The casting of Brosnan as Crusoe inevitably brings with it the intertextual memory of the James Bond films, so that we subliminally align enterprising twentieth-century Cold War heroes with eighteenth-century colonial entrepreneurs like Crusoe, whose gun retroactively seems to foreshadow James Bond-style gadgetry. In this version, William Takaku as a revisionist Friday maintains his pre-colonial faith, becoming a kind of equal interlocutor with Crusoe. As in the Buñuel version, his skepticism about Christianity triggers a crisis of belief in Crusoe himself. Like most adaptations, the film rushes through the early parts of *Robinson Crusoe*, and even the 28-year stay on the island, in order to focus on the Friday/Crusoe relationship. But the cannibal trope is never doubted or reinterpreted; so once again the biracial male buddies struggle against the still-demonized others, the cannibals of the rival tribe.

After almost three centuries, *Robinson Crusoe* has by now become part of the general imaginary, so that relatively new films such as *Blue Lagoon*, *The Beach*, and *Castaway* come to form part of the *Crusoe* textual diaspora, reverberating with distant echoes of the Defoe text and its basic story of castaways on an island. Countless films – *Lethal Weapon*, *Men in Black*, *The Grand Canyon*, *Jerry Mcguire*, and many others – have also played on another seminal theme in the novel, to wit the biracial buddy motif. Robert Zemeckis' *Castaway*, for its part, offers us the Crusoe story in the age of transnational capitalism. Just as Zemeckis updated another eighteenth-century classic, Voltaire's *Candide*, in *Forest Gump*, here he updates Defoe in what amounts in architextual terms to an un-acknowledged adaptation. While the novel's Crusoe formed part of the cutting edge of early eighteenth-century capitalism, and traveled by ocean-going ship, *Castaway*'s protagonist, Chuck Noland (Tom Hanks) is a dynamic, go-getter agent for Federal Express, and he travels by jumbo jet. His name evokes both the cast-away (chuck) and a dystopian "no-land" of solitude. The pre-industrial mer-cantilist Crusoe here becomes the post-Fordist Noland. Unlike the rugged, individualist Crusoe, Noland is at the beginning at least a "company man." Here, Tom Hanks embodies the forces of latter-day globalization – what could be more "global" than Federal Express? – the go-getter master of the universe who is forced by an air disaster to descend into the circumscribed world of the "local," where conditions of life are little different from those suffered centuries earlier by Crusoe.

The medium also shifts: Defoe's verbally described shipwreck becomes the vis-ceral shock effects of ten minutes of disintegrating airplane and flaming waves. Like the original shipwrecked Crusoe, Noland too represents the "bare-forked animal" thrown back on his own resources. But rather than Crusoe's shipful of loot, Noland has only a few random parcels: a pair of ice-skates, some VHS cassettes, a woman's party dress – perhaps an allusion to the Buñuel version – and a document annulling a marriage. Like Crusoe, Noland too is an ardent practitioner of the work ethic. Like the novel, the film emphasizes the prot-agonist's creativity and resourcefulness. Ingeniously, Noland turns the ice-skate into a dental instrument. In a Promethean moment, he manages to kindle a fire, while singing the famous Doors song "Light my Fire." Here, a soccer ball takes the place formerly assigned to Friday as Crusoe's interlocutor, becoming, as Jim Hoberman puts it, "combined pal, pet, and pagan idol," an instance of product placement, since the ball is called by its trade name of "Wilson."[31] In a *Guardian*

Colonial and Postcolonial Classics

Chapter 2

review, Philip French called the ball a cross between a "mute companion and a Cargo Cult fetish."[32] This modern-day Crusoe is more *simpatico* than Defoe's Crusoe, and the whole story is framed by a loving but doomed relationship with his fiancée. Unlike Crusoe's wife, unnamed and dispatched in a sentence, functionally reduced to childbearing and heir providing, here the equivalent of Mrs Crusoe (played by Helen Hunt) has a name, Kelly, and a profession; she is a research scientist. The Oedipal tale is also altered to provide an allegory of beneficent globalization. Rejected by his fiancée, Noland finds his true home in the arms of the transnational cor-poration, as the real-life boss of Federal Express welcomes Chuck back into the FedEx corporate family.

Another, somewhat masked, example of the contemporary actualization of the Crusoe story and ethos might be the hugely popular CBS Television series *Survivor*, which in its way is also a hypertextual variation on *Robinson Crusoe*. Indeed, *Survivor* is the younger American cousin of the 1997 Swedish show *Expedition Robinson*, where the reference was explicit. Set on an island like the Defoe novel, the show features 16 characters who eliminate (by vote) one member of the community every week until only one survivor stands as "King of the Island." The "progress" from many to one parallels the narrative logic of the novel, at least up to the point of Crusoe's encounter with Friday. While on one level a televisual "adaptation" of *Lord of the Flies*, on another it evokes *Robinson Crusoe*. Here once again we find the claim to "realism," now transposed for a mass-media age, in the form of a "reality game show." Like *Robinson Crusoe*, with its mélange of facts about Selkirk and fictions about travel, *Survivor* too mingles fact (characters playing themselves) with fiction, and the characters not only build huts and eat rats but also practice shipwreck-style triage. Although the film features no "Friday," it does feature tribal echoes, for example in the Russ Landau theme music called "Tribal Voices." More important, the "survivors" are now themselves tribalized, equipped with rules and rituals picked up from TV's version of Anthropology 101. Unlike *Crusoe*, the TV fiction has little place for Bible-reading and piety: Derrick is expelled from the island early on. But as in *Crusoe*, the survivor ends up very rich, and is indeed named "Rich." For Rich, as for Crusoe, life is a zero-sum game against other, competing selves, seen as rivals rather than as companions. The prize does not go to the honorable (Rudy) or the female dialogical (Susan), but rather to the calculating. Crusoe too might have adopted the motto "Outwit, Outplay, Outlast."

Much as Marx saw Crusoe as embodying *Homo economicus*, contemporary media critics have seen *Survivor* as allegorizing contemporary politics and cor-porate ladder-climbing. The show-me-the-money Social Darwinism of the show is also revealed in its animal metaphors. Explaining her vote for Richard Hatch, the gay corporate trainer from "Providence" (a name which also resonates with the puritanical *Crusoe* ethos), the tough-talking Wisconsin truck driver Susan **Hawk** (my emphasis) says: "we have come to know to let it be in the end the way Mother Nature intended it to be: for the snake [Hatch] to eat the rat [Wiglesworth]." *Survivor*, like *Robinson Crusoe* in its time, recycles the doxa of its age, in terms surprisingly resonant with *Crusoe* itself: the exterminationist logic of "ten little Indians" (and then there were none); capitalist survival of the fittest; dog-eat-dog competition; cut-throat networking; and nice guys finish last. It is *Crusoe* reinvisioned through Ayn Rand and Alan Greenspan. The notion of surviving and thriving **together**, in the age of neo-liberalism and mass-mediated globalization, is simply ruled out of bounds. Robinson Crusoe, one suspects, would have felt very much at home in the world of *Survivor*.

Notes

1   Marthe Robert, *Roman des origines et origines du roman* (Paris: Bernard Grasset, 1972), p. 33 (my translation).

2   See Samar Attar, "Serving God or Mammon? Echoes from *Havy Ibn Yaqsan* and *Sinbad the Sailor* in *Robinson Crusoe*," in Lieve Spaas and Brian Stimpson (eds), *Robinson Crusoe: Myths and Metamorphoses* (Basingstoke: Macmillan, 1996).

3   Ian Watt, *Myths of Modern Individualism* (Cambridge: Cambridge University Press, 1996).

4   Benedict Anderson, *Imagined Communities: Reflections on the Origin and Spread of Nationalism* (London: Verso, 1983).

5   Cited in Watt, *Myths of Modern Individualism*, p. 171.

6   Homer Obed Brown points out that Crusoe is the only Defoe protagonist who tells his story under the name he was born with. Like Defoe, who added the aristocratic particle "de," and who often wrote under assumed names, their names tend to be unstable and conjunctural; witness, for example, the way that Moll Flanders constantly changes her name for opportunistic purposes. See Homer Obed Brown, *Institutions of the English Novel from Defoe to Scott* (Philadelphia: University of Pennsylvania Press, 1997).

7   Watt, *Myths of Modern Individualism*, p. 169.

8   Derek Walcott cited in John Thirmr, *Postcolonial Contexts: Writing Back to the Canon* (London: Continuum, 2001), p. 53.

9   Daniel Defoe, *Robinson Crusoe* (London: Penguin, 2003), pp. 102–3. All subsequent references will be to the Penguin edition.

10 Daniel Defoe, *Serious Reflections*, quoted in Watt, *Myths of Modern Individualism*, p. 151.

11 Mary Louise Pratt, *Imperial Eyes: Travel Writing and Transculturation* (London: Routledge, 1992), p. 7.

12 Quoted in Watt, *Myths of Modern Individualism*, p. 150.

13 Lawrence Stone has argued that familial love began in England only around 1650, before which men felt very little affection for their wives or children.

14 Leslie Fiedler, *Love and Death in the American Novel* (New York: Stein and Day, 1996).

15 See Peter Hulme, *Colonial Encounters: Europe and the Native Caribbean 1492–1797* (London: Routledge, 1986).

16 Frank Lestringant explores these themes in *Le Cannibale: grandeur et décadence* (Paris: Perrin, 1994), and *Le Huguenot et le sauvage* (Paris: Klincksieck, 1999).

17 See R. Arens, *The Man-eating Myth: Anthropology and Anthropophagy* (Oxford: Oxford University Press, 1980).

18 Recent evidence shows that there were complex civilizations even in the Amazon, long erroneously thought – the metaphor is telling – to be "virgin forest."

19 Peter Hulme, *Colonial Encounters*.

20 Quoted in ibid., p. 21.

21 Michel Tournier, *Le Vent Paraclet* (Paris: Gallimard, 1977), p. 212.

22 I have argued elsewhere that the two – modernism and medieval carnival – are intimately related. See my *Subversive Pleasures: Bakhtin, Film, and Cultural Criticism* (Baltimore, MD: The Johns Hopkins University Press, 1989).

23 Mikhail M. Bakhtin, "Discourse in the Novel," in *The Dialogical Imagination*, trans. Caryl Emerson and Michael Holquist (Austin: University of Texas Press, 1981), p. 421.

24 See Gayatri Spivak, "Three Women's Texts and a Critique of Imperialism," *Critical Inquiry* 12 (Autumn, 1985), 244–5.

25 Lorna Milne, "Myth as Microscope: Michel Tournier's *Vendredi ou les limbes du Pacifique*," in Spaas and Stimpson (eds), *Robinson Crusoe: Myths and Metamorphoses*.

26 See Stewart Brown's and Bridget Jones's contributions to Spaas and Stimpson (eds), *Robinson Crusoe: Myths and Metamorphoses*.

27 All references will be to J. M. Coetzee, *Foe* (London: Secker and Warburg, 1986).

28 Tom Engelhardt, "Ambush at Kamikaze Pass," *Bulletin of Concerned Asian Scholars*, 3, no. 1 (Winter–Spring 1971).

29 For the concept of "regenerative violence," see the work of Richard Slotkin, and especially his trilogy on the American West.

30 Henry Louis Gates, Jr, *Figures in Black* (Oxford: Oxford University Press, 1987).

31 See J. Hoberman, "100 Years of Solitude," *Village Voice* (December 20–26, 2000).

32 *Guardian* (January 14, 2001) available on-line (wysiwyg://9/http://film.guardian.co.uk/ new . . . ver_film_of_the_week/0,4267,422002,00).

Chapter 3

The Self-conscious Novel: From Henry Fielding to David Eggers

Henry Fielding's novels belong like *Don Quixote* to the millennial stream of antique prose fiction and what Bakhtin calls "the Menippea." Whoever reads *Joseph Andrews* and *Tom Jones*, as Margaret Anne Doody puts it, is "in contact with Heliodorus, Longus, Amadis, Petronius."[1] Fielding wrote self-proclaimedly "in the manner of Cervantes," whose pluristylism, comic epic techniques and parodic literariness he clearly emulates. But Fielding was also writing in "the wake of" another, more recent writer: Samuel Richardson, the celebrated practitioner of the epistolary genre of the novel, most notably *Pamela* (1741) and *Clarissa* (1747). While building on the heritage of the antique epistolary novel (e.g. *Chion of Heraklea*), where characters were perpetually reading and writing letters, Richardson also stands at the beginning of a later tradition which includes Rousseau's *La Nouvelle Heloise*, Laclos' *Les Liaisons dangereuses* and, in our own day, even Alice Walker's *The Color Purple*. The epistolary novel usually involves a small number of characters, whose experiences are reported by letter, more or less as they are presumed to occur. (A cyber-romance like *You've Got Mail*, itself a remake/update of *Shop Around the Corner*, constitutes a contemporary update.) While technologically obsolete in the age of faxes and e-mail, the epistolary novel offers the traditional advantage of authorizing the multiple perspectives of various correspondents, while also fostering a subtle dialogical interaction between interlocutors, since the letters are addressed to diverse interlocutors.

Like Defoe, Richardson was from the lower middle class, and, like him, he spoke in the name of verisimilitude. One of Richardson's innovations was to treat women of lower social status as complex human beings. For Leslie Fiedler, *Pamela* gives voice to class war: "its protest against seduction is metaphorical as well as literal; through Richardson a whole class cries: 'We will be raped and bamboozled no more!'"[2] For Judith Mayne, Defoe's *Robinson Crusoe* and Richardson's *Clarissa* illustrate not only the common features of middle-class novels – individual characterization, psychological motivation, attention to quotidian detail, situations drawn from the life of the "middle strata" – but also the "marked differences which separated the journeys of men and women characters." While Crusoe's journey moves constantly outward, Mayne suggests, Clarissa's journey moves ever more inward. While first-person narration dominates both narratives, Clarissa speaks from within the confines of domestic space, and is concerned with female friendship and male–female romance, while Crusoe's journal serves merely as a record of his productive activities. While one novel is a "positive fantasy of reconciliation," the other is a "nightmarish fantasy of reification."[3]

Like Cervantes, Richardson too was critical of romance, but from the very different Weberian standpoint of the commonsensical believer in religious piety and practical success. The title page of his first novel reveals this standpoint and the titillatingly moralistic attractions of this "new species of writing:" *Pamela: or, Virtue Rewarded. In a Series of Familiar Letters from a beautiful Young Damsel, to her Parents. Now first published in order to cultivate the Principles of Virtue and Religion in the Minds of the Youth of Both Sexes. A Narrative which has its Foundation in Truth and Nature; and at the same time that it agreeably entertains, by a variety of curious and affecting Incidents, is entirely divested of all those Images, which, in too many Pieces calculated for Amusement only, tend to inflame the Minds they should Instruct.* What ultimately became the more simplified title of Richardson's novel – *Pamela, or Virtue Rewarded* – is already very revealing. It implies a feminine focalization, a happy ending, and a world where morality and poetic justice hold uncompromising sway. In the novel, the title character Pamela Andrews, who works as a maid/governess for a wealthy landowner, resists his blandishments until he finally marries her. The narrative structure, summed up by some critics as the "principle of procrastinated rape," has obvious appeal for both id and superego, offering the reader both libidinal stimulation and the morally correct doling out of punishments and rewards, and, in social terms, a "mythical" (in Barthes's sense) conciliation between the contradictory aspirations of the lower middle class and the aristocracy.

Pamela was perhaps the first English novel to achieve the status of what would later be called a "media event." The novel's explosive success generated a vast intertextual fallout, even in the first decade after its publication, in the form of parodies, piracies, imitations, and sequels, all gathered in a recent collection.[4]

Unlike Richardson, Henry Fielding was an upper-class, Eton-educated child of the rural aristocracy. Just five months after the first edition of the Richardson novel, Fielding "answered" *Pamela* in his own parody, *An Apology for the Life of Mrs Shamela Andrews* (1741), where he "reveals" Pamela/Shamela to have been a gold-digging adventuress who entrapped the stupid squire, now renamed "Booby." An example of viciously destructive rather than affectionate parody, *Shamela* seeks to destroy the literary prestige of the original. Fielding mocks Richardson's claim of "editing" found letters, as well as his pretense of recording events "immediately" and blow by blow. Richardson's pose of virtuousness, for Fielding, is merely a mask for libidinous sensationalism. In *Shamela*, Fielding turns Richardsonian melodrama into satirical farce, pathos into comic distance and carnivalesque ribaldry.

Fielding renewed the attack on *Pamela* in his next, more ambitious work, *Joseph Andrews*. Rather than simply switch the ethical valence of a literary character as in *Shamela*, here Fielding switches the gender (and the genre) of the Richardson novel. He invents a putative brother for Pamela – Joseph – this time obliged to rebuff the advances of a wealthy **female** employer – Lady Booby. Instead of a powerful man trying to seduce a relatively powerless woman as in *Pamela*, now we have a powerful woman trying to seduce a relatively powerless man, a situation reminiscent, as Fielding himself reminds us, of the Biblical Joseph (Genesis 39) and Potiphar's wife, a situation where refusal of an amorous advance might have very severe consequences. By reversing the terms of the encounter, Fielding reveals the comic/parodic possibilities of the initial situation, while the genre shifts from the female victimization typical of literary melodrama, to (comic) male victimization and satire. The underlying sexist assumption is that sexual harassment of a man by a woman is inherently comic because (1) men almost always want sex and therefore cannot be harassed; and (2) even if the men do not want sex, women are incapable of rape, a view which forgets that rape is as much an act of aggression and violence as it is of desire. By renewing contact with epic, even if via **comic** epic, Fielding was consciously "remasculinizing" the novel after Richardson, seen as suspectly sentimental and gynocentric. In a certain sense, Fielding's work mingles a "progressive" aesthetic critique, and an attack on the hypocrisies of a male author, with a conservative anti-woman backlash, expressed as a parodic denunciation of **female** sexual agency.

As he was writing *Joseph Andrews*, Fielding became conscious of a structural affinity with the work of Cervantes, who in *Don Quixote* had also begun from a parodic premise and gone on to create a masterpiece. Not only is the novel written in "the manner of Cervantes," but also "Joseph Andrews and his friend, Mr Abraham Adams" are reminiscent of Quixote and Sancho Panza. Adams's bookish ineptitude, for example, instantly recalls *Don Quixote*. Fielding also borrowed a basic narrative strategy from Cervantes: to wit, systematic digression within a picaresque plot. The narrator announces his intention to digress, and his decision not to be dissuaded by "any pitiful critic whatever." The novel is narrated by an intrusive and self-conscious narrator who holds forth on literary questions, and even analyzes his own technical problems as storyteller. Like Cervantes, Fielding too weaves interpolated tales and disquisitions on literary criticism into his fiction. In the preface to the first edition of *Joseph Andrews*, Fielding defended his practice as a new species of writing, a "comic epic poem in prose." The work was "comic" in that it dealt with contemporary issues and lower-rank characters, and in provoking laughter at the ridiculous on the way to the conventionally happy ending. It was "epic" in being an ambitious and well-arranged narrative; it was a "poem," finally, in the traditional sense of being a work of the creative imagination, but one expressed in prose.

In *Tom Jones*, meanwhile, Fielding's narrator explores what might be called a "political" dimension of the relationship between author and character. He describes himself as a benevolent despot, the enlightened monarch of the **Aufklarung**. At times the narrator's self-description echoes with the language of colonial settlement, and the absolute domination implied by such rule. The reader, who on one level is Fielding's equal or interlocutor, within this political metaphor becomes the subject of the author's absolute will:

> For as I am, in reality, the Founder of a new Province of Writing, so I am at liberty to make what Laws I please therein. And these Laws my readers, whom I consider as my Subjects, are bound to believe in and to obey; with which that they may readily and cheerfully comply.

But, as an enlightened despot, Fielding hastens to reassure the subjected reader of his charitable intentions:

> I do hereby assure them that I shall principally regard their Ease and Advantage in all such institutions. For I do not, like a **jure divino** Tyrant, imagine that they are my Slaves or my Commodity. I am, indeed, set over them for their own Good only, and was created for their own Use, and not they for mine. (II, i. 77–8)[5]

The ultimate benevolent despot is, of course, God the Almighty, and that analogy too haunts the background of the text. But here we find a relatively secular, or even "Deist" version of what was clearly Protestant Christian in Defoe, i.e. the narrator's "Providential" character, his role as the designer behind the figure in the carpet of the narrative. But Fielding contrasts the relative freedom he grants his readers, interestingly, with the abject condition of "slaves" and "commodities," an allusion embedded in the historical reality of slavery as practiced around the "Black Atlantic."

Writers like Fielding can be seen as the theoreticians of their own literary practice. In a sense they prefigure the "narratologists," i.e. the theorists of the processes and mechanisms of narrative. For example, self-conscious fictioners like Fielding cast suspicion on the central premise of illusionistic narrative: that of an antecedent anecdotal nucleus or substratum from which key blocks have been "extracted." The idea is that a story "out there" in the world pre-exists the actual narrative discourse of the text itself. Fielding implies this pre-existing narrative with the "architextuality" of his title: "A **History** of Tom Jones." In narratological terms, the story seems to both precede and come after the narrative discourse. It is delivered by narrative, yet it pre-exists that very narrative. The use of the past tense, in a novel, asserts this anteriority. And the idea of the "prequel" (i.e. the story of what happened "before" the actions of the novel) implies that novels can be pushed further back into the past, just as the "sequel" implies they can be extended into the future. Illusionism pretends that stories pre-exist their telling, that the events of the story actually transpired and are therefore researchable, verifiable like the positivist's truth. Fielding plays with this pretense of historical referentiality in *Joseph Andrews* by "admitting" that he does not know whether Parson Adams ate "either a rabbit or a fowl [since he] could never with any tolerable certainty discover which . . ."[6] But the joke is double-edged: Fielding's claimed ignorance in this matter can imply either that (1) Adams did eat something, but the narrator doesn't know what it was or that (2) Adams never existed and I am making all of this up.

——————— The Reflexive Stylistics of Henry Fielding ———————

Anti-illusionist novelists mock the documentary strategy of writers who pretend to be the mere editors of correspondence found in the nooks and crannies and attics of circumstantial verism. By claiming to select only "matters of consequence," such novelists imply that their stories antedate their telling. Woody Allen casts comic light on this same illusionistic premise in *Zelig* by having his chameleon man complain that Hollywood, when it bought the rights to his life story, took all the best parts and left him only with his sleeping hours. The presumed artistic selection of an antecedent tale constitutes narrative sleight of hand; in fact, we are given all there is, but the suggestion that there was originally more somehow enhances the ontological status of the story. To speculate, as Fielding often does, about a character's inner thoughts, similarly, is to foster the illusion that the character enjoys some existence outside of the book, that he or she is more than a mere puppet or verbal artifact. The technique recalls, on some levels, the exploitation of off-screen space in the cinema, whereby synecdochic fragments shape in our mind the illusory sense of a continuum extending beyond the frame. The framed, rectangular slice of pro-filmic reality is assumed, by the laws of diegetic implication, to extend beyond the four edges of the frame and to the space behind the set and behind the camera. Off-screen looks or gestures, even those directed at nothing more than a chalked line on a wall, come to imply a larger diegetic space, just as those events of a novelistic character's life that are recounted supposedly form a continuum with those that are not recounted. Just as the filmmaker "fills" the imaginary space surrounding the screen, so the novelist implies the existence of a narrative substratum "below" or "behind" (in spatial terms) or "before" and "after" (in temporal terms) the verbal surface of the text.

"Biological or genetic patterns, genealogical or dynastic sequences," as Homer Obed Brown puts it, "are still conventional metaphoric ways of thinking about causal relationship in both history and narrative . . ."[7] *Joseph Andrews* literalizes the idea of literary lineage and "kinship" through the device of diegetic kinship between Fielding's and Richardson's characters, i.e. Joseph is presented as literally Pamela's brother. In *Joseph Andrews*, Fielding speculates about his protagonist's ancestry. Subsequent to a wild-goose chase after the origin of his hero's name, he conjectures that Joseph Andrews probably "had as many ancestors as the best man living, and perhaps, if we look five or six hundred years backwards, might be related to some persons of very great figure at present." But let us suppose, Fielding continues, "that he had no ancestors at all, but had sprung up out of a dunghill" (I, ii. 63). Superficially directed at an absurd pride in ancestry, Fielding's irony on a deeper level makes a point about the nature of fiction. Fictional characters, Fielding suggests, are not part of a spatial or temporal or, in this case, genealogical continuum. All literary characters, if not sprung out of dunghills, are the product of spontaneous artistic generation, and delivered, to mix our metaphors, by the midwife of literary convention. They can have, therefore, neither ancestors nor, like Lady Macbeth, children. Fielding's playful hypothesizing about Joseph Andrews's lineage reminds us that realistic narrative often "cheats" by implying an existence anterior to the beginning of the story and a futurity that follows the ending. Classical Hollywood films often "cheat" by ending with intimations of marriage and happy conjugal union. (The notoriously phallic train-entering-the-tunnel in *North-by-Northwest*, presumably, foretells years of tumescent sexuality on the parallel tracks of marriage.)

Self-conscious fabulists often seem incapable of telling stories straight, both in the sense of telling them with a straight face and in the sense of telling them in a linear, sequential manner. Their narratives provide comic demonstrations of Mark Twain's essay "How **Not** to Tell a Story." Fielding veils his trickery so thinly that the very whimsicality of his formulation points up the ludicrous inadequacy of the conventional ways of authenticating a story. The Brazilian novelist Machado de Assis, like an inept raconteur who forgets crucial details, interrupts his protagonist Dom Casmurro to correct an oversight: "Pardon me, but this chapter ought to have been preceded by another, in which I would have told an incident that occurred a few weeks before, two months after Sancha had gone away." Here Machado anticipates Cortazar's *Hopskotch* (1963) which invites readers to read the chapters in two different orders. Machado contemplates shuffling the order of the chapters, but decides that it would be "too great a nuisance to have to change the page numbers." (Yet we know that it is Machado himself, in the end, who decides such matters.) Sterne's narrative in *Tristram Shandy*, similarly, on which much of Machado's work was explicitly modeled, is constantly stalled, side-tracked, and derailed. His "choicest morsel," concerning Uncle Toby and the widow, is postponed until the ninth volume.

What was in *Don Quixote* a battle of voices engaged by two paradigmatic characters becomes in *Tom Jones* a battle of rhetorics played out on the register of style, expressed even at the level of the individual sentence. In *Tom Jones*, Auerbach's "separation of styles" between the elite and the vernacular, or Bakhtin's "mutual relativizing" of high and low genres and languages, is staged on the battlefield of diction and syntax. We see this stylistic agon in Fielding's anti-climactic use of epic similes, where lofty grandeur is brought down to earth with a plain English thud. Thus in introducing his heroine Sophie, the author pulls out all the stylistic stops. He begins by invoking, often through circumlocution, a host of classical spirits and divinities. The sheer weight of allusion becomes comically oppressive:

> Hushed be every ruder Breath. May the Heathen Ruler of the Winds confine in iron Chains the boisterous Limbs of noisy Boreas, and the sharp-pointed Nose of bitter-biting Eurus. Do thou, sweetest Zephyrus, rising from thy fragrant Bed, mount the western Sky, and lead on those delicious Gales, the Charms of which call forth the lovely Flora . . . (IV, ii. 154)

Fielding then tries to evoke Sophie's beauty through a series of **recusatios** or ironic declarations of expressive impossibility:

> Reader, perhaps thou hast seen the Statue of the Venus de Medicis. Perhaps too thou hast seen the Gallery of Beauties at Hampton-Court. Thou may'st remember each bright Churchill of the Galaxy, and all the Toasts of the Kit-Cat. Or if their reign was before thy Times, at least thou hast seen their Daughters, the no less dazzling Beauties of the present Age; whose Names, should we here insert, we apprehend they would fill the whole Volume. (IV, ii. 155)

Fielding then tells us, anti-climactically, that we may "have seen all these without being able to form an exact idea of Sophie; for she did not exactly resemble any of them." Resolving to use his "utmost skill to describe this Paragon," Fielding offers the following, rather anti-climactic, description: "Sophie, then, the only Daughter of Mr Western, was a middle-sized woman; but rather inclining to tall" (IV, ii. 156).

Fielding's prose enacts a principle of dramatic as well as stylistic deflation. On a plot level, a character's personal or ideological claims are "interrupted" by events that cast doubt on those claims. Tom's claim that he is incapable of even looking at any woman other than Sophie is "interrupted" by his inability to resist the sylvan attractions of Molly Seagrim. But the same strategy of anti-climax is played out simultaneously on the macro-level of plot/character and on the micro-level of sentence and syntax. The whole pattern, or anti-pattern, as Homer Obed Brown puts it, is one of "accidental interruptions interrupting interruptions."[8] This notion of interruption recalls another definition of epic, one which corresponds neither to Bakhtin's notion of epic as embalming the dead world of the sacred paternal word, nor to the conventional literary notion of epic heroism and spectacular deeds. For Erich Auerbach, the epic style was characterized by a "retarding procedure,"[9] whereby action is frozen in order for the narrator to tell a story of origins, for example that of Odysseus' scar, a procedure typical of the narrated epic as opposed to the directly presentational theater. Cervantes' "modern" seventeenth-century reworking of the Aristotelian notion of comic epic, and Brecht's modernist notion of "epic" and "anti-tragic" and "non-Aristotelian" theater, share the idea of interruption and discontinuity, meant as a counter-weight to the unity of classical tragedy.

In *Tom Jones*, Fielding posits a kind of sliding proportion between story time and discourse time, according to the intrinsic interest of the "protextual" events:

> Now it is our purpose, in the ensuing pages, to pursue a contrary method. When any extraordinary scene presents itself (as we trust will often be the case), we shall spare no pains nor paper to open it at large to our readers; but if whole years should pass without producing anything worthy [of] his notice, we shall not be afraid of a chasm in our history, but shall hasten on to matters of consequence, and leave such periods of time totally unobserved. (II, i. 76)

In another passage, Fielding exercises a tasteful, Lubitsch-like, selectivity in his treatment of an amorous scene:

> Not to tire the Reader, by leading him through every Scene of this Courtship, (which, tho', in the Opinion of a certain great Author, it is the pleasantest Scene of Life to the Actor, is perhaps, as dull and tiresome as any whatever to the Audience) the Captain made his Advances in Form, the citadel was defended in Form, and at length, in proper Form, surrendered at Discretion. (I, xi. 68–9)

By pretending to excise scenes in the name of the reader's patience, or by pretending to be lying in wait for the appearance of "extraordinary scenes" (scenes which the author is, in fact, inventing), and by implying the existence of an underground vein from which all such scenes are "mined," Fielding simultaneously performs and exposes one of the classic confidence tricks of illusionism.

In *Narrative Discourse*, Genette speaks of the special difficulties involved in comparing the duration of story time and narrative discourse time in a literary text.[10] Take, for example, the various attempts to create a strict equivalence between story and discourse time. In both novel and film, rigid isochrony is so rare as to constitute a kind of tour de force. Robert Alter points out an amusing novelistic example in *Joseph Andrews*, where the time it takes to read Fielding's account of Lady Booby's horrified reaction to Joseph's refusal of her advances in the name of "virtue" – roughly two minutes – approximates the time the shocked Lady presumably spent before responding.[11] Such a passage constitutes the novelistic equivalent of the one-shot sequence in the cinema, characterized by a strict isochrony between the duration of the shot and the presumed duration of the fictive event.

In *Joseph Andrews*, Fielding also sheds light on what he calls one of the "mysteries" of the novelistic trade: the practice of dividing works into books and chapters. He likens the spaces between books to an inn or resting place for the reader, and the contents prefixed to the chapters to inscriptions over the gates of the inn. After citing classical precedent to justify his practice, he then compares dividing books to a butcher jointing his meat. The analogy is revelatory of the artificiality of such divisions, for a steer does not naturally apportion itself into neat pieces of shank and rump. Chapter titles in Fielding, as with Cervantes, often highlight this very artificiality. Fielding's titles perform minuscule variations on the same theme – "in which the history is continued," "further continued," "even further continued," and so forth – in such a way as to mock the very idea of novelistic consecution. Fielding's play with titles calls attention to the joints, to the temporal "plumbing" of fiction, instead of using titles as more or less invisible binders in a seamless narrative continuity. The mixing of spatial notations – "containing five pieces of paper" – with temporal ones – "containing the time of a year" – makes us reflect on the complex chronotopic interaction of spatiality and temporality in the novel.[12]

Many of the titles in *Tom Jones* make reference to the potential responses of the reader: "Containing such grave Matter, that the Reader cannot laugh once through the whole Chapter, unless peradventure he should laugh at the Author;" "Containing what the Reader may perhaps expect to find in it." Others serve as a form of stylistic braggadocio and self-promotion: "A short hint of what we can do in the Sublime . . ." At times, Fielding's narrator singles out specific groups of readers, as when he offers caveats for the critics: "Containing Instructions very necessary to be perused by modern Critics." Fielding even makes recommendations about how to read his novel. Those who travel too rapidly through his pages, Fielding warns, will miss the "curious productions of nature which will be observed by the slower and more accurate reader."

Rather than narratorless fiction, where no one speaks and "events seem to tell themselves," reflexive fiction models its discourse on human conversation, which is dialogic by definition; it implies a "you" to whom the utterance is directed. The presence of the reader or spectator is inscribed and signaled in the text, shifting the interest from the diegesis to the intersubjective textual relation which comes to form a kind of parallel plot. Wayne Booth describes the process as it operates in *Tom Jones*: "If we read straight through all of the seemingly gratuitous appearances by the narrator, leaving out the story of Tom, we discover a running account of growing intimacy between the narrator and the reader, an account with a kind of plot of its own and a separate denouement."[13]

Fielding himself metaphorizes the writer/reader relationship as a voyage, on which the reader and the narrator are traveling companions, the real voyage being not so much the picaresque voyage of the literary personage but rather the literary co-travel of reader and narrator. Inscribing the reader/spectator within their own rhetorical space, reflexive texts even perform their own hermeneutics, counseling their audience on certain pitfalls of interpretation. The interest shifts from "meaning" to the productive interaction of reader and text.

────── ## From Novel to Film: *Tom Jones* and *Joseph Andrews* ──────

The cinematic adaptations of self-conscious novels are obliged to wrestle with the challenge thrown up by these reflexive techniques. Tony Richardson's adaptation of *Tom Jones* (1963), in this sense, is frequently held up as a model transposition of the codes of reflexivity from novel to film. The film's off-screen narration, provided by Irish character-actor (and friend of Orson Welles) Michael MacLiammoir, reproduces the novel's narratorial style. The narrating voice, as in the novel, is urbane, tolerant, sophisticated, ironic. The voice-over adopts many phrases and sentences from the book, or at least in the style of the book, in interventions that are "cued" by a harpsichord motif. Highly interventionist, the narrator rushes quickly from Tom's birth, in the opening sequence, to his life as a young man, thus emulating Fielding's policy of passing over "large periods of time in which nothing happened." The narrator also exercises editorial control, as it were, by omitting some of the interpolated tales from the novel.

The narrator also adds episodes (the nick-of-time rescue which saves Tom from the gallows) and provides relevant maxims for our edification: "To die for a cause is a common evil; to die for nonsense is the devil," adding that it would be "the devil's own nonsense to leave Tom without a rescuer."[14] But, generally, the narrator in the film is subordinated to the story/diegesis; he does not expatiate on philosophy or literature, for example. Thus we are deprived, to a certain extent, of the double plot of the novel, whereby the narrator becomes the self-articulating moral center of the fiction. In the Fielding novel, moreover, as Wayne Booth has suggested, the narrator becomes a figure for Providence, the God-like agency that orders the details of the plot.[15] The film's narrator summarizes essential information and provides some ironic commentary, but it includes neither literary criticism nor film criticism, an option which would have been much more audacious and innovative. Indeed, some recent films have toyed with this device. Kevin Smith's film *Dogma* (1994) begins with an intertitle reminding film critics to be gentle and remember that "true judgment belongs only to God." Spike Lee begins *Bamboozled* (2000) with an intertitle showing Webster's definition of satire, as if warning spectators and critics not to commit a "genre mistake" by taking the film literally.

The Richardson adaptation of *Tom Jones* reproduces the "dear reader" direct address characteristic of the Fieldingesque narrator. Although the narrator loses the laboriously constructed ethical centrality of the novel's narrator, he gains, thanks to cinema's synchronous sound, the attributes of a specific voice, accent, and timbre. The direct address in the film is not merely verbal, furthermore; the film also offers a **visual** direct address when the actors wink and gesture toward the camera/spectator, addressed, moreover, as "you" ("Did you see that?"). At one point, Tom covers the lens to shield the half-naked Mrs Waters from our prying eyes. Here literary direct address meets another tradition, that of direct address in vaudeville and silent comedy, where performers often maintained an explicit dialogue with the spectator. While the direct look at the camera was traditionally taboo in dramatic films, it was tolerated in comic films such as the Hope–Crosby "Road" pictures or in the Marx Brothers films.

The Richardson film also foregrounds the censoring capacities of the narrator, who confides that the narrative will not pursue certain risqué scenes, leaving them to the spectator's imagination. Film has the advantage of two forms of narration: the off-screen voice-over narration, and the work of the film itself as narrator. The film conveys this broader sense of narration, the sense of the film itself as the "*grand imagier*" or "grand imager" or "overweening narrative instance," of which narratologists, such as André Gaudreault, have spoken.[16] The film, in this sense, can be seen as exercising its authorial capacity to slow down or speed up the motion, e.g. in the scene where Tom and Sophie mount mules in an instance of speeded up erotic-comic play. Such sequences deploy the same variable-speed proportional relation between story and discourse time to which Fielding calls attention in the novel. In the fast-motion sequences, the story time (e.g. Tom and Sophie riding mules) is the same, yet the discourse time is abbreviated through accelerated cinematography. The freeze-frames that catch the philosopher with his pants down in Molly's closet, in contrast, slow down the action to total stasis, giving a Hogarthian flair to the idea of being "caught in the act."

While it is true that the film version of *Tom Jones* does not offer literary criticism per se, it does reflect indirectly on literary issues, by providing filmic correlatives for Fielding's techniques of allusion. Just as Fielding's novel draws on some very early, time-hallowed literary sources such as the epic simile, the film goes back to early **film** history, and specifically to the slapstick and the melodramas of the silent period. Like the contemporaneous French New Wave directors, Richardson resurrects "archaic" film devices. The opening sequence, for example, clearly mimics (and literally "mimes") the procedures of silent cinema. The sequence is silent not only in the obvious sense of lacking synchronous speech, but also in featuring intertitles (a salient feature of the silent film), while also mocking the histrionic acting of the earliest films (where actors' gesticulations sought to compensate for the lack of voice). The sequence is also comically pleonastic. A character silently screaming an unmistakable "Agh" is redundantly trumpeted by an intertitle: "Agh!" Cinematic freeze-frames, meanwhile, form a marvelous equivalent for the literary freeze-frames that Fielding himself borrowed from the caricaturist Hogarth, i.e. images where a human figure (say a pickpocket) is caught **in flagrante**. The accompanying harpsichord music, finally, has a double function: (1) the instrument (and the style) evoke eighteenth-century classical music, the period when Fielding was writing, while also evoking (2) the kind of improvised piano accompaniment that served to emotionally and dramatically orient the spectators of silent cinema.

Susan Sontag compares the novel's Samuel Richardson to the cinema's D. W. Griffith as two innovators of genius who combine supremely vulgar intellects with a "fervid moralizing about sexuality and violence whose energy comes from suppressed voluptuousness."[17] She might have gone on to point out that silent cinema, after its Richardsonian beginnings, soon took a turn toward Fieldingesque parody and reflexivity. Just as Fielding rendered Pamela's behavior ludicrous by transforming Squire B into the lecherous Lady Booby and Joseph Andrews into the assailed virgin, so filmmakers like Mack Sennett and Buster Keaton ridiculed the maudlin love scenes typical of Griffith's "Pamelas." Even Fielding's reductive comparison of love to a piece of beef finds its literal cinematic counterpart in Keaton's *Go West* (1925), where the ingénue is played by a cow and the lover by Keaton himself. Eisenstein, in *The Old and the New* (1929), provides the cow with a more appropriate mate. After a bovine *coup de foudre* on a collective farm, Eisenstein's editing stimulates the image to a metaphorical climax, followed by a shot of the newly delivered cow and her offspring.

The film version of *Tom Jones* also extrapolates the novel's status as a kind of generic summa (epic, pastoral, literary criticism, comedy, and so on). The film absorbs the traces of these pre-existing literary genres and then superimposes the literary reminiscences on specifically filmic reminiscences of silent comedy, melodrama, farce, historical film. Thus the film substitutes filmic for literary allusion. While the novel alludes in literary terms to Homer and the Bible (for example, the stoning of Molly is compared to that of Mary Magdalene), and in extra-literary terms to Hogarth, the film mingles literary with filmic references, while also being open to painterly, musical, and cinematic intertextuality.

Tom Jones also offers filmic instances of what rhetoricians call "amplification." The fox hunt sequence, for example, gives a clear documentary (direct cinema) inflection to the material. (Tony Richardson began, we recall, as a practitioner of "free cinema" documentary.) The hunt sequence transforms the novel's very brief account of Squire Western's love of hunting into an elaborate, virtuoso sequence with documentary overtones, one which serves a number of functions. On the one hand, the hunt becomes a pretext for the kinds of exuberantly "cinematic" scenes made possible by film technology: aerial shots of sublime landscapes, sweeping crane shots over galloping horses and running foxes. On the other, the sequence makes a social point by foregrounding the cruelty and class-elitism of the chase, the mad cries of the hunters, the crushing of the geese. The sequence hints at the (perhaps unconscious) sadism of the upper classes toward the weak and the vulnerable. It is the poor cottagers' animals, after all, that are trampled by the horses. The love of the hunt is also revealed to be gendered; the men seem to revel in the hunt as a masculine **rite de passage**, while the women appear less enthusiastic about a practice which seems not only cruel but also, for Sophie at least, literally life-endangering.

Another way that the film itself as "impersonal" narrator calls attention to its own imaging is through a dazzling series of optical punctuational effects, especially wipes. (Here again Tony Richardson invokes the French New Wavish practice of resurrecting "archaic" film devices.) Just as Fielding in his novel calls comic attention to the practice of chapter headings, the film's wipes call attention to the divisions and segmentations in the narrative material. In the novel *Tom Jones*, as noted earlier, the chapter divisions call attention to themselves through, for example, the inappropriately precise and material precision of "containing five pages of paper." In the film too the divisions are self-flauntingly artificial, exhibitionistic. Furthermore, the wipes are custom-designed to "match" their immediate narrative context: diamond shapes underline the insincerity of Lady Bellaston's proposal (meant to **discourage** Tom's interest); stripes evoke bars for the prison scene; clockwise wipes evoke passing time; the iris-in (a technique reminiscent of the silent era) isolates the villain (the lawyer Dalloway). Censorship is evoked by a double vertical wipe, reminiscent of the censor's scissors.

The Fielding novel frequently deploys epic similes in the Homeric style, often with comic effect when a pompous invocation of the Greek pantheon and Apollo's fleeting chariot is followed by a brutally direct: "In plain English, it was five o'clock in the afternoon." The novel also develops a sustained analogy between food and sex, for example in the passage where Tom and Mrs Waters, rampant with lust and gluttony, devour both food and each other. The passage vividly illustrates the gains and losses involved in cinematic "translation." On the one hand, the film "realizes" the situation described in the novel: Tom and Mrs Waters wine and dine and desire each other. Performance evokes the exuberant lust of their wine-fueled tryst. Here are the words of the novel: "First, from two lovely blue eyes, whose bright orbs flashed lightning at their discharge, flew forth two pointed ogles. But happily for our hero, hit only a vast piece of beef which he was then conveying onto his plate, and harmless spent their force" (IX, v. 512). What is lost in the film is the novel's virtuoso rendering of the mock-heroic style, incongruously applied to an amorous rather than a bellicose encounter. Also lost is Fielding's hilariously precise delineation of the **differences** between food and sex. While we might **ogle** a desired piece of beef, Fielding explains with gratuitous didacticism, we are not likely to **flirt** with it or **flatter** it in order to achieve our ends. Also missed in the film is the larger sustained overarching epic simile in which the food and sex metaphor is embedded, to wit the analogy of love and war, where love is rendered as a mock epic verbal battle. While film does have language as one of its resources, in this instance it lacks the slow-working allusiveness and flexibility of novelistic prose.

Fielding's novel often exploits the device of "foil characters" with contrasting traits. As usual, Fielding theorizes his own practice. He anatomizes the

The Self-conscious Novel

Chapter 3

Figure 3.1 Sex and food in Richardson's *Tom Jones* (1963), produced by Woodfall Film Productions

"foiling" technique in one of the literary-critical sections of the book, where he speaks of a "new Vein of Knowledge" not yet "wrought on by any ancient or modern Writer," to wit the technique of contrast: "For what demonstrates the Beauty and Excellence of any thing, but its Reverse? Thus the Beauty of Day, and that of Summer, is set off by the Horrors of Night and Winter" (V, i. 212). The case of Tom Jones and Blifil provides an obvious example. Whereas Tom is described as spontaneous and sincere, Blifil is described as calculating and hypocritical. Whereas Tom is instinctively democratic, Blifil is a snob obsessed with hierarchical superiority. Whereas Tom displays sincere, disinterested love for Sophie, Blifil's interest is calculating and opportunistic. Film's "automatic difference," its capacity to take advantage of performance, costume, and *mise-en-scène*, further strengthens its capacity to stage such characterological contrasts.

First, the film deploys performance style. While Blifil is stiff in posture and gait, Tom is loose and ambling. Second, the film exploits costume and decor. While Blifil is formally dressed, almost literalizing the trope of a "stuffed shirt," Tom wears his shirts open, exposing his chest. While Tom is oral, literally open-mouthed, thirsty for life, a man of hearty appetite, Blifil is anal, pursed, with a pinched speaking style. The *mise-en-scène* further reinforces this contrast by foiling backdrops. The film repeatedly places Tom against a forest backdrop, associating him, especially at the beginning, with the freedom of nature and with the violation of social taboos (poaching, for example). Blifil, meanwhile, is filmed against a backdrop of elegantly Frenchified and symmetrical formal gardens. Everything conspires to present Tom as an exuberantly sensuous, unaffected person. He is a "natural child" in the various senses of the expression – "natural" in the sense of "illegitimate," a bastard, but also the "child of nature." Blifil, in contrast, is supposedly "legitimate" but hardly a "child of nature."

At the same time, these "foilings" are intensely gendered. While the association with nature is seen as positive in the case of Tom, it switches valence and becomes negative in the case of Molly. The association with wild nature does not make her an innocent child of nature; rather, it turns her into a whorish wench, lacking in sexual self-discipline. And in this sense Molly is foiled by Sophie. While the dark-haired Molly is associated with wild animals like rutting rabbits and with a disordered hut (rather like an animal's lair), the classy, blonde-haired Sophie is associated like Blifil with well-kept gardens, and with "aristocratic" animals like swans. In this reshuffling of values, class and gender prejudice converge. The nature/civilization binary gets differentially grafted onto a gender division: the contrast of sincere, natural man versus stuffy, unnatural man, applied in the male case to the benefit of Tom, becomes, in the case of women, a contrast between the bad, "natural," lusty girl versus the good, self-controlling, civilized girl/woman.

The sexism of the film version is, in some ways, more severe than that of Fielding's novel, which is more critical not only of Tom's sexual behavior, but also of patriarchal power, forced marriage, and attempted rape. Fielding frequently denounces the cynical rakes who manipulate and deceive women. The novel's narrator excoriates a certain "Nightingale" who practiced many deceits in love, "which if he had used in Trade he would have been counted the greatest villain upon Earth" (XIV, iv. 756). The sexism of the film adaptation is revealed by performing a series of commutation tests. For example, Tom accepts clothes from Lady Bellaston, whom he does not love; in essence he is, if only temporarily, a "kept man." This does not, however, disqualify him as Sophie's suitor. Yet one can imagine the spectatorial outrage had it been a case of **Sophie** accepting clothes from a **male** suitor. Or we can reflect on the scene in which Tom, drunk both with alcohol and with love for Sophie, is wandering in the forest and decides to carve Sophie's name into the bark of a tree. Just then Molly surprises him and flirts with him outrageously, at which point he clumsily and eagerly changes the carved name from "Sophie" to "Molly." No film heroine, one suspects, would ever have been allowed such a quick shift in amorous allegiance; nor would she have been so easily forgiven, since women are usually held to a higher (double) standard.

The challenges in adapting *Tom Jones* are as much aesthetic as ethical. It is fascinating to speculate, in this sense, about the possible stylistic equivalences in film for some of the other rhetorical procedures of the novel. What would be the stylistic-cinematic equivalent of Fielding's oxymoronic expressions (for example, "genteel vices)?" Would a cinematic oxymoron take place only on a verbal register, or might it be transferred to some other register, through the oxmoronic deployment of music track against image track, lighting against dialogue and so forth? Fielding also develops what grammarians call "periodic sentences," i.e. extended sentences which make the reader wait till the end, accumulating information which seems to move in one direction, but which finally ends with a startling reversal. Here is Fielding's account of Captain Blifil contemplating the fortune he will acquire through Mr Allworthy's death:

> But while the Captain was one Day busied in deep Contemplation of this Kind, one of the most unlucky, as well as unseasonable accidents, happened to him. The utmost Malice of Fortune could indeed have contrived nothing so cruel, so mal-a-propos, so absolutely destructive of all his Schemes. In short, not to keep the Reader in

long Suspense, just at the very Instant when his Heart was exulting in Meditations on the Happiness which would accrue to him by Mr Allworthy's Death – he himself – died of an Apoplexy. (II, viii. 109)

In the cinema, this effect might be secured by having a sequence build toward an apparent climax, underlined by a swelling musical crescendo, and then having it suddenly veer away in another, anti-climactic direction. (One thinks of the interminably tumescent coitus interruptus structure of the love-making in Buñuel's *L'Age d'or*.) Or, again, how might one reproduce the effect of verbal deflation for comic purposes, as when Fielding, after a number of literary fanfares introducing his heroine, reveals flatly that Sophie was a "middle-sized woman?" Would the filmic equivalent consist of a drum roll, a stentorian voice-over, followed by a coolly distant long shot of the heroine, without any emphasis or special illumination? While Fielding uses direct address to announce, for example, that he has "interspersed similes" throughout his text for the delectation of critics and readers, a film might have a voice-over proudly announce (à la David Letterman's "thrillcam") that "we have dispersed steadicam tracking shots throughout the film." The film version of *Tom Jones*, as I suggested earlier, does not choose to be meta-cinematic in this sense. Which is not to say that the filmic narration is not, in the main, a resounding success.

Richardson's *Joseph Andrews*

While the Fielding novel *Joseph Andrews* preceded the novel *Tom Jones*, Tony Richardson's film adaptation of *Joseph Andrews* (in 1977) came **after** his adaptation of *Tom Jones*. The major difference between the two adaptations by the same director is that in *Joseph Andrews* Richardson ignores most of the reflexive cues – the whimsical chapter titles, the inclusion of literary criticism (such as the theory of "the comic epic poem in prose"), the reflections on genre and novelistic technique and so forth – provided so profusely by Fielding himself. Most importantly, Richardson discards the loquacious and urbane narrator that he had used to such good effect in *Tom Jones*.

On the other hand, the film is not without its reflexive and intertextual elements. In a kind of transposed reflexivity, Richardson uses the lyrics of musical ballads – "To poverty and hardship the young man was born" – to convey social points, rather in the Brechtian manner of music as **gestus**. The casting of Hugh

Griffith, taking up once again his role as Squire Western (now portrayed as a justice who convicts Adams and Fanny of robbery) – even though Squire Western is not a character in *Joseph Andrews* – constructs an intertextual link to *Tom Jones*. Again like Fielding, Richardson also alludes to earlier texts and genres, this time filmic genres: Errol Flynn-style swashbuckling between Joseph and his kidnappers, cliffhanger rescue scenes, and silent-film-style flashbacks. It is as if Richardson were bringing to the fore a suppressed feature of *Joseph Andrews* itself, to wit its character as the eighteenth-century equivalent of contemporary popular entertainment, replete with farcical slapstick, spectacular violence, scandalous sexuality (the danger of incest!), and dramatic rescues à la *The Perils of Pauline*, along with the usual romanesque claptrap of mistaken identity and tell-tale strawberry marks on forearms and buttocks.

Richardson also transfers Fielding's generic reference to the larger frame of the carnivalesque currents to be found in eighteenth-century England. As C. L. Barber, Peter Stallybrass, and Allon White have all pointed out, England for centuries was the battleground for the survival of a pre-Christian pagan culture against pleasure-hating, Cromwell-style Puritanism. Six years before the translation of Bakhtin's *Rabelais and his World* into English, C. L. Barber, in his book *Shakespeare's Festive Comedy: A Study of Dramatic Form and its Relation to Social Custom*, deployed a slightly modified critical vocabulary – "Aristaphonic" and "saturnalian" instead of "Menippean" and "carnivalesque" – to emphasize the importance of traditions of popular theater and holidays for the understanding of Shakespeare's comedies.[18] Delineating the "saturnalian pattern" of the comedies as a kind of festive epistemology moving from saturnalian release to humorous understanding, Barber traces this saturnalian pattern to many sources: the theatrical institution of clowning, the literary cult of fools and folly, and the real-life community observances of feast days, morris dancing, wassailing, mumming, masques, and pageants. Shakespeare's casual references to popular festivities – "Come, woo me, woo me! for now I am in a holiday humour and like enough to consent" – are premised on thorough audience familiarity with such practices. Barber analyzes these practices, in a manner akin to that of Bakhtin, as embodying liberation from social decorum through raucous eroticism and "gay relativity."[19] The holiday motif brought with it the artistic and narrative strategies associated with carnival: parody and burlesque in the form of the "low take-off of what the high people were doing."[20]

Fielding himself was part of the titanic struggle between the subterranean energies of carnival and the constraining powers of Puritanism; when still a playwright, he had to do battle with puritanical censors. It is highly appropriate, in this sense, that the film begins with an homage to carnival-like revelries. We see Fanny and Joseph at a country May Day festival – precisely the kind of festival invoked by Barber – decked with flowers and dressed in browns and greens. The scene's dancing, jousting, and fantasy costumes mingle the vestiges of the carnivals of the "merry England" of yore with echoes of the "flower-children" of the counter-cultural 1960s. Joseph pulls a leek from between the legs of a female goddess figure and presents it to Fanny as Queen of the May, an expression both of his personal desire for her and also a collective symbol of fertility and seasonal renewal.[21]

All the exuberant naturalness of carnival and young love is then made to contrast with the decadent, calculating artifice of the aristocrats who watch the "vulgar" festival from the safety of their weirdly isolating individual carriages. In the "Author's Preface" to *Joseph Andrews*, Fielding had explained that his satiric method would consist in holding up affectation – "the only source of the true Ridiculous" – to ridicule. Affectation, he further argued, derived either from vanity or hypocrisy. Richardson's film picks up on these cues and even strengthens the satirical element. Ann-Margaret's pancake make-up as Lady Booby, her artificial manner – whose artifice is further underlined by Richardson's initiative of making her a former "actress" from London – and her Frenchified speech patterns all cry out "fake!" It is as if Tony Richardson were staging in film the schematic binarism of another eighteenth-century writer, Jean-Jacques Rousseau, with his contrasting of good, natural, country instincts and the decadent, over-cultivated artifice of the aristocracy. While the sincere young lovers gambol amidst tall grass and blooming flowers, the aristocratic libertines plot seduction in over-decorated boudoirs. While Fielding verbally highlighted the discrepancy between outward behavior and inner motives, the filmmaker has to come up with more concrete indices. (Truffaut once pointed out that it takes more shots to show lies and hypocrisy than to show sincerity, since one has to contextualize what is said through the telltale clues – clenched hands, for example – pointing to mendacity.) Hypocrisy, in *Joseph Andrews*, also has a class dimension. Charity and generosity, throughout the film as in the novel, seem to exist in inverse proportion to wealth and status. And yet "status" itself is also revealed to be highly constructed, for the film is full of social chameleons who are misrecognized as lowly (Joseph) or as noble (Lady Booby). And unlike fake aristocrats like Lady Booby, or slobbering *arrivistes* like Slipslop, Joseph and Fanny stay faithful to their class throughout, and in this sense the portrayal is loyal to the pro-working class attitudes of some of the earlier "Angry Young Men" plays and films, a movement in which Tony Richardson was a key participant.

Apart from eliminating the narrator, Richardson makes a number of other important changes from the book. The various interpolated tales are reduced in

Figure 3.2 Lady Booby (Ann-Margret) and Joseph (Peter Firth) in *Joseph Andrews* (1977), produced by Woodfall Film Productions

number and streamlined by being made relevant to the love of Joseph and Fanny. Parson Adams's six "rival" clergymen, against whom he matches wits, are reduced to two, while Parson Adams is rendered not as the novel's noble amalgam of Hebraism and Hellenism, the Bible and Aeschylus, but rather as something of a clumsy, lovable boob. On the other hand, it could be argued, as James Welsh does, that the "spirit of Adams pervades the film."[22] Richardson also ups the erotic ante in terms of the possibilities of incest – what the malapropian Slipslop refers to as being "intermingled relatively" – hanging over the young couple like a Sword of Damocles. At one point, it appears that Lady Booby is in fact Joseph's mother – to which Lady Booby herself replies "What fucking next?"

As this last bit of dialogue illustrates, the language of Richardson's *Joseph Andrews* is much coarser than that of *Tom Jones*. Squire Western, for example, proposes a "drink to copulation." Stuck in the eighteenth-century equivalent of a "traffic jam," the Squire complains that the "only things that move on this street are the horses' bowels." Sexual innuendo is frequent, as when Lady Booby is said to "bear herself [i.e. **bare** herself] magnificently . . . and frequently." More risqué in sexual terms, *Joseph Andrews* includes the kinds of scenes that the more ironically delicate narrator of *Tom Jones* would probably have elected **not** to follow.

The most misfired sequence in the film, in this sense, is the scene, invented out of whole cloth, in which a decadent lord kidnaps Joseph, Fanny, and Parson Adams. The lord tries to seduce Fanny by staging a Sadean erotic black mass. After prodding the servants to "get the wench well liquored," the lord stages a debauched spectacle involving whorish "nuns" ready to sexually devour Fanny. Richardson crosscuts between the young aristocrat tying Fanny to an altar to rape her, and a drunken prostitute attempting the female equivalent act on a drugged Joseph. Parson Adams, meanwhile, denounces the whole spectacle as "hellish blasphemy." All this might have been a Bakhtinian **parodia sacra** – a carnivalesque parody of religious liturgy – but the tone is much too satanic, as if the film had become suddenly possessed by a debased version of the spirit of the Pasolini of *Salo*.

One pattern that emerges, here and elsewhere, is that women are portrayed as being eminently "rapable." Off-screen cries, in the film, almost invariably cue a rape taking place. Any woman alone seems to be "fair game," not only for highwaymen but also for aristocrats exercising their sexual **droit de seigneur**. At the same time, the women in the film, and the film itself, seem to lust after Joseph's body; female desire is projected as highly visualist, fetishizing, and aggressive. In this sense, Richardson picks up on Fielding's own language in the novel, which compares Slipslop's lust to that of a "hungry tigress" leaping on her prey, or a "voracious Pike" swallowing a little fish. But while the men in the film tend to rape women, and while some women virtually rape men, it is the women who occasionally make false accusations of rape, and who are not always believed when they have actually **been** raped. In the original Fielding novels, as well as in their adaptations, in sum, the representation of sexual violence remains profoundly **gendered** and masculinist.

Machado de Assis: *The Posthumous Memoirs of Bras Cubas*

Literary criticism, as we have seen, forms an integral part of the fictional world of the self-conscious novel. In *Don Quixote*, in *Tom Jones*, in Machado de Assis's

Dom Casmurro, literary criticism does not constitute an alien intrusion but rather a dialectical moment within the process of generation of the text. Many of the cinematic adaptations of self-conscious novels, including the more successful ones, often flounder on precisely this point. While they incorporate certain reflexive devices, they do not metalinguistically dissect their own practice or include critical discourse within the text itself. While Tony Richardson's filmic adaptation of *Tom Jones*, as we have seen, is reflexive on some levels, it still does not address questions of literary (or filmic) criticism or theory.

One exception to this general rule is Brazilian filmmaker André Klotzel's adaptation of Machado de Assis's *Memórias póstumas de Bras Cubas*. Publishing fiction between 1835 and 1908, Machado de Assis has been compared not only to those antecedent writers on whom he consciously modeled his work (Cervantes, Fielding, and Laurence Sterne) but also to contemporaries such as Dostoevsky, Henry James, and Marcel Proust. Although of racially mixed parentage – his mother was Portuguese, his father a Brazilian "mulatto" – and although writing at a time when slavery still existed in Brazil, Machado rarely addressed slavery directly. The theme emerged, however, as we shall see, "between the lines." Regarded as an "honorary white" by the Brazilian literary establishment, Machado became head of the prestigious Brazilian Academy of Letters. His work has been frequently adapted by Brazilian filmmakers, including Saraceni (*Capitu* [1968], based on *Don Casmurro*), Nelson Pereira dos Santos's *Azyllo muito louco* (1970), based on the short story "The Psychiatrist"), and two versions of *Bras Cubas*, one by Julio Bressane (1985), the other by André Klotzel (2001).

Writing roughly a century after *Tom Jones*, Machado de Assis wrote self-consciously in the reflexive tradition of Cervantes, Sterne, and Fielding. As with them, his style is often self-correcting; it is writing, as Derrida would have put it, "under erasure." Machado constantly anatomizes his own expression in an obsessive metalinguistic dismantling of his own practice. His critical sense is forever on the alert, ready to censure his own lapses into bathos or vulgarity. The narrator-protagonist of his *Dom Casmurro*, for example, claims at one point that his forced departure for Europe elicited more tears than all those shed since Adam and Eve. Instantly regretting his hyperbole, he acknowledges the exaggeration, but insists "it's good to be emphatic now and then." Whereas metaphors habitually function as transparent conveyors of analogies, Machado often explicates them. Rather than serve them up as finished products for consumption, he exposes them in their process of elaboration, often proposing metaphors only to discard them as inept: "No, that comparison won't do."

Self-conscious novelists like Machado enlist the reader's active collaboration. They see their texts as indeterminate, full of gaps, as open-ended schemata that need to be filled out by the completing activity of the readerly imagination. Machado breaks the barrier separating writer from reader by having his narrator Dom Casmurro request the reader's help in locating stylistic errors, for example, or by asking the readers to correct his errors for a later edition. The same narrator tells us that he is not disturbed by books with omissions; he simply closes his eyes and imagines everything that was not in the book. He then invites his readers to do likewise: "This is the way I fill in other men's lacunae; in the same way you may fill in mine."[23] At times, Machado enlists the reader's aid in his quest for exactly the right trope. In *Bras Cubas*, he writes: "My idea was really fixed, as fixed as . . . I cannot think of anything sufficiently fixed in this world: perhaps the moon, perhaps the Egyptian pyramids, perhaps the late Germanic Diet. Let the reader make whatever analogy pleases him most . . ."[24] The text, in such instances, ceases to comport itself as a finished corpus, evoking instead some endlessly modifiable work in progress. The writing writes and rewrites itself under the reader's eyes, presumably with the reader's help.

Like Fielding, Machado develops a playful, semi-aggressive relationship with his readers. Just as Godard makes fun of his spectators, Machado mocks his "obtuse readers." We are reminded of Frank Kermode's notion of "underreading," which points to the readers' inadequacies, the ways in which readers filter out or ignore many of the cues present in a novel.[25] In *Bras Cubas*, Machado accuses his readers of being themselves the worst problem with the book: "The worst defect in this book is you, dear reader." This insult to the reader recalls many such aggressive moments in Godard's films; for example, the opening sequence of *Breathless* (1960), where Michel, driving alone, looks directly at us and tells us that if we do not love the sea and the country the way he does, then we can just go "get screwed."

Machado's *Memórias póstumas de Bras Cubas* (literally "Posthumous Memoirs of Bras Cubas," but translated into English as *Epitaph of a Small Winner*) shares with *Don Quixote* its "structure of disenchantment." Rich in reflexion but poor in experience, the title character reflects on a life that includes his first love with the Spanish prostitute Marcela (which lasted "fifteen months and eleven royal **contos**," the currency of the period), his second love with the "beautiful but lame" Eugenia, and the unsuccessful courtship of Virgilia, who ends up marrying Bras's rival, the politician Lobo Neves. Throughout the book, Bras's goals and hopes give way to a disillusionment which **precedes** the attempts to reach the goal. Bras is bored with women **before** he has his romantic adventures. He has brief **élans** – for example, an impulse to elope with Virgilia – but the realization that a **mésalliance** would bring him social embarrassment quickly sobers him up. The structure of disenchantment achieves its (anti) climax in the book's final chapter, entitled "Negatives," where the narrator lists everything he did **not** accomplish:

> I did not achieve celebrity, I did not become a minister of state, I did not really become a caliph, I did not marry . . . [and] upon arriving on the other side of the mystery, I found that I had a small surplus, which provides the final negative of this chapter of negatives: I had no progeny, I transmitted to no one the legacy of our misery. (p. 209)

This pattern of anti-climax, as Roberto Schwarz points out, is deeply rooted in Bras Cubas's status as an upper-class Brazilian whose position and success are virtually impregnable, quietly underwritten by a laboring mass of subaltern humanity.[26] Bras Cubas's inherited class status goes against the very grain and **telos** of the novel as an upwardly mobile genre. As we have already seen in *Robinson Crusoe*, the novel as genre is very much identified with the various forms of social and artistic mobility, whether in the form of the social *arrivisme* of Defoe's Crusoe, the self-realization of Julien Sorel in Stendhal's *The Red and the Black*, the personal self-understanding of Pip in Dickens's *Great Expectations*, or the artistic ambition of Marcel in Proust's *In Remembrance of Things Past*. Bras Cubas, as he himself points out in the final chapter, "didn't have to work by the sweat of [his] brow." Here we are reminded of the narratological truism that narrators cannot be strictly equated with authors. The narrator–protagonist Bras Cubas is decidedly **not** Machado de Assis, the author who **did** have to work by the sweat of his brow, and who went from being a humble typesetter to being the most prestigious literary figure in Brazil.

Bras Cubas is rooted in a very dense intertext. Machado takes from Laurence Sterne his play with the temporal conventions of literature, and the technique of the association of ideas. Like Sterne, Machado plays with the idea of novelistic consecution through a comic retarding procedure. While the narrator of *Tristram Shandy* cannot get himself born, the narrator of *Bras Cubas* has the opposite problem: he is already dead. The novel also echoes *Hamlet*, and more generally the Elizabethan preoccupation with skeletons, corpses, and death, through its dedication: "To the worm which first chewed on the cold flesh of my cadaver, I dedicate, with fond memory, these posthumous memoirs."

In an essay, Machado spoke of his ambition, very much proleptic of the magic realists, to "invent a bird without wings, describe it, make it visible to everyone, so that people end up believing that there are no birds **with** wings." And if *Bras Cubas* on one level looks back to Cervantes, on another it looks forward to magic realism, especially in its frequent, audacious, flights of fancy. The very title of the novel in Portuguese – with its allusion to posthumous writing – is magically supernatural. It suggests that the novel is narrated by a dead man, not an author who has died since **writing** the book, but a dead author, i.e. an author who took to writing after he was dead. This device is literally derived from the Menippean tradition, whose founding text, by the cynical philosopher Menippus himself, was entitled *The Dialogue of the Dead*. The device is first of all anti-realistic, since corpses presumably do not write. We are reminded of a similar device in Billy Wilder's film *Sunset Boulevard* (1950), where Joe Gillis (William Holden) tells his story as he is dead, floating face down in Norma Desmond's swimming pool. But the device also conveys the philosophical idea that death grants the narrator objectivity, or impartiality, since death brings an end to earthly vanity. In his posthumous state, he is "above" the mundane cares of fleshly human beings; his words, therefore, have a higher truth status.

It is also important to remember that Machado deploys the device at an historical moment – 1880 – when many writers around the world are experimenting with narrative voice and point of view, searching for a more impassive or impersonal style that goes beyond the direct editorializing of a Balzac or Dickens. Machado's novel is especially audacious in having Bras Cubas recount his own delirium as he agonizes, a dream-like vision featuring speaking animals and friendly hippopotamuses. Interestingly, the narrator does not actually describe the afterlife; he simply speaks of his own past life from a serene, distanced perspective, as if from "beyond the grave." In his film adaptation, Klotzel plays with the distinction between Bras as living, acting character and as at the same time a dead author. He provokes a split between the two by having the older, close-to-death Bras observe the younger Bras from within the frame. Thus the two "characters" come to coexist side by side.

The narrative structure of *Bras Cubas*, like that of *Tristram Shandy*, is apparently whimsical, proceeding through zigzags and digressions. The novel recounts Bras Cubas's life, but out of sequence, beginning with his death. Bras even overhears, and critiques, the eulogy at his own funeral. Lamenting the fact that only eleven friends – "eleven!" – appeared at his funeral, he mocks his eulogist's banal conceit that, on the rainy day of the funeral, "nature too is weeping" over the loss of Bras. Digressive like *Don Quixote*, *Bras Cubas* features two distinct ways of being digressive. The first consists in narrative interpolations à la Cervantes, and the other consists in the random association of ideas à la Sterne. But unlike *Don Quixote*, in *Bras Cubas* the digressions make a point both about social status and about character. As a member of the elite, as Roberto Schwarz points out, Bras Cubas doesn't **need** to stick to any single idea or endeavor.[27] Thus association of ideas, and the empty parading of useless knowledge and cultural baggage, here becomes the inherited trait of someone who has the luxury of alternating life with whimsical reflections on that life, a life characterized above all by capriciousness. The same point is true in ideological terms. Bras Cubas flirts with, dallies with, as it were, all of the major discourses and doxa of his age – Social Darwinism, Humanism, Liberalism, Scientism, Benthamism, and so forth. But it is all merely whimsical, since the social structure on which he depends will not be radically changed and will continue to support his lifestyle.

The novel *Bras Cubas* is stupendously inventive in its use of reflexive techniques, going far beyond Fielding or anything known at the time. This technique includes such devices as feigning blockage in his own writing, or of introducing tropes or expressions only to withdraw them. He uses the word "enraptured," and then confesses that its use "was merely an effort of mine to lend splendor to my literary style" (p. 71). At another point, he laments that his pen has slipped "into the emphatic" (p. 58). At times, he shares his doubts, as when he intimates that he "had half a mind not to write it" (p. 168), or when he informs us that he has "just written an utterly unnecessary chapter" (p. 188) as if he could not have easily eliminated it without leaving a trace.

Bras Cubas also indulges in shameless self-praise, hailing himself as "the first author" to treat his "own delirium" (p. 16). Or he praises his seamless segues from chapter to chapter. Or, Cervantes-like, he embarks on literary excurses, providing, for example, a mini-essay on the role of the horse in literature, quite different, he points out, within romanticism as opposed to realism (p. 36). Or he takes typographical and formal liberties, leaving an entire chapter completely blank, for example chapter 139, which is entitled: "How I did **not** Become a Minister of State" (p. 191, emphasis added). Machado's experience as an editor and a typesetter, it is worth remembering, made him extremely conscious of the mechanics and formal materials of editing and publishing. In chapter 22 he draws on the jargon of typography, using terms like "in folio" and "in 12," "margins," and so forth. Chapter 55 is even more audacious. It renders the love affair between Bras Cubas and Virgilia through various forms of punctuation, moving from initial converse in the form of asterisks, to foreplay in the form of question marks, through gestural dialogue, and on to lovemaking and even to a simultaneous orgasm of synchronized exclamation points. Rather like those risqué filmmakers laboring under the restrictions of the Hayes Code, Machado manages, in a censorious age, to come up with clever substitutes for explicitly sexual language.[28]

The André Klotzel adaptation of *Bras Cubas* picks up on many of the reflexive cues in the source novel. Unlike many adapters of reflexive novels – *Tom*

Jones is again the exception – Klotzel does not take the easy path of simply relaying the story, while discarding the reflexive devices as so much "static." Klotzel sees the novel for what it is – a self-conscious linguistic/stylistic artifact. In his own comments on his adaptation of the novel, he calls attention to the novel's "ruptures," "instabilities," and "ambiguities." He speaks of its embedded skepticism, which has a skeptical narrator cast doubt even on his character's (i.e. his own) skepticism. The serpent-devouring-its-own-tail structure of the novel reflects the passivity of the narrator/character, who devours himself as it were. Klotzel keeps the self-consciousness and the digressions from the novel; he doesn't clean them up in the name of effective, linear storytelling. In stylistic terms, Klotzel writes: "Machado's lightness, his unemphatic ways of saying things, a tone which is both prosaic and extremely elegant, struck us as fundamental to our adaptation. We worked via analogies, for example by avoiding extremely high or low angles and **recherché** camera movements."[29] The adaptation effectively mimics what Klotzel calls the "sober elegance" of the novel's cool, deadpan and dispassionate style, within a "chamber music aesthetics."[30]

Klotzel also picks up on the novel's eighteenth-century style direct address to the reader by having his narrator/character, both as off-screen voice narrator, and as on-screen presence, refer to "you." But the film further specifies the address to embrace "you spectators sitting there in your movie-theater seats." The aged narrator of the end of the novel is often made to share the frame with the narrator's younger self. As a *magister ludi*, the narrator freezes the frame in order to comment on the action; for example, on an angry encounter with his father. At times the narrator becomes didactic. Bras's lecture on the "essential nature of the Oriental" is illustrated by a real-life guru, sitting in the lotus position, who Bras induces to levitate. At times the film uses "lying" or "subjunctive" narration, i.e. hypothetical sequences subsequently revealed to be untrue. The film has Bras Cubas physically attack his amorous (and political) rival Lobo Neves, for example, but then retracts the sequence that we have just seen, informing us that it "was all just a trick." At another point, the film uses proleptic anachronism, as when Bras conjures up the fantasy of twentieth-century, TV-style commercials advertising his proud, nineteenth-century invention, the poultice.

Klotzel uses a specifically cinematic intertextual device to render Bras's delirium before his death. In the novel, Bras's life appears before him in a series of zany episodes. The film, meanwhile, evokes what Bras calls a "condensation of the ages" through an array of moments from pre-existing films, including silent-era futurist films, Shakespeare adaptations, and Cecil B. de Mille-style Biblical epics. The dedication to the "worm who first chewed on the flesh of my cadaver" is rendered through a silent-era version of the "Alas, poor Yorick"

Figure 3.3 Magical effects in *Posthumous Memoirs of Bras Cubas* (2001),
produced by Cinemate Material Cinematográfico / Cinematográfica Brasileira /
Instituto Português da Arte Cinematográfica e Audiovisual (IPACA) / Lusa Filmes /
PIC-TV / Secretaria de Estado da Cultura (SEC) / Superfilmes

scene of *Hamlet*, where the Shakespearean protagonist is seen parlaying with
Yorick's skull. The cinematic transition from this material to Bras's earlier life
is "covered," meanwhile, by the on-screen narrator's praise of the "brilliant transition" through which he has managed to move smoothly from his death and
funeral to his birth.

The only important element missing in the Klotzel adaptation is the shrewdly
disguised political undercurrent of the novel, and specifically its subtle critique
of slavery and slave society. The full significance of the novel can only be appreciated if we remember that the author, Machado de Assis, can in no way be
equated with the character/narrator Bras Cubas. While Machado was the
descendant of slaves, Bras Cubas is the owner of slaves. As a member of the
hereditary elite, Bras was born at the top of the social foodchain, and social
inertia is likely to keep him there. Machado, in contrast, was an ambitious, hardworking, self-made man, a typographer who worked with his hands – in a society
in which the elite looked down on manual labor – but also with his mind. While
Machado was artistically productive, Bras is unproductive.

Bras is, indeed, precisely the kind of privileged, entitled slacker that people like Machado would be likely to resent. Moreover, Bras as a character forms a critical portrait of the Brazilian elite. He is spoiled by his father, who justifies his injustices; for example, his abuse of a slave boy. In a strange way, Bras is the victim of his own advantages, which prevent him from striving for what he already has. He misses all of the "outs" and possible escape routes for salvation from his own mediocrity. Eugenia might have saved him through her sincere and passionate love, but she is (1) lame, (2) of lower social class, and (3) rejected by his father. In his social solipsism, Bras sees those around him, for example Dona Placida, as predestined by God to serve him (p. 196). In this sense, as Roberto Schwarz points out, *Bras Cubas* is a book written against its own narrator, manifest in "the calculated inadequacy of the narrator's attitudes toward the material he himself represents."[31] The narration forms an act of inadvertent self-disaccreditation, which reveals the protagonist–narrator to be shallow, vain, cruel, despotic, selfish, even inhuman (as in his chilly indifference toward his father's death). In this respect, Machado anticipates other writers who deliberately undermine confidence in their narrators; for example, Dostoevsky in *Notes from Underground*, Robbe-Grillet in *In the Labyrinth* (1957), and Italo Calvino in *If on a Winter's Night a Traveler* (1979).

Despite being a descendant of slaves, as I suggested earlier, Machado rarely addressed the subject of slavery directly. Yet the subject is addressed indirectly, backgrounded but present. In an early passage young Bras "rides" his boy-slave Prudencio. We are reminded that young slaves were perpetually available as objects of aggression for the pampered children of the elite. Later, we learn that the slave Prudencio, after gaining his freedom, himself gets a slave, on whom he vents the same violence that had previously been vented on him. In short, he scapegoats down the social ladder. Although Prudencio is the only enslaved character, we are constantly made aware in the film of many black people quietly performing acts of service. We are reminded that the Brazilian elite was utterly dependent on slaves for their personal comfort, and on slavery as an institution for their wealth and status. The novel makes frequent mention of the slave trade, as when we learn that the character Cotrim does contraband in slaves, since slave commerce had by now become illegal. Throughout, we get glimpses of the epiphenomena of slavery: Uncle Joao telling scurrilous jokes to slave women, Dona Eusebia "scolding a colored gardener," news of shipments of 120 negroes, a piece of news juxtaposed, significantly, with a passage concerning Bras's love of sweets.

We also infer the presence of slavery in the icy calculations and bargaining, reminiscent of Crusoe's contractual bargaining, that take place after the death of Bras Cubas's father. Cotrim wants to inherit the father's black coachman, but Bras Cubas protests that that would force him himself to "buy another coachman." Through a rhetorical zeugma, which yokes slaves and silverware, Machado reminds us of the objectified, commodified status of slaves, as Cotrim jokes that "your father didn't free the silverware, did he?" The novel also communicates a pervasive sense of the elite being **observed** by slaves. Bras Cubas wonders if "the slaves had been spying on [him]" (p. 93). The household slaves, Cubas acknowledges, "found in gossip about us a sort of revenge for their social condition" (p. 112). But the critique takes place as much through style as through content. Bras calls the episode in which the former slave Prudencio brutalizes his own newly acquired slave a "jolly chapter," but the reader has a clear sense that only the narrator, Bras Cubas, and not the author, Machado de Assis, could find a brutal beating "jolly." The inappropriateness of the language points to the ethical limitations of the character.

Even more profound is what might be called Machado's "relational" critique of slavery. At first glance, the novel seems to simply take slavery for granted as a stable, axiomatic, background institution, without ever making an explicit condemnation. Yet a critique does emerge in the interstices, as it were, of the text. The incidents, and Machado's reflections on them, reveal a system of social relations intricately entangled in the social hierarchies typical of a slave society. Thus we intuit the socially approved cruelty inherent in the relation between the young slave Prudencio, who suffers young Bras Cubas's sadistic pranks, and Bras himself, whom his father regards, affectionately, as a "little devil," and whom he never punishes. The son of the elite is presumably seen by the enslaved man for what he is – an abusive, spoiled product of privilege, yet that same slave, once freed, emulates the master's behavior. The interconnected systems of slavery, caste, patronage, and corruption, as Schwarz points out, are "covered over" by a patina of "progressive" ideas borrowed from Europe: liberty, justice, fraternity, equality, and so forth.

Bras Cubas exposes the historical relationalities that link Bras Cubas's spoiled life to the institution of slavery. Take, for example, Bras's conversation with the self-taught vagabond Quincas Borba, where Borba explains that the chicken that he and Bras are eating was:

> fed on corn that was planted, let us say, by an African imported from Angola. This African was born, grew up, was sold; a ship brought him here, a ship built of wood cut in the forest by ten or twelve men and driven by sails that eight or ten men wove, not to mention the rope and the rest of the nautical apparatus. Thus, this

chicken, on which I have just lunched, is the result of a multitude of efforts and struggles carried on for the sole ultimate purpose of satisfying my appetite. (p. 172)

This passage offers an eloquent account of the asymmetrical transnational interdependencies characteristic of the Black Atlantic world, an earlier version of what would later come to be called "globalization." What was already in the nineteenth century a global system nourishes the class advantages of the Brazilian elite embodied by Bras Cubas. We are made to reflect on all the interconnected cogs – the thoroughly **modern**, quasi-industrial cogs – that form part of the machinery of transatlantic slavery. At the same time, the book makes respectful references to Africa, alluding, for example, to "the shores of an ever youthful Africa" (p. 6). (Interestingly, Bras Cubas's humanist learning includes the ancient Greek classics, representing a period when, as Martin Bernal points out in *Black Athena*, Africa was a respected continent to which Greek philosophers and historians made frequent reference.)[32]

Bras Cubas in some ways forms what Fredric Jameson and Ismail Xavier would call "national allegory."[33] Much as *Robinson Crusoe* recapitulates the history of transatlantic slavery, Bras Cubas's trajectory recapitulates the history and social formation of Brazil, including references to independence, to slavery (via the slaver Cotrim), and to cultural colonialism (the hegemony of European ideas). Just as important, style in itself becomes a form of national allegory. The capricious association of ideas which characterizes the style itself, as Schwarz points out, reflects the mental meanderings of a member of the elite, accustomed to having its **caprices** satisfied and even flattered. Thus ideals and discourses borrowed from the European Enlightenment are imposed on a social reality characterized by slavery, injustice, and inequality.

Machado's favored device for dealing with these contradictions is the device of the ironic apologia. The most effective example is Bras's "defense" of the contraband slave-dealer Cotrim. Praising the "deep and fierce sense of honor" in Cotrim's character, Bras "rebuts" the usual charges made against the slaver:

They used to call him avaricious, and perhaps they were right, but avarice is only an exaggerated form of a virtue . . . As his manner was very sharp, he had enemies, who accused him of barbarity. The only fact alleged to support this charge was that he frequently committed slaves to the dungeon and that they were dripping blood when released; but, apart from the fact that he did this only to fugitives and

The Self-conscious Novel

Chapter 3

incorrigibles, one must remember that, as he had long been engaged in smuggling slaves into the country, he had become accustomed to long-established methods of treatment that were somewhat harsher than those practiced in the regular slave trade, and one cannot honestly attribute to a man's basic character something that is obviously the result of a social pattern. Furthermore, although he may have owed kindness to some, he owed money to none. (p. 179)

The boomerang "praise" in this passage is absolutely extraordinary. Under the guise of "defending" Cotrim, the narrator **inadvertently** – but it is not inadvertent on the **author**'s part – reveals the multiple inhumanities of the slave system. It is as if a writer would have a narrator defend Hitler and Nazism by saying: "although people accused Hitler of cruelty, in fact he only exterminated half of the Jewish people, and furthermore extermination was a common practice of European colonialists (think of the Tasmanians or the Herrero), so why should Hitler be held responsible for what was a common practice. Moreover, Hitler was well known for scrupulously paying back his financial debts. While it is true that Hitler expressed genocidal sentiments, it must also be said that the prose style of *Mein Kampf* is impeccable." The narrator's praise of Cotrim shocks us because of the staggering disproportion between the mass cruelty of the whippings and murder of slaves, imaged as "dripping with blood," on the one hand, and on the other the abstract ledger-book correctness of "owing money to none." Within this rigged ethical system, cruelty to slaves merely reflects "a long-established method," while a bourgeois paying of debts reveals intrinsic virtue. But Machado's critique goes even further, for it includes not only the abuses invoked, but also extends to the **blindness** of those like Bras Cubas who justify or normalize such abuses. In this sense, Machado offers a deep-structural anthropological critique of the very exculpatory categories in which the elite of the time **thought**.

The Klotzel film bears few traces of this critique; the ironic praise of Cotrim is excised, as is the scene of the former slave Prudencio beating his newly acquired slave. On the other hand, the film does show slaves as omnipresent and indispensable. While not real, rounded characters, they appear constantly, whether in period engravings, or as the constantly serving black hands, entering the frame just long enough to serve a cup of coffee, or wield a fan, or deliver food, or clean up after the elite. While on the one hand slavery is backgrounded, normalized as part of a picturesque historical drama, on the other the film conveys the clear impression that only black people actually **worked** in nineteenth-century Brazil. And it was this labor that "enabled" Bras's idleness. But, in general, the adaptation's stress is on the reflexivity of Machado's technique and the ironic presentation of a **comédie de moeurs**, not on slavery and its implications.

While successful in stylistic terms as an adaptation of a classic, reflexive novel, one also wonders about some of the adaptational "roads not taken." The music scored is generally European symphonic, although a brief carnival-style moment set in the streets features Brazilian popular music. In this same vein, the film might have developed a more systematic musical/cultural counterpoint, like that developed in other Brazilian films such as *Pagador de promessas* (1962) or *Xica da silva* (1976), between classical European and popular Afro-Brazilian music. Or the film could have featured more point-of-view shots from the perspective of the enslaved characters, communicating their critical perspective on the elite. The director might also have used an embedded double-frame narration. In literature, embedded narration is an ancient tradition, deployed in *The Decameron*, *The Canterbury Tales*, and *The Turn of the Screw*. In this sense, the film might have had an actor representing the author Machado present the narrator/character Bras Cubas. Casting a black actor as Machado would have dramatically changed the racial dynamics of the story, calling attention to the gap between author and narrator, and casting the whole story in a very different and more socially critical light. But perhaps I am asking for too much, and we should be content with what the film does offer us: a very intelligent, thoughtfully reflexive, adaptation of a brilliant and too-little-known literary classic.

From *Bras Cubas* to Postmodern Fiction

A century after Machado's *Bras Cubas*, the kind of reflexivity demonstrated in novels like *Don Quixote* and *Bras Cubas* became a staple within what is now called the postmodern epoch, exemplified by such self-conscious novels as John Barthes's *The Sotweed Factor* (1965), John Fowles's *The French Lieutenant's Woman* (1969), Thomas Pynchon's *Gravity's Rainbow* (1973), Umberto Eco's *The Name of the Rose* (1980), David Lodge's *Small World* (1984), and Dave Eggers's *A Heartbreaking Work of Staggering Genius* (2000).

In the contemporary period, then, reflexivity has become a ubiquitous technique, including in film. Woody Allen's *Manhattan* (1979), in this sense, picks up on a reflexive stratagem already invoked in a 1939 novel, Flann O'Brien's *At Swim-Two-Birds*. That novel opens by a first-person reflection on narrative openings to the effect that a good book might have a number of dissimilar popular beginnings and a hundred possible endings. O'Brien then constructs three

The Self-conscious Novel

Chapter 3

parodic "beginnings," none of which is literally a beginning since they follow the narrator's opening remarks.[34] Allen's *Manhattan* borrows this literary device by having his narrator–protagonist Isaac (Allen) voice different possible beginnings to the novel he is presumably writing:

> "Chapter One. He admired New York City. He idolized it all out of proportion. Now . . . to him . . . no matter what the season was, this was still a town that existed in black and white and pulsated to the great tunes of George Gershwin." Ahhh, now let me start this over. "Chapter One. He was too romantic about Manhattan as he was about everything else. He thrived on the hustle . . . bustle of the crowds and the traffic."

By introducing the author and the question of authorship into the text via a virtuoso collision of possible fictive voices, displaying variable proportions of starstruck romanticism and gritty, disenchanted "realism," all coinciding with Gordon Willis's glistening montage of Manhattan skylines, Allen calls attention to the reflexive modalities of his art.

Our final example of postmodern literary self-consciousness – David Eggers's *A Heartbreaking Work of Staggering Genius* (2000) – has yet to be adapted, despite rumors that an adaptation is imminent. The anecdotal core of this novel, or meta-memoir, is a very personal and indeed "heartbreaking" story about the virtually simultaneous loss of both of the author's parents, leaving the young narrator as the caretaker of his eight-year-old brother "Toph." But this one story is constantly interwoven with reflexive meta-commentary. Here I will concentrate not on the story but only on the ways that Eggers breaks new ground within the larger terrain already explored by Cervantes, Fielding, Sterne, and Machado, bringing to a paroxysm the frame-breaking and dialogic techniques of the self-conscious tradition. The front cover of the book gives the official title – *A Heartbreaking Work of Staggering Genius* – a title which reads less like a title than the blurb for the novel itself. Indeed, in the "acknowledgments," the author recognizes the reader's probable reaction to what he calls the title's direct appeal to "the maudlin and melodramatic." The back cover, which is upside down, is entitled "Mistakes We Knew We Were Making;" it includes "Notes, Corrections, Clarifications, Apologies, Addenda." So if the "real" title evokes a blurb, the "fake" extra title suggests a critical dissection of the book itself.

But the line between the "real novel" and the commentary on the novel constantly blurs, since the "real novel" also includes commentary; for example, "Rules and Suggestions for the Enjoyment of this Book." The first suggestion is that the reader should skip the preface: "Really. It exists mostly for the author, and those who, after finishing the rest of the book, have for some reason found themselves stuck with nothing else to read. If you have already read the preface, and wish you had not, we apologize. We should have told you sooner." Here Eggers picks up on one of Henry Fielding's favorite techniques, as when the narrator in *Joseph Andrews* tells us that "a Chapter or two (for instance this one I am now writing) may be often pass'd over without any Injury to the Whole" (II, i. 120). Here we see a difference between novel and film. Although some avant-garde and militant films, such as the Argentinian film *La hora de los hornos* (Hour of the Furnaces, 1968), did leave intervals during the film for debates among the spectators about the film, it is hard to imagine a conventional feature film advising the audience to go out in the lobby and read the newspaper because the "following sequence relays nothing of importance." The author also recommends skipping what Genette would have called the "paratextual materials" – those materials on the threshold of the narrative that appear alongside the text but not part of the text proper, i.e. acknowledgments, table of contents, and so forth.[35] The author also recommends that the reader skip much of the text proper (he finds pages 239–351 specifically dispensable), since these dispensable passages "concern the lives of people in their early twenties, and those lives are very difficult to make interesting, even when they seemed interesting to those living them at the time."[36]

In the preface, which we have been advised to skip, the author explains that his novel is not actually pure fiction, since much is a fictionalized version of real life. The author also mentions the various passages omitted in the final version, for example some "really great sex scenes," omitted "at the request of those who are now married or involved" (p. xi). The author then offers for our perusal the "out-takes" of the novel, the passages which ended up, as the saying goes, "on the cutting room floor," to wit various occluded sentences, paragraphs, and passages. (Of course, since he has included them in the preface, they are no longer really omitted as he claims.) Finally, the preface lists all the contemplated but finally discarded epigraphs (including "Ooh, look at me, I'm Dave, I'm writing a book"), on the grounds that the author "never really saw himself as the type of person who would use epigraphs" (p. xvii). Eggers stages, in sum, the anxiety of the author at the moment of publication: what to leave in and what to keep out.

Eggers draws comic-ironic delights from the most recondite aspects of novel-writing. His first acknowledgment, which we had been advised not to read, seems improbable in the extreme given the Bay Area bohemian milieu the author/narrator seems to inhabit. The acknowledgment, more appropriate to a science-fiction intergalactic travel film, is to the author's putative "friends at NASA and the United States Marine Corps, for their great support and unquantifiable help with the technical aspects of this story. **Les Saludo, Muchachos!**" Caught up in the momentum of "acknowledgments," the author decides to "acknowledge" as well "the distinguished senator from Massachusetts." And, he adds, "Palestinian statehood." In the spirit of a highly commercialized epoch in publishing, the author makes "special offers" to the readers. For those who prefer not to think that the novel is based on the lives of real characters or to know their real identities, he offers, for a ten-dollar fee, in exchange for the returned copies of the book, "a 3.5 floppy disk, on which will be a complete digital manuscript of this work, albeit with all names and locations changed, in such a way that the only people who will know who is who are those whose lives have been included, though thinly disguised." He then goes on to provide the precise address at Vintage Press to which the books should be sent. Another "special offer," made to the "first 200 readers of this book who write with proof that they have read and absorbed [its] many lessons," involves a $5 check. The problem, he acknowledges, is how to prove that readers have actually bought, and read, and understood, the book. His proposed solution: photos of the person with the book, and the receipt for the book, shown actually **reading** the book. He reminds the readers to center themselves in the photo, and also proffers free advice about lenses and focal length. In an absurd and paradoxical fashion, the literary author proposes that photographic evidence can somehow validate a purely mental/verbal experience, that of reading. The author then speculates on his actual readership, even those who read the book "far in the future," to whom he addresses a number of interested questions: "What's it like in the future? Is everyone wearing robes? Are the cars rounder, or less round? Is there a women's soccer league yet?"

Picking up on something we will ourselves be noting in the next two chapters, the author of *A Heartbreaking Work of Staggering Genius* acknowledges that a novel's success has much to do with "how appealing its narrator is." He then inventories what he sees as his own narrator's attractive features, including "that he is like you," and that, "like you, he falls asleep shortly after he becomes drunk," "that he sometimes has sex without condoms," and so forth. Some of the listed items point to emotional "truths" in the real story, such as the fact that "he never gave his parents a proper burial." As if providing "Monarch Notes" commentary for his own novel, the author also lists the book's major themes, which include such apparently heterotopic items as: "the unspoken magic of parental disappearance," and "the sexual rendezvous . . . as tool for collapsing of time and vindication of self-worth." The author also provides the reader with the following useful items: "incomplete guide to symbols and metaphors;" a list of thematic "threads; the various charts used to plot out the relationships between the characters; and the financial statements delineating agents' fees, taxes." One of the "threads" is the "painfully, endlessly self-conscious book aspect," what the author calls the "knowingness about the book's self-conscious aspect." Using what Bakhtin in relation to Dostoevsky calls "loophole discourse," Eggers anticipates, in a deadpan parody of the competing self-conscious stratagems of writers and critics, all the possible critiques of the novel, along with the answers to those critiques:

> While the author is self-conscious about being self-referential, he is also knowing about that self-conscious self-referentiality . . . he also plans to be clearly, obviously aware of his knowingness about his self-consciousness of self-referentiality. Further, he is fully cognizant, way ahead of you, in terms of knowing about and fully admitting the gimmickry inherent in all this, and will preempt your claim of the book's irrelevance due to said gimmickry by saying that the gimmickry is simply a device, a defense, to obscure the black, blinding, murderous rage and sorrow at the core of this whole story . . .

At another point, the author/narrator has little brother Toph, just before being tucked in at bedtime one night in Berkeley, rather precociously deconstruct the older brother's novel itself.

Eggers carries reflexive frame-breaking to hitherto unheard of extremes, beyond that achieved even by Machado de Assis, bringing the novel into the domain of Andy Kaufman and the *Larry Sanders Show*. Carrying Machado's stylistic self-corrections into real life, the author reports the experience of rereading his own novel aloud in bookstores, and suddenly being appalled by a word choice or passage, and therefore stopping mid-sentence to "furiously cross out the offending words, much to the amusement of the attendees, who thought I was kidding" (p. 7). (Reportedly, Eggers's own readings are somewhat Andy Kaufman-like, involving planted hecklers and Dada-like provocations.)

The author/narrator explains that he telephoned the prototypes of the characters to ask their permission to be portrayed as doing things they had not actually done, even though other scenes involving them are completely accurate. The author then invites us to telephone one of the prototypes, named Meredith Weiss, who, he informs us, lives in Southern California (p. x). The author informs us that he asked the friends featured in the book if they minded his giving out their phone numbers (three did not mind). Surprised that these three people were not deluged, upon publication, with calls from the readers of such a popular novel, the author speculates on the reasons for the lack of calls. A majority of people, he speculates, "either a) assumed the numbers were phony or outdated; b) were exceedingly polite and respectful of the privacy of nonfictional book characters; or c) never actually made it that far into the book . . ." (p. 10).

While many reviewers sensed the novel's affiliation with the self-conscious genre, citing Tobias Smollett and Laurence Sterne alongside J. D. Salinger and Joseph Heller, others predictably accused Eggers of "narcissism," a charge which the book clearly anticipates. The narrator admonishes himself to be "aware of the dangers of self-consciousness" while at the same time "plowing through the fog" of intertextual echoes. But some reviewers took such devices as further evidence of narcissism, reinvoking the ancient charge against reflexivity as onanistic self-abuse. Lydia Millet asks whether a memoir is a "fitting venue for frenzied and public masturbation."[37] At times Eggers talks about these dangers himself. The narrator speaks of an attempt to get a part in the MTV "faux reality" show *Real World*. Within this postmodern tightrope act, the author hopes to imply to any viewer that he is participating for his perverse, but also ultimately pure, amusement. At the same time, he is worried about those clichéd presentations of postmodern media saturation. Here Eggers seems close to evoking the celebrated paradoxes of postmodernism, of complicitous critique and the cultural studies nostrum that mass-mediated texts are both subversive and hegemonic. Irony, the text suggested, can be both a form of managing and distancing intense emotion, or an ethical cop-out, an index of cynicism.

In sum, Eggers picks up on all the auto-referential techniques – the incorporation of literary criticism, and the auto-criticism of discourse – which we have found to be typical of the other writers discussed in this chapter, but he transcodes them in relation to the postmodern world of the simulacrum. In so doing, he provides what amounts to a far-reaching tongue-in-cheek "narratological" analysis of the nature of fiction, realism, authorship, and literary reception. Eggers shows that there is still some life in the old reflexive tradition, that it can even generate a bestseller. Given the current rumors of a forthcoming adaptation of the novel by New Line Cinema, and of Tom Cruise's interest in the leading role (an adaptation which will perhaps be completed, if I may myself break frame for a second, as you read this book), it will be interesting to see if the adaptation respects the reflexive dimension or rather cleanses the book of such "noise" and turns it into a family melodrama.

1   Margaret Anne Doody, *The True Story of the Novel* (New Brunswick, NJ: Rutgers University Press, 1996), p. 298.

2   See Leslie Fiedler, *Love and Death in the American Novel* (New York: Dell, 1960), p. 54.

3   Judith Mayne, *Private Novels, Public Films* (Athens: University of Georgia Press, 1988), pp. 13–39.

4   See Thomas Keymer and Peter Sabor (eds), *The Pamela Controversy: Criticism and Adaptations of Samuel Richardson's Pamela, 1740–1750* (London: Pickering and Chatto, 2001).

5   Henry Fielding, *Tom Jones* (New York: Modern Library, 1985), pp. 77–8. Subsequent page references in the text will be to this edition.

6   Henry Fielding, *Joseph Andrews/Shamela* (London: Penguin, 1999), p. 102. Subsequent page references in the text will be to this edition.

7   Homer Obed Brown, *Institutions of the English Novel* (Philadelphia: University of Pennsylvania Press, 1997), p. 86.

8   Ibid., p. 100.

9   Erich Auerbach, "Odysseus's Scar," in *Mimesis: The Representation of Reality in Western Literature*, trans. Willard R. Trask (Princeton, NJ: Princeton University Press, 1953).

10 Gerard Genette, *Narrative Discourse* (Ithaca, NY: Cornell University Press, 1980).

11 Robert Alter, *Fielding and the Nature of the Novel* (Cambridge, MA: Harvard University Press, 1969).

12 The cinema of the silent period often exploited the unreality of titles and the temporal conventions behind them. Silent film, deprived of the more complete mimesis afforded by synchronous sound, was in some ways more receptive to anti-illusionism. Keaton often pokes fun at the very gratuitousness of the titles that interrupt silent film narrative. In *The Navigator* (1924), Buster casts an anchor. A title, projected for approximately ten seconds, informs us: "ten seconds later," followed by a shot of the anchor floating to the surface. The only conceivable usefulness of such a title is to explain a temporal ellipse; it becomes absurd in a situation of straight continuity. In *The Paleface* (1922) we see Buster in statuesque embrace with his Indian bride. A title then alerts us to a time shift: "two years later." The shot that follows shows us the couple again, identically dressed, in the same position and in the same setting. They pause for breath, and then resume their embrace. The sequence beautifully highlights the non-equivalence of story time and discourse time, for we know that even lovers, with their special respiratory patterns, cannot hold their breath for two years, any more than Don Quixote could hold his sword in the air while Cervantes looked for supplementary sources.

The Self-conscious Novel

Chapter 3

13 Wayne C. Booth, *The Rhetoric of Fiction* (Chicago: University of Chicago Press, 1961), p. 216.

14 See the essay by Judith Bailey Slagle and Robert Holtzclaw, "Narrative Voice and 'Chorus on the Stage' in *Tom Jones*," in James M. Welsh and John C. Tibbetts (eds), *The Cinema of Tony Richardson: Essays and Interviews* (Albany, NY: State University of New York Press, 1999).

15 Booth, *The Rhetoric of Fiction*, p. 217.

16 See André Gaudreault and Philippe Marion, "Transécriture and Narrative Mediatics: The Stakes of Intermediality," in Robert Stam and Alessandra Raengo (eds), *A Companion to Literature and Film* (Oxford: Blackwell, 2004).

17 Susan Sontag, *Against Interpretation* (New York: Bell, 1961), pp. 242–3.

18 C. L. Barber, *Shakespeare's Festive Comedy: A Study of Dramatic Form and its Relation to Social Custom* (Princeton, NJ: Princeton University Press, 1959). See also Peter Stallybrass and Allon White, *The Politics and Poetics of Transgression* (Ithaca, NY: Cornell University Press, 1986).

19 Barber's analysis of Shakespeare is in some ways more "Bakhtinian" than Bakhtin's, whose infrequent remarks concerning Shakespeare's work are rather disappointing. In *Problems of Dostoevsky's Poetics*, for example, Bakhtin discerns "early buddings of polyphony" in Shakespeare's dramas but only across the entire oeuvre. See *Problems of Dostoevsky's Poetics* (Minneapolis, MN: University of Minnesota Press, 1985), pp. 33–4.

20 See Barber, *Shakespeare's Festive Comedy*, p. 46.

21 In their gloss on *Joseph Andrews*, Stallybrass and White point out the satiric, carnivalesque role of pigs, a symbol both of sin, within Christianity, but also of the rustic boorishness of the bourgeoisie. *Joseph Andrews* associates pigs both with the mean-spirited Parson Trulliber and with Parson Adams, who despite "falling in the mire of the pig-sty, resolutely defends his loss of dignity with the cry *nihil habeo cum Porcis*." See Stallybrass and White, *The Politics and Poetics of Transgression*, pp. 51–2.

22 See James M. Welsh, "Henry Fielding Revisited: *Joseph Andrews* (1977)," in Welsh and Tibbetts (eds), *The Cinema of Tony Richardson*, p. 216.

23 Joaquim Maria Machado de Assis, *Dom Casmurro* (New York: Oxford University Press, 1997), p. 112.

24 Joaquim Maria Machado de Assis, *Epitaph of a Small Winner*, trans. William L. Grossman (New York: Noonday Press, 1990), p. 10.

25 See Frank Kermode, *The Art of Telling* (Cambridge, MA: Harvard University Press, 1983), p. 138.

26 Roberto Schwarz, *Um mestre na periferia do capitalismo* (São Paulo: Editora 34, 1990/2000).

27 Ibid., p. 81.

28 Woody Allen is reportedly an enthusiastic fan of Machado de Assis and of *Bras Cubas*. According to John Clifford, who long worked with Woody Allen as his stills pho-

tographer, Allen was amazed to find that a Brazilian author, writing over a century earlier, "sounded like me; he has my voice." At first glance this seems like an expression of vanity and even megalomania on Allen's part, but on closer inspection Allen's comment makes perfect sense. Allen's films, like Machado's writing, are replete with examples not only of dark humor and neurotic narcissism, but also wittily reflexive devices, and fanciful, almost magical realist conceits. In Allen's world, these conceits include chameleon characters who transform themselves into their neighbors (*Zelig*), actors/characters who escape from the confines of the filmic image (*The Purple Rose of Cairo*), characters who are literally "out-of-focus" (*Deconstructing Harry*), blind film directors (*Hollywood Ending*), and so forth. Machado also anticipates the 1950s' "sick humor" that was at the roots of Allen's stand-up comedy. Another Machado novel, *Quincas Borba*, recounts an incident where a drunk, seeing a poor woman weeping next to her still-burning cottage, asks her permission to use the flames to light his cigar. Specific moments in *Bras Cubas* even anticipate specific Allen moments, as when Bras dialogues with the imaginary embryo buried in his lover's womb, reminding us of the parachuting spermatozoa in *Everything You Wanted to Know about Sex*.

29 See André Klotzel, "A Question of Fidelity," from the website for the film (http://www.brasfilmes.com.br.).

30 These comments can be found on the film's website.

31 Schwarz, *Um mestre na periferia do capitalismo*, p. 174.

32 Martin Bernal, *Black Athena* (New Brunswick, NJ: Rutgers University Press, 1987).

33 Fredric Jameson, "Third World Literature in the Era of Multinational Capitalism," *Social Text* 15 (Fall 1986); and Ismail Xavier, "Historical Allegory," in Toby Miller and Robert Stam (eds), *A Companion to Film Theory* (Oxford: Blackwell, 1999, 2004).

34 Flann O'Brien, "At Swim-Two-Birds," in *Flann O'Brien Reader* (London: Penguin, 2000).

35 Gerard Genette, *Palimpsestes: La Littérature au second degré* (Paris: Seuil, 1982).

36 David Eggers, *A Heartbreaking Work of Staggering Genius* (New York: Random House, 2001), first unnumbered page: "Rules and Suggestions for the Enjoyment of this Book."

37 See Lydia Millet, "Rotten Eggers," *Tuscon Weekly*, April 3, 2000 (weeklywire.com/ww/or-03-00/tw_book_html).

Chapter 4

The Proto-cinematic Novel: Metamorphoses of *Madame Bovary*

In the preceding chapters, we have addressed two antagonistic strains within the novel: the documentary-style, "realist" tradition of *The Adventures of Robinson Crusoe*, where the text strives for an overpowering impression of reality, and the Cervantic, parodic, intertextual tradition of *Don Quixote, Joseph Andrews, Tom Jones,* and *Bras Cubas,* as well as their postmodern descendants, all cases in which the text, whether literary, filmic, or televisual, calls direct attention to its status as artifact. *Madame Bovary*, Flaubert's story about a bored provincial housewife who slides into adultery, debt, and suicide, in effect counterposes **both** traditions, playing each off dialectically against the other. More precisely, Flaubert's novel counterpoints the realistic style, traceable to Defoe, with the romantic style, traceable to the chivalric literature mocked by Cervantes. In *Madame Bovary* the shrewd counterpointing of contrasting styles becomes the very key to the novel's aesthetic and narrative strategies.

Flaubert himself time and time again expressed his admiration for *Don Quixote*. For Flaubert, Cervantes' novel "dwarfed" all other books. Indeed, it has long been a critical commonplace to see *Madame Bovary* in the mold of *Don Quixote*, to speak of Emma as the "female Quixote" or "Don Quixote in skirts." Indeed, both *Don Quixote* and *Madame Bovary* treat what might be called "the literary theme." While Don Quixote is inspired, indeed driven virtually mad, by chivalric romance, Emma Bovary is inspired and disoriented by the same kind of literature at a later historical stage, to wit the romantic literature of Chateaubriand, Lamartine, and Sir Walter Scott, a genre of literature itself rooted in the period, if not precisely in the style, of chivalric romance. *Madame Bovary* adheres to what Harry Levin calls the "Cervantic formula of systematic disenchantment."[1] This formula dictates that a protagonist nourished on literary dreams, who sees the world through the deforming prism of readerly idealization, becomes disappointed upon discovering that real life does not "live up" to the hopes inspired by books. The three-dimensional world turns out to be more cruel and pitiless than literature has suggested. Georg Lukács, Harry Levin, René Girard, and Robert Alter have all seen this Cervantic structure as common to many novels central to the European tradition, from *Don Quixote* through Balzac's *Lost Illusions*, on to *Madame Bovary* and even to Proust's *Remembrance of Things Past*. In these fictions, the patterns provided by art prove inadequate to life itself.

Emma Bovary's discourse reflects a mind addled by the reading of romantic literature. Her conversational intercourse with the young law-clerk Leon, for example, amounts to "a continual traffic in books and romances." Her reading, while not medieval per se, is steeped in gothic, medieval memories as recycled by late eighteenth- and nineteenth-century romanticism. And as Denis de Rougemont points out in his classic *Love and the Western World*,[2] European attitudes toward love trace their origins to the medieval period, and specifically to *l'amour courtois* (courtly love), a tradition very much shaped by the love poetry in Arabic that pervaded Iberia and the south of France. Within this **liebestod** tradition, love took the form of pathos (etymologically "suffering" in Greek). Any love worthy of the name was axiomatically impossible, adulterous, and often literally life-threatening. Even the names Emma chooses for her daughter – Amanda, Isolda – emphasize mediated desire and falling in love with love: Amanda etymologically means "to be loved" and Isolda evokes the impossible courtly romance of Tristan and Isolde, precisely the source myth for the occidental cult of love both invoked and demystified in Flaubert's novel. The **liebestod** tradition conjugates love and death together with the third element – religion – in an unstable amalgam exemplified by the eroticized piety of Emma's convent years, or in the passionate kiss – "the most passionate kiss of love she had ever given" – bestowed on the crucifix at the moment of her death. (It was this unseemly neighboring of the spiritual and the carnal, not the carnality itself, that outraged the prosecuting attorney in the *Madame Bovary* trial.)

Since the romance as genre antedates the novel, its social affinities on some levels remain with the aristocracy, the same rather decadent aristocracy waltzing through the Vaubyessard Ball which so enchants Emma. Emma's literary tastes homologize personal biography and literary history. Her reading recapitulates the entire history of romanticism: *Paul et Virginie*, Chateaubriand, Lamartine, Sir Walter Scott, early Balzac. *Madame Bovary* alternates two styles: the cold, detached, lifelike, realistic description of Emma's provincial milieu with another double-voiced, ironically romantic, style consisting of literary pastiches which become indistinguishable, within the free indirect style, from the very consciousness of Emma. Literary style itself becomes a form of consciousness, a symptom of the dissolution of the self into fiction, as in the following passage:

> to savor its sweetness, it would have doubtless been necessary to go off to one of those sonorous sounding countries where the first days of married life are languorously spent. Behind the blue silk shades of the mail coaches they would slowly climb up steep roads, listening to the song of the postilion being echoed through the mountain together with the sound of goat bells and the muffled roar of a waterfall. At sunset, they would inhale the scent of the lemon tree by the shores of the gulfs; then, in the evening, on the terraces of the villas, alone, fingers intertwined, they would gaze at the stars and dream ... Why couldn't she be leaning her elbow on the balcony of a Swiss chalet or indulging her moods in a Scottish cottage with a husband dressed in a black velvet suit with long coattails, soft boots, a pointed hat, and elegant cuffs?[3]

Here we find what Bakhtin calls "double-voiced" writing at its most playfully evocative. Flaubert plays on all the *topoi* of romanticism — sublime nature, aristocratic lovers, the desire for an exoticized **ailleurs** — with a mocking intention, yet without ever becoming explicitly judgmental. Emma's consciousness is rendered through literary allusion, here confounded with her own imagination. Most adaptations of the novel, as we shall see, ignore this fundamental aesthetic strategy, avoiding parody and impoverishing the representation by opting for a **single** homogeneous style.

Characters like Don Quixote and Madame Bovary, according to René Girard, imitate, or believe they imitate, the desires of their chosen models or "mediators." In Lacanian terms, they desire not the "other" per se but rather the "desire of the other." Even as Emma is "finding in adultery all the banalities of marriage," Emma still writes Leon love letters, "in line with the idea that a woman should always be writing to her lover" (p. 272). To depict Emma's mediated desires, Flaubert immersed himself not only in "high" romantic literature, but also in what we now call the "popular culture" of *Keepsakes* and fashion magazines and other "feminine" periodicals. In novels of "external mediation," like *Madame Bovary*, characters also seek a transcendence that goes beyond mere fashion; a religious substratum, therefore, always lurks in the background. Emma's desire, like Don Quixote's, becomes confounded with the ideal image that she

projects onto the mediator, much as a nun's or monk's desire might be confounded with what the desire projected onto Christ.

To put it punningly, Cervantes' "knights errant" turn into Emma's "errant
nights;" her wandering passion gallops after an equally errant object of desire.
In *Madame Bovary*, desire itself rides horseback. And Flaubert's female Quixote,
as Levin points out, has no Sancho Panza to bring her down to earth; she is
foiled only by a dullard husband, a scheming salesman, two mediocre lovers,
along with the boorish M. Homais, avatar of scientific modernity and secular
reason, the incarnation of the *arriviste* "get-rich-quick" spirit of the epoch.

In *Madame Bovary* the structure of disenchantment, the bitter upending of
bookish ideals, takes place not only on the macro-level of plot – Emma's slow
slide into despair, ignominy, and suicide – but also on the micro-level of syntax
and style, notably in the frequently anti-climactic structure of Flaubert's sentences. A discursive devaluation occurs when an idealized romantic metaphor
– often crystallized around "romantic" words like "felicity" and "passion" and
"intoxication," magnet-like fetish words that attract desire within a gravitational
field – is brought down to earth with a thud:

> Love, she believed, should arrive all at once with thunder and lightning – a whirl-
> wind from the skies that affects life, turns it every which way, wrests resolutions
> away like leaves, and plunges the entire heart into the abyss. She did not know
> that the rain forms lakes on terrace houses when the gutters are stopped up . . .
> (p. 111)

Here the currency of the romantic sublime – storms and whirlwinds and chasms
– is devalued into an imagery of stopped-up gutters.

Flaubert's Cinematic Gaze

If *Don Quixote* and *Madame Bovary* generate themes that cinema later takes
up, it is also true that the novel *Madame Bovary* can be seen, on a number of
levels, as "proto-cinematic." Indeed, Eisenstein saw in the "agricultural fair"
chapter of *Madame Bovary* a precursor of cinematic montage. A masterpiece
of verbal *mise-en-scène*, the passage counterpoints two equally fatuous discourses,
that of the grandiloquent politician, and that of the provincial Don Juan:

> From magnetic attraction, little by little, Rodolphe had arrived at the affinities, and while the president was citing Cincinnatus at his plow, Diocletian planting his cabbages, and the emperors of China ushering in the new year by sowing the seed, the young man was explaining to the young woman that the cause of these irresistible attractions derived from some previous existence. (pp. 151–2)

Here, provocative juxtaposition and ironic leveling emphasize the parallels between two modalities (amorous and political) of discursive seduction, two forms of flattery and manipulation. Rodolphe's stream of erotically mystical declarations, consisting largely of clichés about elective affinities and the superior morality of sensitive souls – is interrupted by the more earth-bound phrases of politicians. Rodolphe's mendacious hyperbole that he had wished to follow Emma "a hundred times" is interrupted by the politician's "Manure!" Rodolphe's vow to cherish Emma's memory is followed by "For a merino ram!" And his "I shall be something in your thought, in your life, shall I not?" gives way to "Porcine race; prizes – equal, to Messrs. Leherisee and Cullembourg, sixty francs!"

The concept of the "cinematic" novel has, admittedly, often been abused, bandied about so imprecisely as to mean anything from "sharply imagined" to "featuring physical action" to "having a powerful (film-like) impact" to "using procedures reminiscent of filmic techniques." The concept of the proto-cinematic offers a backhanded compliment to both novel and film, simultaneously implying that the novel already had the qualities of cinema, since it could be "cinematic," but also that films were the *telos* toward which novels were striving, since only films could be **really** cinematic.[4] But, despite the sometimes problematic deployment of the concept, it is nonetheless productive to see a novel like *Madame Bovary* as "proto-cinematic." This quality operates on a number of levels. First, the novel displays a film-script-like precision about the notation of gestures and attitudes. Here, for example, is the novel's account of Charles Bovary's first visit to Emma's family farm:

> One night about 11, they were awakened by the sound of a horse stopping right at their door. The maid opened the attic window and spoke for some time with a man below. He had come for the doctor. He had a letter. Nastasie shivered as she went down the stairs; she unlocked the door and drew all the bolts. The man left his horse and walked into the house. Following right behind the maid, he pulled a letter, wrapped in a piece of fabric, from his gray-tasseled woolen cap and gingerly presented it to Charles, who propped his elbow on the pillow to read it. (p. 35)

The Proto-cinematic Novel

Chapter 4

In its proto-Hemingwayesque directness, this passage reads like a film script; all that is missing are technical notations like "crane shot" or "dolly in." Flaubert offers sensory and compositional cues, as it were, to potential adapters, specifying framing (the maid opening the attic window); involuntary gestures (the maid's shivers); physical actions (the drawing of the bolts); inserted details (the letter wrapped in fabric); costume (the tasseled woolen cap); and physical posture (Charles propped up on his pillow). Subsequent adapters of the novel, like Claude Chabrol, as we shall see, will build on these script-like qualities of the novel.

Flaubert is also extraordinarily sensitive to sound; his ears are as attuned as his eyes are sharp. In a letter of October 12, 1853 to Louise Colet, Flaubert announced his "symphonic" ambitions in the agricultural fair sequence of *Madame Bovary*: "If ever the values of a symphony have been transferred to literature, it will be in this chapter of my book. It must be a vibrating totality of sounds. One should hear simultaneously the bellowing of the bulls, the murmur of love, and the phrases of the politicians."[5]

The fair passage offers us a complex, layered, textured, multi-track sound — one is tempted to say a "Dolby sound." We find the same layered sound in the passage relating Emma's boredom with her marriage: "She would listen in an attentive stupor to each cracked chime of the bell . . . once in a while a dog would howl in the distance and the bell would continue its monotonous, evenly spaced ringing, which faded off into the countryside" (p. 80). We are struck by the acoustic precision of the "cracked" bell, and by the way Flaubertian sound (like Flaubertian light) moves over and modifies space. (Chabrol later picks up on these "acoustic" qualities in his adaptation by duly noting and recording the novel's "sound effects.")

Literary "props" also play a central role in the novel: the silly cap which Charles wears on his first appearance; the bouquet of withered orange-blossoms that metonymize Charles's first marriage; the silk cigar case Emma picks up on the way back from Vaubyessard; the riding crop she gives Rodolphe; the religious statuette which falls from the coach on the road between Tostes and Yonville; the Cupid-decorated bronze clock in the Rouen hotel. We might also speak metaphorically of the mental "props" of Emma's imagination, furnished with imagined stallions and swans, lutes and lyres, balconies and fountains, masked balls and aristocratic horsemen.

Literary critics have spoken, in conjunction with Flaubert, of *le style indirect libre* (the free indirect style or discourse). Although Flaubert is the writer most associated with the technique, he never actually used the term. The "*style indirect libre*" refers to a kind of grammatical-stylistic procedure, an adroit modulation of tenses by which the slow abandonment of pronominal antecedents evokes a slow gliding into an internalized subjectivity. Through the modulation of tenses and modes and parts of speech, the pronoun or proper name ("Emma thought") gradually disappears in favor of the unmediated presentation of a character's thought ("How wonderful it would be to live in a castle in Spain!"). Thought is rendered as reported speech, in the third person and in the past tense, but in a language impregnated by the feelings of the character. The effect is of a "dolly in" to consciousness, an indeterminacy of narrative voice which mingles distance with interiority, molding a sense of intimate access to a character's mind, but without abandoning authorial agency and attitude. This style, revolutionary in Flaubert's time, has become the virtual norm in much of fiction today, largely because it allows for maximum flexibility for the writer, who can regulate distance toward the character, variously deploying description or narration, direct or indirect speech, interior monologue or "inner speech."

The free indirect style in literature enables dialogical interaction between two subjects, two genres, two texts. Extending such ideas to film, Pasolini saw the "free indirect style" as typifying a "cinema of poetry," i.e. a transnarrative "first-person" cinema in which the filmic character becomes a trampoline for the filmmaker's stylistic virtuosity, in which a character's delirium, for example, becomes mingled with the director's brilliant inventiveness.[6] Thus, for Pasolini, "modern" filmmakers exploit sick and neurotic or especially sensitive characters as a trampoline for turning style into the true protagonist of the film. Anomalous lenses, baroque camera positions, decentered framings, mismatched edits, all come to express, simultaneously, the abnormal psychology of the protagonist and the delirious aesthetic ambitions of the director. For Gilles Deleuze, this stylistic inventiveness is associated with the "time-image," where all the cinema becomes a free indirect style operating on the basis of "reality," and where the characters enjoy a free and direct relationship with the poetic vision of the director.

Another way of appreciating the innovations of *Madame Bovary* is in terms of a carefully calibrated gap between style and content. Long before *Seinfeld*, Flaubert claimed that his goal in *Madame Bovary* would be to write a "book about nothing," where "nothing happened."[7] In his novel, Flaubert said, style itself would become "an absolute manner of seeing things."[8] For Flaubert, there are no intrinsically beautiful or ugly subjects; his self-professed goal was to "write well about mediocrity." The artistic challenge, in such cases, is to avoid the "mimetic fallacy," to speak of boredom, for example, without actually **being** boring. Flaubert manages this feat largely through style, by making the objectively boring **stylistically** scintillating, making "fetid" and "foul" subjects aesthetically exhilarating. At times he achieves this exhilaration through the ironic deflation of grandiose metaphors. Flaubert's description of Rouen, for example, as a "small, ignoble Venice," uses the adjective "ignoble" to turn the grandeur of Venice into a boomerang indictment. The vehicular prose of the love-in-a-moving-cab in Rouen, meanwhile, mimics the acceleration of panting sexual desire; a sordid affair is stylistically transmogrified into art, without a single direct reference to adultery or physical lovemaking.

In his analysis of Flaubert's "iterative" rendering, using Genette's terminology, of Emma's mealtimes — "*C'était surtout aux heures des repas*" ("It was above all at mealtimes") — Auerbach brilliantly analyzes the ways that Flaubert's account of dinner *chez les* Bovarys communicates the quiet despair of Emma's married life: "its cheerlessness, unvaryingness, grayness, staleness, airlessness and inescapability."[9] Auerbach portrays Flaubert's technique in strikingly visual terms: "Though the light which illuminates the picture proceeds from her, she is yet herself part of the picture, she is situated within it."[10] Auerbach's characterization of the technique echoes discussion of point of view in the cinema, where analysts have often argued that the strict identification of character with the camera, as in *Lady in the Lake* (1947), is a less effective technique than alternating shots of the character (she is part of the picture) with what the character sees (the picture proceeds from her).

The consciousness within the couple, furthermore, is asymmetrical and non-reciprocal; the husband discerns nothing of his wife's inner misery; their aborted interlocution does not even reach the interactive form of an argument, which would presume some level of actual communication. Life at such moments does not "surge and foam," as Auerbach puts it, "it flows viscously and sluggishly."[11] In terms of cinema, the question becomes: what would be the ideal cinematic equivalent for evoking this slow, benumbed duration, this lugubrious **vécu**? A verbal evocation of ennui by a character? Voice-over narration? Or the literal duration of a long-held shot sequence, where slowness would render the snail like passage of time (a technique used in dos Santos's *Vidas secas*, 1963)? Or one might employ voice-over to literally borrow Flaubert's imperfect tense from the novel (the solution adopted by Chabrol); or use what Metz calls the "episodic sequence" (little scenelets showing a certain trajectory, in this case a trajectory toward boredom, a famous example being the disintegrating-marriage-over-breakfast sequence of *Citizen Kane*). Another approach would be through visual metonymy: a dripping faucet might convey the slow and repetitious drip, drip, drip of time; or slow motion, or the dilation of a shot by editing (whereby the same gesture is repeated ad infinitum), or a well-chosen synecdochic gesture (e.g. distracted doodling). Each approach has its advantages and drawbacks.

The Proto-cinematic Novel

Chapter 4

Anyone who has seen Chantal Akerman's *Jeanne Dielman* (1975) will certainly reject George Bluestone's overly categorical claim in *Novels into Film* that "film lacks the power of language to show habitual behavior."[12] In the Akerman film, seemingly interminable single-shot sequences render the quotidian drudgery as lived by a Brussels' housewife in real time. (Ivone Margulies appropriately borrows the title of her monograph on Akerman – *Nothing Happens* – from Flaubert's description of his own novel.)[13] Other films, which are not adaptations, give us an inkling of how some of Flaubert's tropes and figures might have been handled. The narrator's remark that Emma "rediscovered in adultery all the banality of marriage," for example, constitutes an iterative inversion, the equivalent of which is beautifully evoked in Godard's *Une femme mariée* (1964). In that film, Godard evokes the domestication of platitudinous adultery by having both husband and lover perform the same identical rituals linked to lovemaking – washing hands, undressing, the same sequence of caresses and "I love yous" – and by having them filmed in identical ways.

The historical importance of *Madame Bovary* partially derives from its agile deployment of novelistic point of view, and especially from Flaubert's way of dispersing narrative agency onto multiple delegate characters, without direct authorial intervention à la Balzac. With the author omnipresent but invisible, Flaubert has us slide from one zone of subjectivity into another, experiencing flickering moments of identification with a wide range of characters, while never letting us lose consciousness of the mediating narration. In this sense, Flaubertian narrative conjugates the "spectating" of his characters with the "observing" of his authorial narration. Through an identificatory tag-team approach, Flaubert places us successively within the vantage point not only of major characters like Emma and Charles but also of secondary characters like Rodolphe and even of unnamed characters who never again appear in the text.

This relay process begins with the first sentence of the novel, where we read that "we" (apparently a group of young pupils) "were studying when the headmaster came in, followed by a new boy . . ." The narration "sees" the newly arriving Charles Bovary from the vantage point of a sarcastic group of young cohorts. Significantly, this "we" soon disappears, ephemeral like the loyalty of school classmates. But this is not the only instance of ephemeral identification. Flaubert has two provincial ladies "post themselves in a convenient spot from which they can observe everything going on in Binet's house" (p. 285). Flaubert also has us briefly enter the perspective and even the bodily sensations of the bewildered (unnamed) cab driver who drives Emma and Leon around Rouen as they make love. The driver wonders "what kind of rage for locomotion inspired these people, who did not want to stop . . . he lashed his two sweating nags even more furiously, without paying attention to the jolts, bumping into things here and there, not caring, demoralized, and almost weeping from thirst, fatigue, and unhappiness" (p. 234). The finale of the novel has a "curious soul" observe the widowed Charles Bovary by "[looking] over the hedge and [gazing] in amazement at [an] unkempt, bearded man . . ." (p. 321).

A key critical question about *Madame Bovary* has been the extent of Flaubert's identification with Emma. Although on one level a "tour de force of female impersonation,"[14] Flaubert also contaminates Emma's consciousness with his own, coloring the novel not only with literary reminiscences but also with his own personal memories of trysts and affairs. Yet the fundamental aesthetic premise of the novel, paradoxically, is the suppression of his own personality. In his letters to Louise Collet, Flaubert speaks of his disgust with some of the human material he is treating. But then his project consists in taking exactly such unpromising material – vulgar, provincial, mediocre – in order to show that even such detritus can be alchemized into art. In the novel, Flaubert expresses this ambivalence toward his heroine through what in cinematic terms might be called "variable identification" and "shifting point of view." Although Emma clearly dominates the point of view in the novel, she does not monopolize it.

Flaubert's precise articulation of angle of vision anticipates not only camera "set-ups" but also a favored technique in Robbe-Grillet's novels of clearly marked character vantage points within voyeuristic structures. True to the logic of the proto-cinematic, Flaubert's technique anticipates a signature device of one of the most subjectivizing of directors, Alfred Hitchcock, who also practices rotating point of view among various characters. In *The Birds* (1963), for example, point-of-view shots are accorded not only to the main character (Melanie), but also to other major characters (Mitch, Lydia), as well as to passersby (the unseen "acousmatic" young man who whistles at Melanie in the opening shot; the man on the dock at Bodega Bay who watches Melanie as she gets into her boat). Most innovatively, Hitchcock at crucial junctures grants "the right of regard" to the birds themselves – the aerial/avian views of the burning gas station, the finale that has the birds watch the departing humans.[15]

Like Hitchcock, Flaubert is the master of the manipulation of visual and emotional distance. An abrupt stylistic shift takes us from the verbal "long shot" of the Rouen cab, carrying Leon and Emma making hurried love, to the close detail shot of Emma's "torn-up note," followed by the chilly distanciation which turns Emma into a generic *femme* descending from a vehicle: "Then, about six o'clock, the carriage stopped in a side street of the Beauvoisine section, and a woman stepped down, walking away with her veil pulled down and without looking back" (p. 234). This rotating approach allows Flaubert to achieve a kind

The Proto-cinematic Novel

Chapter 4

of variability of focus and focal length. Its variable focus is ideally suited to the ambivalence in the narrator, who at some points identifies with Emma – *Madame Bovary, c'est moi* – and who at others seems repelled by her. We find here the literary counterpart of "rack focus," the procedure whereby foreground and background are successively made to switch places in terms of clarity and focus. This technique can take us from extreme intimacy on the one hand – Flaubert places us within the very eyes and skin of Emma, so that we look with her, strain our eyes with her, feel our heart beat with her, even enjoy orgasm with her – to an icy and judgmental distance on the other.

Flaubert's portraiture is destabilized, not only in terms of physical milieu but also in terms of character, reminding us again of the cinema, where character is rendered as a flowing composition in time. Not only do Flaubert's characters refuse to sit still for their portrait, the portraitist (Flaubert, or better the narrational camera, as it were) also refuses to stay still. Charles's first encounters with Emma, for example, are not rendered by a static description of Emma's fixed "traits" but rather through Charles's fleeting impressions:

> A young woman in a blue wool dress trimmed with three flounces came out of the threshold of the door to receive Monsieur Bovary, and she invited him into the kitchen, where a large fire was blazing. The farmhands' dinner was boiling around it, in small pots of varying sizes. Some damp garments were drying inside the fireplace. (p. 37)

Emma Bovary, although she is the title character, is not even named: she is simply "a young woman," exactly the status to which she returns after the cab sequence. The encounter with Emma, seemingly rendered from Charles's point of view, is quickly lost in sensuous details which have nothing directly to do with Emma, who at this point has not yet come to rivet Charles's (or the narrator's) attention.

Flaubert the Impressionist

Flaubert reflects a crucial transitional moment within the history of the arts, one that marks the transcendence and supercession of both of the antagonistic traditions mentioned earlier, not only in terms of theme and style but, more importantly, in terms of point of view. I am referring to a moment in the history of

The Proto-cinematic Novel

Chapter 4

literature and of the visual arts when a kind of mobilized regard crystallizes the altered perceptions associated with modernity. Jonathon Crary speaks of a transformation, in this period, in the nature of visuality, a "mutation" in the status of the observing subject. Rejecting the technological (and teleological) determinism which charts an inexorable movement toward a more comprehensive mimesis, Crary suggests that a wide range of nineteenth-century optical instruments were involved in a sweeping transformation of the ways in which the "observer" was figured in a wide range of social practices and domains of knowledge."[16] Popular instruments like the "stereoscope," the "stroboscope," the "zootrope," the "phenakistiscope" and the "diorama," for Crary, reconstructed optical experience. Between 1810 and 1840, exactly the period preceding the writing of *Madame Bovary*, we find an "uprooting of vision from the stable and fixed relations incarnated in the camera obscura," leading to an "unprecedented mobility" abstracted from "any founding site or referent."[17] With "physiological" rather than "geometrical" optics, vision became relocated in the body, leading to scientific studies of the anomalies of vision: retinal afterimages, peripheral vision, and thresholds of attention. Within popular culture, meanwhile, the circulation and reception of "all visual imagery is so closely interrelated by the middle of the century that any single medium or form of visual representation no longer has a significant autonomous identity."[18]

Nineteenth-century novelists in both France and England were fond of the notion of "prose painting," when Henry James published a *Portrait of a Lady* and Conrad spoke of aspiring to the "color of painting."[19] Although Crary does not speak about Flaubert or about the novel as genre, his rewriting of the history of vision helps explain why Flaubert, in 1857, could verbally anticipate the altered gaze associated with Impressionism in painting – where the artist is attentive to what intervenes **between** the object and the eye – and with modernism in the novel, where point of view and "filters of consciousness" become paramount organizing principles. Flaubert, in this sense, offers a new kind of seeing and signification, whereby "vision, rather than a privileged form of knowing, becomes itself an object of knowledge, of observation."[20]

Flaubert is particularly gifted in the verbal recreation of the "feel" of seeing, as in the following passages: "Lying motionless on her back, her eyes in a fixed stare, she could only vaguely discern the objects, even though she was trying to concentrate with a kind of idiot persistence. She focused her eyes on the peeling plaster on the wall ..." (p. 286). Much as contemporaneous scientists study the anomalies of vision, Flaubert often renders disturbed or **encumbered** seeing, witnessed in Emma's frequent squinting, her intermittent loss of focus, her vain attempts to discern objects in the distance. Her very failure to see takes

The Proto-cinematic Novel

Chapter 4

on a metaphoric dimension: "She stared as far as possible into the distance, but against the horizon there were only huge grass fires smoking on the hillside" (p. 204).

This last passage exemplifies still another visual quality of Flaubertian *écriture*, his "Impressionist" attention to atmospheric phenomena. Although writing before the actual advent of Impressionism in painting, Flaubert shows himself to be an Impressionist **avant la lettre**. Although *Madame Bovary* was published seventeen years **before** the label "Impressionism" was attached to the artistic movement (at the first Paris exposition in 1874) and twenty years before it was adopted by the Impressionists themselves in 1877), Flaubert used verbal pigments, as it were, to do what the Impressionists did with literal pigments later. (During the *Bovary* trial, interestingly, both prosecution and defense appealed to the notion of Flaubert as a painter, although their references, inevitably given the time-frame, tended to be to the crude "brushwork" of the "realistic" school of painting.)

In the cinema, the term "impressionism" tends to refer to an avant-garde tendency within the French silent cinema of the 1920s, a movement which invoked impressionism in painting and which was opposed to expressionism. The movement, represented by such figures as Epstein, Delluc, Gance, and Dulac, tried to express feelings through mobile cameras, intense close-ups of faces, and subjectivized editing, rather than projecting feelings outward onto the decor in the expressionist manner. But, in general, impressionism represents the "road not taken" by dominant cinema. The dominant deployment of lighting has aimed at literally highlighting "key" characters and objects and actions in a rather formulaic way. Conventional lighting, at least in the classical cinema, conveyed an ontologically stable world; it called attention to the object, for example, the armchair, but not to the flecks of dust hovering above it. The cinema requires a calculated effort to reveal the operations of light in the atmosphere. As Jean-Pierre Geuens puts it, light can be seen filling space only after smoke, fog, talcum powder, or whatever else is thrown into the air so that the light rays have a chance to "alight upon" particles to "create the sense of a beam of light."[21] Just as Impressionist painting was opposed to the academic style, so any innovative approach to light would have to challenge the "academic" approach to lighting which depends on the hierarchical triad of (1) key light (perceptible and dominant); (2) fill light (supplementary and subordinate); and (3) backlight (barely visible). Light in *Madame Bovary*, interestingly, knows no such hierarchies; it operates democratically, flowing everywhere. Flaubert denaturalizes light by focusing on it rather than on the object itself. Academic lighting in film hides the instability and volatility of light, smoothing it over, much as conventional editing smoothes over the discontinuities of time and space. Yet in fact each successive shot modulates the master shot's original lighting set-up. As Geuens puts it, "transcendental aspirations for a solid world vanish under the weight of vital accommodations."[22] More creative cinematographers like Henri Alekan, meanwhile, speak of producing "impressions" in viewers, using light to set a tone, calling upon our memory to react to physical phenomena such as rain, fog, or heat "to come up with psychological equivalents such as annoyance, sadness, mystery, fear, anguish . . ."[23] A filmmaker like Eric Rohmer (in conjunction with cinematographers like Nestor Almendros) looks precisely for these instabilities of light, the emanations of particular sites and the ephemeral atmosphere of particular moments.

Flaubert develops an anti-academic, Impressionist approach to light, paying close attention to **plein air** effects, to sense impressions, to what is seen and perceived rather than what is known.[24] In the following passage, for example, Flaubert uses words to "paint" the vapors and gases which jostle one another in the atmosphere: "From the heights on which they were standing, the entire valley seemed to be a pale, immense lake, evaporating in the air . . . a brown light hovered in the air between the pines" (p. 160). Or again: "Perspiration was pouring down every face, and a white vapor, like river mist on an autumn day, was hovering above the table between the hanging lamps" (p. 154). Like the Impressionists, Flaubert discerns what is happening **between** the eye and the object being perceived. His verbal depictions anticipate the countless Impressionist paintings where the atmospheric mutations of smoke and vapor play a compositional or textural role: the columns of chimney and factory smoke in Pissarro's *Le Lavoir, Bougival* (1872) and *Usine près de Pontoise* (1873); the locomotive smoke in Monet's *Le Pont de chemin de fer* (1873), *Intérieur de la Gare Saint-Lazarre* (1877), and *Le Chemin de fer* (1973); the dusky wisps of factory smoke in Guillaumin's *Soleil couchant à Ivry* (1869); the smoggy haze in Monet's *The Thames below Westminster* (1871).

Flaubert gives a sense of the dynamic agency of light in modifying appearances, expressed in light-active words which render color, for example, as a perceptual process: *"blanchissaient"* (whitened), *"vernissait"* (varnished), *"veloutant"* (velveted). Visual phenomena in Flaubert's rendition are intrinsically unstable; even Emma's eyes are variously described as brown, black, blue, pallid, changing like the exteriors of Monet's Rouen Cathedral, where Monet took photographs of the cathedral at various times of the day to help shape his famous series of paintings. Like the Impressionists, Flaubert looks for atmospheric and luminous "effects." His language foreshadows the preoccupations of the many Pissarro paintings which spoke, through titles and through technique, of "effects,"

The Proto-cinematic Novel

Chapter 4

whether the "*effet de neige*" (snow effect), or "*effet de pluie*" (rain effect), or "*effet de brouillard*" (fog effect). As Charles rides toward old Rouault's farm, clumps of trees make "regular patches of dark purple against the large gray surface that blended at the horizon into the dull tone of the sky" (p. 38). Light in *Bovary* becomes an active principle:

> The sun's rays, coming through the wooden slats, became long thin stripes that shattered upon contact with the furniture and quivered on the ceiling . . . the daylight coming in through the fireplace made the soot on the hearth look like velvet and turned the cold ashes slightly blue . . . (p. 44)

In Flaubert's prose light has directionality, transformability, energy, and agency; it quivers and breaks and shatters and spreads. It has color and performativity, as "white light [comes] in gentle undulations through the windowpane" (pp. 123–4). In *Madame Bovary*, light alters the appearance of everything it touches. Flaubert's photosensitive prose glimmers and scintillates with "trembling luminous patches of light" and "iridescent light dappling the floor." Just as Flaubert's characters have no essence – they cannot be fixed by an epithet – so his objects have no inherent perceptual traits. As in Impressionist painting, objects have no intrinsic color beyond what light has momentarily and provisionally granted them.

Flaubert also demonstrates an intensely corporeal form of empathy, a sentient feeling for Emma's bodily existence, a capacity which, while not specifically cinematic, does allow him to induce readerly identification with the very body of the heroine, in a way that anticipates the visceral, haptic impact of the cinema. Here is Flaubert's account of Emma's milky forest orgasm:

> The shadows of the evening descended; the horizontal sun passing through the branches was blinding her eyes. All around her, in the leaves and on the ground, luminous patches trembled . . . Silence was everywhere. Something sweet seemed to breathe from the trees. She felt her heart beginning to beat again, and the blood flowing inside her flesh like a river of milk. Then, far away beyond the forest, on the other side of the valley, she heard a strange, long-drawn out cry that hung on the air, and listened to it in silence as it mingled like music with the last vibrations of her throbbing nerves. (my translation)

Thus describing Emma's return to normal consciousness after a sexual swoon, the novel speaks of her "beating heart" and the "vibrations of her throbbing nerves." One wonders how a film might try to achieve the same effect; for example, through dappled forest light, or perhaps through a milkily sensuous kind of music. This corporeal empathy reaches its paroxysm, on a more negative register, in the depiction of Emma's suicide and agony. Here we are made aware of Emma's panting lungs, and the laboring of her ribs "as if the soul were leaping to free itself." Or, again, we find it in the passage where Flaubert describes Emma's reaction to Rodolphe's rejection letter:

> She leaned against the window frame, rereading the letter with sneers of anger . . . her heart was pounding like a sledgehammer, furiously, irregularly, constantly accelerating . . . the beam of sunlight reflecting directly up at her from below was pulling the weight of her body into an abyss. She felt as if the square were swinging to and fro, its ground climbing the walls. The floor was tilting at one end like a vessel in a storm. (p. 200)

This passage, which happens to have been chosen for adaptation by **most** of the filmmakers whose work I will discuss, has the remarkably prescient quality of being more "cinematic" than anything managed by the filmmakers. The deft deployment of interior physical sensation (the sledgehammer pounding of the heart), the sharp impression of light (the beam of sunlight), the sensation of heaviness, and the vertiginous displacements of space, swinging and tilting, anticipate less other instances of literary writing than certain anthological sequences of film history. We are reminded, for example, of *Vertigo* (1958), where Hitchcock combines a forward dolly with a backward zoom shot to make spectators feel in their very viscera the ambivalent push/pull and attraction/repulsion that triggers Scottie's (and our) dizziness.

Flaubert's prose has a kinetic, even kinesthetic quality, which enables it to render the sentient feel, for example, of vehicular movement. Flaubert is particularly adept at verbal "tracking shots," where words convey the progressive revelation of towns and landscapes. Here is Flaubert's rendering of the passing world as seen from a moving carriage: "Finally the brick houses grew more frequent, the ground rang out beneath the wheels, the Hirondelle glided between the gardens, where an opening would reveal statues, arbors, clipped yew trees, and a swing, then, suddenly, the city appeared" (p. 249). Here Flaubert anticipates Proust's mobilized description of the steeples of Combray as observed from a moving vehicle.

Madame Bovary is, above all, relentlessly visualist. In his correspondence, Flaubert described himself as deriving "almost voluptuous sensations from the

The Proto-cinematic Novel

Chapter 4

mere act of seeing . . . the plot is of no interest to me, I aim at rendering a color, a shade . . ."[25] He conceives of himself as a word painter, a concept which itself undercuts the verbal/ visual divide erected by many critics. Interestingly, the appreciative words about reading that Flaubert places in the mouth of Leon might apply equally well to cinema: "Without moving, you walk through the countries you see in your mind's eye; and your thoughts, caught up in the story, stop at the details or rush through for the plot. You pretend you're the characters and feel it's your own heart beating beneath their costumes" (pp. 96–7). Here Flaubert comes close to describing what Metz later called the processes of primary and secondary cinematic identification, the process whereby our thoughts blend with the filmic fiction, mingling with the characters in a strange amalgam of self and other, lived as a virtual, shared experiential durée.[26]

In a famous 1863 essay in *Le Figaro*, Charles Baudelaire used the term "modernité" to designate an art of the "ephemeral, the fugitive, and the contingent."[27] Like the Impressionists, Flaubert's art was "incorrect," anti-academic, the literary equivalent of "broken brushwork." Bypassing the Academy's rules concerning technical procedure, the Impressionists concentrated more on the mode of perception than on the object itself. Flaubert's decentering of the portraiture of Emma corresponds to decentered moments in Impressionist paintings; for example, the inappropriate shadow cast by the parasol in Monet's portraits, or to the intrusive fan obscuring the woman's face in *Berthe Morisot with a Fan* (1872). Like *Madame Bovary*, Impressionist paintings too were accused of being "incoherent," "failures," "and "travesties." The Impressionists were accused of elevating the **ebauche** (sketch) to the status of the finished product. Art critics accused Berthe Morisot, for example, of not taking the trouble to finish her paintings. Flaubert's rendering of Emma's fleeting, inattentive, and selective glance, within what might be called a fragmentary aesthetic of glimpses, corresponds to the selective focus and variable precision of Manet's *Concert aux Tuileries* (1862) where correct composition gives way to a rendering of the modern experience of the **augenblich**, the passing glance and the glimpsing of faces within a swirling crowd. Even Flaubert's choice of writing about "nothing," recalls the Impressionist indifference to subject matter, to Manet's search for the insignificant in his painting, for example. Rather than the grand manner of the **style historique**, the Impressionists, for example in Manet's *Le Vieux musicien* (1862), presented human detritus and lower-class types.

Within this aesthetic of transgression, *Madame Bovary* is a "badly written" novel, much as Godard's *Breathless* is a "badly made film," or *Déjeuner sur l'herbe* a "badly done painting." Even Flaubert's refusal of plot anticipates the Impressionist refusal of grand historical narratives and mythological references.

Flaubert's counterpointing of literary styles, meanwhile, foreshadows the counterpointing of painterly styles that we find in *Déjeuner sur l'herbe*, exhibited just six years after the publication of *Madame Bovary*. What all these works share is their anti-grammaticality, their subversion of the dominant codes of artistic decorum. Indeed, in an illuminating study, Jonathon Culler points out that *Madame Bovary* is less subversive in the surface content of its social portraiture than in its stylistic subversion of a whole gamut of aesthetic norms, notably: (1) **norms of description**, the assumption that every detail must be germane and relevant; (2) **norms of narration**, the assumption that a novel should develop a totalizing meaning revolving around a moral center; (3) **norms of character**, the idea of character as a repository of fixed morals; (4) norms of coherent **theme**. In *Madame Bovary*, the apparent theme – woman corrupted by art – is contradicted by the latent theme – the transparent love of art that animates the book itself. In fact, the theme of the novel cannot be easily summarized; it lacks a teleological movement toward an overriding message. The very interest of the novel, like that of Godard's films, resides in a transgressive "aesthetic of mistakes," in its nature as an "incorrect" and "out of tune" work according to regnant norms.[28]

Madame Bovary, like any text, inevitably enters into the continuing processes of artistic dialogism and intertextuality, leaving new texts in its wake. The novel as hypotext thus generates various hypertexts. The post-text of *Madame Bovary* is vast, and it is both literary and cinematic. Harry Levin mentions a Methodist tract based on the novel, subtitled *The Consequences of Misbehavior*.[29] One of the most inept of the rewritings of *Madame Bovary* is the Italian writer Laura Grimaldi's *Monsieur Bovary* (1991).[30] Dedicated to "All the Men Mistreated by their Wives," the novel aspires to "improve" on Flaubert by upgrading Charles as a character. In a letter addressed to Flaubert himself, the author promises a more logical conclusion seen from Charles's point of view. "*Monsieur Bovary*," she writes to Flaubert, "*c'est moi*." Now Charles is no longer the "paradigmatic cuckold," but rather a sensitive and intelligent being. That relatively rare literary bird called the "misogynistic text by a woman," the "remake" denounces virtually all the women in the novel. The denunciations begin with a somewhat homophobic tirade concerning Charles's mother's miseducation of her son: "it was a miracle that Charles did not turn out effeminate, or worse." They continue with Charles's first "weak and ugly" wife, who Charles began to regard, after a period of insufferable cohabitation, the way he "looked at lizards before he strangled them back in high school." Grimaldi then goes on, in this rewrite aimed at rescuing Monsieur Bovary, to have Charles actually murder his wife, so that her slit throat finally "emitted an agreeable sound," the sound, that is, of her death. The writer acknowledges, in another letter to Flaubert, that the

French author would not have approved of Charles's violent measures, but asks rhetorically: "What other alternative was there?" She re-minds Flaubert of his remark that "women like Emma were crying all over France," but asks him to remember that men like Charles were also crying. In very judgmental, unFlaubertian language, Grimaldi denounces Emma as "hypocritical," "capricious," and "cruel." When Emma strikes their daughter Berthe, Charles wonders if he hadn't "married a monster." It is as if Grimaldi had adopted the perspective, not so much of Charles himself, but rather of one of the unnamed gossips making their hostile observations about their neighbors. Unlike the novel, the rewrite presents a Charles who is completely lucid about his wife's limitations, and when she dies, he does not "shed a single tear." But the rewrite does offer him a (homosocial) happy ending – friendship with Justin, "someone in whom, finally, he could trust." One would like to think that all of this is a feminist satire on machismo, but unfortunately that seems not to be the case.

Renoir's *Madame Bovary*

Madame Bovary is also one of the most filmed of all novels. A partial list would include: two French versions (Renoir in 1934 and Chabrol in 1991); two Hollywood versions, a modern dress update by H. B. Warner called *Unholy Love* (1932) and the Minnelli version in 1949; a German version in 1937; an Argentinian version in 1947; an Italian version in 1969 (*I peccati di Madame Bovary* [Sins of Madame Bovary]); a Russian version by Alexander Sokurov in 1989 (*Spasi i Sokhrani* [Save and Protect]); an Indian (Bollywood) version in 1985; a Portuguese version in 1997 (by Manuel de Oliveira); and a BBC version in 2001. Here I will speak in detail of just four adaptations of *Madame Bovary*, notably those by Jean Renoir, Vincente Minnelli, Ketan Mehta, and Claude Chabrol.

We will not linger much on Jean Renoir's 1934 version of *Madame Bovary*, a film already analyzed in depth by other commentators. Originally three and a half hours in length, the film was cut to two hours at the distributor's insistence, thus giving evidence of a problem encountered only in the cinema. (Renoir joked that the shorter version was interminable, while the longer version seemed much shorter.) What attracted Renoir to the project was the opportunity to work with some of his favorite stage actors, performers like Valentine Tessier (Emma), and his own brother Pierre Renoir (Charles). Renoir's initial motivation seems particularly inappropriate since the novel, with its minimal dialogue, is not theatrical at all. What most strikes us in the Renoir version is its combination

Figure 4.1 Valentine Tessier as Emma in Renoir's *Madame Bovary* (1934), produced by Nouvelle Société des Films (NSF)

The Proto-cinematic Novel

of theatricality (for indoor scenes) and pastoral naturalness (in the outdoor scenes). At the same time, the nature scenes of the film recall in their lyricism the painterly Renoir of *Partie de campagne* (A Day in the Country), reminding us of Jean Renoir's genetic filial link to the celebrated Impressionist painter Pierre Auguste Renoir, famous for his exuberant, luminous renderings of natural scenes and privileged moments of sunlit leisure. In a highly mediated fashion, Renoir picks up on Flaubert's own novelistic anticipations of Impressionist techniques and themes. In the film, Jean Renoir shows great sensitivity to light, to the dappled beauty of the forest leaves during the seduction scene – for example, to the speckled light on Emma's dress – generating a kind of sylvan lyricism.

Although the film never touches directly on what we have called the literary theme – the ways in which Emma is shaped (and misshaped) by her reading – the theme is present in displaced form. Valentine Tessier communicates through her performance style a sense of theatricality and dreamy desire. When she attends the operetta *Lucie de Lammermoor*, she becomes entranced, dizzy; she projects

Chapter 4

herself into the singers' performance. Blind to the erotic nature of her trans-ports, Charles reductively attributes her dizziness to the effect of the gas lamps.[31]

In the Renoir adaptation, Valentine Tessier's theatrical self-staging becomes the performative equivalent of the literariness of the novel. While we do not see Emma read, or hear her speak about reading, or see visual traces of books, she acts out, as it were, the literary commonplaces that have molded her imaginary. For the tension between literature and life, characteristic of the novel, Renoir substitutes the tension between two styles: (1) the (indoor) theatrical acting of the principal players; and (2) the (outdoor) naturalism of the country scenes, with its cows, farms, foliage, and animal noises. The Darius Milhaud music, mean-while – modernist, ethereal, melancholy, subdued, dissonant – might be called "neo-Impressionist," and in this sense provides a musical analogue to the visual impressionism and the proto-modernism of Flaubert's novel. (Renoir's subtle musi-cal choices contrast with the bombastic grandiloquence of the Hollywood-style music chosen for the Minnelli version.) Unlike both the Minnelli and the Chabrol adaptations, the Renoir version eschews voice-over to convey either the voice of the novelist or the voice of the characters. Here the film itself, as the "*grand imagier*" (to use the term Gaudreault borrowed from Albert Laffay) becomes the film's "impersonal" narrator. In this sense, Renoir creates a possible cinematic equivalent for Flaubert's narrator, refined out of existence, dispersed into the characters and their actions, not directly interventionist or judgmental like the Fieldingesque or Balzacian narrator. And Flaubert's intermittent capacity to enter into all his characters without prejudging them here becomes the humanist generosity of Renoir's "everyone-has-his-reasons" approach.

Unlike Flaubert's novel, the Renoir adaptation in a certain sense "desubject-ivizes" Emma's story. The novel, as we have seen, brings us not only into Emma's perspective – we see through her eyes – but even into her very viscera – we feel her heartbeat, sense her dizziness, tingle with her orgasm. The Renoir film, in contrast, lacks even the usual subjectivizing devices of Hollywood cinema. There are very few point-of-view shots to suture us into an individual perspective, few close shots (with the exception of the suicide finale) to convey closely observed emotional reactions, and very little subjectively motivated camera work. On one level, this desubjectivization is typical of Renoir's work, in that Renoir gener-ally favors medium shots or even more inclusive shots, with very few close-ups. Renoir tends to avoid the conventional ping-pong of shot/counter-shot for dia-logue, for example, favoring instead deep focus and multiple spatial planes.

In this sense, Renoir's adaptation might be said to conform to only **one** of the many styles deployed in *Madame Bovary* – the realist style. One might even speak anachronically or transtemporally of the Renoir within Flaubert himself, i.e. the ways in which Flaubert and Renoir share a similar approach to "managing" dialogue and description as part of a sharply imagined space. Both Flaubert and Renoir share a fondness for a multi-planar space peopled with multiple intersecting conversations. Flaubert's journals, in this sense, uncannily anticipate the working notes of a filmmaker. In a letter of September 19, 1852 to Louise Colet concerning the "agricultural fair" passage, Flaubert writes: "I have to place simultaneously, in the same conversation, five or six people (who talk), several others (who are talked about), the whole region, descriptions of persons and things — and amid all this I have to show a gentleman and a lady who begin to fall in love with each other because they have tastes in common."[32] The passage proleptically evokes the future musings of any filmmaker grappling with the challenge of staging the intersecting dialogues of multiple characters against diverse backdrops.

In *Madame Bovary*, Renoir generally adheres to the anti-montage style that is his trademark, emphasizing continuity, long takes, and depth of the field. This rule applies, surprisingly, even in his handling of the very passage that struck Eisenstein as anticipatory of filmic montage: the agricultural fair sequence. In the Renoir version, the juxtaposed speeches of the politician and the Don Juan, which would seem to call for crosscutting and leveling (*mise-en-équivalence*), are dealt with, somewhat counterintuitively, in an anti-montage manner, as if Renoir were deliberately shunning the cues provided both by Flaubert's novel and by Eisenstein's essay.

Renoir does pick up one of the central visual leitmotifs in the novel — mirrors — but with a curious twist. Like Flaubert, Renoir's *mise-en-scène* favors frames within frames, especially in interiors, and on numerous occasions Emma is framed by doors or windows. But, in Flaubert, windows provide a sense both of enclosure and of an opening up onto an elsewhere. In the novel, we look through windows **with** Emma, but in the Renoir adaptation she is **framed by** windows rather than **looking out** of them, a technique which generates a feeling of imprisonment and closure rather than of dreamy escape.

--------------------------- The Minnelli Magic ---------------------------

In 1949, fifteen years after Renoir, Vincente Minnelli also turned to *Madame Bovary*. The Minnelli version has already been rigorously analyzed, by George Bluestone and Stephen Harvey among others, and I will try not to recapitulate what has already been said. Bluestone discusses the adaptation very much within a normative framework wherein both novel and film are seen as having a "vocation for realism," an essential affinity with the natural, material world. For Bluestone, Minnelli "betrays" this vocation by emphasizing the spectacular, the bombastic, the overstated, and the showy. Bluestone speculates that Flaubert, who agonized over refining himself **out** of his work, would be appalled at the "retailing" of Emma's story.[33]

Stephen Harvey, less judgmentally and perhaps more usefully, points out the diverse "mediations" and conjunctural constraints which inflect the Minnelli film: (1) Minnelli's continuing preoccupations as **filmmaker–auteur**: for example, the themes of artistic expression versus conformity, tensions between high and low art, themes which might conceivably align him with Flaubert; (2) the director's **personal problems**, notably the disintegrating mental health of Judy Garland, which led Minnelli to conflate Emma's problems with those of his wife; (3) **professional specialization**: Minnelli's background as art designer makes him emphasize details of decor, costume, and *mise-en-scène*. (One might say that Flaubert's obsession with *le mot juste* becomes an obsession with *le costume juste*); (4) **generic proclivities**, whereby Minnelli's expertise in the musical leads him to search for any possible pretext for grand production numbers in the MGM manner, for example the ball at Vaubyessard; (5) **biography**: Minnelli's "French connection," not only as a designer influenced by Parisian design movements (Art Nouveau, Impressionism, Surrealism) and fashion magazines (*Vogue*) but also because Minnelli at one point aspired to go to Paris to paint; (6) **studio**: MGM as the studio most associated with classy entertainment and a galaxy of popular stars; (7) **censorship pressures**, which led Minnelli to adopt certain strategies for warding off the threat of any potential censorship of the film in the conservative period of the Breen office. By beginning the film with Flaubert's obscenity trial, for example, Minnelli seems to be trying to shame the censors in advance, as if to warn them that any censorship of his film would betray the same short-sighted philistinism displayed by those who persecuted the great writer Flaubert a century earlier.[34]

Minnelli begins, then, with Flaubert's obscenity trial, with James Mason playing Flaubert speaking in his own defense. This brings up a new aspect of "fidelity," in this case fidelity to the historical record. In fact, the *Bovary* trial was nothing like that portrayed in the film. Flaubert did not speak in his own defense, and much of the argument in Flaubert's favor was **ad hominem**, largely resting on Flaubert's status as a bourgeois from a respectable family. The prosecutor, moreover, focused less on the crime of pornography than on the sin of blasphemy, and specifically on Flaubert's constant yoking of sexuality and religiosity.[35]

(The Catholic Church would later accuse Luis Buñuel of the same "sin.") Both prosecutor and defense attorney showed tender concern for the sexually inclined minds of vulnerable young girls (the minds of young boys were presumed not to be in danger). In the film, Minnelli has "Flaubert" (James Mason) speak in his own voice, deploying three classical arguments against censorship: (1) I painted reality ("Madame Bovarys can be found all over France"); (2) I painted vice to exalt virtue; and (3) forgiveness is still among the Christian virtues. But, in fact, the trial was vastly more interesting, a case of warring lawyer-critics deploying divergent **explications de texte**. In advertent witness to the indeterminacy of Flaubert's text, the prosecution quoted passages from the book to show that it was a lascivious portrait of a serial adulteress. The defense contextualized the very same passages to show that the novel portrayed reality in a manner consistent with Christian values and societal norms. In the film, meanwhile, the voice of Flaubert speaking (in synchronous sound) in his own defense at the trial then segues to that same voice, but now with an altered function and status, as voice-over narration for Flaubert's account of Emma's early life.

Narratologists distinguish between the biographical author (here Flaubert) and the novelistic narrator (the narrator of *Madame Bovary*). Minnelli conflates the two by having the voice of "Gustave Flaubert," speaking in his own defense, mutate into the voice-over narration of the film. But quite apart from this theoretically problematic conflation of author and narrator, the tone and content of the voice-over goes against the grain of Flaubert's own aesthetic. Flaubert's narrator in *Madame Bovary* is largely refined out of existence, dispersed into his characters or into a diffuse textual modality of traces and effects. Bluestone is quite right, therefore, in remarking on the strangeness of Minnelli's insistence on reinscribing the traces of a narrational, enunciative presence which Flaubert himself had labored so hard to efface. The novel's narrator is largely implicit, a diffuse agency to be inferred on the basis of style and tone and other subtle textual cues. Minnelli's narrator, in contrast, is physically embodied, particularized through posture, body language, timbre and grain of voice. Minnelli's narrator, unlike Flaubert's, is interventionist; he explicitly condemns Emma's dreams as "silly" and "absurd" and "impossible," in hyper-explicit and harshly judgmental formulations more reminiscent of a Balzac or a Dickens than of Flaubert. James Mason's "Flaubert" argues that Emma is not the shameless hussy described by the prosecutor but rather an unhappy woman victimized by pulpy romances and fashion magazines. Yet here too we discern still another paradox: whereas "Flaubert" defends Emma from her accusers in the opening sequence, the film itself as a whole renders a rather ambivalent, and often harsh, judgment on the heroine.

Instead of Flaubert's impersonal narration, based on partial views and limited perception, Minnelli gives us Flaubert/Mason's know-it-all, voice-of-God commentary, buttressed by the rather manipulative commentative music which virtually dictates our mood and response. Music, in this sense, is "adjectival." It qualifies and characterizes, and directs, rather like an emotional traffic cop, our spectatorial response. It is hard to imagine Flaubert ever being so explicitly moralistic; first, because of his empathy with the heroine; and, second, because his aesthetic was designed to leave a space for the reader's judgment, to leave questions ultimately open. One is struck by Flaubert's indirection in the novel, by his refusal to be explicit, by his way of deploying apparently trivial details to prod the reader to **infer** judgments which he himself refuses to state. The uncut pages of Charles's medical books, for example, lead us to infer that Charles is a mediocre doctor who does not keep up with the research in his field, yet Flaubert never uses the word "mediocre." Similarly, Flaubert shows Emma gazing with admiration at a slobbering and deaf aristocrat at the Ball at Vaubyessard, yet he never describes Emma as "naïve" or the aristocrat as "decadent."

The paradox in Minnelli is that he makes Flaubert, the consummate artist, express philistine opinions about art. The film's Flaubert proffers two of the most hackneyed clichés about art. First, he argues that art simply shows us "reality," drawn simply and directly from "life." What disappears, in this claim, is Flaubert's meticulous care to shape impressions through **le mot juste**. Second, Minnelli's Flaubert claims that he shows us vice in order to preach virtue. This latter point seems more redolent of hypocritical Defoe-style sanctimony (or of the Hollywood ethos of titillating moralism) than of anything the historical Flaubert would have said or thought. And if the Flaubert of Minnelli's film condemns Emma's artsy dreams as "silly," what do we make of Flaubert's notorious identification with Emma, his famous declaration that "*Emma Bovary, c'est moi*?" Through Emma, Flaubert exorcized his **own** love of a certain kind of literature. He identified with Emma's vibrant artistic sensibility – evident in her rapturous response to music, to theater, to literature – and he rendered her consciousness via affectionate pastiches of precisely the romantic literature that he himself had formerly (and perhaps still) loved and which he was now only partially repudiating.

What becomes, then, of the "literary theme" in the Minnelli version? Renoir, as we have seen, shifts the theme to the register of theatricality and performance. In Minnelli it is referenced explicitly – indeed, Minnelli's version has the signal merit of being one of the few adaptations which **does** reference this absolutely fundamental theme – both verbally (through dialogue) and through images and music. Here we do see Emma actually reading, and the frame is frequently filled with books. But the larger theme of literary influence is dispersed onto a more comprehensive entity: the arts, and especially the visual arts. Thus the novel's portrayal of Emma's adolescent passion for bookreading becomes, in the film, a passion for a panoply of **visual** images: book covers, portraits, landscape paintings, fashion magazines, and portraits. The literary theme is expressed through performance, in the emphasis on Emma as a performer who plays various roles: grande dame, caring mother, seducer, desperate for financial help. In a transposed sense, Minnelli reproduces the mingled distance and sympathy which both he and Flaubert share in relation to Emma Bovary; in both novel and film, we look with Emma while also looking at her. Emma is criticized by the off-screen narrator, but she is also herself an artist (like Flaubert and like Minnelli). She arranges her bedroom as an artist would. Indeed, Stephen Harvey points out that Emma's bedroom, evoked in repeated pan shots, resembles Minnelli's own workplace, where he would prepare a scene by tacking suggestive, potentially usable, bits of visuals to the wall.[36]

The narrated sequence which charts the development of Emma's adolescent tastes begins with a mirror and ends with a window, thus picking up on two pervasive imagistic leitmotifs pervading the novel. Interestingly, both mirrors and windows have served as two classic metaphors for the arts in general and for the cinema in particular. Shakespeare's Hamlet asked the players to "hold the mirror up to nature," while Stendhal defined the novel as "a mirror moving along a highway." Both literary fiction and the cinema have also been seen as "windows" on the world, with the difference that the cinema's "window" is quasi-literal: the camera lens as window, the projector lens as window, the projection booth as window, and so forth. In the history of film theory, as well, both of these images – cinema as window and cinema as mirror – have also formed recurrent tropes. More aesthetically Janus-faced than the trope of the window, which is almost invariably associated with realism, the trope of the mirror can evoke either realism, since it reflects what it captures in the world, or reflexivity, since it evokes both narcissism – authors look at themselves in the mirror – and *mise-en-abyme*. The mirror metaphor was explored in depth by Christian Metz, in terms of Lacan's "mirror stage," in *The Imaginary Signifier*, while the idea that cinema is a "mirror of the world" has long been a commonplace of film criticism.

The decor of Emma's bedroom condenses and anticipates a number of themes and later moments in the film. The mirror foreshadows other mirrors in the film: the ornate, oval mirror which frames Emma at Vaubyessard, the clouded mirror in the Rouen hotel, the hand-held mirror that frames her exhausted face on the eve of death. The equestrian paintings anticipate Emma's horse riding and affair with Rodolphe. Many of the images have clear aristocratic class connotations. The image of Lord Byron anticipates Rodolphe as ersatz Byronesque rake, who possesses Byron's legendary sexual prowess but who lacks the English poet's literary talent. The convent scenes show a cloistered, all-female space, yet nevertheless phallocentric and male-centered, without men, yet nevertheless "waiting for men," whether in the iconic form of the crucified Jesus or in the sung male heroism of love ballads. Emma in particular is waiting for her knight on horseback, who turns out to be only a country doctor of modest talents. The sequence of Emma and Charles's first meeting departs from the book, where Charles scarcely notices Emma, to become a dreamlike encounter, in conformity with the Hollywood convention of the **coup de foudre** (love at first sight). In the humble setting of a provincial farm, Charles is surprised to discover a refined young woman who stands out from her humble surroundings, someone with a surprising vocation for elegance. Minnelli thus translates into images Flaubert's notion of Emma as **la fleur poussée dans le fumier**, the flower in the manure pile.

Like the film as a whole, the sequence of the first encounter between Emma and Charles betrays a number of tensions and contradictions. How can one reconcile boredom and spectacle, a "book about nothing" with the spectacular, star-studded entertainment associated with Hollywood in general and MGM in particular? While the voice-over commentary condemns Emma's romanticism, the film itself romanticizes France and, to some extent, adultery. While the commentary condemns art-stimulated dreams, Hollywood, of which Minnelli forms an integral part, was known as the "dream factory." While Minnelli censures romanticism, the very style of his film is romantic. The lush orchestral music and the soft romantic backlighting further nourish this romanticism. Minnelli is especially fond of the romantic trope John Ruskin called the "pathetic fallacy," i.e. the literary procedure which attributes feelings to nature, for example by having the metaphorically charged tempestuous feelings of characters coincide with literal storms, a characteristic device of romantic art, with its relentless anthropomorphization of nature. Flaubert/Mason as voice-over narrator censures "society" for teaching Emma to be romantic, a dreamer, unequipped for the real world, to despise the everyday. But all of these accusations could have just as easily been tendered against Hollywood itself, whose "dream factory" was blueprinted to stimulate the exoticizing fantasies of the provincial Emmas not only of the United States but also of the entire world.

Precisely because the novel *Madame Bovary* is such a stylistically innovative work, the filmmaker adapting it is confronted with a number of rhetorical and stylistic challenges. One has to do with Flaubert's use of the imperfect, or the past habitual tense, as an apt device for expressing the stifling monotony of provincial life. In one scene, Minnelli deals with the challenge of the imperfect through a transposition in tense: he has Emma speak in the future tense as she observes from her doorway what is to her an unbearably tedious provincial scene: "And now Justin will sweep the sidewalk. And now Homais will cross the street and then spit." The technique conveys the numbing predictability of her provincial life, its unending reiteration of the same. The scene also has a self-reflexive dimension, however: Emma's predictive statements, if one switches them into the imperative mode, become uncannily reminiscent of a director's cues to players and extras: "And now Homais, come down the street; and now, Justin, sweep the sidewalk." Here we have yet another sense in which Minnelli sometimes aligns himself with Flaubert but also with Emma.

Not surprisingly, Minnelli often "amplifies" the novelistic passages – for example the Vaubyessard Ball – which suggest even the vaguest excuse for a dazzling production number. In the novel, the ball scene takes only a few pages, but Minnelli turns it into a gigantic production number of the kind for which he was famous. The ball becomes the scene of Emma's exaltation and Charles's humiliation, with both conditions hyperbolized in the Hollywood spectacular style; Emma's enchanted elegance contrasts with Charles's inebriated boorishness. The only man at the ball not graced with a mustache, Charles is ignored by the aristocratic guests; even the butler looks down on him. But this humiliation is also clearly gendered. Unlike Charles, Emma possesses corporeal and cultural capital: her body, her looks, her literate charm, make her desirable for the aristocrats, as mistress, at least, if not as wife and potential heir. This gendered system is then mapped onto the Hollywood star system. Emma/Jennifer Jones becomes the **star** of the ball, as she was not in the novel. The novel's Emma is a minor player at the ball, in a situation where sexual liaisons between a middle-class woman and an aristocrat would most likely have to be kept secret. The film's *mise-en-scène*, in contrast, has all eyes converge on her, thus constructing her as "star." Minnelli also has Rodolphe dance with Emma, whereas in the novel Rodolphe was not even present at the ball. In this sense Minnelli adheres to the Hollywood principle of narrative streamlining, of emphasizing the long-term trajectories of couples as a structuring identificatory principle.

In musical terms, Minnelli commissioned composer Miklós Rózsa to write a "neurotic waltz," which would reproduce Emma's disoriented exhilaration, which is achieved in the film not only through the music but also thanks to a camera that waltzes through a series of 360-degree pans, in a cinematic equivalent of Flaubert's mimetically waltzing prose. Like the novel, the film makes us feel Emma's corporeal sensations. While many adaptations of *Madame Bovary*, for example Chabrol's, simply record the pro-filmic dance, Minnelli has the camera,

Figure 4.2 Emma as star in Minnelli's *Madame Bovary* (1949), produced by Metro-Goldwyn-Mayer (MGM)

as if by contagion, itself dance, in a kind of bourgeois version of Jean Rouch's ethnographic **cine-transe**. Indeed, the contagion of character and style evokes, again, Pasolini's "cinema of poetry" as the filmic equivalent of Flaubert's **style indirect libre**, whereby the character's frenzied emotional state – in this case the swirling vertigo of the dance – becomes the pretext for stylistic virtuosity.

A kind of interior crosscutting within the scene alternates shots showing Emma drunk on dance and flirtation, with shots of Charles stumbling around in an ever-more drunken state. In this beautifully orchestrated and choreographed sequence, the spectator divides sympathies between both Charles and Emma, feeling sorry for the former and happy for the latter. Yet ultimately Charles's social **gaucherie** becomes an annoying obstacle to the naughty, graceful glide of adulterous pleasure and enchantment which we as spectators also want. But the real climax is reached in the highly stylized shot of Emma regarding herself in the oval mirror, surrounded by elegant aristocratic suitors, where it becomes unclear whether we are seeing reality or Emma's idealized fantasy of it. Minnelli's "promotion" of Emma to a starring position also has a clear cultural/political dimension. In the novel's depiction of the ball, Emma suffers the slings and arrows of social injustice and middle-class **resentment**; she notes, for example, that much less attractive women are admired more than she is simply because of their social status. But in the film, her triumph at the ball gives voice to a profoundly American vision of equal opportunity and meritocracy. In the land of Hollywood, everyone presumably can be a star, just as in the US "anyone can become president." Class, an insurmountable obstacle in the novel, is of trifling importance in the American film.

Minnelli "mines" the novel, as it were, not only for possible production numbers but also for potential melodramatic and spectacular scenes. This melodramatic penchant, often associated with the "women's picture," dominates Minnelli's treatment of the passage where Emma receives Rodolphe's note informing her that he is not going to elope with her. The novel has Emma receive the note and grieve because of it. Flaubert makes us identify with her beating heart, with her blurred vision, with her nauseated vertigo. In the film, Minnelli manages events so as to place Emma in a lonely street, breathlessly waiting for the coach that she is certain that Rodolphe has arranged for her, and then have her become disoriented when the coach fails to stop for her. The scene resonates with bravura sound effects: the loud rumble of the horses' hooves; the "sympathetic weather" thunderstorms; the grandiloquent music, reminding us of the etymological link of music and **melo**drama. On every register, Minnelli cultivates an aesthetic of crescendo and excess, in contradiction, again, with a dedramatized "novel about nothing," but effective in terms of mainstream entertainment norms.

The film carries other traces of dominant Hollywood norms. The style of the film is, generally speaking, what linguists call "redundant," i.e. it repetitively conveys the same message through the diverse tracks. Music, dialogue, performance, for example in the just-analyzed sequence, all reinforce the same melodramatic effect. While Flaubert prefers irony and inference without explicit statement, Minnelli seeks above all clarity of judgment and motivation so that the spectator will not be confused by complexity. Thus Minnelli has Charles call attention to his own inadequacies: "I'm not exciting, Emma . . . I'm not a good doctor." The explicitness is not only characterological, it is sociological, as when Charles explains to Emma that "we are peasants," much as characters in an Ionesco play might explain to each other that "we are middle-class characters living in the suburbs of London." Moreover, perhaps in conformity with the gendered decorum of Hollywood films of the period, Minnelli "improves" the image of Charles Bovary. Minnelli's idealizing representation contrasts with the novel's clear belittling of Charles, where Charles is an uxorious, pathetic cuckold. Minnelli's Charles, in contrast, is depicted as wise, caring, understanding toward Emma, and courageous in relation to others. Aware of his limitations, Minnelli's Charles, unlike Flaubert's, **refuses** to perform the operation on Hippolyte's clubfoot. Minnelli's Charles is more lucid and more virile, even administering the standard masculine corrective slap to Emma when she misbehaves. Played by a very popular actor of the period (Van Heflin) often cast for war-hero roles, Charles here undergoes a kind of patriarchal upgrading, as if what later came to be called "family values" could not allow for the humiliation of the paterfamilias. And in a zero-sum game, the upgrading of Charles goes hand in hand with the downgrading of Emma.

Rodolphe too gets a masculinist upgrading. In the novel, Rodolphe is a cynical rake, a provincial Don Juan. He calculates mentally that seducing Emma would require only "three words of gallantry," but he worries **in advance** about how to get rid of her ("*comment s'en débarrasser ensuite*"). The film, in contrast, makes Rodolphe, as incarnated by the stellar French lover Louis Jourdain, more sincere, less mediocre, and here too the image of Emma suffers correspondingly. While in the novel Rodolphe is a charlatan posing as a romantic, in the film he is closer to a **real** romantic, a plausible avatar of Emma's literature-fed dreams.

In its acerbic satire on the corruption embodied by Homais, and more generally in its indictment of Emma's social surroundings, Flaubert's novel is clearly more socially corrosive than the Minnelli adaptation. Emma's slow slide into debt, for example, can be seen as a proleptic version of pathological consumerism, a literalization of the "shop-till-you-drop" imperative. Emma's consumerist mania is as destructive as her adulteries; in her purchases and borrowing she finds death on the installment plan. Emma's sexual desire runs parallel to what might be called her "consuming desires," skillfully stimulated by her "pusher" L'heureux, whose very name incarnates the "happiness," the **promesse de bonheur**, implicitly promised the consumer. (Zola called his Paris department store "Au Bonheur des Dames.") The film, in contrast, shies away from social critique. Relatively apolitical, Minnelli seems to think that the basic problem in nineteenth-century French society was not its inequitable division of wealth or its penchant for rewarding dishonesty but rather its tendency to implant impossible dreams in the minds of young girls. Minnelli's choice of eliminating virtually all of the scenes in which Emma does not play a role, furthermore, has the effect of muffling Flaubert's incisive social satire. L'heureux, for Flaubert the incarnation of greed and manipulation, in Minnelli seems more like a normal businessman. Homais too, Flaubert's prototype of the secular, complacent, servile bourgeois, undeserving winner of the prestigious Legion of Honor, is rendered by Minnelli as somewhat less repulsive than in the novel.

Although Minnelli deserves credit for being one of the few directors to capture the art/life dialectic that animates the novel, his film also reflects a kind of aesthetic mainstreaming. The stylistic experimentalism of the novel – what Jonathon Culler sees as its systematic subversion of descriptive, stylistic, and ethical norms[37] – largely disappears in the film. Indeed, to my knowledge, no adaptation of *Madame Bovary* has tried to subvert the stylistic norms of dominant cinema the way Flaubert subverted the stylistic norms of the canonical "well-written" novel.

Chabrolian Realism

At first glance, Chabrol's 1991 adaptation of *Madame Bovary* offers the kind of "match" between author and filmmaker missing in both Renoir's and Minnelli's versions. Not only did Chabrol frequently express admiration for nineteenth-century realist writers like Balzac and Flaubert, but also both he and Flaubert formed part of innovative movements – the classical French nineteenth-century novel and the French New Wave – both linked to the ideal of "realism." The New Wave expresses its link to realism through its admiration for Italian neo-realisms, through Bazin's preference for *mise-en-scène* over montage, or through **boutades** like Godard's "cinema is truth 24 times/second." Like Flaubert, Chabrol has been the chronicler of provincial boredom (for example, in *Le Beau Serge*), middle-class adultery (*La Femme infidèle*), and the self-

The Proto-cinematic Novel

Chapter 4

destructive pursuit of illusory desires (*Les Bonnes femmes*). Like Flaubert, Chabrol has been the acerbic critic of bourgeois duplicity, for example in *Le Boucher*. And Flaubert's "book about nothing" anticipates Chabrol's essayistic defense of *"des petits sujects,"* i.e. modest quotidian subjects as opposed to grandiose themes – a provincial love affair rather than the Battle of Waterloo. Like Flaubert, Chabrol can be seen as the ironic anatomist of mimetic desire and social aspiration. In *Les Biches*, the young bisexual Why appropriates the identity of her beloved/hated lesbian lover Frederique (the plot was loosely based on Patricia Highsmith's *The Talented Mr Ripley*). Like Flaubert, Chabrol is fascinated by intelligent women who tower over the mediocre men who circumscribe them. The female characters of *Les Bonnes femmes* (1960) and *Les Noces rouges* (1973) all remind us, in their way, of Emma Bovary.

To prepare for his adaptation, Chabrol looked not only at *Madame Bovary* itself but also at Flaubert's letters, at critical analyses of *Madame Bovary*, at illustrations of the novel, at extrapolations and parodies, and even at Flaubert's preparatory drafts. Just as Flaubert got physically sick while writing about Emma's suicide, nauseated by "the taste of arsenic" in his mouth, Chabrol became ill while filming the same scene. Chabrol's film is above all the fruit of an immense admiration for Flaubert. Unlike Minnelli, Chabrol consciously strove for "fidelity," his professed goal being to make the film Flaubert would have made had he had a camera instead of a pen. Here the metaphor of the **camera-stylo** (camera-pen), coined in 1948 by Alexandre Astruc, resonates with a specific approach to adaptation. Chabrol went so far as to claim that the very rhythm of Flaubert's sentences determined the montage of the film. Whenever the novel indicated an angle of vision, which, as we have seen, it often does, Chabrol respected Flaubert's verbal "set-ups" to the letter. *Madame Bovary*, Chabrol remarked, provides a "ready-made script," since Flaubert worked like a filmmaker, researching locales and dialogue. For Chabrol, "fidelity" entailed the detailed reconstruction of the Norman countryside, with hundreds of extras dressed in period costumes fashioned by Corinne Jorry from portraits by Winterhalter and the Duboffe Brothers. If Flaubert mentioned a specific forest (e.g. the Forest of Argueil), Chabrol tried to film there. This fastidiousness about detail, reminiscent of Flaubert's own careful research into provincial life, even included looking for textiles and clothing in Parisian flea markets, or having it made on handlooms by silk manufacturers.

The Chabrol adaptation betrays the influence of the Renoir version, both in the selection of incidents treated and in its basically realist aesthetic. Chabrol also shows a Renoir-like tenderness for nature. If the Minnelli film favors a "gothic" look based on chiaroscuro, the cinematography in the Chabrol film at

Figure 4.3 Chabrol's *Madame Bovary* (1991), produced by CED Productions / Club des Investissments / Conseil General de L'Eure / Conseil Regional de Haute-Normandie / France 3 Cinéma / MK2 Productions

times creates a diffuse, impressionist look, with shots of mist-laden pastures and fuzzy images of flowers that recall the paintings of Monet's garden. Like Renoir, Chabrol also downplays the "literary-parodic" side of the novel, although he does use bits of voice-over narration borrowed from the novel. A male voice, evocative of the Flaubertian narrator, reads a series of passages. During Emma's agony, a pause in the dialogue opens a space for the reading of what Chabrol called "five of the finest lines Flaubert ever wrote." The final shot of the film is made to coincide with the last paragraph of the novel. Yet Chabrol's approach to the narrator is very different from Minnelli's. While Minnelli conflates the biographical Flaubert with the actor James Mason as character, in order to provide an ideological rationale for the adaptation, Chabrol emphasizes the literary status of the text through the voice-over. The film illustrates and translates the words of the novel, and the voice-over comes to the rescue whenever visual translation seems impossible. Chabrol, and his narrator, present themselves modestly, as what François Jost calls the "servants of the text."[38]

Chabrol, the *cineaste* of lost illusions, makes surprisingly little of Emma's illusions. He selects for the voice-over narration the relatively "flat" passages

– prose which, like Charles's conversation, is "as flat as a sidewalk," not the bravura "anthological" passages of literary pastiche. Nor does Chabrol depict Emma as particularly dreamy. There is little reference in the film to her reading, to her convent-year daydreams, or to her wild ambitions. While Minnelli exacerbates and hyperbolizes Emma's romanticism, Chabrol alludes to it indirectly through the verbally evoked romantic *topoi* – sublime nature, the power of music – engaged in the flirtatious conversations with Leon. As a result, Emma here seems to match her environment; we do not have the sense of a personage whose violent and romanesque imagination scrapes against and **transcends** her environment.

Unlike Minnelli, Chabrol does not idealize Charles; rather, he insists on his banal, uncomprehending nature. The fact that Chabrol elides both the beginning and the end of the book, i.e. Charles's childhood and the passage where Charles reads Rodolphe's letters, further diminishes our sympathy with Charles. The master of the manipulation of point of view and an admirer of Alfred Hitchcock, Chabrol disperses the point of view, having it oscillate between characters. Like the book, the film at times locks us into Emma's perspective and at other times sutures us into the vantage point of other characters such as Charles, Leon, Rodolphe, L'heureux, and Homais. Like Flaubert himself, Chabrol seems to want to simultaneously embody the perspective of everyone, and of no one. In this sense, Chabrol approximates Flaubert's view of the author as comparable to the "God of creation," invisible yet dispersed into his creation.

At times, Chabrol deploys something close to what we earlier called Flaubert's technique of "variable focus," moving us in and out of various subjectivities. During Emma's agony, for example, zoom-outs take us away from close-ups of Isabelle Huppert's face to a more cold and distanced perspective on the other witnesses at the scene. Occasionally, a "soliloquy" technique allows the spectator to "overhear" Emma articulating her most intimate feelings, as when she ecstatically repeats her mantra: "I have a lover! I have a lover!" And Chabrol uses reported speech to have Rodolphe soliloquize about the elegance of his well-crafted "Dear Emma" rejection letter, thus emphasizing the snide insincerity that Minnelli tended to obfuscate. By having Rodolphe look at his own letter and "pronounce it good," Flaubert/Chabrol has him echo God's words about the Creation, while also recalling Flaubert's analogizing of lower-case literary creator with upper-case Divinity.

Chabrol deploys diverse strategies to render Emma's subjectivity. First, he exploits performance, in the form of Isabelle Huppert's acting, which begins as somewhat bloodless, but comes alive as the film proceeds. (Huppert enacts this same metamorphosis, from cold and repressed to passionate and obsessive, in the more recent film *The Piano Teacher*, 2001). Under Chabrol's direction, Huppert counterpoints two acting styles; one bland and inexpressive, when she is bored and out of sorts, the other passionate and vibrant, with her face flush with blood. Huppert shows an Emma transfigured by passion; while she normally looks pale and depressive, she comes alive and radiates erotic energy when she is in love. Huppert portrays Emma as a person of appetite, orally inclined, as when she licks the blood from her own wound, or probes the bottom of the cup with her tongue. Her repeated expression "I'm thirsty" takes on a quasi-metaphorical quality. During the deathbed scene, out-of-focus shots render Emma's confusion, the equivalents of the perturbed vision offered by the novel. Emma's hallucinations prior to her suicide, meanwhile, are rendered by *Marnie*-like fades to bright red.

Huppert remarked that she deliberately went in and out of character, as someone simultaneously inside and observing her character – "*Emma Bovary, ce n'est pas moi*" as she herself put it. In an instance of performance as interpretation, this interpretative move recapitulates Flaubert's own narrational procedures on the register of performance, and particularly Flaubert's oscillating and variable identification with Emma. At times, virtuoso camera movements give voice to the expansive side of Emma's personality. During the Vaubyessard Ball, for example, the camera rises elegantly to give a sweeping aerial view of the dancers, and then descends again to floor level. When she and Rodolphe have made love in the woods: the camera rises ecstatically into the foliage, to the accompaniment of choral music. For Guy Austin, these rising and falling movements encapsulate the pattern of Emma's life; the camera returns to earth, rather like her dreams which, we are told in a voice-over from the text, fall into the mud "like wounded swallows."[39]

The sumptuous clothing in *Madame Bovary* in some ways compensates for Isabelle Huppert's relatively cool style of acting, while also conveying a message about Emma's emotional trajectory. As Emma Wilson puts it, Chabrol's Emma "begins in virginal white" but progresses toward "rose pink and dove grey and an illicit scarlet evening dress, then gauzy black silk with fitted bodice, dashing hats with veils and ribbons, and trailing laces." As a "clothes fetishist," Emma enlists style into her bookish performativity, embellishing the tawdriness of her everyday life. Her "masquerade of femininity" hides her "disenfranchised status."[40] *Mise-en-scène*, furthermore, conveys her changing positionality vis-à-vis her two lovers. Chabrol's *mise-en-scène* places Emma on a higher level than Leon, for example, instantiating Flaubert's judgment that "Leon was more her mistress, than she his."

Like most adaptations of *Madame Bovary*, the Chabrol version eliminates Charles's first marriage, beginning instead with Charles's visit to Emma's family farm. Streamlining Flaubert's story, Chabrol leaves out most of what comes before Emma's first encounter with Charles, along with virtually everything that comes after her death (Charles reading Rodolphe's letter, the meeting between husband and lover). Worried that male spectators, especially, would identify too easily with the male figure rather than with Emma, Chabrol downplays identification with Charles without eliminating it altogether. Chabrol reminds us that Flaubert said "*Emma Bovary, c'est moi;*" he never said: "**Charles** Bovary, c'est *moi.*" Nonetheless, Chabrol did actually film a key passage ignored by all the other adaptations, to wit the opening gambit of the novel where young pupils (whom we never encounter again) observe the newcomer Charles's awkward premiere at school. He eliminated the sequence from the final version, however, finding that it disturbed the overall coherence of the point of view. Chabrol recognized, if only by indirection, the provocative "incorrectness" of Flaubert's opening.

Chabrol inventoried and recorded Flaubert's myriad references to sound in the novel – animal noises, church bells, and so on – and used them to "fill out" the sound track. We are reminded again of film's "automatic difference," and especially of its capacity to incorporate **actual** performed sounds and music. While Flaubert mentions a Scarlatti sonata which "made Emma dreamy," a filmmaker like Chabrol has the option of playing the sonata on the sound track, thus making not only his **character** dreamy but also making the **spectator** dreamy, without ever having to use the phrase "making dreamy."

In generic terms, *Madame Bovary* constitutes Chabrol's foray into the "heritage genre," i.e. the wave of quality costume dramas from the 1980s and 1990s, a genre parallel to the "nostalgia" films of the same period. In some ways a reincarnation of the "tradition of quality" tradition so excoriated by Truffaut and the New Wave, the heritage genre, as exemplified by films such as *The Bostonians* (1984), *A Passage to India* (1984), *A Room with a View* (1985), and *The Age of Innocence* (1993), tended to favor historical and literary themes pursued within a classical aesthetic, usually featuring international stars, aristocratic locales, high production values, and lush symphonic music. According to Andrew Higson, the genre favors long takes and deep focus rather than close-ups and rapid cutting. Chabrol's *Madame Bovary*, the work of the most aesthetically conservative of the New Wave directors, both conforms to and departs from this schema.[41] It relays the literary and historical theme with high production values within a long-take and deep-focus style, but the players are all French and the "lush music" is kept to a minimum.

The Vaubyessard Ball sequence offers a good example of the "heritage" style. This four-and-a-half minute sequence, composed of thirty-one shots, begins with a wide-angled shot of the uniformed musicians, revealing an impressive display of wealth and opulence and cultural capital. Chabrol shows Charles's awkward out-of-placeness in this milieu, for example, by having him confuse the name of the wine being offered him by a servant with the servant's own name. Emma, meanwhile, tries to distance herself from Charles by walking ahead of him, looking away from him, and waltzing out of his range of vision. While Charles frets about his physical discomfort in formal dress, she eavesdrops on the conversations of other guests, awed by their cosmopolitan banter about gambling, love, and foreign travel. The overheard name of "Berthe" becomes the inspiration, later, for the choice of name for her own child. While Charles looks adoringly at her, she ignores him to look with insatiable curiosity at what is for her the brave new world of the provincial aristocracy.

Chabrol handles the Vaubyessard Ball scene quite differently from Minnelli. While, for Minnelli, Emma is the star and the center of attention, for Chabrol, she is an outsider, a spectator with her nose pressed against the window, admiring an elite world to which she has no real access. Unlike the Minnelli version, in Chabrol it is not Emma who complains about the heat – leading to the breaking of the windows – but another guest. While Minnelli is hyperbolic and spectacular in his treatment of the ball, Chabrol is flat, discreet, understated, almost minimalist. While Minnelli has his camera dance along with Emma, Chabrol has the camera, here identified with Charles's look, coolly observe Emma dancing. François Jost suggests (somewhat overstatedly) that in the Chabrol version "all interiority vanishes. The visualizable becomes the visible and the audible, reduced to a few pertinent elements, as we remain outside of the character, in no way sharing her perceptual point-of-view whether ocular or auricular. In short, Flaubert as re-envisioned by Robbe-Grillet."[42] I would suggest, rather, that the sequence orchestrates interiority and exteriority in a manner which approximates Flaubert's free indirect style. The conjunction of close-shots of her face with conversations overheard by her aligns us with her mental universe; we "see her overhearing," as it were.

Unlike Renoir, with his *mise en-scène* and depth-of-field approach, Chabrol treats the agricultural fair sequence by crosscutting Rodolphe's romantic declarations with the political declarations from the square below. Chabrol's rendering of this passage recalls both Eisenstein's comments on the passage as anticipatory of cinematic montage and Pudovkin's comments on how to handle crowd scenes. Chabrol follows Pudovkin's recommendation that such scenes be filmed from various angles and heights, mingling general views with shots of small subgroups seen from the ground. But, at the same time, he strictly follows Flaubert's cues about where to cut between contrasting snippets of conversation, thus counterpointing two forms of flattery and seduction, sexual and political.

The Proto-cinematic Novel

Chapter 4

Chabrol renders Flaubert's imperfect tense, meanwhile, not through the future tense (à la Minnelli) but rather through a combination of voice-over narration (quoting Flaubert's observations in the imperfect about the predictabilities of provincial life), combined with the *mise-en-scène* of events in the film's present. One such scene presents a typical Sunday, where Leon recites a poem – Lamartine's *Le Lac* – which has to do, significantly, with the passage of time. The scene counterpoints multiple temporalities: the romantic time of the Lamartinian "stay-moment-thou-art-so-fair" motif ("*O Temps, suspends ton vol*") which favors the mythic eternalization of privileged moments, and the quotidian time of domesticity, boredom, and repetition. The scene "conjugates" diverse times both in the grammatical and the dramaturgical sense: the time and tense of the voice-over (in the imperfect), the time of the poem read by Leon, and the time of the *mise-en-scène* of the typical activities, forming, to use terms drawn from Metz's "*grande syntagmatique*," at once an "ordinary sequence," a "scene," and a "bracket syntagm," all deployed so as to convey a sense of what Genette calls the "iterative."[43]

Like Renoir, but unlike Minnelli, Chabrol does not play up the literary side of *Madame Bovary*. Apart from a reference to Emma having won a "reading prize," and her own claim that she has "read all the books," there is only one shot of Emma actually reading (while lunching with Charles). Perhaps Chabrol did not regard the act of reading as terribly visual or cinematic. Three slow pages in a novel, the director pointed out, do not destroy the experience of the reader, but three tedious minutes in a film can destroy the spectatorial pleasure (and thus the commercial potential) of a film. While Renoir stages literariness through theatricality, and Minnelli evokes it though the visual arts, Chabrol achieves the same effect through dialogue, by having the characters (especially Emma and Leon) mouth the *topoi* of romantic literature: the sublimity of mountains and the sea, music as the language of the soul, and so forth.

From Bollywood to Woody Allen

Every adaptation of *Madame Bovary* filters the novel through the grid of a national culture and through a national film industry, with its generic corollaries and so forth. The Minnelli version clearly, and perhaps inevitably, "Americanizes" Flaubert. The Indian version of *Madame Bovary*, meanwhile, Ketan Mehta's *Maya Memsaab* (1992) – "Maya" is Hindi for "illusion" – "Indianizes" the Flaubert novel. In the Mehta version, the French novel is filtered and channeled not only through the conventions of the "art film" but also through the conventions of Bombay ("Bollywood") popular cinema. *Maya* straddles and to some extent scrambles the frontiers between a number of genres: mystery, musical, erotic film, popular, and art cinema. While relatively realist within Bollywood norms, *Maya* also features the extravagant musical production numbers typical of Bombay cinema. Through a generic division of labor, the non-musical episodes represent life in a fairly verisimilar manner, while the songs represent life as dreamed and fantasized. (Film analysts have often said that music, in the American musical for example, forms its "id," its latent desire, while the narrative proper represents the reality principle and the superego.) While the plot resembles life, as Ratnapriya Das puts it, the songs represent dreams.[44]

Unlike the novel, *Maya* begins as a murder mystery, with two investigators trying to discern whether Maya/Emma died by suicide or by murder. The film then gives way, à la *Citizen Kane*, to successive testimony from witnesses who knew Emma: the pharmacist who sells her the poison, the servant who reads her diary, Charu (Charles Bovary), Lalit, Rudra, and even the crippled beggar. The occasional voice-overs, interestingly, are not given (as in both the Minnelli and the Chabrol versions) to the narrator, but rather to Emma/Maya herself. As Maya is cradling her baby, Chaya, for example, she muses: "For many days nothing happened. Oh, I have a daughter now – Chaya. Maya's chaya (shadow). Everyone says I'm lucky – I have everything. Now the dreams don't come anymore." Maya's words ironically echo Flaubert's own words about *Madame Bovary* as a novel in which "nothing happens." Mehta also makes a substantial change in Emma's social status. Wealthy thanks to her inheritance, Maya is rich from the outset; she lives in a mansion, surrounded by mirrors. The wealth that Emma only half-consciously strives for in the Flaubert novel – the desire for wealth is implicit in her desire for a "higher," more aristocratic love, and in her enthusiasm for the horseback riding and elegant balls characteristic of the aristocratic ethos – belongs from the beginning to Maya, thus stripping Emma of the quiet but tenacious social *arrivisme* that characterizes her in the novel.

Along with Govind Nihalani, Mrinal Sen, and Shyam Benegal, Mehta belongs to a kind of "third way" within Indian cinema, a style that negotiates between apparently antagonistic traditions. Mehta strives for a "middle cinema" located between the fantastic, colorful, dance-dominated, and very popular Bollywood cinema, on the one hand, and the austere, low-budget, independent, and programmatically realist "New Indian Cinema" on the other. The foiling of different genres and styles in Mehta's film, I would argue, forms an analogue to Flaubert's own counterpointing of the romantic and the realistic style throughout *Bovary*. In Indian terms, as Ratnapriya Das points out, *Maya* violated a

The Proto-cinematic Novel

Chapter 4

number of taboos, much as Flaubert's novel did in its time. The director displays Deepa Sahi, the director's real-life spouse, well known as an actress in alternative cinema, in a state of passion and nudity. (The invocation of a wifely presence recalls, if only by analogy, the indirect referencing of Judy Garland in the Minnelli version.) Whereas the eroticism of Bombay films was customarily sublimated into highly eroticized dances, while paying "lip service" to the taboo on kissing and erotic contact, this film is openly and straightforwardly erotic. The love scene with Lalit features the usual *topoi* of "erotic" filmmaking: bare breasts, love bites, shredded pillows, and, importantly, female orgasm. The finale of the film evokes still another genre, the Hindu mythological. Maya's body disappears in a blaze of light – with nothing left – thus underlining the core trope of the film, inherent in the protagonist's name : "Maya" (illusion). But to convey this translation into another realm, Mehta appeals to the magical conventions of the mythological.

It is revealing to compare the various versions of *Madame Bovary*. Both Chabrol and Renoir, for example, adopt the passage where Emma tries to confess her spiritual and erotic frustration to an uncomprehending priest. (In an ironic inversion, the priest speaks only of earthly things, of sick cows and hungry peasants, while Emma speaks of the spiritual.) Minnelli, perhaps worried about censorship pressures from the Catholic Church, omits the scene altogether. What is perhaps most disappointing in virtually all of the adaptations of *Madame Bovary* is that no filmmaker seems to really have managed to forge the equivalent of Flaubert's specific stylistic achievement: to wit the counterpointing of styles which pits the exalted, romantic, metaphoric, and grandly literary style against the flat, boring, banal, metonymic style, and to do this in terms of specifically cinematic techniques and genres, through lighting, camera movement, music, and so forth. Minnelli evokes the literary theme, but the sustained high and melodramatic pitch deprives us of the counterpoint of provincial boredom. Chabrol takes the opposite tack: he emphasizes the boredom and platitude, but neglects the literary exaltation. (Mehta perhaps comes the closest to a real counterpoint by contrasting the Bollywood style musical sequences with a more realistic style.) Nor has any filmmaker tried to create the cinematic equivalent of Flaubert's painterly Impressionist style, the active light, the attention to gaseous movement in the atmosphere, although the cinema is superbly equipped for such effects. (Renoir and Chabrol very occasionally do achieve such effects through a kind of dappled, forest lyricism.) Nor has any adaptation tried to actualize the satiric and socially critical side of the book. There has been no feminist adaptation of *Madame Bovary*, for example. For all these reasons, there is more than enough room for new "hypertextual" variations on Flaubert's infinitely suggestive text.

The various adaptations of *Madame Bovary*, then, form hypertextual readings, or better rewritings, of Flaubert's text. They come in the wake of literal rewritings, for example the Gérard Genette pastiche, entitled "Charles Bovary's Secret," in which it is Charles who encourages Emma to cheat because he is already so busy cheating himself. In some cases, we find **literary** rewritings of *Madame Bovary* that generate **filmic** rewritings. Such is the case of the Portuguese writer Agustina Bessa-Luis's rewriting of *Madame Bovary* as *Vale Abraão* (Valley of Abraham, 1993), an extrapolation written in order to be adapted by Portuguese filmmaker Manoel de Oliveira in 1997. Flaubert's novel becomes hypotext for Bessa-Luis's hypertextual literary variation, which in its turn becomes hypotext for Oliveira's filmic adaptation. Bessa-Luis takes the themes of the novel – provincial milieu, social *arrivisme*, the literary theme – and filters it through less-than-exhilarating prose. Indeed, her prose commits the "mimetic fallacy" in that it not only treats the subject of boredom but is itself boring. The novel switches the scene to Portugal and the time to the present, but many of the main characters retain their names: Emma remains Emma, while her husband becomes "Carlos," the Portuguese equivalent of Charles. Here too a woman from a provincial milieu (Tostes/Vale Abraão) is married to a doctor whom she does not love. The woman commits numerous infidelities (three rather than Bovary's two) and finally commits suicide (or perhaps it was an accident). Emma's nickname, in the Bessa-Luis version, is "Bovarinha" (the little Bovary), and a rather long passage in the novel is devoted to whether she actually deserves the epithet. In this new version, a lover's speedboat replaces Rodolphe's horses, and guests at the Vaubyessard Ball dance to recorded music rather than to a live orchestra. In this version, Emma leaves her lovers before they leave her. Leon is bifurcated into two characters, Fortunato and Narciso. Bessa-Luis keeps Flaubert's third-person omniscient narrator, but in this case the narrative voice is more remote and authoritative, rarely entering Emma's psyche as does the narrator of *Madame Bovary*. Indeed, Bessa-Luis takes a step backward in terms of the historical trajectory of narrational technique, in that she crowds the texts with opinions, rather in the Balzac than the Flaubert manner.

The Manoel de Oliveira adaptation picks up long swaths of the Bessa-Luis text, rendered as an almost constant voice-over narration, but transfigures them by superimposing on the text wonderfully discreet and poetically understated images. He restores the narrational audacity lacking in the Bessa-Luis rewrite through what Pasolini would call a "cinema of poetry," a kind of contamination between directorial style and what Oliveira intuits as Emma's romantic imagination. Oliveira also installs a reflexive device: he has the novel's Emma read a novel – *Madame Bovary* itself! His adroit *mise-en-scène*, more evocative than

Figure 4.4 Leonor Silviera as Ema in Manoel de Oliveira's *Vale Abraão* (1997), produced by Gémini Films / Light Night / Madragoa Filmes

literal, has the poetic qualities of Flaubert's own style. Thus Oliveira rejoins Flaubert, but at another level, through the visual "rhymes" of repeated shots, and through images whose power "exceeds" that of the Bessa-Luis rewriting. Oliveira's style seems at first static, anti-kinetic, yet in fact it is contemplative, immobilized in what Madalena Galamba calls a "poetic stillness that allows the spectator to scan the image in synchrony with the tranquil rhythm of the film."[45] Thus the filmmaker "rewrites" a pre-existing rewriting (Bessa-Luis's) in such a way as to better approximate the strategies of the "original" writing by Flaubert.

Some adaptations of *Madame Bovary*, interestingly, have not even been recognized as adaptations. Woody Allen's *The Purple Rose of Cairo*, for example, as a story about a provincial woman trapped in an oppressive marriage but longing for romance, clearly constitutes a cinematic update of *Madame Bovary*, in which Hollywood films occupy the functional slot that romantic literature occupies in the Flaubert novel. Indeed, the key sequence in the Woody Allen film, where Mia Farrow imagines that the film star is addressing her directly, was already anticipated in the novel itself. Attending a performance of *Lucie de Lammermoor*, Emma starts to conjure up a love affair with the opera singer

Lagardy. She fantasizes that "they might have been lovers" and becomes convinced that the singer is singing just for her. "Then a mad notion struck her: he was looking at her, she was sure of it! She wanted to run into his arms, to take refuge in his strength as in the incarnation of love itself, and to say to him, to cry out: 'Take me away, take me with you, let us go!'" (p. 218).

In fact, Woody Allen has surreptitiously adapted *Madame Bovary* not once but twice, once in *The Purple Rose of Cairo* and again in a short story, "The Kugelmass Episode." In the story, the title character, a professor of humanities at New York's City College, finds himself in the Bovary-like situation of boredom and unhappy marriage. Rather like Emma complaining to her priest, Kugelmass tells his psychoanalyst that he wants a more romantic and exciting life. When the analyst responds that he is not a magician, Kugelmass terminates his therapy and goes in search of – a magician. He finds him in the Great Persky, a literary shaman/pimp who has the power to arrange amorous trysts between his clients and famous women characters from literature. After rejecting Sister Carrie and Hester Prynne, Kugelmass asks Persky for a French lover. Offered Zola's Nana, Kugelmass protests that she is a prostitute and he prefers not to pay. He ultimately settles on Emma Bovary. Emma, he learns, has "always dreamed that some mysterious stranger would appear and rescue [her] from the monotony of crass rural existence." Kugelmass sees a window of adulterous opportunity if he can enter the novel before page 120, before Emma hooks up with Rodolphe. Transported into Emma's bedroom in Yonville, Kugelmass is delighted to discover that Emma spoke "in the same fine English translation as the paperback." What he did not realize was that at that very moment students in classrooms around the world were asking their teachers why a bald Jewish guy was kissing Madame Bovary on page 98 of the novel. Kugelmass, meanwhile, is amazed that he, who always got failing grades in literature courses, has somehow managed to sleep with Emma Bovary. He brings Emma to New York, where she is enthralled by Kugelmass's tales of Broadway night life and Hollywood premieres. Literature professors, at this point, are shocked by Emma's disappearance from the novel. "First a strange character named Kugelmass," notes one Stanford professor, "and now Emma's gone from the book. Well, I guess the mark of a classic is that you can reread it a thousand times and always find something new." At this point, the magician's technique falters and he is unable to get Emma back into the book, which worries Kugelmass since he is a married man with classes to teach, while Emma is concerned that Charles will miss her. Emma gives Kugelmass an ultimatum: "Get me back into the novel or marry me!" Some professors, meanwhile, have sighted Kugelmass in the novel and threatened to tell his wife Daphne. Kugelmass, finally, gets released from

Emma, but at the end of the story he is accidentally projected into an old text-book (*Remedial Spanish*) and chased over rocky terrain by a hairy irregular verb.

The novel *Madame Bovary* leads outward not only to Woody Allen's parodic retailing and Agustina Bessa-Luis's retelling, but also to many subsequent styles of novelistic writing. Within one strain, his realistic (as opposed to his romantic-parodic) style can be seen as leading to Zolaesque naturalism, since Flaubert too called in his correspondence for a stylistic method which would emulate the precision of the physical sciences. Just as the sketchy impressionism of Monet gave way to the "scientific" impressionism of Seurat, so Flaubert's critical realism gave way to the scientific naturalism of Zola's **roman experimental**. Within another strain, Flaubert's recounting, via the indirect free style, of Emma's interior imaginings can be seen as leading to what became more programmatically called the "stream of consciousness" novel of Virginia Woolf and James Joyce, or, in its more stylistically conservative version, the "reflecting consciousness" novels of Henry James. Indeed, Flaubert became a constant reference in the Lubbock–James school. But Flaubertian realism also leads to the "*choisisme*" of Robbe-Grillet. The practitioner of the nouveau roman brings to its paroxysm Flaubert's precision about angle of vision. Robbe-Grillet combines the most complete subjectivity (that of personal obsession) with the most complete objectivity, relayed by rigorous, mathematical, description, rigorously cleansed of the anthropomorphic and the metaphoric, the prose of the engineer that Robbe-Grillet almost became. But, in the next chapter, we shall examine just one eddy within these post-Flaubertian currents: that of the ironic, subjectivized, and often deeply neurotic, narrators of writers like Dostoevsky and Nabokov, before turning, in chapter 6, to the cine-roman of Robbe-Grillet, Duras, and the French New Wave.

The Proto-cinematic Novel

Chapter 4

Notes

1 Harry Levin, *The Gates of Horn: A Study of Five French Novelists* (New York: Oxford University Press, 1966).

2 See Denis de Rougemont, *Love in the Western World* (New York: Harper and Row, 1977).

3 Gustave Flaubert, *Madame Bovary*, Signet edition (New York: American Library, 1964), p. 60. Most of the passages cited in the text will be taken from this edition. On rare occasions I will offer my own translations (marked as "my translation") based on the Garnier-Flammarion edition (Paris, 1966).

4 See Kamilla Elliot, *Rethinking the Novel/Film Debate* (Cambridge: Cambridge University Press, 2003).

5   Quoted in Vladimir Nabokov, *Lectures on Literature* (New York: Harcourt Brace, 1980), p. 156.

6   See Pier Paolo Pasolini, *Empirismo eretico* (Rome: Garzanti, 1972).

7   Gustave Flaubert, *Correspondance*, vol. II, ed. Jean Bruneau (Paris: Gallimard, 1973), p. 31.

8   Ibid., p. 229.

9   Erich Auerbach, *Mimesis: The Representation of Reality in Western Literature* (Princeton, NJ: Princeton University Press, 1953), p. 483.

10 Ibid., p. 484.

11 Ibid., p. 490.

12 See George Bluestone, *Novels into Film* (Berkeley, CA: University of California Press, 1957).

13 Ivone Margulies, *Nothing Happens: Chantal Akerman's Hyperrealist Everyday* (Durham, NC: Duke University Press, 1996).

14 Levin, *The Gates of Horn*, p. 251.

15 This process begins even with the film's logo – the whirling globe of Universal – on which is superimposed the cries of birds (implying an avian point of view) and is invoked again in the final shots, where it is implied that a line of birds is watching the departure of Melanie and Mitch and the others from a scene that the birds have come to reappropriate from human beings.

16 Jonathon Crary, *Techniques of the Observer: On Vision and Modernity in the Nineteenth Century* (Cambridge, MA: MIT Press, 1995), p. 7.

17 Ibid., p. 14.

18 Ibid., p. 23.

19 See Elliot, *Rethinking the Novel/Film Debate*, for an extended discussion of this topic as it applies to English literature.

20 Crary, *Techniques of the Observer*, p. 70. Crary is, of course, not speaking of Flaubert in this passage.

21 See Jean-Pierre Geuens, *Film Production Theory* (Albany, NY: State University of New York Press, 2000), p. 164.

22 Ibid., p. 157.

23 Quoted in ibid., p. 159.

24 Alan Spiegel also makes this point in his *Fiction and the Camera Eye: Visual Consciousness in the Film and the Modern Novel* (Charlottesville: University of Virginia Press, 1976).

25 Flaubert, *Correspondance*, vol. II, p. 229.

26 Christian Metz, *The Imaginary Signifier* (Bloomington, IN: Indiana University Press, 1981).

27 Charles Baudelaire, *The Painter of Modern Life and Other Essays*, trans. Jonathan Mayne (London: Phaidon, 1964/1995), p. 13.

28 See Jonathon Culler, *Flaubert: The Uses of Uncertainty* (Ithaca, NY: Cornell University Press, 1985).

29 Levin, *The Gates of Horn*, p. 262.

30 See Laura Grimaldi, *Monsieur Bovary*, originally published in Italian by Leonardo in 1991. My references are to the Spanish translation by Celia Filipetto, published in Madrid by Anaya and Mario Muchnik in 1994. All translations are mine.

31 The staging of Emma's spectatorship in her *loge* reminds us of the many Impressionist paintings portraying spectatorship, not only Renoir's own father's *La Loge* (1874) and *La Première sortie* (1876), but also Mary Cassatt's *Woman in Black at the Opera* (1879) and *Lydia Seated in a Loge, Wearing a Pearl Necklace* (1879).

32 Quoted in Nabokov, *Lectures on Literature*, p. 147.

33 Bluestone, *Novels into Film*, p. 198.

34 See Stephen Harvey, *Directed by Vincente Minnelli* (New York: Harper and Row, 1989).

35 For a discussion of the trial and its implications, see Dominick LaCapra, "*Madame Bovary*" *on Trial* (Ithaca, NY: Cornell University Press, 1982).

36 See Harvey, *Directed by Vincente Minnelli*, p. 204.

37 Culler, *Flaubert: The Uses of Uncertainty*.

38 François Jost, unpublished essay entitled "La Transfiguration du Bal" kindly given to me by the author.

39 Guy Austin, *Contemporary French Cinema: An Introduction* (Manchester: Manchester University Press, 1996), p. 165.

40 Emma Wilson, *French Cinema since 1950: Personal Histories* (New York: Rowman and Littlefield, 1980), p. 117.

41 For Higson's analysis of the heritage genre, see Andrew Higson, "Re-presenting the National Past: Nostalgia and Pastiche in the Heritage Film," in Lester Friedman (ed.), *British Cinema and Thatcherism: Fires Were Started* (London: University College London Press, 1993).

42 Jost, "La Transfiguration du Bal."

43 Gerard Genette, *Narrative Discourse: An Essay in Method*, trans. Jane E. Lewin (Ithaca, NY: Cornell University Press, 1980).

44 Ratnapriya Das, unpublished paper written for my "Film and Novel" course.

45 Madalena Galamba, "Flaubert, Bessa-Luis, and Oliveira: A Trilateral Dialogue in *Vale Abraão*," unpublished manuscript.

Chapter 4

Chapter 5

Underground Man and Neurotic Narrators: From Dostoevsky to Nabokov

In our discussions so far, we have already encountered a wide spectrum of narrators: (1) the pseudo first-person reporter–narrator of *Robinson Crusoe* (in Genette's terms the "autodiegetic narrator"); (2) the amiable, digressive, dialogic, outside-observer narrators of *Don Quixote* and *Tom Jones* (in Genette's terms the "heterodiegetic narrator"); (3) the first-person "homodiegetic" narrator who both narrates and plays a role in the fiction (*Bras Cubas*); and (4) the variable-distance, infinitely flexible, at once intimate and impersonal, narrator (*Madame Bovary*).[1]

The conventional terms of discussion, unfortunately, do not account for even this limited spectrum of styles of narration. The traditional analysis of narration in both literature and film was rooted in concepts based in language and grammar, such as "first-person narrator" (subdivided into "first-person observer and first-person participant narrators); and "third person" narrator (subdivided into omniscient, limited omniscient, and dramatic narrators). But such grammar-based terminology creates more confusion than clarity, since designating a narrator "third person" actually tells us very little about specific narrational processes in novelistic texts. Third-person narration is presumed to be omniscient, but that is not always the case. A strictly grammatical approach obscures the fact that a writer can shift person, as we have seen Flaubert do in *Madame Bovary*, moving easily from an occasional "I" or a "we" to a mixed **style indirect libre**, constantly changing the relation between the narrator and the fiction. Even a "third-person" narrator like the narrator of Fielding's *Tom Jones* sometimes says "I." More important than the grammatical "person" is authorial control of intimacy and distance, the calibration of access to knowledge and consciousness, all issues which function above and beyond and below the issue of grammatical "person." A wide array of techniques can be deployed with any "person." Within "free indirect discourse," as we have seen, the narrator can adopt the voices and attitudes of diverse characters. Furthermore, a narrator can be "dramatic" in relation to one character, showing only what the character says or does (for example, Blifil in *Tom Jones*), and "limited omniscient" in relation to another (for example, Sophia in the same novel). Part of the fascination of a novel like *Lolita*, as we shall see, is that it offers no direct access to Lolita's subjectivity. It is always refracted through Humbert's solipsistic fantasies; we can only imagine what she herself might **really** be thinking.

With indirect interior monologue, a favored technique in the work of Henry James, the "reflector character" becomes a kind of co-narrator with the narrator, within a hybridized focalization. The free indirect style, similarly, also offers a hybrid discourse, a contamination between author and character, which for Pasolini finds its cinematic counterpart in a "cinema of poetry," where character becomes a pretext for self-flaunting authorial virtuosity. In direct interior monologue, the character takes over as narrator (as in certain passages of *Madame Bovary*) while "stream of consciousness" (as in James Joyce) shows the non-linear associative processes characteristic of unmediated thought, the idiosyncratic forms of what Vygotsky and Bakhtin (and Eisenstein) called "inner speech." The contribution of Bakhtin's discursive approach to narration, meanwhile, was to depersonalize the issue of point of view by emphasizing not the psychic integrity of the character but rather the diverse discourses assumed, relayed, refuted, resisted, or internalized by a character or a narrator, an approach especially relevant, as we shall see, to Dostoevsky's novels of ideas.

As Wayne Booth points out in *The Rhetoric of Fiction*, we react to narrators as we do to persons, finding them likable or repulsive, wise or foolish, fair or unfair.[2] Narrators vary widely on a broad spectrum, not only in terms of likability but also in terms of reliability. Some are honest brokers, while others are pathological liars. What interests me in this chapter, however, is not narration in general but rather a particular kind of narration, to wit **unreliable** narration. The modern period has been especially fond of (1) changing narrators and (2) unreliable narrators. Changing narrators alter their discourse and ideas as they narrate; they mutate before our eyes. This trait is especially true of the **Bildungsroman** or novel of development (for example, *Great Expectations*); part of the plot, in such novels, is not just **what** happens but how the narrator changes **in function of** what happens; for example, when Pip learns about the true source of his fortune. Although the technique of unreliable narration can be traced back to the prose fictions of antiquity, it is modern novelists since Dostoevsky who have especially exploited the device. The challenge of reading, with unreliable narration, consists in ferreting out the narrator's inconsistencies and neuroses, penetrating the veil set up by the narrators to hide their vices (or even their virtues). Sometimes the reliability of a narrator becomes a "crux" in interpretation, the case of Ellen Dean in *Wuthering Heights* (1848) or of the governess in Henry James's *The Turn of the Screw* (1898). In the cinema, Kurosawa's *Rashomon* (1951), in which the story of a crime is told in four radically different, yet equally plausible ways, constitutes a tour de force of problematic narration.

Dostoevsky's novella *Notes from Underground* (1864) was a key text in this process of elaborating ever-more subtle techniques of unreliable narration. There is no reason to trust the narrator's account of his relationship with Liza, the vulnerable prostitute on whom he projects the "motiveless malignity" of his own masculinist hostility. Unable to wreak revenge on his social superiors (Zerkov) or even on his social inferiors (his servant Apollon), Underground Man turns his aggressions instead on her. Unreliable narration in this sense can produce insight into the gendered nature of human blindness, exposing the distorted grids through which some men see women as only traitors or victims. Unreliable narration thus constitutes a clear historical shift within the history of the novel. Whereas the narrator of a Balzac or a Dickens novel addressed the audience in terms of presumably shared values, a proto-modernist like Dostoevsky adopts a narrational stance of aggressive destabilization, leaving the reader in an off-balance state of anxiety about the norms of the text and the true relations between author and narrator. In such narratives, the difficulties of the narration become part of the subject.

Rather than being only a retrospective, well-thought-out autobiographical memoir, *Notes from Underground* gives us the impression of a man talking to himself, telling a story which he is trying to explain both to himself and others. An extraordinarily prescient text, *Notes from Underground* anticipated any number of subsequent modes of thought: Freudianism, existentialism, modernism, and even postmodernism. All we know about the narrator/protagonist of the novella is that he is a former civil servant, that he is around forty years of age, that he has a maid and a servant, that he lives off his income from rents, and that, like Don Quixote, he has spent much of his life reading. Although the novella omits many of the basic indicators of selfhood – name, family, position in life – this insubstantial figure, like Don Quixote or Emma Bovary, has achieved the status of an identificatory archetype.

The Dostoevsky novella provides the model for an important strain in modernist fiction, one in which the story is told by a self-conscious, tormented, and unreliable narrator. If we reflect on the narrators of Thomas Mann's *Doctor Faustus*, of Gide's *Les Faux monnayeurs*, of Huxley's *Point Counter Point*, of Sartre's *La Nausée*, of Camus' *L'Etranger*, of Ralph Ellison's *Invisible Man*, of Nabokov's *Lolita*, of Desnoes' *Memories of Underdevelopment*, and of Clarice Lispector's *Hour of the Star*, they all have in common this intrinsically problematic and untrustworthy character. (Needless to say, these unreliable narrators cannot be simplistically equated with the authors who contrived them.) It is hard to disentangle the true from the false in what they are saying. In this chapter, then, we will explore a number of novels featuring problematic narrators in the Dostoevskyan tradition, beginning with Dostoevsky himself, and moving on to other writers in the same tradition, notably Edmundo Desnoes, Clarice Lispector, and Vladimir Nabokov, always examining both the source texts and the adapatations based on them.

Notes from Underground and its narrator/protagonist occupy an extremely important place in literary and cultural history, the point of convergence of many trends. On one level, *Notes from Underground* reflects the culmination of a long historical process, to wit the increasing subjectivization of the novel, the transition from what Ian Watt calls "the objective, social and public orientation of the classical world to the subjective, individualist and private orientation" of modern life and literature.[3] On another level, the novella, or more accurately its protagonist, stands at the end of the historical process traced in Stephen Greenblatt's *Renaissance Self-fashioning* whereby human beings became more and more self-conscious about human identity as a manipulable, artful process, leading to a malleable, cosmopolitan sense of self.[4] Put differently again, this trajectory coincides with what Bakhtin sees as the melancholy downward trajectory of carnival from a public space of collective *jouissance*, in the Middle Ages and the Renaissance, into a privatized realm of personal insurrections and *ressentiment* in the modern period.

A paradox about *Notes from Underground* is that while, on the one hand, it exhibits a sense of lonely, monadic, idiosyncratic subjectivity, at the same time it also exhibits a kind of objectivity, in that Dostoevsky gives voice to a wide range of actually existing, socially generated voices. This technique produces what Bakhtin calls "polyphony," whereby the author becomes the orchestrator of independent and mutually relativizing discourses. Bakhtin's analysis takes off from what had always been the pivotal question within Dostoevsky criticism: the relation between Dostoevsky as author and his vociferous gallery of opinionated characters. The traditional question which oriented Dostoevsky criticism was exactly

But for Bakhtin this is the wrong question, since Dostoevsky is to be identified not with one or another voice within his novels, but rather with the agency that orchestrates the polylogue of distinct and even antithetical voices, the textual plurality of unmerged voices and consciousnesses. Polyphony deploys juxtaposition, counterpoint, simultaneity in its treatment of its favored subject: the dialogue of consciousnesses within the sphere of ideas. The lack of an originary personality or homogeneous style is not a flaw in Dostoevsky's work; it is, rather, "of the essence;" it allows the artist to juxtapose discourses in a process of mutual illumination. Yet Dostoevsky is by no means the passive compiler of others' points of view; he is at once composer, orchestrator, performer, and discursive disk jockey. The author is profoundly **active**, alert to the dialogic tissue of human life, to an array of voices which the author reproduces, answers, interrogates, amplifies, and places in relation to one another.

Notes from Underground is a metadiscursive work, consisting of "speech about speech" and "discourse about discourse." The novella also constitutes **literary speech about literary speech**, in that it parodies such works as Chernyshevsky's *What is to Be Done?* (1861). The book instantiates what Bakhtin calls "the auto-criticism of discourse," in which artistic discourse is tested in its relationship to social reality. Within this "line," Bakhtin cites two types. The first type concentrates on the critique and trial of literary discourse around the hero – a "literary man" – who tries to live according to the rules of literature. (*Don Quixote* and *Madame Bovary*, as we have seen, provide two obvious examples.) The second type introduces an author in the process of writing the novel, not as a character but rather as the real author of the given work (Bakhtin cites *Tristram Shandy*). Alongside the apparent novel there are fragments of a "novel about the novel."

In generic terms, *Notes from Underground* is affiliated with the "confession" genre – indeed, Dostoevsky's original title was "A Confession" – a genre whose most distinguished representatives are Saint Augustine and Jean-Jacques Rousseau. The confession as genre evokes a spiritual quest, mingled with the guilty pleasures of self-pride. Autobiographical writing often mingles disgrace and exposure, truth and masquerade. Rousseau sought perfect candor in his *Confessions* (1781), but many symptomatic critics have found him dishonest and manipulative. Mark Twain caught the double nature of autobiography when he called autobiographies the "truest of all books." Despite the "shirkings of the truth" and the "partial revealments," Twain argued, "the remorseless truth is there, between the lines, where the author-cat is raking dust upon it, which hides from the disinterested spectator neither it nor its smell . . . the result being that the reader knows the author in spite of his wily indulgences.'[5]

As these remarks suggest, an undercurrent of vanity animates the confession, since the confessor assumes that the world is fascinated by every twist and turn of the confessor's thought, no matter how vicious or culpable. "It is sometimes possible," Underground Man tells us, "to pin full-fledged crimes on ourselves out of vanity."[6] Underground Man pins innumerable "crimes" on himself, beginning with the novella's startling first lines: "I'm a sick man . . . a mean man. There's nothing attractive about me." Within the opening pages, he informs us that he is "morbidly superstitious," "spiteful," and lower than "an insect." He later compares himself to a "dwarf," a "hunchback," and a "mouse in his mouse-hole." In Underground Man, self-hatred and misanthropy go hand in hand. "I derived pleasure," he tells us, "from the blinding realization of my degradation." No accusation is too harsh, as long as he is the one making it.

In linguistic terms, Underground Man lives, as it were, in the subjunctive mood – "if I **were** to confront the officer." More precisely, he lives in the self-idealizing, often delusional world of the modals (the wouldas, couldas, and shouldas of discourse), the ideal linguistic terrain for retrospective rationalization. Underground Man wards off finalization and self-definition through a systematic policy of anticipatory self-depreciation. Even in the midst of his self-flagellations, Underground Man retains the "last word" on himself, always maintaining a positional superiority. Bakhtin calls this strategy "loophole discourse." "A loophole," Bakhtin writes in *Problems of Dostoevsky's Poetics*, "is the retention for oneself of the possibility for altering the ultimate, final meaning of one's own words."[7] Underground Man constantly tries to destroy the restrictive framework of other people's words about him, words that might fix and finalize and suffocate him.

For Bakhtin, art does not offer direct access to the real, but only to the discourses and ideologies that refract the real. Thus Underground Man is not real, but the social tendencies and the discourses that he relays **are** real. And in this sense, Underground Man is both weirdly idiosyncratic and absolutely typical. While on one level intensely personal, his discourse is on another emblematic of a more general condition. As Dostoevsky puts it in the first "note" to the novella, the "Notes" and their author are "fictitious," yet people like Underground Man "must exist in our society, if we think of the circumstances under which that society has been formed." Underground Man's neuroses and obsessions resonate, as it were, with those of his age.

During the course of the novel, Underground Man constantly replays, and re-edits, as it were, the memory tapes of scenes that occurred many years earlier.

After exposing his rebarbative personality in the opening section, the protagonist recounts his humiliation at the hands of some acquaintances in a second section, climaxing with his own attempt to simultaneously humiliate (and somehow redeem) the prostitute Liza in the third part. In thematic terms, Underground Man rails against humanism, idealism, utopian/socialism, rationalism, utilitarianism, and romantic notions of the "good and the beautiful." Unimpressed by Enlightenment notions of "progress," Underground Man sees human beings as incorrigibly selfish, giving more value to a "single drop of their own fat" than to a "hundred thousand human lives." *Notes from Underground* undermines any notion that literature humanizes its readers, for Underground Man is at the same time exquisitely literate and horrifyingly inhumane. Anticipating Walter Benjamin's lucid observations about civilization's intrinsic barbarism, Underground Man notes that the "most bloodthirsty tyrants" are often "exquisitely civilized." (Here Dostoevsky foreshadows the widely noted, and only apparently paradoxical, truth that well-educated Nazi officers loved Wagner, Goethe, and Beethoven.) And anticipating by more than a century Jean-François Lyotard's ideas about postmodernism and the "end of metanarratives," Underground Man expresses skepticism not only about the **grands récits** of science, progress, and revolution, but also about the **petits récits** of personal development and the acquisition of wisdom. As a story of aborted self-fashioning and failed emplotment, *Notes from Underground* relays its protagonist's misfired attempts to narrativize even his own mediocre life in a coherent fashion.

Notes from Underground further reworks the Cervantic theme of bookishness and disenchantment which Flaubert, only seven years before, had already reworked in *Madame Bovary*. Underground Man can no longer separate what he really feels from what he has picked up from books. Like Quixote, Underground Man provokes laughter by speaking in inappropriately literary language. The good, normal citizens, he speculates, "would have laughed at [him] when [he] spoke up in literary language" (p. 46). Like Emma Bovary, he spends most of his time reading and dreaming. Underground Man reminds us that "we are all secretly agreed that the way it is presented in literature" – nowadays one might add cinema – "is much better" (p. 203). His loves, too, are vicarious and literary, consisting of what he himself calls a "leisurely, rapturous sliding into the domain of art, that is, into the beautiful lives of heroes stolen from the authors of novels and poems . . ." (p. 92). His diatribes are "contrived, literary, stuff," and Liza accuses him of sounding "just like a book" (p. 179). "Left alone without literature, we immediately become entangled and lost – we don't know what to join, what to keep up with; what to love, what to hate; what to respect, what to despise" (p. 203).

Underground Man's habit of "imagining everything happening the way it does in books" prevents him from seeing the simple truth: that Liza had discerned his **own** unhappiness. His vengeance too takes literary form; while afraid to confront the arrogant officer in the flesh, he does dare to attack him in the much safer mode of a satirical short story. His real-life "victories" — he claims to have stood his ground when the arrogant officer tries to push him off the sidewalk — are Quixotic, in that the officer never becomes aware of any "defeat," even though Underground Man insists that the officer was only "pretending not to have noticed." But our knowledge of the unreliable narrator convention leads us to suspect that the officer **really** did not notice Underground Man's "heroic" action.

While Underground Man as a character is afflicted by a virulent Slavic strain of Bovarysme, the narrational technique which presents him as a character is quite distinct from Flaubert's. While Flaubert offers a mobilized, impressionistic portrait of Emma, Dostoevsky never even describes his narrator/protagonist, making him more of an empty actantial slot, an abstract point of interlocution with the reader. If Flaubert offered portraiture destabilized in visual terms, Dostoevsky gives us portraiture destabilized in **ideological** and **discursive** terms. Dostoevsky dialogizes **le style indirect libre**, while further relationalizing the Flaubertian character. Flaubert's Emma was constructed out of the fleeting impressions of others (for example, Charles's first glimpses of her) combined with her sense perceptions (her blurred vision) mingled with Flaubert's quasi-parodic rendering of the romantic literature which also shaped her psyche. Dostoevsky's Underground Man, in contrast, is constructed out of the character's imaginary dialogue with what he projects as the possible discourses of others about him. There is nothing we can say about Underground Man, as Bakhtin puts it, that he has not already said himself:

> At all the critical moments of his confession he tries to anticipate the possible definition or evaluation others might make of him, to guess the sense and tone of that evaluation, and tries painstakingly to formulate these possible words about himself by others, interrupting his own speech with the imagined rejoinders of others.[8]

While Emma Bovary (and her creator) also dialogue with literature, and with other characters **through** literature, Emma is never portrayed as constantly imagining the perceptions and discourses of others, such as L'heureux or Homais, **about** her. Nor does Flaubert have Emma constantly shift her ideologies and discourses for opportunistic or polemical purposes. Like Underground Man, Emma too dreams of the sublime and yet sinks into the mud, but she lacks the gnawing, toothache-like self-consciousness of Underground Man, who himself states: "The more conscious I was of the good and the beautiful the deeper I sank into the mud . . ." (p. 94). Unlike Emma, Underground Man is lucid, up to a point, about his own tendency to make neurotic projections: "Now, it is absolutely clear to me that, because of an infinite vanity that caused me to set myself impossible standards, I regarded myself with furious disapproval, bordering on loathing, then ascribed my own feelings to everyone I came across" (p. 124).

Underground Man looks at himself "in the mirrors of other people's consciousness;" he is conscious of all the possible refractions of his image in those mirrors. While Flaubert offers a visual polyperspectivalism through the literary equivalent of "point-of-view shots," Dostoevsky gives us discursive polyperspectivalism, through a character whose psyche itself forms the arena for an ideological agon. In a way, the two authors play on the diverse facets of "point of view," which is at once perceptual/visual (for Flaubert), and discursive/ideological (for Dostoevsky).

From the first sentence, the hero's speech cringes and breaks and cracks under the pressure of the anticipated words of another, with whom the hero enters into what Bakhtin calls "internal polemic." Thus the text is dotted with linguistic "tics" symptomatic of dialogic (and often paranoid) anticipations: "I know you'll say . . . ;" "you are probably imagining . . . ;" "I don't want you to think . . . ;" "I'll bet you think . . ." He is constantly answering an imagined interlocutor. It is as if we were hearing one side of a telephone conversation, left to infer what is being said on the other side. We are reminded of a frequent cinematic technique in Godard's films, where actor/characters (for example, Juliette in *2 ou 3 choses que je sais d'elle*) respond to questions which we as spectators do not hear. While linguists speak of "phatic communication," i.e. communication designed merely to keep open the channels of communication, Underground Man practices "anti-phatic" speech, i.e. a hectoring nastiness that effectively closes off communication through escalating aggression. His proactive verbal strikes generate the "Mutual Assured Destruction" of human interlocution. Yet all this aggressivity merely masks his desperate dependence on the other, since even when he fears that the other might recognize his own fears he is still demonstrating his connection to the others, even while affecting to despise them. "I wanted terribly to show them that I could easily do without them, but at the same time, I was stamping my feet on purpose. But to no avail. They really paid no attention to me" (p. 156).

Underground Man's infantile, egocentric acting out, then, is still aimed at the other. Underground Man exists in dialogue, however hostile, with the other. He is always aware of third-party observers as a kind of invisible jury; in what Bakhtin calls "triple-directed discourse," he "squints his eyes to the side, toward the listener, the witness, and the judge." His "solution" of refusing to be circumscribed by the discourses of others does not free him, ultimately, from interrelational dependency on others. That such a nasty character as Underground Man is also "dialogical" shows that Bakhtin never saw dialogism as an ideal speech situation, a touchy-feely, Oprahesque love-in, as some of Bakhtin's critics would have it. While dialogism is inherent in human interaction, it is only **potentially**, not necessarily, humane and progressive.

For René Girard, Underground Man represents the last stage in the novel's evolution toward abstract characters whose desire is necessarily unsatisfiable. Like Woody Allen's Zelig, Underground Man successively identifies with and discards a series of "mediators." Unlike Quixote, who is at least faithful to the grand chimera of his madness, the Underground Man is for Girard only "a human rag . . . a ridiculous weather-vane placed atop the ruins of Western humanism."[9] For Girard, Dostoevsky is laughing at his hero's illusions; romantic critics are wrong to idealize Underground Man as an exemplar of existential freedom and rebellion. Dostoevsky's ferocious parody of the myths of his time ends with an arbitrary interruption by the metanarrator who closes down Underground Man's discourse in the name of the reader's patience, thus offering the final (textual) humiliation: "Actually the notes of this lover of paradoxes do not end here. He couldn't resist and went on writing. But we are of the opinion that one might just as well stop here" (p. 203). The effect is rather like that of the insolent fade-outs that interrupt some babbling character in Jim Jarmusch's *Stranger than Paradise* (1984), suggesting, in effect, "pay no attention to this inconsequential muttering, you will miss nothing if I halt its flow."

One of the challenges for a would-be adapter of *Notes from Underground* is how to represent the conflicted, internally dialogic discourse of a neurotic narrator/protagonist. For in the Dostoevsky novella even less "happens" than in Flaubert's novel; most of the events are purely mental and discursive. Each of the two adaptations I will examine here deals with this challenge differently. The Argentinian adaptation by Nicolas Sarquis – *El hombre del subsuelo* (1980) – updates the novel, not to the present of the production but rather to the 1930s. The film begins with the protagonist, here named Diego Carmona (played by Alberto Mendoza), learning of his inheritance. The film then gives us the sullen battle of wills between Carmona and his resentful Buster Keatonish deadpan servant Severo (modeled on Dostoevsky's Apollon, and played by Miguel Ligero). Sarquis translates the character's self-conciousness not through voice-over but rather through performance and *mise-en-scène*. Rather than the verbal "loophole discourse" of the novella, the film associates the protagonist with various **optical** devices — looking glass, telescope, camera — and with the constant presence of mirrors. Although there is a modicum of self-deprecatory voice-over at the very beginning of the film — "I never finished anything. I'm not even an insect" — that soon gives way to staged dialogue among a series of characters: the servant Severo, the actress Liza (played by Brazilian soap-opera and film star Regina Duarte) and former school pals, headed up by McKinley (based on the novella's Zerkov, played by Ignacio Quiroz). The philosophical debates about idealism and realism and politics are all elided, but idealism is invoked at other levels, for example by the operatic and popular music we hear on the sound track. While the novella is cosmopolitan in its **intellectual** references (for example, to French and German Enlightenment thinkers), the film is cosmopolitan in its atmosphere and in its **cultural** references, with echoes of France, the US, and Argentina. The bookish theme is invoked when Liza says of Underground Man that he has "read more books than all the rest of you put together," but generally this Underground Man is more concerned with examining photographic **images**.

The Sarquis adaptation externalizes what was internal (dialogized) monologue in the novella. Underground Man is shown as constantly venting his spleen and spoiling for a fight. He seethes with resentment toward both those socially below him and above him. He explodes in rage against his servant, but his servant maintains a supercilious hostility throughout. Underground Man berates Liza for not being married, telling her that her life has no meaning, but she berates him back, saying he of all people has no right to preach to her. Yet his insults do elicit her tears. The unhappy consciousness of Underground Man is conveyed through the *mise-en-scène*, through an annoyingly ticking clock, and through the protagonist's heavy breathing. When Underground Man dons a woman's dress, his overbearing servant sarcastically tells him: "Dinner is served, **senora**!" As in Hegel's dialectic of master and slave, the servant, ironically, has the dignity and confidence that the "master" lacks. The film portrays Underground Man more as an incorrigible cynic than the frustrated idealist who only pretends to be cynical that we remember from the novella. As a result, the film lacks the Don Quixote/Sancho Panza-like dialectics of cynicism and idealism. At the same time, the film conveys a pervasive sense of social malaise through its powerful atmospherics, conveyed through lushly photographed yet oppressive interiors, reminding us, perhaps, of a contextual element: this film was made during the period of dictatorship, of censorship, and of the "disappeared," at a time when truths were unsayable.

Reflexivity in *El hombre del subsuelo* takes the form not only of a film-within-the-film, but also of a portrayal of Underground Man as a voyeur, constantly peeping through windows or through doors left ajar. The *mise-en-scène* makes us always conscious of his presence, even when he is not speaking and others apparently dominate the image and the sound track. The very fact that he is the **only** one not speaking calls attention to him. The film culminates in a dystopian banquet scene, a party for "McKinley," which reveals Underground Man's complete isolation. The scene brings echoes not only of Argentinian director Torre-Nilson and his *Fin de fiesta* (1956) – one of the screenwriters of *El hombre del subsuelo* is Beatriz Guido, wife and longtime collaborator of Torre-Nilson – but also of Buñuel and the aristocratic chaos of *Exterminating Angel* (1962). Underground Man watches the drunken revels of the stag party with a jaundiced eye, with hunched posture and resentful visage, until he explodes in a tirade in which he denounces them all as hypocrites and degenerates. In an awkward speech, he speaks of his dreams of **la verdadera solidaridad** (true solidarity) but he stumbles and it comes out as **la verdadera soledad** (true solitude). His denunciations, within the logic of mimetic desire, are in the end motivated by a desperate search for companionship. Despite these humiliations, the Underground Man character is nonetheless much more forceful than we imagine him to be in the novella. In the novella, we intuit a gap between the narrator's self-portrait, alternately self-abusing and egomaniacal, and what we imagine to be his actual performance in life. The unreliable narration of the novella, in sum, is more or less discarded in *El hombre del subsuelo*.

Gary Alan Walkow, in his 1995 American adaptation of *Notes from Underground*, takes a slightly different approach. A low-budget feature strongly influenced by the avant-garde, shot in eighteen days on sound stages in Sylmar, California, the film's low production values form the objective correlative of the protagonist's genteel poverty. In the Walkow film, the "underground" habitat of the "Underground Man" meets the experimental aesthetics of "underground" cinema. The underground cinema of the 1950s and 1960s, also known as "New American Cinema," was characterized by aesthetic experimentation, first-person narration (in some ways rooted in expressive romanticism), and the violation of social taboos. The Walkow film draws on a specific genre, that of avant-garde documentary autobiography, a tradition that includes Jonas Mekas's film diaries, Stan Brakhage's *Scenes from Under Childhood* (1967), Shirley Clarke's *Portrait of Jason* (1967), Hollis Frampton's *Nostalgia* (1971), Jerome Hill's *Film Portrait* (1971), James Broughton's *Testament* (1974), and, especially, Jim McBride's *David Holtzman's Diary* (1968).

Like the McBride film, *Notes from Underground* stages the protagonist's confession as a direct-to-camera soliloquy. In the McBride film, "Holtzman" begins to record, on videotape, in real time, all the moments of his life, arguing that since "film is truth 24 frames a second," a non-stop constant filmic portrait would result in the whole truth, all the time. But ultimately the film plays a modernist trick on the spectator, undermining its own documentary "truth value." The film encourages the spectator in a series of contractual generic assumptions – that the film is a courageously truthful documentary, and that the director and narrator and the pro-filmic character are all the same person – yet the final credits reveal that the director is James McBride, and that an actor is pretending to be "David Holtzman." It is as if McBride were making a theoretical/practical critique of the interpretative conflations of director/actor/character.

To adapt the Dostoevsky novella, Walkow shifts the story in both time and space, locating it in the present and shifting the locale from St Petersburg in the winter to Southern California in the summer. In this altered setting, Underground Man is the misfit loner out of synch with the yuppified, celebrity-obsessed Los Angeles of the 1990s. Unfortunately, Walkow largely excises the novel's first philosophical section, where Underground Man rails against assorted intellectual demons, thus downplaying the discursive dimension of Underground Man's malaise. Most of these ideological demons could have easily been actualized to fit a present-day setting where nineteenth-century discourses of "progress" and "rationality" have given way to discourses of "success," "upward mobility," "gentrification," "stardom," and "postmodernism." But instead of emphasizing these ideological tensions, the film foregrounds the novella's literal face-to-face human encounters, and particularly the dinner-party fiasco, and the equally disastrous sequel, Underground Man's encounter with Liza.

In a case of chronotopic transposition, one partially due to the change of medium, Walkow fleshes out the relatively sparse visual description of the novella by placing Underground Man (Henry Czerny) in a small, crowded studio apartment graced only by a few filtered rays of light from outside. The atmosphere is one of cloistered claustrophobia and bookish solitude. In Walkow's adaptation, the novella's psychological reflexivity – morbid consciousness watching itself morbidly consciousing, as it were – becomes the film's **artistic** reflexivity – the film watching itself film. This direct-address reflexivity takes both linguistic form (the character's direct verbal address to the spectator) and visual form (the actor/character's direct look at the camera/spectator). The reflexivity is further underlined by having Underground Man record his life on videotape. The camera becomes an epistemological instrument, the catalytic device which might help the protagonist make sense of his life. In words that stay fairly close to the original, the Underground Man addresses the camera directly:

> I am a sick man.
> I think it's my liver but I refuse to see a doctor.
> From spite. I am a spiteful man . . .
> I was a bad civil servant. I was uncivil . . . spiteful . . .
> No, that's a lie. I am not spiteful. I am not . . .
> I am not anything.

The fact that **we as audience** become Underground Man's interlocutors – by looking at the camera he is also looking at us – cinematizes the implied verbal interlocution of the written text. The camera (and therefore the spectator) takes the place of Underground Man's imaginary interlocutors. What Metz calls the cinema's "missed rendezvous" of actor (present only at the moment of production) and spectator (present only at the moment of reception) is represented here as simultaneous interaction. The technique illustrates, on a different register, Bakhtin's idea that even our most solitary acts – looking in the mirror, masturbation, dream, even suicide – are ultimately dialogic in that they are addressed to someone. The film's characterological encounters, in this sense, are doubled by intertextual encounters; just as Dostoevsky dialogues with St Augustine, Rousseau, and Hegel, so Walkow dialogues not only with Dostoevsky but also with Jonas Mekas, Stan Brakhage, and Hollis Frampton.

Avant-garde cinema has generally been reflexive, denaturalizing the assumed voyeurism of conventional "fourth-wall" dramatic cinema. As Emma Marciano points out, Walkow portrays Underground Man's struggle specifically as one of confrontation with one's own image, as opposed to a written revisitation of one's own memories.[10] The camera, Underground Man hopes, will allow him to "see himself saying it" and thus exorcize his demons and bad memories. And as Underground Man's confession proceeds, as Marciano further points out, the camera becomes more distant, as if the character were driving away the camera in the same way that Underground Man drives away all those with whom he comes into contact. With the Liza story, the camera dollies backward as if in disgust.

But on another level, the film turns the solitary, remembered exchanges of the novella into the performed interlocution typical of the more "embodied" medium of film. Through film's "automatic difference," the dialogue is contextualized and framed by the lighting and color and *mise-en-scène*, all of which signify the mood of the character/narrator, while simultaneously shaping our mood as well. Thus film can make us share the feelings of a character, by placing both character and spectator, almost literally, in the same environment, even as it

Figure 5.1 Henry Czerny in Walkow's *Notes from Underground* (1995), produced by Renegade Films Inc. / Walkow-Gruber Pictures

distances us from this very same character. Whereas in the novel we as readers imagined Underground Man's voice and gestures and facial expressions on the inner stages of our mind, now they are realized for us by a performer, filtered through Henry Czerny's acting style, with its grimaces, mannerisms, twitches, frowns. Dostoevsky's verbal cues become in the film a specific manner of speaking, a timbre, a grain of voice. The narrational stance is thus subtly altered. Whereas the reader of the novella has to take an active role in discerning the cowardice hiding behind Underground Man's verbal bravado (toward the officer, for example), in the film this work is partly performed for us, predigested as it were. In a sense, the novella makes it easier to project ourselves into the verbal posturings of Underground Man, as we transform a series of verbal cues into a virtual, holographic presence that we ourselves have partly shaped. The overpresent screen image, in contrast, is heavily overdetermined with paradigmatic choices and visual details. The novella never describes Underground Man physically, leaving it to the reader's imagination, leaving open the possibility that Underground Man might resemble the reader. The actor in the film, however, does not necessarily look like us, so we have more trouble seeing him as a man like ourselves, or like the Underground Man that we imagined.

As noted earlier, the Walkow adaptation largely skips over the protagonist's rantings about philosophy, progress, and "the good and the beautiful," plunging us instead into his early office days, followed by his various abortive attempts to "embrace humanity." The protagonist crashes the party of the pompous former schoolmate Zerkov. Some obscure masochistic impulse leads him to seek out for company people whom he dislikes and who equally dislike him. Unsurprisingly, the dinner encounter with Zerkov quickly degenerates into a social disaster. Despite the unwelcoming atmosphere, Underground Man invites himself along on their trip to a bordello, leading to the encounter with Liza, on whom he vents all his rage and frustration. Since he lacks the courage to spill his anger directly onto Zerkov, the protagonist scapegoats down the social ladder, displacing his aggression onto Liza. At the same time, he indulges in a Quixotic fantasy of rescuing and "redeeming" Liza. In this sense the character anticipates Travis Bickle's "rescue" of the young prostitute (Jodie Foster) in *Taxi Driver* (1976), a film itself influenced by *Notes from Underground*, whose director, Martin Scorsese, at one point wanted to film the Dostoevsky novella.

In both novella and adaptation, Underground Man is a voyeur. Acutely conscious of his inability to sustain any alien gaze, Underground Man prefers to look without being looked at. Voyeurism has been a theme as well both in the mainstream film (Hitchcock's *Rear Window* [1954], Powell's *Peeping Tom* [1962]) and in the avant-garde cinema (Noel Burch's *Correction Please or How*

We Got into Pictures [1979]). At the end of the film, the Underground Man makes his final declarations direct to the camera, at which point we realize that his confession is being watched in a classroom by Zerkov and others, as if Underground Man had become a specimen for scientific analysis.

An interesting feature of the Walkow adaptation, as Emma Marciano points out, is its strategy of using what Gary Saul Morson and Caryl Emerson, in another context, call "sideshadowing," i.e. of revealing other possible times, other possible alternative comportments or attitudes on the part of the protagonist. Morson and Emerson evoke "a ghostly presence of **might have beens** or **might bes**," of other narrative and narrational possibilities.[11] During the calamitous dinner, for example, the film "realizes," in a kind of cinematic equivalent of the subjunctive mood – what if I **were** to physically attack you! – the protagonist's fantasy of smashing a wine bottle over the heads of his hated dinner companions. In the taxi on the way to the bordello, Underground Man has a falsely proleptic vision of the redemption of Liza. In another slow-motion sequence, he quixotically imagines himself arrested, convicted, imprisoned, and, after his release from prison, going to Zerkov to beg for forgiveness. (The imaginary embrace of the "enemy" corresponds to Girard's analysis of the mediator/scapegoat figure who is at once loved and hated.) A final "sideshadowing" offers a fairytale ending with Liza, with Underground Man caring for her, educating her and eventually marrying her.

In his adaptation, Walkow does not generally choose the path of Pasolini's "cinema of poetry," whereby a character's delirium becomes the trampoline for authorial virtuosity. The protagonist's confusion does not "contaminate" the *mise-en-scène* itself. Marciano points out that the film has a very distinct palette, with "blues and grays dominant in the confession segment, while reds and browns dominate in the flashback sequences."[12] But Walkow does take advantage of a resource available only to film. While literature has the capacity to play on the page with Derridean "split writing," or orchestrate a counterpoint of typographical fonts, cinema can create a dialectic between various film stocks and formats (35 mm, 16 mm, video, digital). And indeed the Walkow film does distinguish between the two temporal "series" – present and flashback – by aligning each with contrasting formats. The confession (the protagonist's present) was first shot on HI8, recorded on Beta, and then blown up to 35 mm, resulting in a crisp image with clear contours, while the memory sequences were shot directly on 35 mm, resulting in softer edges with warmer dominant tones of brown and blue. But while the novella characterizes Underground Man as a shifting, unstable figure in constant movement – both the representer and the represented are in flux – the film's camera is largely static. Like the novella, the film ends ambiguously, without us knowing why Zerkov is watching this confession, or what has happened to the protagonist. While hardly a brilliant adaptation, the Walkow film does manage to deploy the specific resources of film, in this case variable formats, to convey the morbid dialogism and the self-critical "loophole discourse" of Underground Man.

I suggested in the Introduction that filmmakers sometimes realize the transposition of the literary techniques of a given work or author without actually adapting the novel in question. Some of the true heirs of Dostoevsky's Underground Man and the other neurotic narrators, in this sense, are contemporary stand-up comedians. Like Dostoevsky, these artists turn their psychic turmoil and neurosis into a certain edgy strand of comedy. In this sense, Underground Man's encounter with Liza forms the novelistic equivalent of the stand-up comic's story about a bad date: "I had a disastrous date the other night. Well, it wasn't really disastrous . . . it's just that . . ." In this sense, Underground Man anticipates the self-mockingly neurotic world of Lenny Bruce, in an earlier period, and Seinfeld and Gary Shandling and Richard Lewis later. The masks of the clown, Bakhtin writes:

> grant the right not to understand, the right to confuse, to tease, to hyperbolize life; the right to parody others while talking, the right not to be taken literally, not "to be oneself" . . . the right to rip off masks, the right to rage at others with a primeval (almost cultic) rage, and finally the right to betray to the public a personal life, down to its most private and prudent little secrets.[13]

Bakhtin's words carry the echoes of Underground Man as he teases and hyperbolizes and parodies, railing at others with primeval rage while betraying private secrets. At the same time they anticipate contemporary comics – the "cultic rage" of a George Carlin or John Cleese, the "comic spasms" of a Jim Carrey or John Belushi, the "hyperbolizations" of a Richard Prior or a Chris Rock, the manic free-association "confessions" of a Robin Williams. Imagining Underground Man as the nineteenth-century equivalent of the stand-up comic reveals even certain **formal** affinities. Like *Notes from Underground*, stand-up too can be seen as a form of what Russian literary critics call **skaz** (from the root "to say, speak, relate"), a form of discourse which incorporates oral models and subliterary materials. Like a stand-up comic, Underground Man is given to attention-grabbing overstatement: "It's indecent, vulgar, and immoral to live beyond forty! Who lives beyond forty! Answer me honestly. Or let me tell you then: fools and good-for-nothings" (p. 92). Like the stand-up comic, Underground Man examines the humiliating minutiae of everyday life. Isn't a riff on intellectuals and their toothaches exactly the kind of material favored by stand-up comics like Jerry Seinfeld?

The two worlds – Dostoevsky and stand-up – meet in the figure of Woody Allen.
Indeed, the Allen stand-up comic persona has much to do with the Dostoevskyan figures that Allen must have encountered in his early reading. Indeed, it comes as no surprise that Woody Allen has written a pastiche of *Notes from Underground*. It is entitled "Notes from the Overfed" and subtitled "(After reading Dostoevski and the new "Weight Watchers" magazine on the same plane trip)." The essay's opening clearly echoes Underground Man in its nauseating self-portraiture:

> I am fat. I am disgustingly fat. I am the fattest human I know. I have nothing but excess poundage all over my body. My fingers are fat. My wrists are fat. My eyes are fat. (Can you imagine fat eyes?) I am hundreds of pounds overweight. Flesh drips from me like hot fudge off a sundae.

The pastiche takes off, perhaps, from Dostoevsky's own reference to the inordinate value that human beings place on their own fat, and the persona of the story resembles Underground Man in his relentless self-absorption, his penchant for cheap philosophizing, and his being subject to quick emotional turnabouts. Sandy Bates, the neurotic filmmaker of *Stardust Memories* (1980), in this sense, is clearly a latter-day descendant of Underground Man. Allen casts himself as a celebrity-director who reluctantly attends a retrospective in his honor, where he has to listen to the fawning praise of his fans and the inane censure of his critics. The studio executives screen what is retroactively revealed to be a clip from "Suppression," Bates's latest film, find it "horrible," "a disgrace," "pretentious," "shallow," and "morbid." Like Underground Man, Sandy Bates practices a policy of anticipatory self-deprecation, a "loophole discourse" designed to ward off all unsympathetic finalization. Sandy Bates's loophole consists in demonstrating his advance knowledge and refutation of all possible criticisms of himself and his work. Each statement anticipates reactions and answers them in advance; indeed, each response answers the imagined responses to the **answers**.

Reflexive films (perhaps even more than reflexive novels) have often been "bad objects" for critics, who resent their sabotaging of the conventional pleasures of illusion and identification. It is surely no accident that Woody Allen's most widely despised film is also his most self-conscious and avant-gardist. The same strategies tolerated or even praised in Allen's fiction and essays are condemned in *Stardust Memories*. Foster Hirsch, who condemns *Stardust Memories* as "narrow," "parochial," "meanspirited," and "misanthropic," praises in Allen's book *Side Effects* (1980) the same techniques he had condemned in reviews of *Stardust Memories*.[14] It is only because of the differential expectations applied to literature and the cinema that the disruptive techniques lauded in prose fiction are rejected as self-indulgent in film.

Our next problematic narrator, Sergio from *Memorias de subdesarollo* (Memories of Underdevelopment, by Edmundo Desnoes), is clearly a latter-day descendant of Underground Man. Here the "under" of "Underground" becomes the "under" of "Underdevelopment" of a country suffering "under" neo-imperial domination. The novel's Sergio, like Dostoevsky's protagonist, is full of self-loathing, comparing himself to an "insect" and a "fly." He too is a voracious reader of books; he too has disastrous relationships with women; and he too is ultimately very much isolated. Indeed, Alea's initial interest in the story had to do with showing the trajectory of a man who "ends up alone." Like many Dostoevsky characters, Desnoes' protagonist heads toward self-dissolution. Although he lives "overground," in a penthouse, Sergio is as alienated as Underground Man. Like Dostoevsky's protagonist, Sergio otherizes and alienates all those close to him. In the ouverture sequence of the film, after a chilly farewell to wife and family at the Havana airport (Sergio disgustedly wipes off the traces of his wife's kiss), Sergio writes at the typewriter: "All those who loved and nagged me up to the last moment have already gone . . ." (He does not say: "all those I have loved.")

Just as Dostoevsky, from the beginning of his career in the 1840s, was interested in political issues of revolution and the liberation of the serfs, so Desnoes sets his tale against the backdrop of the Cuban revolution. Reflecting on the dangers of radical revolt in the St Petersburg of the 1860s, Dostoevsky warned, in words anticipatory of Desnoes' discussion of "underdevelopment," that "every society can accommodate only that degree of progress that it had developed and begun to understand."[15] The Desnoes novel clearly derives, then, from the line instituted by Dostoevsky in *Notes from Underground*, i.e. the tradition of the irritable, spiteful, inconsistent, unreliable first-person narrator, who is undeserving of our confidence or respect. While the protagonist of *Notes from Underground* railed against all utopias (socialist or otherwise), which he compared to the crystal palace and the ant hill, the protagonist of the Desnoes novel shows ambivalence not about theoretical utopias, but rather about "actually existing socialism" in Cuba at a precise historical moment, that of Playa Giron (The Bay of Pigs), the 1961 US-supported invasion of Cuba (which met ignominious defeat) and the 1962 "Cuban missile crisis."

The narrator/protagonist of *Memories of Underdevelopment* is a Cuban intellectual, living, if not off rents like Underground Man, at least off the fees paid in compensation for his inherited apartment building confiscated by the Cuban government. He decides to stay on in Cuba after the revolution, partly out of curiosity, partly out of conviction, and partly out of disgust for his middle-class cohorts abandoning Havana for Miami. After his wife leaves, Sergio tries unsuccessfully to write, while indulging in, remembering, and fantasizing about a series of sexual affairs. Sergio is the man in-between, neither revolutionary nor anti-revolutionary, divided between his bystander status in relation to the Cuban revolution and his revulsion for what he calls the "stupid Cuban bourgeoisie."

The narrator's persona in the Desnoes novel recalls many of the unreliable narrators of modernist fictions. He has the self-disgust of Roquentin, in Sartre's *La Nausée* (1938), finding himself "mediocre," and even, in an allusion to Gregory Samsa in Kafka's *The Metamorphosis* (1915), a "worthless cockroach." The novel proliferates in the existentialist *topoi* of the postwar period: bad faith, le regard d'autrui, the hostile glances and controlling looks of "witnesses all around and everywhere." In another sense the novel draws on the taproot of the reflexive literary tradition, with its *mise-en-abyme* techniques and self-correcting style. After writing that the brakes of a bus "groaned," the novel's narrator instantly regrets the anthropomorphic nature of the comparison – an allusion, perhaps, to Robbe-Grillet's attempt, in the same period, to rid literature of anthropomorphic imagery – concluding that the comparison was "a stupid idea. Machines never complain or do anything remotely like it."[16] And of another of his own descriptions, the narrator writes that "it's all so boring that I don't know why I'm describing it" (p. 166).

Both book and adaptation of *Memories of Underdevelopment* provide interesting examples of the sometimes unpredictable circuitries of film-literary intertextuality. In this case we have the following sequence of texts in different languages and media. The novel was first published in the US in 1963 as *Inconsolable Memories* (New York: NAL Press), followed by the script in Spanish for the film, followed by a second version in Spanish incorporating scenes from the script in 1967, followed by the film itself in 1968.[17] The original title *Inconsolable Memories* was a reference to a line in *Hiroshima mon amour* (1959) where the Riva character expresses a desire for an "inconsolable memory." The phrase resonates on many levels, since it could refer to the memory of Sergio's various lovers, or to the memory of life prima della revoluzione (before the revolution), or to the love and death themes that pervade both the novel and the film. The reference to *Hiroshima mon amour* also reminds us that like the Resnais/Duras film, *Memories of Underdevelopment* also concerns private and public catastrophes, nuclear threats and erotic dreams.

Memories of Underdevelopment constitutes one of those relatively rare cases where an adaptation decidedly improves on the source novel. Indeed, the author

Figure 5.2 Sergio and his mirror in *Memories of Underdevelopment* (1968), produced by Cuban State Film / Instituto Cubano del Arte e Industrias Cinematográficos (ICAIC)

himself upended conventional notions of "fidelity" by praising the adaptation as "wonderfully treasonous:"

> I don't share the indignation of some writers who feel betrayed by evil filmmakers. I don't deny the treason of the adaptation; rather, I celebrate it. [Alea] has objectivized a world which was inchoate in my head and still abstract in the book. In the film, he combines social density with the subjectivity of a diary.[18]

In the film version Alea achieves the filmic transcoding of a wide gamut of novelistic techniques. But the fundamental technique, one not shared with the novel, is collage. On the one hand, this newspaper-like collage technique can be traced back to Dostoevsky; the newspaper, with its inherently collage-like juxtaposition of random materials, was central to Dostoevsky's aesthetics. For

Bakhtin, it was the key to his "polyphonic" style, since newspapers are "the living reflection of the contradictions of society in the cross-section of a single day, where the most diverse and contradictory material is laid out, extensively, side by side . . ."[19] The newspaper metaphor was also a force within the avant-garde documentary film, as implied by Vertov's term **Kino-Pravda** (Cinema Truth) – which referred simultaneously to the truth of cinema and to the official Soviet newspaper *Pravda* – and as practiced in Santiago Alvarez's documentaries.

But collage was also one of the signature devices of painterly and cinematic modernism, and this modernist collage technique is designated within the film itself. When the protagonist brings a young Cuban woman, Elena, to see his friend, an unnamed film director (played by Alea himself) shows them some porn clips that he plans to include in his next film. The film, he tells them, will be a "sort of collage." The collage technique is referenced as well in the form of a newspaper article about "cutting and pasting," as well as in the modernist collages – for example, the collage showing the Pope framed within a toilet seat – that grace Sergio's apartment walls.

The special power of collage derives from its capacity to bring into close and intensely meaningful association apparently unrelated objects and images and texts, all reframed within the new space of a refashioned creative totality. The aesthetic potency of collage derives from its semiotic openness, its capacity to stage provocative neighborings, generating a structured aleatory which reconciles the formal rigor of art with the randomness of life and what the Surrealists called "the definitive by chance." It is this semiotic openness that makes it possible to see *Memories* scores of times and yet always find something fresh and new, precisely because the spectator never exhausts the open-ended reverberations across the collaged segments.

In "For an Imperfect Cinema," an essay roughly contemporaneous with *Memories*, Cuban filmmaker/theorist Julio Garcia Espinosa warned against the "temptation" of perfection. Technically and artistically perfect cinema, he argued, is almost always a reactionary cinema. Imperfect cinema, in contrast, proposes an art energized by the "low" forms of popular culture. Rather than a self-sufficient cinema, imperfect cinema proposes art as endless critical process.[20] Rather than imitate the unattainably high production values of First World cinema, imperfect cinema turned strategic weakness into tactical strength by using waste materials, turning aesthetic poverty into a badge of honor. In the same period, Cuban filmmaker Santiago Alvarez, whose documentaries on the war in Vietnam and the US civil rights movement are "quoted" in *Memories of Underdevelopment*, practiced "imperfect cinema" by making innovative documentaries like *LBJ* and *Now*, based on the creative collage of found materials.

Such, then, was the historical/aesthetic context of Alea's deployment of collage. But in what ways is the film a collage? The film is, first of all, a **generic** collage. Among the genres of material invoked are: archival news material (the speeches of John Kennedy and Fidel Castro); Cuban TV news reports (about Guantanamo military base, for example); newsreels from the Battista era showing bourgeois debutante balls, life "before the revolution;" quoted documentaries (such as Santiago Alvarez's *Now*); quoted fiction films (e.g. Marilyn Monroe singing "I'm Through with Love"). Alea thus destabilizes the frontiers between documentary and fiction, since the film offers various modalities of the New Wavish mixing of fiction and documentary. The materials worked over by the film range on a spectrum that includes not only the various forms of archival material but also purely staged sequences (e.g. the love affair with Elena), partially staged sequences (actor Sergio Carriere as Sergio at Havana Airport, performing against the backdrop of **actual** departures of Cubans for Miami), and purely subjective sequences (flashbacks to childhood, the relationship to Hanna, the eroticized fantasy about Noemi's baptism).

In *Memories*, characters themselves become, à la Walter Benjamin, assemblages of quotations. The speech of Sergio's lover Elena, for example, forms a collage of pop citations, and especially of her beloved **boleros**. Sergio's psyche, like that of Underground Man, is the arena of a discursive/ideological struggle. If we are, as Bakhtin has suggested, the voices that speak us, then Sergio's mind forms a veritable polyphony of voices – the speeches of Fidel, the poems of Neruda, the aphorisms of Ortega y Gasset, the siren images of Hollywood. But Sergio revoices and recasts what he quotes. To Fidel's famous exhortation "this great mass of humanity has begun to move" Sergio adds an ironic addendum "yes . . . to Miami!" Sergio's character brings with it a vast intertext at once literary and cinematic, and especially the heritage of modernist literature and cinema. In cinematic terms, the character recalls the tormented protagonists of the European art film (for example, Fellini's artists in crisis such as Guido in *8½* [1963], intellectuals in crisis as in *La Dolce Vita* [1960], joyless womanizers in crisis as in Antonioni's *Aventura* [1960] or *Eclipse* [1962]). But Alea's point is precisely that Cuba is **not** Italy, and that he is not Antonioni. As the politicizing title, with its evocation of "underdevelopment" suggests, ennui takes on a different connotation when set against a Caribbean backdrop of oppression and revolution. In the early 1960s, Alea implies, Cubans did not have the **luxury** of ennui.

But these "points" are never made in a preachy or didactic manner but rather through the reciprocal undermining of apparently incompatible genres; in this case the mutual relativization of, on the one hand, the European art film – with its melancholy protagonists, its *flâneur*-style perambulations, its modernist music and montage, and its open endings – and, on the other, the militant documentary, with its social engagement and clear political position-taking. Each genre gains as a result of this reciprocal osmosis: the art film gains social density and critique, and the militant film gains subtlety and humanity. In using documentary and archival footage, Alea draws on a resource uniquely available to the cinema. Admittedly, novelists can include written documents in their fictions, as Doctorow or Ivan Angelo sometimes do. Any number of films deploy actuality footage within literary adaptations – the World War I stock footage in *Jules and Jim* (1961), or the TV reportage footage of the 1968 Soviet invasion of Prague in *The Unbearable Lightness of Being* (1988). But few directors have used archival footage and documentary in the manner that Alea uses it – as part of a critical contextualization of a **character**. In this sense, Alea brings the contextualizing power of cinema to its paroxysm, in a manner perhaps unique within the history of adaptation.

The generic dialogue in *Memories* is very much linked to Sergio's double function as simultaneously character and narrator. As a narrator, he is aligned with the director and the norms of the text. In that capacity, he orchestrates discourses and citations, and he provides the voice-over narration of the mini-documentary segments concerning such subjects as the Bay of Pigs, Hunger in Cuba, and so forth. As a character, however, he is only partially aligned with the director. Indeed, Sergio as a character is indirectly criticized by the very documentary segments that his voice narrates. The documentary segments contextualize Sergio, creating a counterpoint between the subjective and the objective. One documentary segment "stages," as it were, passages drawn from Leon Rozitchner's book about the Bay of Pigs entitled *Bourgeois Morality and Revolution*.[21] Thus the adaptation features an "adaptation within the adaptation" in the form of a filmic version, not of a novel, but of a work of non-fiction. The Rozitchner book speaks of the "dialectical relationship of the individual and the group," a phrase that resonates with Sergio and **his** relationships. Although Alea never falls into the Manichean temptation of demonizing Sergio as a detestable and selfish bourgeois, the *mise-en-scène* does subtly undercut the character through telling details. The decor of his apartment with its ultimately innocuous avant-garde props, for example, constitute pseudo-radical gestures without real-world consequences. At one point, Sergio regards himself in the mirror, while his interior monologue comments proudly that "I think I affect a certain dignity." Sergio's smug self-satisfaction is then violently interrupted when Elena's "*guapo*" brother bursts into the apartment to accuse him of molesting his sister, threatening to beat him up if he does not marry her, an intervention which obviously wreaks havoc with Sergio's claim to "dignity."

Alea began his film career by making documentaries, and was schooled in Italy at the Centro Experimentale, a school very much under the aesthetic/political influence of Rossellini, another director who systematically mingled documentary and fiction techniques. *Memories* betrays the influence not only of neo-realism but also of various documentary traditions. While some of the documentary segments cite pre-existing films, other portions were invented for the film itself. The "excess seeing" of the documentary sequences help us to see what Sergio as a character cannot see, exposing the shallowness of Sergio's pose of proudly defiant solitude. His illusion of being apolitical and above the fray seems risible in the context of an imminent threat of a nuclear war, where existential solitude has lost its heroic aura. Sergio is alone, yet life continues around him. The juxtaposition of his isolation with the missile crisis points up what Bakhtin saw as the theoretical and practical **impossibility** of solitude. In a nuclear holocaust, individual attitudes are absolutely irrelevant; mere sensibility is laughably ineffective.

In this sense, *Memories of Underdevelopment* carries out the theoretical/aesthetic project outlined by Alea in his book *Dialectica del espectador* (Dialectics of the Spectator), where he calls for multiple, simultaneous "dialectics" of contrary impulses and values, between the epic and the everyday, between fiction and documentary, between emotion and distance, between celebration and critique, between the **verfremdungseffekt** of Brecht and the **pathos** of Eisenstein.[22] Within this dialectic, *Memories* produces an oscillation of identification and critique. In characterological terms, Sergio is handsome, intelligent, and urbane, the center of the film's attention and focalization. Many of his affirmations ring true, especially in so far as he functions as off-screen narrator of the documentary-style segments. At the same time, the film critiques his elitist tendency to see everything through Europeanized eyes. For Sergio, who has self-proclaimedly "always tried to live like a European," Europe is the ultimate ontological measure, the reality in relation to which the rest of the world is mere shadow. And this Eurocentric attitude is profoundly gendered. The novel's Sergio complains that the fate of underdeveloped intellectuals is to "masturbate over the image of first world women." The film's Sergio scorns Cuban woman as full of black beans, inferior not only to idealized fantasy figures like Marilyn Monroe, but also to his former lover Hanna, who, unlike Elena, "is not an underdeveloped Cuban girl."

Sergio's literary pilgrimage, symptomatically, is not to the home of a **Cuban** writer but rather to Hemingway's. Rather than show Sergio reading Alejo Carpentier or Nicholas Guillen, the film shows Sergio reading Hemingway and Nabokov. The Desnoes novel develops this theme even more assertively. There the narrator describes Cuban intellectuals as completely derivative: "That's all we deserve, copies. We're nothing but a bad copy of the powerful and civilized countries, a caricature, a cheap reproduction" (p. 138). Both French novels and American consumer products, the novel's narrator complains, make him feel inferior. Sergio buys into a series of hierarchies which always inferiorize Cuba: European and American writers over Cuban writers; European cuisine over Cuban black beans; the blonde Hanna over the **morena** Elena. But rather than discuss these themes explicitly, as in the novel, the film evokes them through juxtaposition and *mise-en-scène*, indirectly refuting the view that film is inevitably less subtle than literature.

At the same time, Sergio as narrator is acutely aware of the limitations of First World artists and the folly of trying to emulate them. This awareness emerges especially during the visit to the Hemingway house/museum, a visit which forms part of Sergio's crusade to remold Elena according to a classy and Europeanized standard. Sergio's goal is to educate Elena, to endow her with information about painting and literature as forms of what Bourdieu would call "cultural capital." Sergio's voice-over, in this sequence, offers a devastating critique of Hemingway's persona, and notably his machismo and the desperate race against death which culminated, ironically, in his suicide. But the sequence also reverberates ironically in relation to Sergio himself, drawing attention to the subterranean currents linking him to the American author. The story Sergio reads aloud – "The Short Happy Life of Frances Macomber" – bears on the adolescent immaturity of a male character. The *mise-en-scène* also makes the point: both Hemingway and Sergio live in towers, and both are hunters – one of animals, the other of women. But while Hemingway was at least productive, Sergio is blocked, stalled, artistically impotent, or to use the word on which his typewriter jams – **jodido** ("fucked up").

Many of Sergio's critical words about Hemingway end up boomeranging against himself. His claim that Hemingway was "never really interested" in Cuba applies equally to himself. The critique of Hemingway's Eurocentric decor applies equally to Sergio's own apartment. Sergio's mockery of Master Hemingway's attempt to mold his servant into an ideal "Gunga Dinn" resonates ironically with his own attempt to mold Elena into a cultivated **bourgeoise**. His idea that Cuban women, after a certain age, turn into "rotten fruit" describes himself as well. His observation that Elena "doesn't connect things" pinpoints his own intellectual blindness to social relationality. Even the term "underdevelopment," which he extends patronizingly to Cuba and to people like Elena, points accusingly back at him.

The encounter with the "urban reform committee" is especially telling in this regard. In this sequence, two government officials come to evaluate Sergio's living space. A man and a woman ask Sergio a series of questions about the size and layout of the apartment. We realize that now "the people" are boss, and that they observe Sergio with a critical eye. (The sequence ends with a shot of an enormous eyeball.) The woman investigator's appearance and concerns – she asks about the maids' quarters – suggests that she might have been a maid before the revolution. Sergio acknowledges, somewhat awkwardly, that the apartment has five bathrooms. Although the officials are not hostile, Sergio has difficulty sustaining their gaze. The fact that Sergio and the officials are generally not filmed together within the same space suggests that they inhabit two very different social/cinematic worlds. Sergio seems not to have really thought about his own apartment, since he has trouble estimating its size and scope. While writers are supposed to be observant, those on whom "nothing is lost," Sergio is unaware even of his own "habitat." If he cannot account for his own environment, one wonders, how can he as a novelist possibly register the lives and feelings of others?

The urban reform sequence points to two key "chronotopic elements" – architecture and decor – which can be evoked verbally in literature but which play a significantly more "concrete" role in film. *Memories of Underdevelopment* repeatedly contrasts the Underground Man-like solitude of the writer, associated with the interior space of his apartment, with the public spaces of the outside world. "Did the city change," Sergio asks, "or did I?" Referring to the decaying buildings of old Havana, Sergio compares the scene spread out before his eyes to a movie set. As a Third World *flâneur*, Sergio is often seen walking alongside walls, so that even exteriors come to have a claustrophobic feeling. But more generally, Alea deploys architecture or urban backdrops to comment on the action. Many of Sergio's childhood flashbacks, for example, take us to the old, decaying center of historical Havana, a reference to his social origins, but also, perhaps, to his own decaying self. The brawl with Elena's outraged family about what they see as her defloration, similarly, is staged in front of a window display of virginal white wedding dresses. *Mise-en-scène* and performance also underline Elena's discomfort, as a person from "*el pueblo*," in more bourgeois settings such as Sergio's apartment and Hemingway's house, both of which evoke a material standard and style of life from which she feels removed. In Sergio's apartment, she switches the music from classical to pop, thus acoustically molding the space in conformity with her own popular tastes.

Both novel and film express mild, cautious, critiques of the Cuban revolution, at times leading some North American critics to see it, mistakenly, as a "dissident" film, when in fact it was made under the official auspices of the Cuban

Institute of Cinematic Art and Industry.[23] As his airport bus passes a pro-Fidel billboard, Sergio as narrator laments the fact that "people need someone to think for them." When Sergio visits his (formerly Catholic) childhood school, we note that a portrait of Lenin has replaced the Virgin — the Communist portrait substitutes the Catholic icon — implying a religious substratum within Cuban-style Marxism. The Hemingway sequence makes fun of Russians taking photographs of Elena as the "beautiful Cuban senorita."[24] In the bookstore, Sergio has to make his way past reams of pro-Soviet propaganda about Soviet astronauts before getting to the book that really interests him — *Lolita*. The Nabokov reference also reverberates ironically with Sergio, since *Lolita* too concerns a cultivated and Europeanized older man who prefers the company of younger, less educated, more "popular" women.

In his published essays, Alea rejected Stalinist purism and defensive nationalism in the cultural realm, calling instead for modernist internationalism. As an island, Alea argued, Cuba needs ideas from elsewhere, precisely to compensate for its insularity. During what seems to be an actual Conference (at the National Library) dedicated to the subject of "Literature and Underdevelopment," Sergio as both observer and off-screen narrator endorses the critique of the Conference offered by American playwright Jack Gelber, who asks why revolutionary intellectuals would resort to an archaic, constipated form like the roundtable discussion to convey their ideas. (Here we find a filmic version of the Cervantic practice of including passages of literary criticism.) A true revolution, Gelber argues, would revolutionize the forms as well. This rather remarkable sequence, perhaps unique in the annals of adaptation, shows the actual author of the novel, Edmundo Desnoes, seated as part of the panel. In a rare instance of an adaptation poking fun at a physically present author of the source novel, the film has Sergio, perhaps spurred by his envy of an actually published writer, silently heckle Desnoes in his voice-over commentary: "You must feel pretty important. Here you don't have much competition. Outside of Cuba you'd be a nobody." Like Underground Man, Sergio launches quiet, mental attacks but does not usually voice his aggressive thoughts publicly. The scene also calls attention to the vestiges of racism in Cuba. At the panel, Desnoes claims that as a Cuban in New York he suffered racism; he was regarded as a "spic," a black man — "I was a spic, we're all blacks." But the film problematizes Desnoes' equation of the social oppression of white and black Cubans by showing, at precisely this moment, an elderly black man serving water to the panelists, i.e. a black Cuban reduced to a classically subservient role. But in all of these instances, the critique of Cuban society is made from the left, not from the right. That is, the critique implies a desire not for the **status quo ante** but rather for a revolution that is **more** egalitarian, **more** equal, and **less** racist and Eurocentric than the actually existing revolution.

What I have called the "ironic boomerang" effect also operates in other sequences. The porn loop sequence, for example, shows porn materials from the Battista period in a treadmill succession of coitus interruptus repetitions. The scene interrupts Sergio's dinner with Elena in a Chinese-Cuban restaurant. Sergio's description of the life of an actress as one of mere repetition – "the same words, the same words" – gives way to footage of a man and a woman making love on a rocky shore, the man endlessly mounting the woman thanks to the loop effect. The repeated shot then segues to other porn footage, subsequently revealed to be material destined for inclusion in a forthcoming film by Sergio's director-friend (Alea himself). The porn sequence makes a number of points, including pro-revolutionary propaganda points: (1) that the Mafia produced porn in Cuba under Battista; (2) that pornographic materials, formerly censored by the Battista regime, can now be shown in the era of the revolution (i.e. Cubans are now freer, after the revolution, to see such scenes, and without the moralistic hypocrisy of the Battista period). At the same time, the porn loop evokes Sergio's pornographic imaginary – while dining with Elena he is actually thinking of sex – as well as the iterative vacuity of a life of meaningless sexual conquests.

Alea's collage technique performs constant variations on the same thematic materials. The opening sequence, of a salsa party, works by repetition, in that the salsa itself has a refrain. This special "*montuno*" section of the salsa consists of instrumental repetition and the refrain: "*donde esta Teresa*?" Later the same dance is seen again, and we realize that the protagonist Sergio was present at the party, that he perhaps witnessed a murder. The second time around the very **lack** of sound makes the scene eerie and ominous. Any number of scenes are repeated in a different register: Sergio's tape-recording of his wife Laura is first heard as Sergio, in a very Buñuelian fetishistic sequence, tries on his wife's clothes. His placing of a stocking over his head (rather like a criminal dressing for a crime) coincides with her recorded words "You are a monster." The second version of the same material suggests that his wife, exasperated with his sadistic taunts, has left Cuba precisely in order to leave **him**. The sequence ends with Laura biting her fist, which segues to him brushing his teeth. The baptism of the Protestant maid, Noemi, similarly, is seen twice. As Sergio first imagines it, she arises from the water like Venus from the half-shell, accompanied by Chopinesque music, her erect nipples poking through the wet robe. The second time the same scene occurs with lifelike "flatness." A pastor baptizes her while surrounded by his congregation, without music and with no breasts visible. Finally, even the seduction of Elena is repeated, first as staged drama, and the second time verbally at the trial, framed in legalistic language: "the defendant did then take the plaintiff to his apartment etc." To comic and ironic effect, the same scene is recalled "through" the abstract precision of legalistic jargon.

At times, Sergio's relation to Elena reminds us of both Buñuel's *Viridiana* (1961) and Hitchcock's *Vertigo* (1958), films where erotically obsessed male protagonists dress up their objects of desire so that they resemble former lovers. Sergio asks Elena to literally wear his wife's clothes, a fetishistic repetition reminiscent of both the Buñuel and Hitchcock films. *Memories* also intimates a euphemistic form of prostitution: Sergio offers Elena his wife's clothing, in an exchange which suspiciously resembles a quid pro quo for sex. (Elena's family, in their stubborn, lower-class directness, make the charge explicit: "You think you can sleep with our daughter in exchange for some of your wife's old clothes!") Speaking more broadly, a certain schematic quality informs Sergio's relations to women, in that the women range widely in terms of class, religion, and political affiliations. Hanna, who is Jewish in the novel but only implied to be possibly Jewish in the film (we are told that her family fled from the Nazis), is blonde, refined, and lives in New York. Laura, the wife, is fake blonde, Americanized, likes Colgate toothpaste, and reads American bestsellers. Noemi is Protestant, virginal, an object of fantasy. And Elena for him represents "the Cuban people," much as Susan Alexander, for Charles Foster Kane, represented the "American people."

Sergio sees women, especially, from a distance, as if through translucent glass. He observes his wife through the glass windows at the airport, his apartment features bottled up erotic pictures, and so forth. Alea also introduces a crucial prop absent from the novel — Sergio's telescope — with which he scans Havana, and especially the bikinied women at the swimming pool of a neighboring hotel. At first, Sergio sees people from the secure heights of his apartment, with a sense of superiority. On one level, *Memories of Underdevelopment* is structured in the same way as *Rear Window* (1954), Hitchcock's famous anatomy of cinematic voyeurism. The central trajectory of *Memories*, like that of *Rear Window*, "consists in the progressive shattering of [Sergio's] illusion of voyeuristic separation from life."[25] As in *Rear Window*, Sergio's apartment space becomes more and more vulnerable to outside intervention. At the beginning of the film, Sergio, like Jeffries in the Hitchcock film, enjoys the power of an unreciprocated gaze. Many shots in *Memories* situate Sergio as apartment-bound voyeur, and one shot, in which he scratches his back with a backscratcher, evokes an almost identical moment involving Jimmy Stewart, immobilized in his cast and wheel-

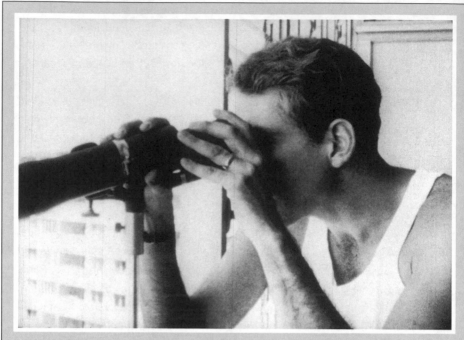

Figure 5.3 Sergio as voyeur in *Memories of Underdevelopment* (1968), produced by Cuban State Film / Instituto Cubano del Arte e Industrias Cinematográficos (ICAIC)

chair, in *Rear Window*. The basic logic of the film, like that of the Hitchcock film, is the ironic reversal of the gaze. The man with the telescope, in *Memories*, like the man with the telephoto lens, in *Rear Window*, observes others from an apparently safe distance. But in the end, the observer becomes the observed. Within a regime of scopic inversion, the voyeur is **vu**. Sergio the cool observer, "monarch of all he surveys" (to use Mary Louise Pratt's suggestive phrase), becomes himself the object of scrutiny.[26] The reform committee looks over his apartment and scrutinizes his reaction. In the trial, the judge insists that Sergio "look at him." As the film progresses, Sergio becomes less and less the subject of the gaze and more and more the object of scrutiny. The film's finale points to the political dimension of the gaze. The news report of John F. Kennedy's speech shows American spy-satellite footage of a Cuban base, a form of surveillance; in a word, a form of geopolitical voyeurism. But Castro refuses this voyeurism, proudly warning that "no one inspects our country." (One wonders, of course, whether such heroic posturing means much in an age of high-tech surveillance.) In any case, here we find just one of the many ways in which

Memories sets up suggestive parallels between private voyeurism and public surveillance, in media-specific ways that transcode the themes and strategies of the novel.

The Metamorphoses of *Lolita*

Roughly a century after *Notes from Underground*, Vladimir Nabokov picks up, albeit in a parodic mode, some of Dostoevsky's narrative techniques in his *Lolita* (1955), his masterwork about a middle-aged European intellectual absorbed in the pursuit of murder and nympholepsy. I will not rehearse the details of the story of *Lolita* here, since the very name "Lolita" has become synonymous in the popular mind with exactly the kind of story that the novel tells. Ironically, Nabokov was never especially fond of Dostoevsky, whom he called a "claptrap journalist and a slapdash comedian" who wrote "irresponsible and somewhat antiquated novels."[27] Nabokov's list of favorite authors includes Joyce, Proust, Pushkin, and even Poe, but not Dostoevsky. While finding some of Dostoevsky's texts amusing, Nabokov claimed to detest his "soulful prostitutes" and "sensitive murderers."[28] Indeed, *Lolita* might be seen as the ultimate spoof on the theme of the "sensitive murderer."

Yet despite Nabokov's expressed hostility toward Dostoevsky, his narrator in *Lolita* clearly carries the genetic traces, the literary DNA, as it were, not only of Don Quixote (since the memoirs are the ravings of a hyper-literate obsessive), but also of Dostoevsky's Underground Man. Like the narrator of *Notes from Underground*, the narrator of *Lolita* is unreliable in the extreme. Indeed, he is self-declaredly mad, sometimes "losing contact with reality" and given to what he himself calls "bouts of insanity." As with *Notes from Underground*, here again the perverse pleasure of the text partially consists in reading between the lines, in detecting the inelegant, not to say grotesque, behavior hidden "beneath" the elegant style. "You can always count on a murderer," Humbert reassures us, "for a fancy prose style."[29] Yet one of the dangers of unreliable narration is that hermeneutically challenged readers will take liars at their word. Thus some readers were seduced by the murderer's fancy style, as when critic Robertson Davies summed up the story as "the exploitation of a weak adult by a corrupt child."[30] It is ultimately up to us to discern, in the interstices of all the circumlocutions and literary display of *Lolita*, exactly what is going on. Indeed, at times we have to figure out that sexual acts are taking place, to realize, for example, that when Humbert's tumescent prose speaks of being "proud like a

Turk in his tower" as Lolita sits in his lap, for example, he is referring to his erection, and that going "over the abyss" means he is having an orgasm.

Lolita is written in the first-person confessional point of view, a latter-day descendant, in a long literary-historical perspective, of the celebrated "confessions" of St Augustine and Jean-Jacques Rousseau. Like his forebears, Nabokov too was skeptical about the possibilities of honest autobiographical revelation, even within the intimacy of a diary. (Hermann, the narrator of Nabokov's *Despair*, calls the diary "the lowest form of literature.")[31] Nabokov picks up his narrational technique, more particularly, from the neurotic, unreliable, self-deconstructing narrators of Dostoevsky novellas such as *Notes from Underground*. Divinely egocentric and solipsistic, the Humbert of the novel controls his own self-presentation; consequently, we get only glimpses of what Nabokov called "the vain and cruel wretch" who "manages to appear touching." So the challenge is to distinguish between the authorial voice, which Nabokov calls "an anthropomorphic deity impersonated by me," and the narrational voice of the character Humbert.[32]

Nabokov's imaginary had always been shaped by the cinema. Already in the 1920s he was writing scenarios. In the early 1930s former Moscow art theater director Sergei Bertenson invited Nabokov to Hollywood to devise story lines. Both *Camera Obscura* in 1932 and the rewrite *Laughter in the Dark* in 1938 revolve around a man who falls in love with an usherette who dreams of becoming a film star. An early avatar of the Humbert Humbert character in the novel *The Enchanter* (1986) watches young girls at play but perceives only the "senselessly smooth movement of slow-motion film."[33] Nabokov's *Bend Sinister* (1947) includes camera notations such as "photographed from above" and notes to the "actors."

By crowding *Lolita* with references to movies and stars and spectatorship, Nabokov brings Girard's notion of "triangular" and "mimetic" desire into the age of the mass media. The societal imaginary is no longer inflected by romantic literature, as in *Madame Bovary*, but rather by Hollywood films. Everyday life is shown as shaped by cinematic art. The film industry functions as pedagogue; behavior too is learned from movies: in *Lolita*, kissers close their eyes "as Hollywood teaches." As Alfred Appel, Jr lovingly delineates in *Nabokov's Dark Cinema*, the novel is littered with movie references.[34] Humbert, after a lover's spat with Valechka, regrets having merely slammed the door, when he could have delivered the "backhand slap" more in conformity with the "rules of the movies." Humbert describes himself, for example, as "a great big handsome hunk of movieland manhood." Here the narrator's abuse of a poetic device – alliteration – becomes the aesthetic correlative of the clichés of fan magazines.

Allusions to movie stars, at this point in literary history, become a kind of descriptive shorthand premised on readerly cine-competence, as in Humbert's account of Charlotte as "a weak solution of Marlene Dietrich."

Interestingly, Humbert Humbert himself thematizes the issue of the narrative capacities of film vis-à-vis novel. Humbert at one point calls himself an idiot for not having **filmed** Lolita: "Idiot. Triple idiot. I could have filmed her. I would have had her now with me, before my eyes, in the projection room of my pain and despair" (p. 59). Witnessing such a scene, Humbert imagines himself "a humble hunchback abusing [himself] in the dark." In the "seduction" scene, Humbert notes that he "seemed to have shed [his] clothes and slipped into [his] pajamas with the kind of fantastic instantaneousness which is implied when in a cinematographic scene the process of changing is cut" (p. 118). In another suggestive passage, Nabokov's narrator expresses a kind of envy of the cinema. Gleefully reporting his wife Charlotte's providential death by car crash, Humbert deplores the fact that he:

> has to put the impact of an instantaneous vision into a sequence of words; their physical accumulation on the page impairs the actual flash, the sharp unity of impression . . . At this point, I should explain that the prompt appearance of the patrolmen, hardly more than a minute after the accident, was due to their having been ticketing the illegally parked cars in a cross lane two blocks down the grade; that the fellow with the glasses was Frederick Beale Jr, driver of the Packards . . . and finally that the laprobe on the sidewalk (where she had so often pointed out to me with disapproval the crooked green cracks) concealed the mangled remains of Charlotte, who had been knocked down and dragged several feet by the Beale car as she was hurrying across the street . . . (p. 91)

Humbert laments the incorrigible, frustrating linearity of the linguistic signifier, the plodding deliberateness of prose fiction, with its subordination to linear consecution, its congenital incapacity to seize the moment in its multifaceted simultaneity. At the same time, style itself becomes symptomatic of a severely disturbed sense of human values. The meaning of the "mangled remains" of a person well known to the narrator (and who had shown him only kindness) is obscured by the disproportionate attention to the trivial details of green cracks and laprobes. Charlotte's death is subordinated to a writer's maniacal obsession with getting the details right. The very syntax is perverse, as Charlotte is "killed off" in a dependent, subordinate clause ("Charlotte, who had been knocked down . . ."). The same moment as staged in Kubrick's *Lolita* (1962), in contrast, **does** offer simultaneity: we see the crash as we hear it, along with the commentative music which conveys a tragically suspenseful atmosphere which matches and underlines the events presented. Yet Nabokov, paradoxically, conveys more sense of discontinuity between theme and style – between the tragic motif of untimely death, on the one hand, and the flip, cynical style of Humbert's presentation of that death on the other – than does Kubrick, who decides not to take advantage of the potentially discontinuous multiplicity of tracks available to the filmmaker.

In another passage of the novel, Humbert tries his hand at genre criticism. Delineating Lolita's tastes in movies, the narrator explains:

> Her favorite kinds were, in this order: musicals, underworlders, Westerners. In the first, real singers and dancers had unreal stage careers in an essentially grief-proof sphere of existence wherefrom death and truth were banned, and where, at the end, white-haired, dewy-eyed, technically deathless, the initially reluctant father of a show-crazy girl always finished by applauding her apotheosis on fabulous Broadway. The underworld was a world apart: there, heroic newspapermen were tortured, telephone bills ran to millions, and, in a robust atmosphere of incompetent marksmanship, villains were chased through sewers and storehouses by pathologically fearless cops . . . Finally, there was the mahogany landscape, the florid-faced, blue-eyed roughriders, the prim pretty schoolteacher arriving in Roaring Gulch, the rearing horse, the spectacular stampede, the pistol thrust through the shivered windowpane, the stupendous fistfight, the crashing mountain of dusty old furniture, the table used as a weapon, the timely somersault, the pinned hand still groping for the dropped bowie knife, the grunt, the sweet crash of fist against chin, the kick in the belly, the flying tackle; and immediately after a plethora of pain that would have hospitalized a Hercules . . . nothing to show but the rather becoming bruise on the bronzed cheek of the warmed-up hero embracing his gorgeous frontier bride. (pp. 155–6)

The passage vividly evokes readerly memories of hundreds of cinematic scenes. Nabokov's mimetic prose conveys not only the images but also the feel of the editing of the films, as in the quick-cut succession of "close shots" in the account of the Western, where the gutturals and the fricatives and the dentals and the sibilants and the plosives – the thrust pistol, the stupendous fistfight, the crashing furniture, the grunt and the crash and the kick and the tackle – convey the visceral violence of the genre.

As the previous passage suggests, Nabokov is also an extraordinarily sound-sensitive writer. In the screenplay to *Lolita*, Nabokov requests that the director reproduce the "the hot, moist sound . . . the tickle and the buzz, the vibration, the thunder of [Lolita's] whisper." The same acoustic sensitivity is evident in the account of the seduction night in the Enchanted Hunters Hotel:

> There is nothing louder than an American hotel . . . the corridor would brim with cheerful, resonant and inept exclamations ending in a volley of goodnights. When that stopped, a toilet immediately north of my cerebellum took over. It was a manly, energetic, deep-throated toilet, and it was used many times. Its gurgle and gush and long afterflow shook the wall behind me. Then someone in a southern direction was extravagantly sick, almost coughing out his life with his liquor, and his toilet descended like a veritable Niagara, immediately beyond our bathroom. And when finally all the waterfalls had stopped, and the enchanted hunters were sound asleep, the avenue under the window of my insomnia, to the west of my wake . . . degenerated into the despicable haunt of gigantic trucks roaring through the wet and windy night. (pp. 119–20)

If we could "see" the films described in the earlier passage about genre, here we can virtually "hear" the sounds evoked, thanks to the use of onomatopoeia ("gurgle" and "gush") and to the evocative, anthropomorphic language (the "manly" and "energetic" toilet). In an uncanny way, Nabokov anticipates innovations in multitrack sound which came to the cinema only decades later. Nabokov's almost comic precision about directionality – "north of my cerebellum . . . in a southern direction . . . to the west of my wake" – provides the literary equivalent of stereophonic and later Dolby sound, where one becomes conscious of the location and thrust and directionality of sound. (One possible way of adapting such a passage would be to have the screen go blank, while the various noises emerge from the speakers spread around the screen and the theater.)

Before becoming a film, *Lolita* the novel took an intermediate narrative form, that of Nabokov's 400-page screenplay, conceived by its author as a "vivacious variant" of the novel, of which Kubrick used but a small portion. The screenplay is rather more audacious than the film, although Nabokov himself recognizes in the preface that the "author's goal of infinite fidelity" may be a "producer's ruin." In the published screenplay, Nabokov contrasts what he sees as the beatific solitude of literary writing with the chaotic collectivity of filmmaking, which Nabokov compares to a "communal bath where the hairy and the slippery mix in a multiplication of mediocrity."[35] Speculating on how he might have directed the film himself, Humbert imagines himself an *auteur*-tyrant of the kind imagined by certain versions of *auteur* theory:

> I would have advocated and applied a system of total tyranny, directing the play or the picture myself, choosing settings and costumes, terrorizing the actors, mingling with them in the bit part of guest, or ghost . . . prompting them, and in a word, pervading the entire show with the will and art of one individual.[36]

The screenplay also makes frequent allusion to Edgar Allen Poe, appropriate given both the gothic tone of the story and the nympholeptic tendencies of the American writer. The screenplay also includes a cameo role for Nabokov himself, a Hitchcockian touch that recalls his guest appearance in his own *Despair*, and which would have constituted the filmic equivalent of his anagrammatic presence in *Lolita* in the form of "Vivian Darkbloom."

The Nabokov screenplay also develops the embedded narration featured in the book. Expanding the role of the pedantic Dr John Ray, Jr, it develops a constant interplay between Ray's presentation of Humbert's notes and Humbert's own self-presentation. The screenplay in this sense creates a dual alter-ego narration, another doubling like that of Humbert and Quilty. The screenplay also promotes a dialectical interplay between direct and indirect narration. Valeria screaming "I hate you!" at Humbert segues to Dr John Ray's voice commenting that "she had never been more voluble." The screenplay is more prone than the Kubrick film to comic interruption and dedramatization. For Charlotte's fateful car crash, the screenplay has the film cut to traffic policemen examining diagrams of the accident, a narrative dislocation which visually translates the nonchalantly perverse syntax of Humbert's account of his wife's death. The stress in the Nabokov screenplay is on mediations of all types: photographs that come alive, a tape-recording of a Humbert lecture. The narrator of the screenplay is more interventionist than that of the Kubrick film; he requests specific shots, a technique "faithful" to certain passages in *Lolita* where the narrator actually addresses any future adapter of the book: "If you want to make a movie of my book, have one of those faces gently melt into my own, while I look" (p. 203). The suggestion anticipates precisely the technique adopted two years later by Alfred Hitchcock in *The Wrong Man* (1956), where the face of the wrongly accused Henry Fonda is lap dissolved into that of the actual thief. The screenplay also features completely fantastic images, for example a "ripply shot" of a knight in full armor on a black horse or of the graceful specter of his mother "holding a parasol and blowing kisses to her husband and child who stand below. Looking up, hand in hand."[37] The last vignette is anticipatory of the shots of Woody Allen's mother floating in the sky over Manhattan in *New York Stories* (1989). Had they been filmed, these vignettes would have formed part of a completely different film, featuring an anti-illusionistic aesthetic more reminiscent of Fellini or Woody Allen than of the early Kubrick. Nabokov's screenplay also constantly anthropomorphizes the camera, having it "glide," "slide," and "slither," so as to suggest an active, constantly moving camera functioning almost as a kind of narrator. One *Rear Window*-like sequence, entitled "Various Rooms," has the camera "glide from room to room at dawn [so as to] construct a series of situations contrasting with the atmosphere in Room 342."[38]

The Nabokov screenplay also brings up interesting questions relevant to the theory of adaptation. It reveals the instabilities of textual production, the fact that so-called definitive works are actually only one version arbitrarily frozen into definitive status. The screenplay, for example, includes scenes rejected from the final draft of the novel yet reinstated in the screenplay, as well as dialogue unlike anything in the novel, all of which elicits a fascinating question: if a novelist has written a novel, but also provided a screenplay which is already "unfaithful" to the novel, to which text is the filmmaker to be "faithful?"

Nabokov's own reaction to the Kubrick film was contradictory:

> I discovered that Kubrick was a great director, that his *Lolita* was a first-rate film with magnificent actors, and that only ragged odds and ends of my script had been used. The modifications, the garbling of my little finds, the omission of entire scenes and all sorts of other changes may not have been sufficient to erase my name from the credit titles but they certainly made the picture as unfaithful to the original script as an American poet's translation from Rimbaud or Pasternak.[39]

Nabokov also offered his own analysis of the Kubrick film in the form of a poem, entitled "Pale Film" in an allusion to his own *Pale Fire*. In the poem, anatomized by Richard Corliss in his study of *Lolita*, Nabokov speaks of himself as the "novelist who watched/as each of his books-into-films was botched," where "similes were debased into a smile," where he "intersected with the movies' gaze/as Humbert saw the young Dolores Haze:"

> I saw my words made whispers, twelve made teen
> Back roads made backlots, US made UK
> And green made gold, and me an émigré
> From Lo, whom I conceived but could not save . . .

Referring to his work as an extra in German cinema, Nabokov compares himself to "the larval author lurking in costume/as Hitchcock did, or Vivian Darkbloom." Applying his "writer's sleight-of-hand" to these "film-besotted wretches," Nabokov finally consoles himself with an assertion of the ultimate superiority of the verbal medium of literature: "nitrate reels will decompose, but each good reader will preserve my prose."[40]

Kubrick cleans up Nabokov's "messy" protagonist and "mainstreams" the relationship with Lolita. Partially as a sop to the censors, the Kubrick version makes an important structural change, also made in Nabokov's screenplay, by creating a circular structure whereby the murder of Quilty begins and ends the film. The change generates a shift in genre from erotic confession to murder mystery: the hermeneutic tease is no longer **who** killed Quilty or who Quilty is but rather **why** a specific person — Humbert — killed Quilty. Through this framing device, Kubrick downplays the novel's eroticism, thus giving Kubrick a strategic advantage in his inevitable struggles with potential censors. In the novel, we know that Humbert is a murderer but we do not know whom he has murdered. In the film, we know whom he has murdered but not why he has murdered.

The generic shift has the corollary benefit of placing Quilty center stage, thus authorizing more space for the mercurial performance of Peter Sellers. (Kubrick's long-take style, furthermore, allows room for Sellers to spread his wings as a performer.) Along with Quilty, Sellers also plays the unnamed guest in the Enchanted Hunters Hotel, the psychologist Dr Zemph, and the (unseen) salacious phone-caller from the morality squad. The Quilty character becomes a shape-shifter, incarnating some of the protean, Menippean spirit that animates the novel. Sellers, who comes from the world of stand-up comedy, radio parody sketches, and the *Goon Show*, thus shares an affinity with the genre that surreptitiously permeates Kubrick's later *Dr Strangelove* (1964), where many of the routines could easily have been drawn from the repertoires of stand-up comics like Mel Brooks, Sid Ceaser, Mike Nichols, and Elaine May. Through a kind of displacement from narrative to character, Quilty becomes a kind of ambulatory intertext, a performative embodiment of the Nabokovian style, no longer as literary citation but rather as allusive improvisation.

Many of the specific features of the Kubrick adaptation can be partially explained by the pressures of censorship. The film combats the censors, or better censors itself, for example, by normalizing the relationship between Humbert and Lolita. Unlike both the novel and the Nabokov screenplay, the film does not explain the origins of Humbert's nympholepsy. Everything conspires to create the impression, when Humbert first meets Lolita, of love at first sight, the only taboo being an age difference slightly greater than what was conventionally seen as acceptable between two lovers. In sum, the film offers what seems more a case of an adult's normal lust for an attractive teenager than a case of incest or nympholepsy. (Could it be this reluctant "normalization" that triggered Sellers/Quilty's obsessive repetition of the word "normal" in the dialogue between Quilty and Humbert in the Enchanted Hunters Hotel?)

The theme music by Nelson Riddle subliminally reinforces this normalization effect, by supplying a static, pre-modernist, rather syrupy muzak-style love theme. The very lack of dissonance and discontinuity in the music, and the fact that it does not change or progress either rhythmically or melodically, implies a lack of dissonance in the relationship; it empties the relationship of the tantalizingly taboo atmosphere that renders the affair deliciously illicit and dangerous. The standardized "love-theme" music seems to "bless" the relationship, wrapping the incest in an innocuously romantic glow. The choice of James Mason, as opposed to the other players contemplated as possibilities (Laurence Olivier, David Niven, Marlon Brando), also contributes to this normalization. Understated, stern, paternal, Mason throughout most of the film seems more the harried father than the dirty old man, although he does at least fit Nabokov's description of Humbert as "attractively Simian, and boyishly manly" sporting "thick black eyebrows and a queer accent," although one might not want to attribute to Mason "a cesspoolful of rotting monsters between his slow boyish style." But here too the film transforms the process of readerly/spectatorial inference. In the film, we witness Humbert's clumsiness, including his **verbal** clumsiness, resulting in a reversal: while in the novel we have immediate access to Humbert's verbal brilliance, and have to **infer** his clumsiness, in the film we witness his clumsiness, and have to infer his brilliance.

The film also makes a significant adjustment in narrational technique. The novel features twenty-nine passages of direct address by Humbert to the reader, variously referred to as "readers" as well as "jury," "doctor," and even "printer." Humbert is aware of his dependency on the reader – "I shall not exist if you do not imagine me . . ." He reminds the reader that his "gloomy good looks" should be "kept in the mind's eye if [the] story is to be understood." Humbert also asks for the collaboration of "learned readers" in the scene he is about to replay. Thus Nabokov's technique mingles the direct address of a Henry Fielding narrator with the continuing swirl of internal self-consciousness of a Dostoevskyan character. In the film, in contrast, Humbert's voice-over narration is only intermittent, and it exercises much less control over the point of view. The unreliable narrator of the novel, whose neurotic voice echoes with the overtones of the *Notes from Underground* tradition, becomes the reliable narrator of the film, in that the film never casts any serious doubt on Humbert's account of events. The voice-over is generally only informative, providing basic exposition rather than glimpses into Humbert's feelings or fantasies. The voice-over narration becomes an anchor of truth, unlike the novel, where the narration forms a shifting, ambiguous, unanchored space of mendacity. Kubrick achieves this normalization of narrational voice, in part, by eliding the more outrageous things that the Humbert of the book has to say. What is lost, unfortunately, is the novel's shrewdly constructed gap between the elegant, courtly style of the narrator and the sordid behavior of the child-abuser, the dirty old man lurking "behind" the style, hiding, as it were, in the interstices of the prose.

While the novel's narrator is what Genette would call "autodiegetic" (i.e. the author generates and narrates a story within which he is the main protagonist), the film is closer to what Genette calls "homodiegetic" (i.e. the narrator is involved with the story but is no longer the only protagonist). What becomes clear in the film versions both of *Notes from Underground* and *Lolita* is that filmic narrators based on novels featuring unreliable narrators must struggle against a basic feature of the film medium. The discursive power of unreliable autodiegetic narrators is almost automatically relativized by film. In a novel, the narrator controls the **only** track – the verbal track. In a film, the narrator can partially control the verbal track – through voice-over – but that control is subject to innumerable constraints: the pressure to include voiced dialogue, to dramatize, to tell stories visually, and so forth. In a film, the other characters instantly gain a physical presence denied them in the novel. Even minor figures like Lolita's husband, completely marginalized in the novel, achieve, however briefly, a certain embodiment. They cannot be safely "solipsized," as Humbert solipsizes Lolita, since they are now present as speaking, moving, gesticulating characters. The narrator/character from the novel is also relativized through contextualization; he now has to compete for attention not only with the other characters but also with the decor, the music, the color, the light. Of course, I am not suggesting that it is impossible to relay unreliable first-person narration in the cinema, but only that it would require relentless subjectification on various cinematic registers: uninterrupted voice-over, non-stop point-of-view editing, constantly motivated camera movements, always marked subjective framing, in a way that approximates Pasolini's "cinema of poetry." The Adrian Lyne version of *Lolita* (1997), as we shall soon see, takes a few, tiny steps in that direction.

Questions of narration are inseparable from questions of style. *Lolita* (1962) was made at a certain point in Kubrick's career, and at a certain point in film history. Kubrick in the early 1960s was primarily the "realistic" director of *The Killing* (1957), *Paths of Glory* (1957), and even *Spartacus* (1960). He was not yet the satiric reflexive director of *Dr Strangelove* and *Clockwork Orange* (1971). At the time of *Lolita*, Kubrick had an instrumental view of novelistic style, something a writer "uses" to convey his feelings and thoughts. Yet style in Nabokov's novel is not instrumental or decorative; it is arguably "of the essence," completely inseparable from content, and the means by which we find clues to

Nabokov's attitude toward his character. The Kubrick film, although made three years after Godard's jazzy and polyrhythmic *A bout de souffle* (Breathless, 1960) and Resnais' modernist *Hiroshima mon amour*, deploys a relatively conventional pre-New Wavish style. While Godard renders car-driving sequences as a nervous, jump-cut orchestration of shrewd and discontinuous editing mismatches, Kubrick exploits the rather old-fashioned device of matte-shot (back projection) effects. The mainstream fiction film's relative impermeability to reflexivity partially explains the film's aesthetic failure of nerve and its consequent incapacity to create a filmic equivalent to the novel's self-flaunting artificiality. While the novel constantly flaunts its own status as linguistic artifact, the film is largely cast in the illusionistic mold, presenting rounded characters in plausible settings, filmed by a self-effacing camera. While the book forms a veritable palimpsest of virtuoso parodic turns – Dostoevsky, Sade, Poe, Proust are all spoofed – the Kubrick film is at best intermittently parodic, as we see in the clumsy homage to Chaplin's tussle with a bed in *One A.M.* (1917), in Quilty's allusion to Kubrick's own *Spartacus*, in the disorientingly direct cut to *The Curse of Frankenstein* (1957), but never as consistently or as effectively as the novel. In terms of cinematic allusion, paradoxically, the film is less "filmic" than the novel. Yet in another sense, however, the film displaces the literary spirit of Nabokovian wit onto the register of spoken performance, and especially that of Peter Sellers as Clare Quilty. Sellers's shape-shifting capacity to mimic diverse personages makes him an ambulatory intertext, a comic constellation of impromptu "quotations" whose very modus operandi is parodic in the best Nabokovian sense.

Occasionally, Kubrick does achieve a sense of the stylistic discontinuity of the novel; for example, in the scene of Quilty's murder. In the book, the scene takes roughly ten pages (discourse time) and portrays an hour in the fiction (story time). The film also creates a certain gap between the decor and the lighting. Quilty's Pavor Mansion is the gothic castle *par excellence*, yet the lighting is high-key, not expressionist as would be the norm in horror films. The scene is beautifully choreographed, and, more importantly, reproduces the sense of a gap between style and content, since a very serious event – a murder – is treated In the tone of a black-humored prank. Kubrick's long-take style allows room for Sellers to spread his wings as a performer.

Many sequences are brilliantly filmed and performed: Humbert drunk in his bath, sipping wine to commemorate Charlotte's death, while his friends and neighbors worry that he might be contemplating suicide (rather than nympholepsy) and where they insist that he do exactly what he is doing anyway: "Try to think of Lolita." In a number of scenes, Kubrick "traps" Humbert in the act of voyeurism. Often we see Humbert, satyr-like, peeping at Lolita from behind books,

Figure 5.4 Humbert (James Mason) as voyeur in Kubrick's *Lolita* (1962), produced by Anya / Harris-Kubrick Productions / Seven Arts Productions / Transwood

newspapers, and flower arrangements. At one point he is lasciviously ogling Lolita wiggling with her hula hoop, when Charlotte takes his photo, catching him **in flagrante**. A number of shots feature a triangular composition, fitting for a situation of "mediated desire." The shot where Humbert, making love to Charlotte, draws erotic inspiration from Lolita's photo strategically placed next to Charlotte's bed. This triangular structure informs the book as a whole, where Humbert marries one woman (Valeria) because he admires her father, where he marries another (Charlotte) because he lusts for her daughter, and where he desires Lolita because she reminds him of his lost love Annabel.

While Nabokov constantly highlights the verbal factitiousness of his text, Kubrick finds no filmic equivalent for this self-referential device. While the novel frequently plays with or violates the reader's expectations, the film rarely surprises (the sudden cut to the drive-in Frankenstein film constitutes a rare exception). The novel consistently disorients its reader, especially as to the degree of "sincerity" of the text, while the film guides the spectator gently by the hand. While the novel develops a systematic tension between **what** we are told and **how** we are told it, the film, in the main, is stylistically homogeneous. In short, Kubrick substitutes three-dimensional illusionism and stylistic continuity for the recklessly flamboyant anti-illusionism of the book. That is why the Kubrick film is more pleasurable on a second viewing. Lovers of the Nabokov novel can forget the specifically literary qualities of the book to better appreciate the film's specifically cinematic pleasures: its fine-tuned performances and subtle *mise-en-scène*.

Over three decades after the Kubrick version, the Adrian Lyne adaptation of *Lolita* (1997) was made in an overwrought social atmosphere that harmed the film's possibilities for distribution. On the one hand, the 1990s would seem less censorious than the early 1960s, for by then pornography had entered the mainstream, so that the film looked relatively tame compared to the offerings of cable television or even of "Enchanted Hunters" style motels and hotels. On the other hand, the US, at least, was obsessed with pedophilia and the sexual abuse of children by teachers and caretakers. It was the period of the Jon Benet Ramsay case, and of the Orin Hatch "Child Porn Prevention" bill. As a result, the film was denounced by conservatives in the US and the UK. Given the difficulties of finding a distributor, it finally premiered on cable TV; *Showtime* became the contemporary media equivalent of Paris's Olympia Press.

Lyne's *Lolita* went through various scriptwriters – James Dearden, Harold Pinter, David Mamet, and, finally and definitively, Stephen Schiff. Each version entailed dramatically different choices. The Dearden version did not include Annabel, and had Humbert distributing books by Stephen King and Norman Mailer. David Mamet wanted to have the same actress play both Annabel and Lolita to stress the sense of ritual repetition and déja vu. The Pinter version, interestingly, seemed to read *Lolita* through *Notes from Underground*, as is evident from the opening lines of his screenplay: "My name is Humbert. You won't like me. I suffer from moral leprosy."

While the Kubrick *Lolita* treats a contemporaneous story, the forty-two years that separate the original novel from the Lyne adaptation turn the film into a period piece, now set in the late 1940s. While the foreign-born Nabokov had shown himself to be a master observer of Americana, paradoxically, the American-born Kubrick had filmed the novel as if he were a foreigner, partially because Kubrick at that time was living in England, where his version (apart from some second-unit work) was actually filmed. The Englishman Lyne, again paradoxically, shows a better grasp of Americana than did Kubrick, both in terms of an anthological sound track filled with pop hits by Louis Prima and Ella

Fitzgerald, and in terms of locations which privilege the tackier aspects of an industrialized American landscape. What in the novel was **literary** allusion here becomes pop culture musical allusion. Pop songs are deployed to ironic effect, as when we hear "That's Amore" as Lolita is jiggled by a coin-operated massage-bed. And we hear Louis Prima's "barbaric yawp" against civilization – "Bongo, bongo, bongo/I don't want to leave the Congo/Oh no, no no!" – coincide with the couple's picaresque journey across the United States, suggesting that Humbert prefers the uncivilized (i.e. taboo) relationship with Lolita to a return to "civilization" and respectability.

Whereas one thinks of Kubrick as an anti-erotic and misogynistic director, who prefers the world of men alone and at war (*The Killing* [1956], *Paths of Glory* [1957], *Dr Strangelove, Full Metal Jacket* [1987]), Lyne is associated with films laced with frank eroticism: *Foxes* (1980), *Flashdance* (1985), *9½ Weeks* (1987), *Indecent Proposal* (1993), and, most recently, *Unfaithful* (2002). Unlike the Kubrick version, but like the Nabokov screenplay, the Lyne version reserves a privileged place for the Annabel episode in the form of a sensuous, soft-focus French Riviera flashback. A voice-over reveals the traumatic effect of Annabel's untimely death:

> Whatever happens to a boy the summer he's fourteen will mark him for life. The shock of her death froze something in me. The child I loved was gone, but I kept looking for her, long after I left my own childhood behind. The poison was in the wound, you see, and the wound wouldn't heal.

The sequence, seen as if through the soft-focus haze of memory, traces the genesis of Humbert's nympholepsy to a cruelly interrupted relationship: "If it wasn't for Annabel," Humbert's voice-over informs us, "there might never have been a Lolita." Thus Lyne, like Kubrick, normalizes, or more accurately "humanizes," Humbert, but differently. By positing Humbert as victim in the first instance, and repentant in the last, Lyne foregrounds the trajectory of Humbert's moral growth, and his melancholy realization that he has abused Lolita. He thus closes the novel's gap between the narrator's self-presentation and the author's.

The Lyne version also uses music to make a point about character. Lolita's character is very much identified with the late 1940s' and early 1950s' diegetic pop music in the film, which she sings, mouths, dances, or otherwise performs. Humbert, meanwhile, is associated with the more complex music scored for the film. The scored music is impressionist, dissonant, harmonically complex,

Figure 5.5 Jeremy Irons and Dominique Swain in Lyne's *Lolita* (1997), produced by Guild / Pathé

evocative of the ethos and psyche of the European intellectual and the aesthetics of the art film. As a hybridization of the romantic and impressionist/modernist modes, the Ennio Morricone music "carries" the melancholy and even tragic overtones of a dissonant romance. And the tragic sensibility belongs to Humbert, while the pop sensibility belongs to Lolita. The close shots in which complex and contradictory emotions play over Jeremy Irons's face, together with the music's evocation of interiority, all help shape Humbert as a complex and ultimately moral figure. Yet this normalization of Humbert as a multi-faceted and sensitive human being enters into conflict with another aspect of the film, its soft-core erotic aesthetic, the sensuous pastels, the filtered smoky lighting, reminiscent of champagne commercials, which make the spectator, and especially the voyeuristic male spectator, complicitous with Humbert's nympholeptic desire.

Music and close-ups are just a few of the many cinematic registers used to align us with Humbert's feelings. Both Kubrick and Lyne emphasize Humbert's voyeurism. But, in Kubrick, we do not peek with Humbert; rather, he has us watch Humbert watching, often catching him in flagrante, as when Charlotte photographs him as he is admiring Lolita's undulating hula hoop. Many of the shots in the Kubrick version are pointedly **not** point-of-view shots, as when a shot of Lolita getting into a car on the way to camp, framed through Humbert's window, is subsequently revealed **not** to be from Humbert's point of view, since he is shown sleeping. Kubrick thus simultaneously identifies us with Humbert's voyeurism and distances us from it through the refusal of the reaction shot that might have sutured us into the character's gaze. Lyne, in contrast, rigorously identifies us with Humbert's perspective by having us look **with** Humbert through carefully constructed point-of-view shots. Countless shots show Humbert straining to get a glimpse of Lolita. Humbert peers from behind obstacles, looks through half-open bathroom doors to glimpse her bare legs and the unrolling toilet paper. Repeatedly, Humbert positions himself strategically in order to afford himself (and the spectator) the best possible view. Lyne in this sense reproduces Nabokov's quasi-Flaubertian precision about point of view, for the novel too posits precise vantage points: "I happened to glimpse from the bathroom, through a chance combination of a mirror aslant and a door ajar, a look on her face . . . an expression of helplessness" (p. 283). At times, Humbert's strategic scopophilia does, admittedly, take on a comic dimension, as when Humbert, seated on the porch swing with Charlotte, has to strain his neck to catch Lolita's whimsical Charleston, while the swinging has him pop up and down, in and out of the frame.

But even when not deploying literal point-of-view editing, the Lyne film aligns us with Humbert's feelings and sensibility. Humbert's first epiphanic vision of Lolita, for example, is rendered in aquatic, dripping, sprinkly slow-motion. On other occasions, the film's canted frames render Humbert's "slanted" point of view. Even the leitmotif of impeded vision, or blocked scopophilia, lubricates the mechanisms of spectatorial desire, through a striptease of fragmented body parts. Here an aestheticized deviancy comes close to Pasolini's "cinema of poetry;" the implied author's style becomes virtually indistinguishable from the perverse sensibility of the character. The net result is to give a much greater sense of what Genette calls "internal focalization" or of what Murray Smith calls "alignment," which weds us to Humbert's, rather than Lolita's, feelings and perspective.[41]

Kubrick emphasized the comic dimension of his source by casting stand-up comedian Peter Sellers in three distinct roles. The rather cold lighting in Kubrick tended toward the *noir*ish, as in the seduction passage: "The door of the lighted bathroom stood ajar . . . a skeleton glow came through the Venetian blind from the outside arclights; these intercrossed rays penetrated the darkness of the bedroom . . ." (p. 130). The Lyne film, in contrast, quarantines expressionist techniques to those sequences featuring Anthony Minghella as Quilty. (If Kubrick misses the style of the novel, Lyne misses its humor.) And if the lighting of the

Kubrick *Lolita* tended toward gothic chiaroscuro, the Lyne version prefers the pastels of a commercialized version of painterly impressionism. The Kubrick aesthetic, speaking more generally, favors depth of field, a fairly static camera, and shots of relatively long duration, while Lyne prefers an aesthetic of close-ups and glimpses, with a constantly moving camera restlessly crawling along surfaces. In generic terms, the Lyne film adheres to a relatively timid version of the conventions of the European art film genre (the genre with which Jeremy Irons was associated), while the lighting favors backlit sunbeams and overly pretty landscapes. At times, the light becomes impressionist, almost pointillist, as when the hazy, filtered, gaseous and smoky look favored by Lyne literalizes the haziness of the memory of the adolescent tryst with Annabel. In the Lyne film, a love affair with filtered light and textured style in some ways substitutes for Nabokov's love affair with language. Just as Humbert's elegant style constitutes a form of seduction which masks his perversity, so the filtered light and smoky effects and sunlit nymphetry of Lyne's film obscure the sordid nature of the events depicted.

While Nabokov in *Lolita* was self-declaredly "not concerned with so-called sex at all" — a fact which triggered disappointment in hard-core porn-lovers — Lyne is very much concerned with sex. This concern is reflected in the soft-core porn aesthetic — an erotic version of TV champagne commercials — and in the gratuitous states of undress for Dominique Swain and in the generally "taste-ful" titillation characteristic of the film. The result is a kind of aestheticization of child-molesting. But the contemporary prevalence of real porn has had the perhaps salutary effect of revealing soft-core porn's basic falsity, as if real porn's "money shots" had torn away the fig leaf of the artsy sexuality of the art film. In an erotic version of Marshall McLuhan's "rear view mirror" theory, real porn has had the retroactive effect of revealing the basic dishonesty of soft-focus "erotica."

In terms of character, Lyne's Lolita is more spontaneous and lively and intel-ligent than Kubrick's somewhat bland heroine, more in keeping with Nabokov's own notion of "courageous, undefeated Lolita." Dominique Swain shows a talent for improvisation, as when she exhibits her skill in chin-wobbling. When Humbert stumbles in his attempt to find the right word to characterize their relationship, Swain's Lolita supplies the precise substantive — "incest." In her singing and dancing and acting, she is more creative than Kubrick's Lolita. Her unrelenting attack on Humbert's body, along with her constant verbal mockery, constitute a form of agency, since it puts Humbert on the defensive even while charming him. Interestingly, Lolita often impedes Humbert's ability to see, whether by knocking off his glasses, or by wrapping her legs around his face, or by placing a bag over his head while he drives. But what Lolita gains in agency she loses in dignity and autonomy. Whereas the novel repeatedly stressed that Lolita "never vibrated to my touch," Lyne portrays Lolita as seductive and taking sexual pleasure from the relationship with Humbert. In the Lyne version, then, Lolita seems more accomplice than victim. She even seems, on rare occasions, a victimizer.

The derisive portrayal of Charlotte, in both the Kubrick and the Lyne adaptations, not only conveys the narrator's attitude but also points to our own perversity as spectators. Like the novel, neither of the two adaptations prods us to sympathize with Charlotte. While conventional morality would have had us side with the exploited mother and sincere wife Charlotte, the structure of the film and the dynamics of the performances lead us to empathize with Humbert. Not unlike the novel's murdering protagonist, we too begin to see Charlotte as an annoying obstacle to a liaison that we as spectators desire as well. (It is that desire, after all, that brought us into the theaters.) Lyne also downplays the role of Quilty. While Quilty is a major player in the Kubrick *Lolita*, in the Lyne version he seems like a generic extraterrestrial, someone who seems to have wandered in from another studio's backlot.

While the voice-over narration in Kubrick is pedestrian, giving us little more than basic information, the voice-over in Lyne is poetic in style and emotional and soul-baring in content, still another way in which the film aligns us with Humbert. At the same time, the adaptation "translates" Nabokov's poetic prose through audiovisual correlatives for poetic devices. And in this sense it is possible to analyse the film in terms of the devices and tropes of classical rhetoric such as metaphor, metonymy, and synecdoche. At times, Lolita's off-screen voice, or her shadow, synecdochically "stands in" for her real presence. When she escapes from Humbert, she remains present through cherished vestiges – chewed gum, bottle caps, photographs. But other characters and emotions too are evoked through partial objects: suds in a car wash, for example, evoke Humbert's tears. Even the electric bug-zapper can be seen as a metaphor, whereby Humbert is the moth attracted to the "light" of Lolita.

Both the beginning and the end of the film show Humbert's drunkenly weaving car, which clearly metaphorizes a man out of control; the violation of traffic rules evokes the transgression of more serious taboos such as incest and murder. In fact, the voice-over in the sequence picks up on Humbert's own analogy in the novel: "Since I had disregarded all laws of humanity, I might as well disregard the rules of traffic" (p. 279). The voice-over narration literally conveys Humbert's description of driving on the wrong side of the road:

> Gently, dreamily, not exceeding twenty miles an hour, I drove on that queer mirror side . . . Cars coming towards me wobbled, swerved and cried out in fear . . . With a graceful movement I turned off the road, and after two or three big bounces, rode up a grassy slope, among surprised cows, and there I came to a gentle, rocking stop.

The Lyne version renders this sleepy, strangely peaceful finale – including the surprised cows – with great aplomb. The *mise-en-scène* communicates the feeling that Humbert, as his pursued car shudders to a halt, is relieved to be caught. The finale has Humbert contemplate the landscape as he remembers Lolita, just as the police catch up with him. What in the novel is presented as a trans-temporal memory here becomes present time. Everything about the sequence – the point-of-view shot, the hilltop vantage point, the music, the voice-over, screams: Epiphany! In words that vary slightly from Nabokov's, the voice-over tells us: "What I heard then was the melody of children at play, nothing but that. And I knew that the hopelessly poignant thing was not Lolita's absence from my side, but the absence of her voice from that chorus." This moment, more than any other, seals Humbert's redemption as a character. It is the "moral apotheosis" promised by John Ray, Jr in the novel's preface, the "socially redeeming" message that rescues the film's kiddie-porn indulgences. The scene fulfills the drift of the entire film, the trajectory that leads from Humbert's initial victimization – in the Annabel episode – through his exploitative relationship (but with which we are made complicitous) – through his final repentance and redemption.

Whatever its problems, the film's style does succeed in matching theme to aesthetic. Throughout the film, a synecdochic aesthetic of close-ups provides a formal corollary to the protagonist's fetishistic pathology, rooted in a "cut-off" experience of adolescent love interrupted by Annabel's sudden death. Here we see the metonymic displacements typical of fetishism. Literally a fetishist, Humbert dives into Lolita's closeted clothing after her departure for camp, provoking the maid's sarcastic "what's he doing in there?" But throughout the film, Lyne develops an aesthetic of synecdoche, of part for whole, whereby objects come to stand for persons or feelings. Lolita, especially, is evoked through objects – the bobby pin, the dripping underwear, the ejaculatory milk on the lip (now a cliché of eroticized milk commercials) – which render her as an object of desire and nostalgia – ink pot, insect-zapper, typewriter, telephone, hotel fan, braces. But many shots take on metaphorical resonances. We are constantly given body parts – Lolita's knees, elbows, and so on – and partial views. The film also proliferates in metonymical slidings in various forms: sexual innuendo, where words suggest something taboo ("Has Lolita been keeping you up?"); names that slide into other names (Lola into Dolly, Dolores, Lolita; Quilty into Vivian Darkbloom); the sliding appearance of Dominique Swain as Lolita, as she shifts in appearance from girl to woman to adolescent to child to mother; Quilty's ever-changing signature and his sliding homophones ("you lie, she's not" becomes "July was hot"). The camera also slides metonymically over Lolita's body, much as her body slides up and down Humbert's when she says goodbye on her way to camp. Thus Lyne transposes the poetry of the novel, its rhetoric of stylistic devices, into a homologous rhetoric shaped for another medium; Nabokov's poetic prose style is now rendered as cinema. The only difference is that while Nabokov's poetic prose is distanced and ironic, Lyne's is painfully sincere and sometimes overwrought.

The novel *Lolita* has generated an intricate and voluminous post-text which includes not only the two filmic adaptations but also Nabokov's voice reading albums of the novel (in 1959); the original screenplay (offered to Kubrick in 1960); the revised published screenplay (worked over by Nabokov in 1970, published in 1974); a Broadway-style musical (in 1971), and a play adapted by Edward Albee (in 1981). But the "Lolita" diaspora goes far beyond these explicit adaptations. Internet pornographers use the name "Lolita" to sell illegal images of children, while tabloid journalism dubbed the sexually precocious teenager Amy Fischer the "Lolita of Long Island." Lolita also lurks in the background of films like *American Beauty* (1999) and *Guinevere* (1999). And just as *Robinson Crusoe* was rewritten from Friday's point of view, and *Moby Dick* from the point of view of *Ahab's Wife*, so *Lolita* has been rewritten from Lolita's point of view, in *Lo's Diary* (published in Italian in 1995), Pia Pera's polemical (and lawsuit-ridden) recasting of the novel.

In the Pera version, Dolores Haze becomes Dolores Maze; Humbert Humbert becomes Humbert Guimbert; Charlotte becomes Isabel; Ramsdale is Goatscreek; and Clare Quilty becomes Gerry Sue Filthy. In this version, John Ray, Jr, an editor at Olympia Press, is approached by Dolores Schlegel (Schiller in Nabokov), who did not die in childbirth as Humbert would have us believe but who is now happily pregnant with her second child by her husband Richard. Humbert, who it turns out never did kill Filthy/Quilty, is now living out his last days in Paris with a younger wife. Lolita is eager to have us hear the true story. In fact, she claims that her version is the original, and that Humbert's prison confession is the parasite, the "adaptation," as it were.

According to Pera's John Ray, Lolita scribbled out her diary in various public restrooms during the course of the cross-country journey with Humbert. Any reader expecting the rewrite to offer not only a feminine but also a **feminist** version of the events of *Lolita*, one which denounces the masculinist fantasies of Nabokov/ Humbert, will be sorely disappointed. In *Lo's Diary*, Lolita is the manipulative, knowing seductress. She is narcissistic, self-pitying, cynical, cruel (she tortures her hamster), and almost sociopathic. For her, Humbert is a "guinea pig" for her "new seduction technique," since she fears that Mom's pre-war strategies "could easily let him get away."[42] Lo complains that her mother is blind to the obvious fact that "the only way for an older woman to get herself married is to get the absent-minded man to fall in love with the child first" (p. 85). Nor is Lo an unwilling accomplice. In the famous "orgasm-on-the-lap scene," Lo describes herself as "dying with longing" and "with a burning desire to press myself against him" (p. 91). This rewrite novel by a European inverts the sophisticated European/naïve American cliché by having Lolita find Humbert erotically unsophisticated. After their first session Lo writes: "That's that. Hummie's definitely a bore in bed. He doesn't know anything interesting. In spite of his vast 'experience' . . . he lies there like a straw man. A real sexual parasite. Aside from stammering some French poetry, he brings nothing of himself" (p. 129).

Lo complains that Humbert does not take the time to make her come, leaving her "naked and dirty and wet and irritated" (p. 153). In feminist terms, it could be argued that Nabokov's *Lolita* – and Nabokov is far from being a feminist – gives more hints of patriarchal victimization than does *Lo's Diary*, since Nabokov at least supplies us with innumerable clues pointing to the unreliability of Humbert's narration. Even Humbert himself lucidly describes the situation as that of a "lone child, an absolute waif," with whom a "heavy-limbed, foul-smelling adult" had had strenuous sex several times the same morning. Pera's Lo is a stranger to female solidarity, and she feels nothing but hatred for the person she calls "Plasticmom." Before her death, she herself contemplates killing her: "pull out the IV, give her the wrong medicine, whatever, since a shit like her for sure doesn't deserve to go on living" (pp. 134–5). For Lo, the death of the mother she calls "the hen" only "opens up interesting prospects" (p. 137). Needless to say, *Lo's Diary* is not a major contribution to literature. Gone are the hermeneutic tensions of unreliable narration, and the sharply observed Americana.

──────────── Gendered Narration: *Hour of the Star* ────────────

With the exception of *Lo's Diary*, most of the unreliable and neurotic narrators discussed up to this point – Underground Man, Sergio, and Humbert Humbert

– have been male. (And although Lo is a narrator, she is not an unreliable one, and she is more cynical than she is neurotic.) And there is a kind of deep cultural and anthropological sense in these neurotic narrators being male. Does one imagine women scapegoating a male prostitute, as Dostoevsky's protagonist does in *Notes from Underground*, or marrying a man to have sexual access to his son, as occurs in *Lolita*? The point is not that women are not capable of such actions, but whether such attitudes could be presented, as they are in Dostoevsky, for example, as convincingly **typical**. What happens, then, when the author, and the adopting filmmaker, are women? In this sense, it is worthwhile to analyze the narrational strategies of another novel featuring an unreliable narrator, to wit Brazilian novelist Clarice Lispector's *A hora da estrela* (Hour of the Star, 1977), and those of the screen adaptation by Suzana Amaral in her *Hora da estrela* in 1984.

Hour of the Star tells the story of Macabeia, a poor and uneducated girl from the Northeast who migrates to the poor neighborhoods of Rio de Janeiro. Her self-definition is sexual ("I'm a virgin"); professional ("I'm a typist"); and culinary/consumerist ("I drink Coca-Cola"). And on one level, the Lispector novel features the same kind of neurotic, self-torturing, unconvincingly flippant narrator that we have encountered in *Notes from Underground* and *Memories of Underdevelopment*. The novel is narrated by a certain Rodrigo S. M. – for some critics the "s.m." evokes "sado-masochism." The novel's narrator has the hyper-consciousness that Macabeia herself lacks. But the novel's narration is also gendered and in some ways bifurcated along gender lines. The dedication hints that the "real" author/narrator of the book is Clarice Lispector, yet the narrator S.M. is putatively male, although we are never entirely convinced by this case of narrational transvestism. The narrator, we are told, **has** to be a man because a woman would weep at the heroine's condition. Through this distancing device, the narrator's constructed masculinism, for Lispector, keeps the character, and the emotion generated by the character, at a safe, presumably "manly" distance. (We are also reminded of the strong tradition of literary cross-dressing incarnated by writers like George Sand and George Eliot, who wrote as if they were men.)

A clear social distance separates narrator and character, a feeling of distance combined with sympathy, linked to a sense of injustice, a sense that this poor character might, in other circumstances, have **been** the author or narrator. This distance is also implied by the fact that the narrator – rather like the filmmaker Sullivan in *Sullivan's Travels* (1941), who pretends to be poor in order to make a film about the poor – feels obliged to experience poverty in order to write about it: "In order to speak about the girl I mustn't shave for days. I must acquire dark circles under my eyes from lack of sleep; dozing from sheer exhaustion like a manual laborer. Also wearing threadbare clothes . . . [all] to put myself on the same footing as the girl from the Northeast."[43]

In a sense, the narrator, to switch our field of reference, adopts the procedures of a method actor, like Robert de Niro, who rehearses and prepares for the role, and who might even overeat in order to play an obese person. In order to write the novel, Lispector's narrator decides not to shave, to eat only fruit, to stay at home and avoid all newspapers, as if such "sacrifices" would really constitute the equivalent of crushing, ongoing poverty. The issue of class difference between narrator and character in *Hour of the Star* thus gets mapped onto another order of difference, that of the interrelated power differentials between author and character, on the one hand, and narrator and character on the other. In his study of Dostoevsky, Bakhtin contrasts those authors who delegate power and autonomy to their characters, and those "puppeteer" authors who merely exploit their characters as mouthpieces for their own opinions. At the same time, clear points of identification — shared Northeastern roots, a strong interior life, and their common status, in a sense, as writers — link the biographical author, Lispector, and the character Macabeia. Like Melville's Bartleby the scrivener, Macabeia is a secretary (however incompetent) and in this minimal sense is a writer like the author.

The dedication of *Hour of the Star* comes before the title and clearly implies that the author ("alias Clarice") is a woman named Clarice, a device which contradicts the claim that the narrator is a man, since readers are likely to confound authors and narrators. As French critic Hélène Cixous points out, the novel gives us a series of alternative titles, as if Lispector could not make up her mind which one to choose.[44] The first of these possible titles is interrupted by Lispector's signature, immediately after the words "the right to protest," which reminds us that the novel was written during the Brazilian dictatorship that lasted from 1964 to roughly 1984. Each alternative title hints at another dimension of meaning. Just as Lispector has trouble finding the right subtitle for her story, she also has trouble beginning it. She postpones starting it for twenty pages. Rather like the **cine-romans** *Hiroshima mon amour* (1959) and *Last Year at Marienbad* (1961) discussed in the next chapter, the novel refuses, at least at first, to name its major character, as if the novelist were afraid the name might trigger the wrong associations. Emphasizing only gender and social geography, the narrator just calls her "the girl from the Northeast." Strangely, the book offers us extremely intimate details about Macabeia (for example, her penchant for cheap cotton underwear full of "suspicious stains") before we have really met her or even know her name. It is as if a fiction film were to show us the underwear of a major character before showing her face. The very hesitation communicates fear, or repulsion, or a doubt about the writer's right or capacity to represent such a figure.

Another "incorrect" feature of Lispector's style is that the narrator affects not to know certain details about the character s/he is creating. "Was Macabeia tubercular?" the narrator asks, and answers: "I don't think so." The narrator addresses the reader directly: "So, dear readers, you know more than you imagine, however much you may deny it." Picking up on the reflexive tradition of Cervantes, Fielding, Sterne, and Machado de Assis, the narrator foregrounds the choices involved in writing, wondering, for example, if "he" should introduce some "difficult, technical terms." Like many self-conscious, neurotic narrators, Rodrigo lambastes his own writing, protesting that "this story is so banal I can hardly stand it" and that the novel "has no technique, not even in matters of style" (p. 35). The narrator also inventories all the points he would like his character to make but cannot. Rather like Laurence Sterne, who constantly bewails the quotidian hassles that derail his writing, the narrator complains that his cook threw away three pages of his manuscript, and that he is now obliged to remember them. Although some films – *8½*, *Stardust Memories* – and many novels – Gide's *Faux monnayeurs*, and, as we have just seen, Desnoes' *Memories of Underdevelopment* – thematize the difficulty of finishing creative works, this kind of writing mishap rarely makes its way into a finished novel, just as faulty film footage is usually thrown into the editing-room trashcan.

Unlike the novel, the Suzana Amaral film adaptation (1984) not only has no marked narrator, it is also, generally speaking, not reflexive. By eliminating the narrator, the site of reflexivity in the novel, Amaral switches the emphasis away from self-conscious mediation toward realism and exteriority. Amaral's basic choice here also takes on a gendered dimension. It is as if the film director rejected the novel's narrator, literally masculine and associated with stereotypically masculine traits such as objectivity and distance (even though he was invented by the woman novelist), and has now herself replaced him by **becoming** the narrator. "For me," as Amaral put it repeatedly in interviews, "I was the narrator." This substitution, to use somewhat hyperbolic language, constitutes a kind of feminine/feminist writerly *coup d'état* against Clarice Lispector's own choice to speak through a constructed masculine narrator. In the film, Amaral (and the cinema) become the new narrators.

Reflexivity, in Lispector's work, often takes psychologized form; her novels work through the character's unfolding interior life. In the Amaral adaptation, in contrast, interiority is implied by exterior signs alone. The film's aesthetic, while modern, is no longer modernist. Indeed, reflexivity is not really compatible with Suzana Amaral's basically realist aesthetic. Nor does it conform to her modus operandi in filmmaking, which is to read and re-read the source novel, but to forget it completely at the moment of shooting, thinking only in terms of cinematic rather than novelistic logic. Amaral was quite conscious and explicit in this rejection of reflexivity, or what she calls "metalanguage." In an interview with Susana Rossberg, she said:

> Metalanguage doesn't work. It's really just a question of film language. Films which speak about films, stories wrapped inside of stories, all these *mise-en-abyme* constructions. I thought all that would be very complicated for our public. People wouldn't understand. So I decided to tell the story directly, "straight to the point" (in English). In other words, I eliminated the narrator because in my mind I was the narrator.[45]

This passage is especially interesting because it actually invokes different orders of argument. One aspect of the argument bears on the issue of reception, the idea that "our" Brazilian public is not ready to understand a difficult, reflexive film. (This argument forgets that Brazilian audiences have often been very receptive to audacious, provocative, and even avant-garde films like *Red Light Bandit* [1968], and that the history of Brazilian cinema is full of *mise-en-abyme* framestory films such as *Amuleto de Ogum* [1974] and *Tent of Miracles* [1977].) For Amaral, cinematic logic entails a refusal of reflexivity, discarded as inessential "static" and "noise" which distract us from what really matters – the story. In this sense, Suzana Amaral has done what many adapters of reflexive novels have done. She has filtered out the modernism of the original in favor of presenting the straightforward core anecdote imagined as somehow "behind" all the self-conscious artifice.

Hour of the Star, in this sense, pursues a very different aesthetic project from the novel. The camera does not, generally, call attention to itself. Nor does the film artificially postpone the entrance of the main character. Instead, the first shot thrusts us into the action *in medias res*, showing Macabeia at her desk in the office. Nor does the story have any trouble "starting." In the novella we learn the heroine's name only on page 43, almost halfway through the book, while in the film we learn it immediately. I do not bring up these differences to suggest that the film would have been stronger had it been reflexive – the film is strong as it is – I am merely pointing to the basic aesthetic option for realism and transparency. Any novel offers a dense network of informational cues, available for the filmmaker to pick up or ignore. Quite apart from aesthetics,

Figure 5.6 Macabeia (Marcelia Cartaxo) in *Hour of the Star* (1984), produced by Kino International Corp. / Raíz Produções Cinematográficas

there were also sound economic reasons for Amaral's shunning of reflexivity, since reflexive, self-deconstructing films are often failures at the box office. Mainstream audiences have been made accustomed to lose themselves in the story; they often resent having stories interrupted and deconstructed and questioned as they are in the Lispector novel.

In the novel, Macabeia is clearly constituted as a body through very physical processes, almost never characterized from outside in judgmental ways through descriptive evaluations like "naïve." She is defined, rather, like Flaubert's Emma, through her viscera and her physical perceptions — but here through grossly physiological processes such as urinating and coughing, through corporeal traces like menstrual stains, through indispositions like heartburn, through crude gestures like wiping her nose on her blouse or eating chicken while on the toilet, and (in the film at least) through vomiting. This last picks up on a physical characteristic of Macabeia, her lack of control over bodily functions. Macabeia cannot even masturbate successfully; her clumsy self-groping provokes only a coughing fit, emblematic of an exiled relation even to her own body. And there is little sense of liberation in this corporeal grotesquerie, none of the exuberance of what is commonly called the "carnivalesque." Macabeia does find a few moments of transcendence, however. She is moved by music, enchanted by a rainbow, by a red flower (which her "friend" Gloria appropriates). Her capacity for joy is rendered in the film by her dance with a bed sheet as if it were a wedding dress.

Although the film version of *Hour of the Star* eliminates the narrator, the narrator's **opinions**, at least, are spread around the film, dispersed onto the dialogue of other characters such as Macabeia's landlady, her boss, and so forth. But one corollary of the elimination of the narrator as a **structural** element is that we become less conscious of the bourgeois universe of the narrator, and consequently more immersed in the lower-class working woman's story. On the one hand, this choice might be seen as less "elitist," in that it identifies us more with the lower-class character. But, on the other hand, it elides the reality of class by making us less conscious of the social differences between the narrator and the character. These social differences are now shifted to another register – between the **characters** – where the social spectrum is much more restricted. So in another sense the film could be seen as **more** elitist, in that the consciously acknowledged social differences between character and narrator are rendered in a pseudo-objective way. The "impersonal" narration of the film displays Macabeia's social difference by revealing all the ways in which she falls short of bourgeois norms of socially correct behavior, norms that do not have to be stated because they have been internalized by the middle-class audience which judges characters according to these norms.

Hour of the Star ends with a sequence in which a handsome blond man driving a Mercedes – evoking a romantic/commercial fantasy of an imaginary amorous encounter – runs over Macabeia. The finale brings to their paroxysm a whole series of references, which alludes to dimly perceived worlds of cinema, stardom, and advertising. Lispector calls her novel "a story in Technicolor" and Macabeia dreams of being a star, like her beloved peach-colored Marilyn Monroe. Her very death becomes associated with consumerist fantasy. The sequence evokes the seductive lure of advertising, as well as the social resonance of a poor person being literally run over by a representative of the elite. In her imagination, the man runs to embrace her in cinematic slow motion, but in fact he is a hit-and-run driver. She has achieved her 15 seconds of fame, she has become the "star" of the title. Although most readers, and most viewers of the film, did not necessarily see the "star" of the title as referring to **that** kind of star, the moment forms a quite logical finale, carefully prepared for by the entire film.

In this chapter, we have examined a series of novels (and their adaptations) and cultural phenomena (such as stand-up) that involve unreliable, complex, neurotic narrators. Their unreliable approach destabilizes narration, placing in the reader's lap the burden of interpretation, as the reader has to intuit the gap between what the narrator claims has happened and what we suspect might have happened, between what the narrator says things mean and what they might actually mean. Each adaptation deals with this challenge differently. Walkow cinematizes the theme through "underground" cinema. Alea in *Memories of Underdevelopment* politicizes the narration by contextualizing fiction **through** documentary. Both Kubrick and Lyne, in their versions of *Lolita*, reduce the gap between narrator and the "norms of the text," thus making the narrator more normal and **less** unreliable. Suzana Amaral eliminates the narrator and substitutes herself (and the cinema as impersonal narrator). Each novel, and each "adaptation," I have tried to show, enriches and complicates some of the lines opened up by Dostoevsky and *Notes from Underground*.

Notes

1   My categories here derive from the terms developed by Wayne Booth, in *The Rhetoric of Fiction* (Chicago: University of Chicago Press, 1983), and Gérard Genette, in *Narrative Discourse: An Essay in Method*, trans. Jane E. Lewin (Ithaca, NY: Cornell University Press, 1972).

2   Booth, *Rhetoric of Fiction* (see note 1).

3   Ian Watt, *The Rise of the Novel* (Berkeley, CA: University of California Press, 1957), p. 176.

4   See Stephen Greenblatt, *Renaissance Self-fashioning* (Chicago: University of Chicago Press, 1980).

5   Letter to William Dean Howells, quoted in H. Peter Abbott, *The Cambridge Introduction to Narrative* (Cambridge: Cambridge University Press, 2002), p. 63.

6   Fyodor Dostoevsky, *Notes from Underground* (New York: New American Library, 1961), p. 122. Subsequent page references in the text will be to this edition.

7   Mikhail Bakhtin, *Problems of Dostoevsky's Poetics*, ed. and trans. Caryl Emerson (Minneapolis, MN: University of Minnesota Press, 1984), p. 233.

8   Ibid., p. 52.

9   René Girard, *Deceit, Desire, and the Novel* (Baltimore, MD: The Johns Hopkins University Press, 1961), p. 94.

10 See Emma P. Marciano, "Polyphonic Screens: A Study of Dostoevsky and Film," unpublished PhD dissertation, Comparative Literature Department, New York University, May 1998.

11 Gary Saul Morson and Caryl Emerson, *Mikhail Bakhtin: Creation of a Prosaics* (Stanford: Stanford University Press, 1990).

12 Marciano, "Polyphonic Screens."

13 Mikhail Bakhtin, "Forms of Time and the Chronotope in the Novel," in *The Dialogical Imagination*, trans. Caryl Emerson and Michael Holquist (Austin: University of Texas Press, 1981), p. 163.

14 Foster Hirsch, *Love, Sex, Death and the Meaning of Life: Woody Allen's Comedy* (New York: McGraw-Hill, 1981), p. 209.

15 Quoted in Brian Price, dissertation in progress on Bresson's adaptations of Dostoevsky, New York University.

16 Edmundo Desnoes, *Inconsolable Memories*, included in *Memories of Underdevelopment and Inconsolable Memories* (New Brunswick, NJ: Rutgers University Press, 1990), p. 118. Subsequent page references in the text will be to this edition.

17 See Fernandez Grossvogel Monegal, "3 on 2: Desnoes/Gutierrez Alea," in *Diacritics* (Winter 1974), 51–64.

18 Cited in "Sergio habla de Sergio," *Cine Cubano* 152 (April–June 2001), 45.

19 Bakhtin, *Problems of Dostoevsky's Poetics*, pp. 29–30.

20 Espinosa's essay is included in Michael Chanan (ed.), *Twenty-five Years of the New Latin American Cinema* (London: British Film Institute, 1983).

21 Leon Rozitchner, *Moral burguesa y revolucion* (Buenos Aires: Tiemp Contemporaneo, 1968).

22 See Tomas Gutierrez Alea, *Dialectica del espectador* (Havana: Udiciones Union, 1982).

23 See Julianne Burton, "*Memories of Underdevelopment* in the Land of Overdevelopment," *Cineaste* 8: 1 (1977), included in *Memories of Underdevelopment and Inconsolable Memories*, pp. 232–47.

24 On a recent trip to Cuba, I heard many ironic comments about the Russians; for example, in answer to a question about the impact of the Russian presence in Cuba, I got the answer: "Were the Russians here?"

25 See Robert Stam, *Reflexivity in Film and Literature* (New York: Columbia University Press, 1992), p. 49.

26 See Mary Louise Pratt, *Imperial Eyes: Travel Writing and Transculturation* (New York: Routledge, 1992).

27 Vladimir Nabokov, *Lectures on Don Quixote* (New York: Harcourt, Brace, Jovanovich, 1983), p. 147.

28 From a *Playboy* interview with Nabokov, quoted in Vladimir Nabokov, *The Annotated Lolita*, ed. Alfred Appel, Jr (New York: Random House, 1970), p. 368.

29 Vladimir Nabokov, *Lolita* (New York: Berkeley Medallion, 1977). Subsequent references in text will be to this edition.

30 Robertson Davies, "Mania for Green Fruit," *Victoria Daily Times* (January 17, 1959).

31 Vladimir Nabokov, *Despair* (New York: Putnam, 1966).

32 Preface to Vladimir Nabokov, *Lolita: A Screenplay* (New York: Random House, 1974).

33 Vladimir Nabokov, *The Enchanted*, trans. Dimitri Nabokov (New York: G.P. Putnam's Sons, 1986).

34 For a thoroughgoing account of the cinematic references in *Lolita*, see Alfred Appel, Jr, *Nabokov's Dark Cinema* (New York: Oxford University Press, 1974).

35 Nabokov, *Lolita: A Screenplay*.

36 Quoted in Appel, *Nabokov's Dark Cinema*, p. 237.

37 Nabokov, *Lolita: A Screenplay*, p. 45.

38 Ibid., pp. 111–12.

39 Ibid., prologue, pp. xii–xiii.

40 The poem is included, and commented on, in Richard Corliss, *Lolita* (London: British Film Institute, 1994).

41 Murray Smith, *Engaging Characters: Fiction, Emotion, and the Cinema* (Oxford: Clarendon Press, 1995).

42 Pia Pera, *Lo's Diary*, trans. Ann Goldstein (New York: Foxrock, 1999), pp. 74–5. Subsequent page references in text will be to this edition.

43 The Portuguese version of the Lispector novel is *A hora da estrela* (Rio de Janeiro: Nova Fronteira, 1984). The reference here is to the English translation. *The Hour of the Star*, trans. Giovanni Pontieri (New York: New Directions, 1992), p. 19. Subsequent page references in text will be to this edition.

44 Hélène Cixous, *Coming to Writing and Other Essays*, ed. Deborah Henson (Cambridge, MA: Harvard University Press, 1991).

45 The interview with Amaral is included in Susana Rossberg, "Quotro adaptacoes filmicas: por un cinema politico claramente narrado," unpublished masters thesis in the Department of Portuguese and Brazilian Studies at Brown University, December 1998.

Chapter 6

Modernism, Adaptation, and the French New Wave

While previous chapters have dealt with the filmic "progeny" of specific literary texts, this chapter reverses direction by taking off from film, or more precisely from a film movement, and then moving back, or better "over," to literature. What interests me here is the multifaceted relation between literature, adaptation, and the French New Wave. By "New Wave" I refer, of course, to that movement of film renovation, beginning in the late 1950s, thanks to which scores of relatively young directors managed to make their first fiction features, in the process revolutionizing film language and altering the course of film history.

Michel Marie argues persuasively that the phrase "New Wave," despite its journalistic provenance, is not an arbitrary rubric; rather, the New Wave has all the earmarks of an artistic movement or "school," one of the "most coherent in the history of cinema." More specifically, for Marie, the New Wave has: (1) a corpus of doctrinal works and manifestos (the essays of Astruc, Truffaut, Bazin, Godard); (2) an aesthetic project (roughly summarizable as a conjugation of modernist reflexivity with Bazinian realism); (3) a theory linked to a strategy (*auteurism* as a means to forge a place for new directors); (4) a corpus of films exemplifying the criteria outlined in the manifestos; (5) a constellation of artists and artisans (directors, screenwriters, performers, editors, set designers, and so forth); (6) a journalistic support apparatus (led by *Cahiers du Cinéma*) equipped to disseminate the group's views and achievements; (7) a leading theoretician (Bazin); and (8) strong adversaries (Marxists, the tradition of quality) who diacritically define the group and prod it into clarifying its positions.[1]

There are myriad possible approaches to exploring the complex relation between the New Wave and literature. One approach might focus on the actual practice of adaptation by New Wave directors, for example on Truffaut's adaptation of Henri-Pierre Roche's *Jules and Jim* (1961) or David Goodis's *Shoot the Piano Player* (1960), or Jacques Rivette's adaptation of Diderot's *La Religieuse* (1966) and so forth. What literary corpus was favored for adaptation by the New Wave? While the antecedent French "tradition of quality" preferred to adapt prestigious classical novels from the French realist tradition (Stendhal, Balzac, Zola), the New Wave directors favored less canonical (often foreign) and more contemporary writers such as David Goodis or Ray Bradbury. Another approach might treat the more covert, even subterranean literary influence on directors who did not actually adapt novelists and yet were affected by them: the influence of Balzac on Chabrol, or Faulkner on Godard, or Proust on Resnais. In this sense, Resnais's obsessive search for lost cinematic time makes him a "Proustian" director, even though he never actually adapted *A la recherche du temps perdu*. Still another approach might emphasize the strikingly innovative approach to literature–film relations in the *"cine-roman"* films by "left-bank" directors like Alain Resnais and Marguerite Duras. Alternatively, one might examine the role of polemics about adaptation within the New Wave's formulation of its own aesthetic. In what follows, I shall try to do a little bit of all of the above, making some general comments about the "literariness" of the New Wave, but also looking more closely at three early films, notably *L'Année dernière à Marienbad* (1961), *Hiroshima mon amour* (1959), and, in much greater detail, *Le Mépris* (1963).

The *Cahiers* critics who subsequently formed the nucleus of the French New Wave were profoundly ambivalent about literature, which they saw as both a model to be emulated and an enemy to be abjured. Haunted by the overweening prestige of literature in a country that had always venerated its writers, the *Cahiers* critics forged the concept of the *cineaste* as **auteur** as a way of transferring the millennial aura of the established art of literature to the relatively fledgling yet industrial art of film. Novelist/filmmaker Alexandre Astruc prepared the way with his landmark 1948 essay "Birth of a New Avant-garde: The Camera-pen," in which he argued that the cinema was becoming a new means of expression analogous to painting or the novel.[2] Within this view, film was no longer the rendering of a pre-existing written text; rather, the shooting process itself became a form of writing through *mise-en-scène*. With its first issue in 1951, *Cahiers* became a key organ for the propagation of la **politique des auteurs**. *Auteurism* formed a palimpsest of cultural influences, combining romantic expressive notions of the artist, existentialist notions of authenticity and freedom, modernist–formalist notions of medium-specific reflexivity and discontinuity, and a "proto-postmodern" fondness for "lower" arts and genres like the musical and the B-film. Paradoxically, a theory that traced its ideological roots to pre-modernist romanticism – with its idealization of the artist as visionary, seer, magus, and "unacknowledged legislator of mankind" – helped generate films which were resolutely modernist in aspiration and aesthetics.

In the postwar period in France, in sum, both film and literary discourse came to gravitate around such concepts as "authorship," "*écriture*," and "textuality." A "graphological trope" informed a wide spectrum of coinages and formulations from Astruc's "**camera-stylo**" to Resnais's **cine-roman** to Varda's **cinécriture**. The New Wave directors' fondness for the scriptural metaphor was scarcely surprising given that many of them began as film journalists who saw writing articles and making films as simply two variant forms of expression. For Godard, writing criticism was already a way of making films, just as making films was a way to continue writing criticism. "Whether in the studio or before the blank page," as Godard put it somewhat melodramatically, "we are always alone."[3] Agnes Varda, about to make *La Pointe courte* (made in 1954, released 1956), announced that she would "make a film exactly as one writes a book."[4] In Eric Rohmer's case, the "transfer" was even more direct, in that he began as a novelist and then proceeded to "adapt" his own stories. Rohmer (aka Maurice Scherer) defended the idea that the novel as genre was the best model for film: "Cinema should recognize the narrow dependence which links it, not to painting or to music, but to the very arts from which it had always tried to distance itself – literature and the theatre."[5]

The New Wave began to formulate its aesthetic principles, symptomatically, precisely around what came to be called the "**querelle de l'adaptation**." In a series of articles, Bazin argued that filmic adaptation was not a shameful and parasitical practice but rather a creative and productive one, a catalyst of progress for the cinema. In "Defense of Mixed Cinema," Bazin mocks those who express outrage over the outrages against literature supposedly committed by film versions, arguing that culture in general and literature in particular have nothing to lose from the practice of adaptation. Filmic adaptations help democratize literature and make it popular; "there is no competition or substitution," Bazin writes, but "rather the adding of a new dimension that the arts had gradually lost . . . namely a public."[6] In another essay, "Adaptation, or the Cinema as Digest," Bazin suggests that the adaptation, far from being illegitimate, has been a perennial practice in all the arts. While admitting that most films based on novels merely usurp their title, Bazin also argues that a film like *Day in the Country* shows that an adaptation can be "faithful to the spirit of Maupassant's story while at the same time benefiting from . . . Renoir's genius." With Renoir, adaptation becomes "the refraction of one work in another creator's consciousness." For Bazin, Renoir's version of *Madame Bovary* (1934) reconciles a certain fidelity with artistic independence because here author and *auteur* meet as equals.[7]

Bazin's admirer and onetime disciple, François Truffaut, in his manifesto essay "A Certain Tendency in French Cinema" (first published in *Cahiers* in 1954), also turned to the issue of adaptation. Distancing himself from his mentor's cautious approval of adaptation, Truffaut excoriated the "tradition of quality" which turned French literary classics into predictably well-furnished, well-spoken, and stylistically formulaic films. The prestige of the "tradition of quality" partially derived from the borrowed luster of the literary sources it adapted, so Truffaut was striking at the sources of canonical prestige. Truffaut especially lambasted adaptation as practiced by two "quality" screenwriters: Jean Aurenche and Pierre Bost. In his 1948 "Adaptation, or the Cinema as Digest," Bazin had suggested that Aurenche and Bost simultaneously "transformed" – in the manner of an electric transformer – but also "dissipated" the energy of their source novels.[8] Truffaut, in contrast, is much more harsh and unforgiving. Truffaut accuses the two screenwriters of being disrespectful to both literature and film. He mocks the two screenwriters' claim to have revolutionized adaptation through a "creative infidelity" which produced "equivalencies" between literary and cinematic procedures. What this amounts to in practice, Truffaut argues, is a cynical triage which discards whatever is arbitrarily decreed to be "unfilmable." Every novel becomes an excuse for Aurenche and Bost to smuggle into the adaptation the same old anti-clerical and innocuously anarchistic themes. Since one cannot be "faithful" to the style and spirit of writers as diverse as Gide, Radiguet, Colette, and Bernanos, the screenwriters are faithful instead to their own myopic vision. Basing his critique on actual adaptations of Bernanos' *Journal d'un curé de campagne* (Diary of a Country Priest, 1951) and Radiguet's *Le Diable au corps* (1946), Truffaut argues that the "quality" screenwriters simply exploit their source texts to introduce a limited set of secularist, anti-militarist, and left-wing ideas. The result is a flattening out of the heterogeneity of literary sources. But, even more gravely, the search for "equivalencies" for the putatively "unfilmable" passages from the novel masks a profound scorn for the cinema, seen as fundamentally incapable of ever achieving the grandeur of literature. For Truffaut, adaptation, too, is a "*question de morale*." (In retrospect, Truffaut clearly mingled valid insights with a passionate oedipal hostility to what was symptomatically called "*le cinema de papa*," and Bazin gently rebuked the violence of Truffaut's language in his own response to Truffaut's polemical tract.)[9]

Truffaut denounced "quality" adaptations in the name of "fidelity," but, since the time of the New Wave, adaptation studies have oscillated between a "fidelity" discourse and a more theoretically sophisticated "intertextuality" discourse. It was the "realist" Bazin, ironically, who anticipated some of these currents in his 1948 "Cinema as Digest" essay. There he argued for a more open conception of adaptation, one with a place for what we would now call "intertextuality" and "*transécriture*." Bazin's words about adaptation in 1948 ironically anticipate both *auteurism* and its critique. The "ferocious defense of literary works" vis-à-vis their adaptations, Bazin suggests, rests on a "rather recent, individualist conception that was far from being ethically rigorous in the 17th century and that started to become legally defined only at the end of the eighteenth."[10] Here Bazin anticipates Foucault's devalorization of the individual author in favor of a "pervasive anonymity of discourse." Bazin also anticipates Roland Barthes' prophecy of "the death of the author" by forecasting that "we are moving toward a reign of the adaptation in which the notion of the unity of the work of art, if not the very notion of the author itself, will be destroyed."[11] Thus Bazin, whose "humanism" later made him the whipping boy for film structuralists and semioticians, ironically foreshadowed some of the later structuralist and post-structuralist currents which would indirectly undermine a fidelity discourse in relation to adaptation.

The question of adaptation stands at the point of convergence of a number of crucial issues: cinematic specificity, modernist reflexivity, and inter-art and inter-semiotic relations. But these questions are all inextricably interconnected, in the sense that the foregrounding of specificity is often linked to a modernist stance, while filmic modernism necessarily passes through an interplay with other, more markedly modernist, arts. It is hardly surprising, in this light, that the *Cahiers* writer/filmmakers constantly draw suggestive comparisons between film and other arts such as painting, music, and sculpture, usually in terms of their relative coefficient of mimetic realism or modernist reflexivity. In his 1955 series of "Celluloid and Marble" essays, Eric Rohmer, picking up on the old theme of "film as synthesis of all the arts," successively compares film art to painting, poetry, music, and architecture, ultimately concluding that film embodies the best of both modernism and classicism.[12] The 1959 *Cahiers* roundtable devoted to *Hiroshima mon amour* also elicits frequent inter-art comparisons. Rohmer describes Resnais as a "Cubist" and the first "modern" filmmaker of the sound film. For Pierre Kast, *Hiroshima* combines the "greatest cinematic ambition" with "the greatest literary ambition." And, for Godard, *Hiroshima* can only be appreciated in relation to other arts, more like "Faulkner plus Stravinsky" than the combination of any two film directors.[13]

The advent of the New Wave coincided with the emergence of various avant-garde-inflected movements in criticism and the arts in France: Barthes and **nouvelle critique** in literary theory; Beckett and Ionesco and absurdism in the theater; Boulez in music; and the "new novel" in literature. It was no accident that the subtitle of Astruc's 1948 "Camera Stylo" essay was "For a **New Avant-garde**" (emphasis added). What would differentiate the "new avant-garde" of the late 1940s from the "historical avant-gardes" of the 1920s was its hybrid character as a compromise formation negotiating between entertainment and vanguardism. While the avant-gardists of the 1920s called for "pure cinema," the New Wave preferred a "mixed cinema" which mingled a certain formal audacity (reflexivity, sound/image disjunction) with the pleasures of mainstream cinema (narrative, performance, desire, spectacle).

An important question, for all the various "wings" of the New Wave movement, then, was that of the cinema's relation to modernism. The New Wave posed the question of modernism in terms of the specific spatio-temporality of film, and especially in terms of "continuity" as the very kernel of the dominant style. The New Wave questioned the aesthetic cornerstone of dominant cinema: the reconstitution of a fictional world characterized by internal coherence and by the artfully fashioned simulacrum of a seamless **continuity**. This continuity, as I suggested in the Introduction, was classically achieved through a series of devices for introducing scenes, for evoking the passage of time (dissolves, iris effects), for rendering imperceptible the transition from shot to shot, and for implying subjectivity and identification. The conventional Hollywood film in the dominant style was expressive of the individual desires of believable characters, within coherent, cause–effect linear plots, revolving around "major conflicts," and deploying a traditional spatio-temporal decorum which conveyed a feeling of seamlessly lived duration. Everything was designed to avoid provoking spectatorial discomfort, to avoid sudden contrasts of sound or light or tone, while also nourishing interest and suspense through the narrative striptease of hermeneutc stimulation. Continuity devices, meanwhile, disguised the actual **dis**continuities of film production, covering them over in the name of a fluid narrrative illusionism.

One key factor in the questioning of the norms of dramatic realism and normative continuity as a style was the pervasive influence of the theories and practice of the German dramatist Bertolt Brecht. The performances of Brecht's Berliner Ensemble in Paris, in this period, inspired enthusiastic essays by critics such as Roland Barthes and Bernard Dort.[14] In his own writings, Brecht argued for an

Chapter 6   Modernism, Adaptation, and the French New Wave

art of disjunction and distantiation. Partially as a response to the viscerally mani-pulative spectacles of Nazism, Brecht wanted to cultivate an active, critical, think-ing spectator who did not identify emotionally with heroes or with the fiction. Brecht proposed specific strategies to achieve this goal, for example through a fractured, interrupted narrative structure, through direct address to the specta-tor, and through a distanced approach to acting, whereby actors deliberately act as if they were "quoting." The point was to avoid the voyeuristic premises of the "fourth-wall" convention, which staged events in such a way that it appeared that spectators just "happened" to be able to observe other people while being themselves unwatched.

Brecht also argued for a thoroughgoing reflexivity, for an art which would reveal the principles of its own construction. In the cinema, this meant calling attention to the apparatus (the camera and the boom, for example), to the con-text of production of the fiction (the studio, the editing room), to the makers of the fiction (the producer, the director, the screenwriter, and so forth), or to the intertext of the fiction (the various genres and films which influence the film in question). Brecht promoted an aesthetic of contradiction based on the "radical separation of the elements." Each film track – music, dialogue, lyric, lighting – was to exist autonomously, in tension with other tracks; the music might go against the image, or the lyrics against the music, for example. The New Wave adaptations, in this sense, reflect a certain "theatricalization," reflected in virtually all of the films discussed in this chapter; one medium – theater – mediated the filmic adaptations drawn from another medium – the novel.

The **nouveau roman** (new novel) and the **cine-romans** by the "left-bank" direc-tors – the older cohort of filmmakers coming from other arts – constituted one response to the challenge of modernism. The first works of the New Novelists, toward the end of the 1950s, coincided with the first shorts and fiction features by the New Wave directors. Thus more or less simultaneous with films such as Chabrol's *Le Beau Serge* (1958) and Truffaut's *Les Mistons* (1957) we find novels such as Michel Butor's *La Modification* (1957), Alain Robbe-Grillet's *La Jalousie* (1957), and Marguerite Duras' *Moderato cantabile* (1957). The term **cine-roman** (film-novel) is somewhat misleading, in that it might erroneously suggest (1) a novelization of a film or (2) an illustrated novel, when what is really intended by "*cine-roman*" is a sort of parallel artistic creation, which takes two simultaneous forms: prose fiction and film. The text is meant for the screen – and in this sense it resembles a screenplay – but it also has an autonomous literary existence as well. For the theorists of the *cine-roman*, the film–literature relation did not entail even a **soupçon** of subordination or hierarchy between the two arts. At times this equality in status, this lack of theoretical anteriority, was literalized through simultaneous publication/release of novel and film. Each medium was seen as having its own invaluable strengths and particularities. Neither text was prior or superior in value; instead, a parallel and criss-crossing movement of creation would benefit both film and literature. Through a reversible, two-way artistic current, each medium could energize the other through a process of reciprocal actualization. In the case of the *cine-roman*, then, it is misleading even to speak of "adaptation," which Resnais has often compared to "reheating a meal." We are dealing, rather, with a transartistic cross-media collaboration by two artists with sibling sensibilities and aesthetics. It is therefore less a question of "adaptation" than of a dialogic co-creation, a synergistic transfer between a film-literate writer and a literarily minded director. And if conventional adaptation is like "reheating a meal," then the *cine-roman* is rather like inventing a new form of cuisine.

Last Year at Marienbad (1961), a collaboration between the writer Robbe-Grillet and the filmmaker Alain Resnais, wonderfully illustrates this process. It is well known that Resnais almost always chose to collaborate with writers (often with little initial experience of the cinema) – Raymond Queneau, Jean Cayrol, Marguerite Duras, Jorge Semprum, Robbe-Grillet – in an atmosphere of symbiotic mutual admiration. Resnais's practice was to ask the writer for an original text, in relation to which he was the first and privileged reader, and then, cinematic executor. For Resnais, transpersonal collaboration, somewhat paradoxically, facilitates **personal** expression. Through a kind of salutary contagion, many of Resnais's collaborators (Robbe-Grillet and Duras, for example) subsequently became filmmakers themselves. In the case of Robbe-Grillet, the collaborative **écriture** generated two texts: a film by Alain Resnais and a screenplay/novel by Alain Robbe-Grillet. (*Marienbad* was the first of four **cine-romans** by Robbe-Grillet.) The process demonstrates what we will be calling the "automatic difference" between literature and film. Even though Resnais "scrupulously respected" every detail of the screenplay, even sending telegrams "every time he wanted to change a comma," as Robbe-Grillet himself pointed out, at the same time Resnais also "transformed everything."[15] Robbe-Grillet also revised his text after seeing the film, thus showing the mutually impacting process of what Gaudreault would call a dialogical **transécriture**.[16]

In his theoretical book *Pour un nouveau roman* (1956) Robbe-Grillet had already expressed admiration for the cinema as a medium, lauding its perpetual present tense, its highlighting of objects ("*chosisme*"), and its inescapable specificity about point of view. By its very nature, the cinema demands a vantage point; the necessity of choosing a camera set-up dictates a specific point of view, even if only that of the camera itself. Echoing earlier Surrealist ideas about film's

> It isn't the objectivity of the camera that enthuses them, but its possibilities in the domain of the subjective, of the imaginary. They don't conceive of cinema as a means of expression, but of research, and what most claims their attention is, naturally, what was most lacking in the means of literature; namely, not so much the image but the sound track – the sound of voices, different noises, atmospheres, kinds of music – and above all the possibility of acting on two senses at once, the eye and the ear.[17]

Thus, with Robbe-Grillet, a novelist already inflected by film and its "looks" meets a filmmaker inflected by a novelistic regard.[18]

As a novelist, Robbe-Grillet writes puzzle-texts, in which key elements are missing and have to be inferred by the reader. In *Le Voyeur* (1955), the reader has to divine a missing murder, buried within the interstices of the text. In *La Jalousie* (1957) – the title puns on the words for "jealousy" and "Venetian blinds" – the reader must deduce the missing key character lurking "behind the prose," as it were, inferred only from the words of the story. The technique forms the literary counterpart, in some ways, of the literally subjective camera (the classical example being *Lady in the Lake*, 1947) where the camera is closely identified with the vantage point of a character, yet whom we never actually see in the frame (except in a mirror).

Robbe-Grillet's novels offer an innovative approach to the role of novelistic description. While description had been more or less absent from the Cervantic tradition rooted in *Don Quixote*, and while it played only a minimal and "instrumental" role in novels like *Robinson Crusoe*, it became a vital factor in referential illusion only in nineteenth-century realist fiction. In a novelist like Balzac, description made thematic points: in a relationship at once metonymic and metaphoric, the decor (for example, la maison Vauquer in *Père Goriot*) osmotically resembled and at the same time shaped the character. But in Robbe-Grillet, this link is broken. Description no longer "serves" the story; it becomes autonomous. Film, it has often been said, obviates the need for description, since filmic "monstration" (showing) effectively presents the characters and decor in all their physical plenitude, often making it difficult to distinguish between "description" and "narration." In the case of *Marienbad*, the Robbe-Grillet text verbally describes images and sounds which are more directly perceptible in the film, rearticulated through the cinema's five tracks. The space of the chateaux, for example, is described (often inaccurately) by the narrator's voice-over, while it is simultaneously "plowed through," as it were, by Resnais's relentlessly tracking camera.

Last Year at Marienbad is not an adaptation, but rather a collaborative effort by two artists trying to instantiate their vision of a radically modernist art, while still respecting the specific traits and potentialities of their respective media. Two parallel and mutually enriching modernisms shape novels and films which are each discontinuous, in ways appropriate to the two media in question, and which pursue a shared interest in the exploration of mental time. Few films provide a better refutation of the mistaken idea that films are ill equipped to portray subjectivity. For Resnais, cinema does not represent an event but rather stages and enacts and models the operations of the mind itself. Cinema, like sex, occurs within the brain. As a kind of film manifesto of the *cine-roman*, *Marienbad* offers an exhibitionistic display of cinematic specificity, a demonstration of all the things films can do and novels cannot do, or what they can do only in very different terms. Rigorously formalist, Resnais and Robbe-Grillet agreed on stylistic questions — the orchestrating of off-screen glances, an approach to montage — even before settling on the core story or anecdote. A truly modernist cinema, for them, entailed a more active, participatory role for the spectator. *Last Year at Marienbad*, in this sense, turns the film experience into a perceptual puzzle. Like the famously labyrinthine Robbe-Grillet literary texts, *Marienbad* is a maze and the spectator has the feeling of being lost in a maze. Those who try to make linear sense of the film, to discern a coherent cause-and-effect logic or a plausible trajectory of plot or character development, Robbe-Grillet suggested, will be doomed to failure, frustrated, finding the film incomprehensible.

Last Year at Marienbad itself thematizes this process by having its fictitious characters try in vain to establish the "true" antecedent story of "last year at Marienbad." Robbe-Grillet's introduction to the novel even casts doubt on the very idea of a pre-existing story.[19] The characters, he tells us, "do not exist." And as for the "past which the hero introduces forcibly into this closed and empty world, we have the impression that he invents it while he speaks." In sum, "there is no last year, and Marienbad is not to be found on any map." In fact, the characters begin to exist, as Robbe-Grillet pointed out, with the first page of the novel (or the first shot of the film) and cease to exist with the final page (or shot). The spoken words are not there to be understood; the screenplay/ novel points out on various occasions that we do not understand the words: "The words, by the end of the credits, have become normally comprehensible" (p. 20); "these fragments being only partially comprehensible" (p. 29); "their words are

Figure 6.1 The ghostlike dance in *Last Year at Marienbad* (1961), produced by Argos Films / Cineriz / Cinétel / Como / Cormoran Films / Les Films Tamara / Precitel / Silver Films / Société Nouvelle des Films / Terra Film

at first indistinct, virtually incomprehensible" (p. 30); "what they say is indistinguishable" (pp. 32–3); "the text is virtually inaudible" (p. 68). The normative *telos* of story here gives way to what Deleuze calls "pure optical and sound situations." We could not be farther from the conventions of novelistic realism, from Defoe's "no appearance of fiction," or of Fielding's "true history" of Tom Jones. Instead of the "story of an adventure," as Jean Ricardou puts it, we are given the "adventure of a story."[20]

In a sense, the film constitutes a sardonic gloss on the spectator's complicity in filmic illusion. The title calls attention to the twin chronotopic coordinates of filmic fiction – time (last year) and space (Marienbad). The lack of a realistic story is reinforced by the artificial setting: an old-style spa, relic of an archaic, isolated, and stuffy world lacking the usual points of reference such as known city landmarks or recognizable streets, or familiar social institutions such as cafés or modern media such as radio or television. The actors' voices, according to Robbe-Grillet's directions, are "theatrical," but without any particular intonation. Rather than convey what Derrida would call "presence," they offer only a flow of articulate sound. The film posits spatial and temporal impossibilities in the form of single images which condense, rather like De Chirico paintings, various times in the day, or in the form of characters who disappear only to reappear in improbable places, or objects that jump around inexplicably in space. *Marienbad* thus disorients its spectator through "reality effects" that point not to the real but only to the "really" impossible.

At the same time, the film's tale of seduction allegorizes the relationship between film and the spectatorial protocols of the conventional fiction film. Like a film director, X tries to persuade A that something happened, elsewhere, the previous year. He tries to persuade her to see things, as it were, through his framing lens. In Deleuze's words, the question is whether A will allow herself to be attracted into X's sheets of time, or if X will be unhinged by A's resistances.[21] X orchestrates realistic details intended to convince her of the truth of his story. The spectator, like A, is the object of a seduction; in both cases, complicity is required for the seduction to work. Thus *Marienbad* offers a stylized, exemplary, and strangely unsettling demonstration of the spectatorial processes constitutive of all fiction films.

Marienbad has been interpreted in myriad ways.[22] But rather than pursue the chimera of a single interpretative key to the film, it strikes me as more productive to approach the film in terms of "what's wrong with this picture?" What about the film seems strange, anomalous, disconcerting, incoherent? How are the usual conventions and continuities scrambled or upended? Here, I will explore just a few segments as samples of the creative possibilities of discontinuity in the cinema, always against the backdrop of aesthetic modernism. The sequence – if one can call it that since the film as a whole maintains a kind of seamless fluidity throughout, without marking off specific sequences – has to do, once again, with the attempt by the man X (the characters are never named, but played by Giorgio Albertazzi) to convince A (Delphine Seyrig) that they had met the previous year in Marienbad. (The film's "plot" has been compared to an extended riff on the hackneyed pick-up line: "Haven't I met you somewhere before?")

The sequence opens with a single, continuous shot which lasts roughly two and a half minutes. Delphine Seyrig is standing alone in a vast hall in a chateau. We hear what we assume to be X's off-screen voice, but which seems to be addressed to her and to which she seems to react. We do not see him; we see only her alone. The camera reframes very slightly, almost invisibly, and we are surprised to see X, the source of the off-screen voice, appear in a space exactly to the right of Seyrig, space the film had just shown as completely devoid of human beings. Seyrig had been looking screen-left, moreover, so that if X were to appear anywhere, the conventions of eyeline match and direction would normally dictate that it be in the space toward which Seyrig was looking, not in the space to screen right. Thus Resnais/Robbe-Grillet perversely mix up the usual eyeline and position matches, destabilizing spatial relations and de-anchoring, and then re-anchoring, the voice.

Even before X appears, Seyrig's spoken "You're mistaken" offers the first indisputable clue that she has heard what X is saying. We are obliged to redefine the status of what we have seen: what we assumed to be off-screen narration has been now transformed into on-screen synchronous dialogue. The camera then tracks right, and we are surprised to discover that the same hall which we had assumed to be empty – since no images of people or sounds of conversation had alerted us to any human presence – is now crowded with people. While the camera tracks right and abandons X, his voice continues at exactly the same volume, thus shifting its status once again back to off-screen narration. The segment constitutes a long single-shot sequence tracking shot, which entails by definition the **literal** traversal of physical space and precise temporal duration, with no room for the kinds of manipulative trickery made possible by montage. We are therefore surprised all the more when the tracking camera picks up X again, now standing at a point quite distant from the place of his original conversation with Seyrig, and now facing in the opposite direction (screen right). Neither his voice, nor his breathing, nor his bodily posture, betray the slightest symptom of expended effort or prior movement. At the end of this extremely long tracking shot, we are surprised once again to encounter Seyrig moving toward the camera on a balustrade, at a point quite distant from where we had earlier seen her standing. She too betrays not the slightest symptom of exertion.

Through a strange inversion, the camera in *Marienbad* is generally more active and mobile than the film's human figures, who remain immobile, stiff, hieratic. The people are frozen in position, like statues; they seem dead, while the camera's relentless tracking makes it seem "alive." The characters' snail-like pace and the general lack of triggering movements to prepare for cuts clearly violate the Hollywood continuity rules of "movement matches" and "cutting on movement." The characters simply appear at their new stations, like apparitions, without betraying the symptoms either of their imminent departure from one place or their imminent arrival at another. Indeed, one can imagine a hilarious "making of" film about *Marienbad* which would show all the out-of-breath and frantic scurrying around of the impeccably dressed, stuffed-shirt characters trying to arrive before the camera at their designated points of arrival. The "making of" film, more Keystone Cops than European art film, would highlight the comic gap between production and product. The atmosphere of frenzied kineticism would contrast dramatically with the hieratic frieze-like stasis classically associated with *Marienbad*.

The next series of shots shows A and X engaged in the matchstick game, various versions of which structure and punctuate the film. The matchstick game is just one of many games in the film, along with poker, dominoes, checkers, and theatrical plays. The game, not unlike the "game" of cinema itself, is one of controlled dominance. More significant than the game itself is the paradigmatic role of games within the film in general, where games come to metaphorize the film's stance, at once ludic and aggressive, toward the spectator. Moreover, the characters constantly offer diverse theories about the game: the person who begins wins, they speculate, or the winner has to always take an uneven number of matches, and so forth. The attempts to interpret the game come to homologize our own attempts to learn the rules and resolve the enigma of the film itself as a game. Throughout, the statues seem more alive than the human beings, reminding us of Gorky's impressions of the cinema as a "kingdom of shadows" which offers not life but its shadow, not motion but rather a "soundless specter" where "gray silhouettes" glide "noiselessly along the grey ground."[23]

After the game, the camera proceeds through the corridors of the castle. In fact "the" castle is actually an optical illusion created by the montage of shots featuring **different** chateaux – Schlessheim for the park and façade, Nymphenberg and Paris studio sets for the interiors – which have been spliced together to form the simulacrum of a single space. A fractured chronotope (in the production) is artfully reassembled into an apparently seamless unity. Throughout, Resnais and Robbe-Grillet deploy the same primordial trick; they combine impeccable continuity on one track, for example on the image track, with radical discontinuity on another track such as the sound track. The basic technique involves what Resnais calls "*faux raccords;*" that is, shrewdly calculated conjugations of editing matches and mismatches, where absolutely flawless continuity on one level is calculatedly mingled with disturbing discontinuities on another. Two successive shots might display razor-sharp precision and flawless continuity in terms of decor, position matches, and camera movement, yet be discontinuous in terms of costume, since the actress is wearing a different dress in each shot. Or the camera might track at different points through the very same door, yet the contiguous space will differ markedly. (In the postmodern age, these formerly avant-garde techniques have become a staple of TV commercials; the difference is that the commercials **are** anchored in the "real" of soft-selling commodification.) Or the off-screen narration will contradict what we see in the image. While the off-screen narration tells us that the corridors are empty, the film reveals corridors crowded with people. A subsequent shot shows us four people seated together, yet their sightlines shoot off in four completely different directions, evoking a choreographed randomness of the gaze, a calculated **impossibility** of looking relations. This technique violates the dominant regimen of the cinematic gaze, whereby every eyeline is carefully calculated to show who is looking at whom, not in "reality" of course, but rather in terms of a purely cinematic logic of visual implication.

The next segment, set outside the castle, shows us the couple speculating about the meaning of some statues. Here Resnais deploys some of the same techniques he developed in his art documentaries of the 1940s and 1950s (*Van Gogh* [1948], *Guernica* [1950], *Les Statues meurent aussi* [1953]). In these films, Resnais deployed zooms and pans and reframings to "animate" static two-dimensional materials, turning Picasso's *Guernica*, for example, into a simulated battle, or using tricky eyeline matches to create an artificial sense of "dialogue" between two characters in a painting. One moment especially encapsulates the perverse decorum of the glance in *Marienbad*. Arguing a certain interpretation, X invites Seyrig to "look over there" at the statues of which he speaks. In any conventional film, the following shot would show exactly what was to be seen "over there." Yet *Marienbad* denies us this counter shot, as if in a sadistic refusal of the habitual coddling of the spectator of dominant cinema.

Like the various games, and like the film itself, the statues too provoke hermeneutic surmises; the characters can only speculate about their meaning. The characters present hypotheses about the statues, just as we as spectators formulate hypotheses about *Marienbad*. While the spectator of *Marienbad* tries to cognitively map the film, to force it to "make sense" in cause–effect narrative terms, the film frustrates that desire. Indeed, *Marienbad* virtually begs for close shot-by-shot analysis, not because analysis might "make sense" of the film but rather because only close analysis reveals how the film is constructed, David-Byrne-like, so as **not** to make sense. The film forms an unstable amalgam of signifying layers within an exploded narration unanchored in any secure sense of the "real." As Deleuze describes it, the narration consists of distributing different presents to different characters, each plausible in itself but "all of them together" are, in Deleuze's coinage, "incompossible."[24] Rationalism and cause–effect logic break down, and the spectators, if they are to retain their sanity, must surrender to the sentient flow of images and sounds. They must abandon the search for depth and content themselves with surfaces, since the forging of a coherent story would be a Sisyphean task, doomed to failure. Cinematic resources usually deployed to solder and integrate and normalize the film experience are here used to explode it. In a sense, Resnais has incorporated into the very structure of the film the irrationalist aesthetic principles of the Surrealists that he so admired, achieving what Genevieve Rodis-Lewis has called the "vertigo of **amour fou**."[25] The film multiplies and fractures and disperses the energies of the various tracks, offering the spectator a flux of images, sounds, and words, with little anchorage in a stable diegetic world. Robbe-Grillet and Resnais thus reveal the cinema's capacity to disturb and destabilize the reader/spectator's perceptions. We feel at a loss, at the mercy of a somewhat sadistic narrator. Even Robbe-Gillet's written text builds into the story the spectator's **failure** to comprehend – "the spectator does not understand the spoken words . . . due to a strong reverberation" or "X's words have become absolutely incomprehensible."[26] Rather than merely talking about the "hermeneutics of suspicion," the film instantiates and stages a systematic sense of doubtfulness. It is in this way that *Marienbad* mounts a double assault, simultaneously against the realist novel and against the classical realist/illusionist film.

When *Marienbad* was first screened, reviewers praised it, or condemned it, largely in thematic terms. As if entrapped by what Robbe-Grillet had called "*le mythe de la profondeur*," they glossed the film as an exercise in existentialism, or a critique of elite society, or a lament about the "failure of communication" (a critical cliché of the period), or a meditation on death. Few reviewers caught the inside joke, that the film was essentially a ludic deconstruction of the dominant codes of continuity editing. Resnais and Robbe-Grillet discerned that the key to the dominant form of cinema, the key to its anti-modernism, was its fetish of continuity, and it was precisely continuity which they chose to undermine. Rather than cinema as a slice of life, they revealed it to be, as Hitchcock once put it, "a piece of cake," or as A's guardian says of the *mise-en-abyme* painting of "the" chateau, a "matter of pure convention."

The Violent Yokings of *Hiroshima mon amour*

Another Resnais film, *Hiroshima mon amour*, directed by Resnais and written by the experimental writer Marguerite Duras, also performs a radical interrogation of conventional continuity. With *Hiroshima mon amour*, as with *Last Year at Marienbad*, it is misleading even to speak of "adaptation." In language that echoes Barthes's "death of the author," which gives "birth to the reader," Duras has said that adaptations construct themselves out of the destruction of their novelistic source. But it is "this massacre which is the bridge which leads to the place of reading."[27] Moreover, both Resnais and Duras are experimental artists, Resnais in film, Duras in the novel and theater (and later in film as well). Here we find a confluence of obsessions, Resnais with memory and art, Duras with relationships, silence, and voice.

Duras, who has compared her own life to "a badly dubbed, badly edited, and badly acted film,"[28] came to *Hiroshima* in the wake of a series of disappointments with adaptations of her own work by other filmmakers. Unimpressed by René Clément's 1958 film version of *The Sea Wall* (*Barrage contre le Pacifique*), Duras began to toy with the idea of writing for cinema. But, interestingly, Duras does not condemn other filmmakers' adaptations of her work in the name of "fidelity:"

> If I had to transpose another of my novels to the screen, I think I'd make a good job of it. I could take liberties with my book that an adapter wouldn't dare take. In the final analysis I think adapters are too faithful to the original. I could rewrite any scene for the screen, in the same spirit, without it having anything to do with the book. If one wants to remain faithful it is essential to preserve the tone.[29]

Resnais, meanwhile, saw Duras as a writer rich, precisely, in "tone." Having just read *Moderato cantabile* and liking *The Square*, whose musicality he found moving, Resnais approached Duras about working on *Hiroshima mon amour*. He asked her for two different plots set in two different time periods. Duras had nine weeks to write the script, guided only by Resnais's demand that she "write literature, without worrying about the camera."[30] And indeed the written version has no technical, filmic notations. Since Resnais wanted Duras' voice and intonation, he asked her to make tape-recordings of the script. Since Duras had written the love story in Nevers as a separate story, the Nevers episode was not part of the original film script. Duras insisted on the theme of nighttime, and especially on the dark night of the cellar where the young woman was locked up because of her forbidden love, as terribly appropriate to the period of the Occupation.

The basic story of *Hiroshima mon amour* is well known. It revolves around the tale of an unnamed French "she" (played by Emmanuelle Riva), an actress making an antiwar film in Hiroshima, who has an affair with an unnamed Japanese "he" (played by Eiji Okada), an architect whose parents were killed by the A-bombing of Hiroshima. The affair in Hiroshima reawakens her repressed memories of a love affair, in Nevers, with a German soldier during World War II.

To appreciate *Hiroshima mon amour*, the contemporary spectator has to try to reimagine its shocking effect when it was first screened in 1959. The film shocked, first of all, by its completely fresh approach to an historical episode – the atomic bombing of Hiroshima and Nagasaki – whose unprecedented, horrific violence had been largely repressed, sanitized, "pacified" as it were, within the

European and American consciousness. The massive destruction triggered by the bombing had been sublimated and prettified through a Eurocentric and patriotic grid, crystallized and rendered inoffensive as "the event which ended the Second World War." A kind of pan-white racism clearly played a role in the discriminatory channeling of empathy; few in Europe or North America grieved over the death of those commonly referred to at the time as "Japs." At that point in history, European and North American spectators had never been prodded to imagine the nuclear holocaust as lived by its Japanese civilian victims. In this sense *Hiroshima* catalyzed a return of the historically repressed.

Secondly, the film shocked by "humanizing" a number of the conventionally defined "enemies" of the immediate postwar period. First, it humanized the Japanese, who, as members of the Axis powers during World War II, were presumably the enemy of the Allies, yet with whom the film empathizes as victims of the bombing, while also featuring a sympathetic male Japanese lead. Second, the film humanized Vichy collaborators, those Frenchmen who had various forms of relation with the occupying forces, and more particularly the women who had slept with German soldiers during the war. In an orgy of vindictiveness, such women, many of them lower-class, were scapegoated by many French as "the enemy within," to be tonsured, paraded, and generally humiliated in the streets of France after the Liberation, victimized even, at times, by those who had themselves collaborated in other, non-sexual ways. Yet *Hiroshima mon amour* presents the affair between the French woman and the German soldier sympathetically, and the woman mourns the loss of her German lover throughout the entire film. (Duras explained in interviews that an earlier draft of the script had clarified that the German character actually formed part of the anti-Nazi resistance, in a situation where few French men were romantically available, but no hint of this potentially crucial information made its way into the final film.) These sympathetic portrayals of internal and external "enemies" came, furthermore, from two artists very much associated with the left and the anti-fascist resistance.

Thirdly, the film's love affair itself would normally be seen as shocking in 1959, although not necessarily for the obvious reasons. The apparent taboos and obstacles to romance – adultery, racial difference – are given absolutely no importance. Both the French and the Japanese lovers are happily married and love their mates, and race seems not to be an obstacle. (Duras was obviously partially inspired by her own adolescent memories of the "North Chinese lover.") As for the taboo of adultery, Riva puns at one point that she is a "person of doubtful morality" (*de moralité douteuse*), clarifying that she is not a person of doubtful morality but rather a person who "casts doubt on morality itself."

Fourth, the film shocked by challenging the dominant masculinist codes of the period. *Hiroshima* offered a relatively outspoken and liberated heroine, reminiscent of the "new woman" incarnated, in different ways, by such contemporary figures as the actress Brigitte Bardot and the pop novelist Françoise Sagan, within the postwar situation of male dominance and female resentment theorized by Simone de Beauvoir in her groundbreaking *The Second Sex*.

Fifth, the film shocks in its treatment of death, which breaks with a number of the unstated conventions regnant in the mainstream feature fiction film. In *Hiroshima*, death is not a plot device, nor a pretext for violent spectacle. Instead, the film confronts us with death in the form of incinerated, deformed, decomposing bodies. The dominant cinema, which over the years has aggressively promoted the spectacle of death in war films, action blockbusters, and disaster movies, has generally favored a choreographed and antiseptic image of death. It has seldom given us death in the style of *Hiroshima mon amour*, a style interspersing images of real-life suffering, or better the traces of such suffering, combined with philosophical commentary about its meaning. Feature fiction films usually sweeten and prettify death through what Joseph Conrad, in a different (colonial) context, called a "redeeming idea," through chimerical ideas suggesting a vague promise of redemption or resurrection. Thus dominant cinema, or at least classical cinema at the time of *Hiroshima mon amour*, tended to offer death in the name of patriotism, or death in the name of a "better world." Rarely did films offer **this** kind of death — corrosive, decaying, death deforming "to the point of ugliness," death falling absurdly and invisibly from the sky, death with such irrefutable and grotesquely palpable impact on actual human bodies.

The opening image of *Hiroshima*, on which the credits are superimposed, is fascinatingly polysemic. Spectators seeing the film for the first time often misremember this opening shot. Asked immediately after seeing the film to describe the first shot, my students almost invariably cite later shots such as those of the intertwined lovers or even the later documentary-style material of the nuclear museum. When I remind them that one shot precedes even the shots of the lovers, they tend to recall a wide variety of other shots: a Japanese ideogram, an aerial shot of a city, a scorched scalp, a forest, a city map, and so forth. Very few remember the actual image — that of a plant fossil imprint burned into the Hiroshima pavement. In short, the students substitute for the actual first shot their memory of shots which appear later in the film. Yet this "misremembering" is itself an uncannily appropriate and "correct" response to the film, since the film itself is **about** remembering and misremembering. It is about the memory of Hiroshima, of World War II, of collaboration, of liberation, of tonsured women, of the need to remember not to forget. The students are therefore not wrong to

Figure 6.2 Polysemy and memory in *Hiroshima mon amour* (1959), produced by Argos Films / Como / Daiei Studios / Pathé Entertainment

superimpose on the opening image their filmic memory of later images; the film itself solicits such misrememberings. They have recapitulated precisely the process portrayed, or better incarnated, in *Hiroshima mon amour*, the process of the destabilization of memory, of remembering and repressing, of misrecognizing and forgetting, images from the past. The opening shot of a fossil does foreshadow all those other images: the fossil **does**, indeed, remind one of the Japanese ideogram we see later, or the scarred, scorched head; it **does** evoke a forest, map, or the aerial view of a city, its network of rivers and streets. Thus the opening image forms a visual matrix which generates the film as a whole.

In her writing of *Hiroshima mon amour*, Duras was partially inspired by the memory of the lava fossils of Pompeii, with its lovers permanently frozen by heat, as it were. In a different context, Deleuze speaks of cinematic images which resemble "radioactive fossils," which haunt the present with their tacit and dangerous injunction to excavate the past.[31] With the fossil, living animal, vegetable or human tissue has become petrified. The choice of precisely this image, of a fossil imprint, to begin this film, is also uncannily appropriate to a highly reflexive film which constantly calls attention to the cinema and to its own status as artifact. A fossil too constitutes a memory trace, a form of witness, just as the cinema is based on the witnessed traces left by photo-chemical processes. For Bazin, photography and cinematography were indexical imprints of the world, rather like a mummy or a death mask. The fossil thus evokes both film itself and more broadly the processes of physical and psychic scarring linked to traumatic memory. Riva's voice-over for the museum sequence recurrently mentions the indexical role of photographs, which we depend on *"faute d'autre choses"* (for lack of anything better). In a mass-mediated age, we rely on such metonymic traces – photographs, films, footage, video – **faute d'autre chose**. The rich polysemy of the opening image, then, provides an ideal overture for a multi-layered film about traces. The museum images, furthermore, also have anticipatory value for the film itself: the shots of hair falling out foreshadows Riva's loss of hair when she is tonsured during the liberation; the burned bicycle frame anticipates the bicycle Riva rides to visit her German lover, and her bicycle ride to Paris after the war.[32]

In terms of adaptation and the comparative capacities of cinema and literature, the overture sequences of *Hiroshima mon amour* develop a technique, that of the disembodied voice, available, in a certain way, **only** to the cinema. A novel might presumably posit an unmarked voice, a voice of mysterious origins. Robbe-Grillet's novel *La Jalousie*, for example, does feature a narrational voice, but the "I" of the narration is absent; it remains unidentified. But the cinema's multi-track nature allows it to construct what Michel Chion, following Jean-Pierre Schaeffer, calls the "acousmatic voice," i.e. the voice that is heard, which features a specific timbre and grain and "voiceprint," but whose source is unclear.[33] The early images drawn from the Hiroshima museum are "covered," for example, by a voice-over narration, which we perhaps presume to be that of the woman, yet the film withholds – for 132 shots – the sight of Riva's mouth actually articulating the words in synchronous speech. It is only when the camera pans up to Riva's face, and the two players begin to adopt a more natural voice and intonation, that the voice and moving lips achieve synchronization. Our ears and our eyes are finally reconciled, as the phonetic sounds are anchored in a human voice. (For some reason, New Wave directors were particularly fond of this acousmatic technique; we find it as well in the beginning of *Cleo de 5 à 7* [1962] and in the opening poem read by an invisible off-screen Jeanne Moreau in Truffaut's *Jules and Jim* [1961]). After a brief slip into naturalistic and synchronous dialogue, Riva's voice during the holocaust museum sequence modulates again into a kind of voice-over narration.

Throughout, *Hiroshima* generates this indeterminacy of meaning and status. The polysemy of the opening shot, the ambiguity of the shots of the lovers – are we seeing elbows or knees? are they covered with sweat or radioactive ash? – the characters without names, the acousmatic voice with its strange incantatory style, everything conspires to warn us: what we are seeing is definitely not a slice of life; it is stylized, hieratic, artificial.

Hiroshima mon amour has already been analyzed ad nauseam, and I will try not to retrace here already well-worn paths of interpretation. My goal here is to look at *Hiroshima mon amour* through a prism not often applied to the film, one supplied by the inventory of tropes of classical rhetoric. A fundamental rhetorical device structures *Hiroshima* as a whole. That device, I will be suggesting, is the oxymoron, the violent yoking of opposites. The oxymoronic procedures of the film are announced already in the title. The first word, "Hiroshima," is redolent of the very worst in human experience, to wit nuclear holocaust, mass death to no purpose whatsoever. Hiroshima in this sense does not refer to a city but to a hecatomb, a seared necropolis. The final words in the title, *"mon amour,"* meanwhile, evoke the polar opposite of mass death, calling attention to what is most cherished in human experience – life, love, tenderness, sexuality.[34] The title also indirectly invokes a venerable tradition within occidental art, one we have already encountered in *Madame Bovary*, to wit the oxymoronic **liebestod** tradition, the interplay of love and death, Eros and Thanatos. In the *liebestod* tradition, going back to courtly love and Tristan and Isolde, love was lived as pathos (etymologically "suffering). Love was impossible, usually involving adulterous love where desire both confronts (and is generated by) obstacles and challenges, in which arbitrary Law engenders passionate Desire. In *Hiroshima*, ironically, the ordinary obstacles – racial difference, nationality, the civil status of the partners – are treated as irrelevant, yet the love remains impossible.

Hiroshima mon amour "nuclearizes" the *liebestod* tradition. The passionately impossible love of Tristan and Isolde lives again in the mingled pain/pleasure of the lovers in Hiroshima. A love affair is illuminated, as it were, by the memory of radioactive flashes of a nuclear firestorm. Much of the dialogue and voice-over narration explicitly touches on this theme. Riva speaks of her hunger for "infidelity, adultery, lies and death" and an "inconsolable memory." (The phrase provided the title for one version of *Memories of Underdevelopment*.) The theme of love/death, the love "which kills and does one good," permeates the entire film. The **liebestod** provides both the film's overarching macro-theme, informing its very architectonics, as well as its local micro-leitmotifs, articulated in the details of language and *mise-en-scène*. This oxymoronic passion is expressed verbally, linking love to ugliness, for example (*"Deforme-moi jusqu'à la laideur"*), and in tortured ecstasies that offer a more refined version of the sublime/grotesque minglings typical of the erotic writing of Georges Bataille.

Oxymoronic love is realized, furthermore, through image/text juxtapositions. A shot of the eyeless visage of a woman, a victim of the nuclear blast, coincides with the off-screen words "just as in love," reminding us of proverbial expressions like "love is blind," while also calling up the Surrealist film heritage and the notorious shot of the slicing of the woman's eye in Buñuel's *Chien Andalou*. The Resnais/Duras film inherits the penchant for the oxymoronic that has characterized certain movements in the arts, notably the Baroque, the Elizabethan, and especially Surrealism, a movement which was philosophically and aesthetically inclined to transcend conventional oppositions such as male/female, life/death, through oxymoronic figuration.

The title of *Hiroshima mon amour* thus heralds a crucial procedure throughout the film: the tense yoking of contraries, designed to trigger both attraction and repulsion. Oxymoronic in generic terms as well, *Hiroshima* mingles documentary and fiction modes. The oxymoronic principle operates even at the level of grammar, in the pronouns deployed in the film. In grammatical/linguistic terms, pronouns constitute examples of what linguists call "shifters," i.e. deictic terms whose meaning depends on the speaking situation, on who is speaking to whom, in what circumstances, and from which location. Thus "I" has no essential meaning beyond "the person saying the word I." In the film, Resnais/Duras exacerbate this shifting quality of pronouns, so that the Japanese man confounds two grammatical "persons," in this case the second and third person, telling Riva that "she" (i.e. you) had a German lover. Elsewhere, Riva addresses the Japanese man as "you," yet the words that follow make clear that she is referring to the German lover. When the Japanese man asks "Am I dead?" the "I" refers not to himself but to the German. Even life and death become mingled, as when Riva claims, paradoxically, that there was "no difference" between the German's dead body and her live body.

Theatrical and cinematic performance, by the same token, can also be seen as an exercise in pronominal shifts. Riva tells the Japanese man that "she is an actress playing a nurse in a film." But what is acting if not a form of pronominal transference, by which an "I" pretends to be a "you" or a "he" or a "she." Acting involves impersonation and transvocalization; the actor, at least in the Stanislavski or "method" traditions, takes on the attitudes and suffering of others in a transfer of pathos with Christological overtones. Even the psyche can be a stage for the interaction of various personae, a polylogue of the pronominal voices that constitute us as selves. During her mad ordeal in the cellar in Nevers, Riva evokes this psychic interplay of selves by using expressions like "beside myself" or "not myself," expressions which suggest that "*je est un autre*," that the self is another, that the self can contain the negation of self, that it can become alterity, constituting a fissured multiplicity of voices and discourses. At times lighting or *mise-en-scène* works to evoke these pronominal shifts. One underlit shot of Riva in the cellar, for example, makes her briefly resemble her Japanese lover; woman becomes man, French becomes Japanese. Many critics, furthermore, have compared the process by which the Japanese man elicits Riva's traumatic memories to a psychoanalytic "talking cure." And psychoanalytical "transference" can also be seen as a shift in pronouns, this time within the psychoanalytic drama. Indeed, in a Lacanian perspective the subject constructs itself on the basis of such pronominal shifts and identifications.

Hiroshima mon amour proliferates in rhetorical figures of contradiction, procedures broadly related to the oxymoron in their figuring of impossibility. As a trope of impossible contradiction, the oxymoron is uncannily appropriate to a film which tries to express the inexpressible. As Duras put it, "It is impossible to speak of Hiroshima. All we can do is speak of the impossibility of speaking of Hiroshima."[35] Thus the film offers examples of what rhetoricians call "*recusatio*," the device whereby statements appear to deny what they in fact affirm, as when a poet professes an incapacity to describe his or her beloved. In such cases, speakers do precisely what they claim not to be doing. Riva's claim that "Nevers I have forgotten you," for example, simultaneously means "Nevers, I have forgotten you" and, thanks to the English word "never," also its opposite: "I have **never** forgotten you, Nevers."

Hiroshima mon amour is oxymoronic even in narratological terms, in that it interweaves, through a narratological **faux raccord**, two very different, "unmatchable," stories, one tellable (a love affair that ended in death) and the other, far more difficult to tell, of mass carnage and destruction. If the film had not been commissioned, Duras wrote, she would never have written about Hiroshima, and when she finally did it she "decided to place the innumerable deaths of Hiroshima up against the invented story of the death of a single love."[36] Resnais, too, was acutely aware of the danger of juxtaposing these two incommensurable stories. One term, the love or the death, might easily overwhelm the other. If the erotic theme were to drown out the theme of nuclear holocaust, the film might easily have become pornographic by trivializing catastrophe. The film conjures away this danger by carefully, delicately, constructing links between these two incommensurate stories. The film links them, first of all, through a temporal coincidence: the Riva character recounts that she left her prison in Nevers and bicycled to freedom in Paris on August 6, 1945, the very day that Hiroshima was bombed.[37] But, more importantly, a series of metaphoric connections link Riva's private trauma to a very public catastrophe, homologizing the reconstruction of a devastated city with the reconstructing of a devastated life. As a result, the stories mutually strengthen, rather than undercut or sabotage one another.

The film's oxymoronic thrust is also temporal. Past and present, conventionally regarded as opposites, become inextricably intertwined, partially through instances of what Proust, following Bergson, would have called "voluntary" and "involuntary" memory. Riva demonstrates voluntary memory when she declares that she "wants to see Nevers tonight." But she also exemplifies involuntary memory when the sight of the Japanese man's hand leads her irresistibly back to the memory of the hand of the dead German lover – the first hint of the repressed memories of Nevers. The film is structured as a day in the present, repeatedly invaded by traumatic memories from the past. In narratological terms, the film offers what Genette calls "mixed analepses," not flashbacks in their "pure" state but rather past times that erupt into the present, and which are fleshed out over the course of the film.[38] (Hitchcock's *Marnie* provides another example of this "fleshing out" of a traumatic memory in the present.) What is more interesting than this theme of memory per se is its specifically cinematic realization, the ways in which Resnais exploits the resources of the cinema to communicate and even mimic mental processes. Relentless forward tracking shots, for example, embody the oxymoronic backward/forward thrust of memory and consciousness by moving, thanks to the editing, across the space of two geographically distant cities. Much as *Marienbad* mingled two times of day in the same shot, the editing of *Hiroshima* weds night shots of Hiroshima with day shots of Nevers, indissolubly linking them through camera movement, forging a connection between mental and cinematic processes, in a manner analogous to the condensations and displacements typical of the "dream work." *Hiroshima* in this sense proleptically demonstrates Deleuze's claim that film too can be a philosophical instrument, a generator of concepts which renders thought in audiovisual terms, not only in language but also in blocks of movement and duration.[39]

The oxymoronic yoking of opposites operates on virtually all of the registers of the film. The music forges an identity between the German and the Japanese man, for example, by associating both men with the same musical leitmotif. The film stages a constant play of contradiction and redundancy between the various tracks – image, text, music, and voice. The image is of Nevers yet the sound (e.g. the tearoom jukebox) is in Hiroshima. We see the moving lips of a tour guide addressing tourists in a bus, yet we do not hear what the guide is saying. Or the music contradicts the tone of the image: cheerful, Satie-style piano music, for example, accompanies the horrific materials showcased in the museum.

Hiroshima mon amour forges a synthesis, in a sense, between two distinct modernist traditions, both of which favor an oxymoronic attitude. On the one hand, the film derives from Surrealism, with its striving to transcend conventional hierarchies and oppositions through such procedures as dislocation, displacement, and automatic writing. On the other, the film derives from the theory and practice of Bertolt Brecht, a reference made explicit when Riva speaks of her "*histoire de 4 sous*" (her "four penny story"), a clear allusion to Brecht's "Three Penny Opera." Indeed, *Hiroshima* was made at a time of intense Brechtian influence on French cinema, shortly after the Berliner Ensemble had performed in Paris, provoking admiring essays by such prominent commentators as Bernard Dort and Roland Barthes.

Although it would be a travesty to reduce *Hiroshima* to an exercise in Brechtianism, the film clearly manifests a number of Brechtian principles. It incorporates Brechtian "reflexivity," the injunction to art to reveal its own nature as art, by having Riva tell the Japanese man (and the spectator) that she is "acting in a film." The Brechtian aesthetic too, after all, is fundamentally oxymoronic, a yoking of opposites, in that it favors a conflictual aesthetic of simultaneous identity and contradiction, whereby music, for example, goes against the tone of the dramatic moment, or where a song's lyrics contradict the feeling of the music. This oxymoronic aesthetic of optical/acoustic collision can be seen metaphorically as "horizontal" and syntagmatic, on the one hand, in that it strives for demarcated, autonomous scenes, separated off one from the other, and on the other hand as "vertical" (much as Eisenstein spoke of "vertical montage") in that it favors contradictions between the diverse superimposed tracks or layers that coexist simultaneously within the text. *Hiroshima* calls attention to the material heterogeneity of the tracks, highlighting their individual and specific processes. Thus one can easily listen to the music of *Hiroshima* not as "mood music" or "commentative music" designed as support for the film's story, but rather as an independent composition, a theoretically isolatable "series" (to use Formalist language) or set of musical materials, just as the clearly marked tracking shots (eighty-nine of them out of 450) call attention to the camera work as autonomous and independent. Even the finale of the film reflects a Brechtian refusal of "suspense." The climax of the film – the naming of the characters as "Hiroshima" and "Nevers, in France" – consists of what would usually constitute the **beginning** of a film, i.e. conventional exposition concerning the basics of setting and character. To sum up, rarely has a film so fully achieved an oxymoronic aesthetic of contradictory unity within difference, as has *Hiroshima mon amour*.

Jean-Luc Godard has been one of the most provocatively irreverent practitioners of adaptation. His writings and interviews are full of innovative, even outrageous suggestions for forms of adaptation, simply to film the **pages** of the adapted novel, for example, or to show an actress preparing for her role in an adapted play. This irreverence also finds expression in Godard's actually realized adaptations. In the case of *Masculin féminin* (1965), supposedly based on a Guy de Maupassant story, Godard kept little from the source text beyond the names of a few characters, to the point that the owners of the rights decided that the story had not even been used. *Le Gai savoir* (1968) was commissioned as an adaptation of Jean-Jacques Rousseau's *Emile* but its title was drawn from Nietzsche (*Frohliche Wissenschaft*) and the film has more to do with twentieth-century audiovisual communication than with the eighteenth-century *philosophe*. Godard "adapted" *King Lear*, but claimed, perhaps as a *boutade*, that he had never read the play. (Needless to say, the non-reading of the source renders absurd the very idea of fidelity in adaptation.) And in adapting the canonical Ur-text – Holy Scripture – in *Je vous salue Marie* (Hail Mary), Godard sent the Virgin Mother to a decidedly anachronistic gynecologist, thus provoking the wrath of the militant **right-wing** Catholics who called for the banning of the film.

Le Mépris (Contempt, 1963), for its part, is irreverent in that it is inspired less by admiration for the source novel – Alberto Moravia's *Il disprezzo* (Contempt, 1954) – than by indifference and even hostility. Godard expressed "contempt," ironically, for the novel itself, which he called a "railroad station novel . . . vulgar and pretty, full of old-fashioned sentiments, even though the situations are modern."[40] Godard claimed, nevertheless, that his adaptation was both faithful to and different from its source: "I kept the basic materials and transformed a few details, on the principle that whatever is filmed is automatically different from what is written, and therefore original."[41] In this sense, *Contempt* is one of the **least** irreverent of Godard's adaptations.

Alberto Moravia's socially **engaged** novels generally offer critical portraits of a postwar Italian society largely peopled by depressed middle-class intellectuals. But Moravia's *Contempt* specifically draws on the author's direct experience of the cinema as a screenwriter and film critic, his insider knowledge of the Italian film industry, and his close friendship with Pasolini, all of which enabled Moravia to speak knowledgably about films and about the film milieu. Especially relevant to *Contempt*, which concerns the production of a film based on *The Odyssey*, Moravia had closely followed the production of Mario Camerini's *Ulysses* (1955).

Like Joyce's *Ulysses*, the Moravia novel plays itself out against the backdrop of *The Odyssey*. Within the epic schema of the Moravia novel, Emilia (Camille in the film) is Penelope, and Ricardo Molteni (Paul in the film) is Ulysses. The producer Battista (Prokosch in the film) stands in for the suitors courting Penelope. Again like *Ulysses*, *Contempt* exploits the typically modernist device of contrasting epic prototypes with the modern characters who form their diminished shadows. An anti-Ulysses, Paul Javal does not fight heroically for his wife; rather, he appears to encourage her infidelity for his own ambiguous purposes. Indeed, Michel Marie points to one quasi-comic sequence, very close to the end, which encapsulates this mock-heroic aspect: the actor playing Ulysses makes a menacing gesture toward Paul, as if to say: "I'm your prototype, and you don't measure up."[42]

Godard's description of the Moravia novel as modern in its situations but pre-modernist in its style is somewhat inaccurate, given that the novel is also, in its way, reflexive and modernist. Not only does the novel reflexively foreground a neurotic writer/narrator/protagonist – in some ways reminiscent of the neurotic narrators discussed in chapter 5 – but it also thematizes the process of writing. Moravia even orchestrates a vigorous debate on the subject of adaptation itself. The director Rheingold and the screenwriter Molteni worry over how to convey the "poetry" of *The Odyssey*; Rheingold argues for a psychologistic interpretation; Molteni calls for classical respect for epic values; while Battista simply wants spectacular entertainment. In Rheingold's "strong misreading" of Homer, *The Odyssey* is an interior drama. Rejecting Rheingold's psychologizing, Molteni laments the cinema's tendency to "change everything for the worse," and points to the "massacres" (p. 99) occasioned by the film industry's predatory seizure of literary properties.[43] Molteni defends the "innocence" of literature, and himself as a man of letters, against what he sees as the corrupting power of the film industry. Yet since Molteni turns out to be wrong about so many things, for example about his wife, we wonder if he might not also be wrong about the relations between literature and cinema.

Anticipating the Godard adaptation, the Moravia novel also foregrounds the subject of voyeurism. Emilia compares Ricardo's way of looking at her naked body to that of "a boy peeping through a crack into a bath house" (p. 134). (The film transfers this adolescent-style peeping to Prokosch, who gleefully drools over some naked mermaids in the film version of *The Odyssey*.) As Molteni watches Emilia kissing Battista, it "seemed to [him] that [their] eyes met," a peeping-Tom moment picked up directly in the Godard film. At one point, however, the narrator does imagine a quasi-reciprocal gaze. On the shore watching a ship,

> I thought of the people over there looking from their ship at the coast of Capri;
> their eyes would perhaps be brought to an unwilling halt by an isolated white spot
> on the coast, and they would not even suspect that that white spot was the villa
> and that I was inside it and with me was Emilia and we two did not love each
> other . . . (p. 204)

Here the narrator at least imagines another perspective with a reversible gaze,
even if the stress is on what that gaze "would not suspect."

The Moravia novel is narrated in the first person by screenwriter Molteni (Paul
in the film). The entire novel is the tortured reminiscence of a problematic
narrator striving to make retroactive sense out of the precipitous decline of a
conjugal relationship. Through the process of reading the novel, we slowly realize that the narrator's account is less than trustworthy. In this sense, Molteni
too is a latter-day descendant of Dostoevsky's Underground Man. Although everything is seen from his point of view, we become suspicious of that point of view.
Since he is the focalizing character, we know everything through him, yet this
focalization does not induce us to **identify** with him; the cognitive and the emo-
tive do not coincide. We become skeptical about the narrator's interpretations
not only because they constantly keep changing, but also because with Molteni,
self-preoccupation does not translate into self-awareness. Although he portrays
himself as a rational, detective-like figure, we sense that he embodies a certain
(usually male) type: the middle-aged man on the verge of a nervous breakdown,
hysterically over-invested in his own sense of reasonableness and mastery.

The novel features a double time-frame, the narration of the events themselves,
and the narrating of the writing. Indeed, the novel ends with the words: "I decided
to write these memoirs in hopes of finding her again." The novel repeatedly reflects
on this double time-frame by calling attention to the disconnection between the
actual moment or incident and a person's later interpretation of that moment.
Molteni's account proliferates in retrospective re-evaluations of the past, hardly
of a fine-tuned Proustian quality but insistently present nonetheless, evidenced
in such phrases as: "at the time I hardly noticed" (p. 7); "all this I reconstructed
later" (p. 11); and "at the time I didn't realize" (p. 136). Since he and his
wife never really communicated, everything becomes subject to revisionary speculation. The film, in contrast, collapses the two schemas into a single continuous time: the events as they occur parallel the events as they are narrated by

the film itself, with only very rare flashbacks on the part of Camille and Paul. Instead of the novel's highly personal narration, the film offers what Metz calls "impersonal narration," whereby the film itself seems to tell the story without mediation, without any characterized narrator. The first-person point of view of the novel becomes the "no-person" point of view of the film. Since the film has no marked narrator, the question of narrational "reliability," so essential to the novel, does not even come up.

Like Underground Man, Molteni is by turns self-aggrandizing and self-flagellating, subject to huge (bipolar) mood swings. As readers, we infer multiple possible causes for Emilia's contempt for him: his cowardice, his hysteria, his unfairness, his absurd rescue fantasies. His own words reveal a violent streak: "I seized her by the wrist" . . . "I wanted to kill her." (Godard picks up on this violence by having Paul slap and threaten Camille, whose response – "Don't start again, Paul" – implies that it is not the first time.) Although Molteni channels all the information – and here we have a sure sign of unreliable narration – it is Emilia who ultimately seems the more cogent of the two. Even though Molteni maligns Emilia's interpretations of events, we have a sneaking suspicion that **her** versions are more plausible. Molteni's obsession with her lack of love for him, furthermore, has the feel of a self-fulfilling prophecy. His neurotic syllogism might be summed up as follows: "I am afraid that she does not love me, therefore I shall act in such a way as to ensure that she in fact no longer does love me, thus confirming my original hypothesis."

Nor do Molteni's contradictions end there. This "progressive" Communist is full of elitist class prejudices, and he joins the Party largely out of petty **ressentiment**. This "friend of the workers" patronizingly sees workers as "closer to nature," and women as "children." Although he deems himself "civilized" in contrast with his "primitive" wife – a case of orientalist otherizing at the level of the couple – it is she who is paradoxically smarter than "the intellectual" who is baffled by the most elementary human exchanges and emotions. Even through his account we sense that Emilia unfailingly understands his motives and even intuits his inner thoughts – and here we find a parallel to Liza in relation to Underground Man – while Molteni is reduced to bewildered speculation about **her** motivations. He projects Emilia as grossly materialistic, uncultivated and simple-minded, while idealizing himself as a man of profound artistic sensibility. He even scapegoats her for his own artistic failures, since he "sacrificed" his artistic ambitions for her. Like the Underground Man, Molteni abuses two prejudicial mechanisms toward women – scapegoating and rescue fantasies – to maintain his own positional superiority. He scapegoats Emilia for his own inadequacies and falsely claims to have rescued her from a useless secretary's life. Our growing suspicions about the reliability of his account are confirmed, in the end, by his slow descent into hallucinatory madness. He literally begins to imagine "ghosts," and even projects his wife's accidental death, egomaniacally, as a "last supreme act of hostility" toward him.

What seems to have triggered Godard's interest in *Il disprezzo* was the novel's film-industry setting, a theme appealing to Godard's penchant for reflecting on the film medium and on film technique. While less cavalier than with his other adaptations, Godard performs a number of "operations" and "transformations" on the Moravia source text. In generic and narrational terms, Godard transforms a novel of psychological analysis, rooted in Dostoevsky-style unreliable narration, into a multi-generic film, at once tragedy, satire, documentary, film-about-film, and (dystopian) romance. And, in diegetic terms, while the novel emphasizes the pre-production phase, especially the scripting of *The Odyssey*, the film emphasizes the production phase, the rescripting, and the shoot itself.

Godard also operates a temporal **condensation**. The novel covers nine months in Rome and three days in Capri, a total of two years. The film, in contrast, condenses all the events into a period of two days, a gesture toward the temporal unities of classical tragedy. Indeed, Godard called the film a "tragedy in long shot," a phrase which rewrites Chaplin's famous dictum that "tragedy was close up and comedy long shot." The result is a generic hybrid, a tragedy treated with comic distance rather than melodramatic pathos. The temporal condensation also reflects the theatricalization typical of Godard's work of the period. (*Masculin féminin* and *2 ou 3 choses*, for example, also have this 24-hour day structure.)

Contempt's oxymoronic plot revolves around the simultaneous destruction of a couple and the construction of a film. The American producer Jeremiah Prokosch (Jack Palance) invites scriptwriter Paul Laval (Michel Piccoli) to collaborate on a film version of *The Odyssey*. Prokosch expresses dissatisfaction with his director, Fritz Lang (played by Lang himself). Paul's wife Camille (Brigitte Bardot), meanwhile, tells Paul that she has contempt for him, for reasons that remain obscure but which presumably have to do with Paul's apparent readiness to pander her to Prokosch to advance his own career. In Capri for the filming, she allows Paul to see her kissing Prokosch. Camille and Prokosch then take off together, but die in an automobile accident, while Lang continues filming *The Odyssey*.

More important than the details of Godard's alterations is their tendency, their **drift**. The net effect is not only of theatricalization, but also of depersonalization. The novel is personalized, psychologized, crowded with memories and emotions which feed into a swelling paranoia, and in this sense it is analogous to

Proust's study of jealousy in *A la recherche du temps perdu*, although far from the high literary achievement of the Proust novel. The film, in contrast, is impersonal, with the cinema itself serving as kind of abstract character/narrator which replaces the psychologized narrator of the novel. The emphasis shifts from one character/narrator's subjective perceptions of a relationship to the "objective" relationship between a series of characters directly or indirectly linked to the world of the cinema.

Godard also alters the dynamics of international exchange that characterize the Moravia novel. The Italian screenwriter Ricardo Molteni of the novel becomes the French screenwriter Paul (Michel Piccoli), while the Italian wife Emilia becomes the Frenchwoman Camille. The central cultural polarity in the novel pits the Germans, portrayed as morbidly introspective and gothic, against the Italians, portrayed as sunny, lighthearted, and extroverted; as Battista puts it: "two worlds, two sensibilities." But while the novel mocks German misconceptions about Italy in particular, the film mocks American ignorance about Europe in general. The producer Battista, Italian in the novel, becomes the American Jeremiah Prokosch in the film. The novel's intra-European dialogue here becomes a tense standoff between Hollywood and its European interlocutors. Indeed, Godard constantly stresses the cultural advantages of the Europeans in terms of classical culture. It is the Europeans like Paul and Francesca who recognize Lang's literary allusions or the identity of the Greek deities represented by the statues. It is they who say "yes, that's Hölderlin," or "that's Dante," or "that's Homer."

Godard also slightly shuffles Moravia's characters in relation to their expressed opinions. The configuration of characters — producer (Battista in the novel, Prokosch in the film), writer (Ricardo in the novel, Paul in the film), wife (Emilia, Camille) and director (Rheingold, Lang) — is homologous but the names are changed and their opinions are redistributed. The producers in both film and novel envision the film adaptation of *The Odyssey* as a spectacular proto-blockbuster or action film: "Homer put monsters and prodigies in the *Odyssey*," as Prokosch puts it, "and I want you to put monsters and prodigies into the film." But Godard melds the traits of the novel's Battista with features of the actual producers of *Le Mépris*: Carlo Ponti and Joseph Levine, both of whom had been associated with the "spaghetti epics" mocked by the Godard film. While in the novel the writer defends the idea of the untarnished heroism of the Homeric world, in the film version, it is the director (Lang) who defends that position. The psychologizing penchant typical of Rheingold in the novel is attributed in the film to the scriptwriter Paul, who emphasizes the interior drama of Ulysses, onto whom he projects his own present-day marital anxieties. Which leads us to ask a theoretical question about character in adaptation: if the ideas of a character are changed in the process of adaptation, are we still dealing with the same character? Can the discursive/ideological content of character be altered without changing the character itself?

Contempt as a film calls attention to its own cinematic and literary "transtext." Its recapitulation of *The Odyssey* in another medium inserts itself into the broad history of the arts over the centuries, part of a long, Janus-faced intertextual chain that looks back at least as far as *The Odyssey*, an epic poem itself rooted in millennial oral traditions, and looks forward to Joyce's *Ulysses* and the Coen Brothers' *O Brother Where Art Thou?* (2000). In Genette's terminology, both Virgil's *Aeneid* and Joyce's *Ulysses* are "hypertextual" re-elaborations of *The Odyssey* as "hypotext."[44] For classical Greek and Roman literature, the work of Homer formed a vast reservoir of stories and meanings, which generated its own sequels. *The Diary of the Trojan War* (*Ephemeris Belli Troiani*), for example, offered a fresh telling of the Trojan War story, including strong dissents from the Homeric version, yet always premised on the assumption that the reader remembers *The Iliad* and *The Odyssey*. Two millennia later, Godard's film picks up on this same tradition.

Godard's rewriting of epic asserts the irrelevance of the classical ethos in the contemporary world. Quite explicit about this theme, Godard called *Contempt* the "story of castaways of the western world, survivors of the shipwreck of modernity."[45] Within the Western tradition, "Greece" has often signified an ideal homogeneous totality, a kind of proto-Europe, a point of origin and the locus of an impossible nostalgia. The loss of the idealized Greek world of epic, according to Lukács, forms the background for the emergence of the novel as the "expression of transcendental homelessness."[46] *Contempt* stages this sense of loss, illustrating Hegel's reflections of epic as a world out of tune "without present-day machinery and factories together with the products they turn out . . ."[47] In this sense, *Contempt* can even be seen as fundamentally Cervantic, in that it charts a "trajectory of disenchantment" whereby romantic epic yields to bland middle-class existence. Indeed, it is perhaps symptomatic that Godard places the modern-day counterparts of Ulysses and Penelope, quite literally, on the toilet.

This anti-epic quality pervades both the world of the film itself and the world of the film-within-the-film. At a time when the word "epic" is more likely to evoke a costly and spectacular film genre rather than *The Odyssey*, the film-within-the-film also fails to bring the Homeric ethos to life. The director, who both is and is not Fritz Lang, strives for Olympian grandeur but the film's rushes betray his grand designs. Athena, Jupiter, and Neptune are gaudily colored statues (although in this sense Godard was being historically accurate since Greek statues **were** painted) and Ulysses struggles awkwardly onto the rocky shores of a putative Ithaca. The tired nymphs do not sing each to each, and Nausicaa is a graceless model lip-synching an Italian *yé-yé* song. One shot – showing the actor playing Ulysses swaying from side to side to mimic the movements of a boat rocked by high seas – especially encapsulates the epic deflation. Filmic illusion is shown to depend on the synecdochic isolation of objects from their contexts. What better way to demystify cinema, and the epic genre, than by showing an epic protagonist not in the glorified isolation of a low-angle close-up but rather in long shot, surrounded by the cumbersome machinery of cinematic representation: dollies, lights, cameras, recording equipment?

Lang has difficulty conveying the grandeur of the gods because of distance in time – the modern ethos accords no place for ancient divinities – and differences in medium. In the realm of art, as in that of language, as well as in the realm of adaptation, *"traduire, c'est trahir"* ("to translate is to betray"). Francesca's hurried translations of Lang's poetic quotations illustrate the point: they invariably miss a nuance or exclude an ambiguity. Her translations of Prokosch's words, similarly, soften their brutality considerably. *Contempt*, in this sense, can be seen as a meditation on the unavoidably problematic and interested nature of all translation and adaptation. At the same time, the film shows that art renews itself though creative **mis**translation. Every artist is inserted within a tradition, constantly betrayed and constantly renewed, indeed renewed **though** betrayals of the kind that Harold Bloom called "misprisions" and "strong misreadings."[48] In a form of "revolutionary nostalgia," the past becomes a source of renovation. Godard reminds us of cinema's infancy by placing Lumière's misguided dictum that the "cinema is an invention without a future" directly under the projection room screen. The cinema, Paul suggests, should resurrect the more artisanal methods of Griffith and Chaplin. Figures like Lumière and Meliès, Griffith and Chaplin, we are reminded, were in a sense the Homers of their medium, yet in cinema as in literature there is no point of origin, no unchanged Ithaca to which one can return.

The same lack of a precise point of origin, as we have seen throughout this text, applies to filmic adaptations; there can be no inviolate return to an originary source. Indeed, the brilliant opening sequence of *Contempt* reveals all the things that film can do but literature cannot. The film is prefaced by a quotation from André Bazin: "The cinema substitutes for our gaze a world in accord with our desires. *Contempt* is the story of that world."[49] The quotation not only calls attention to one of the critical gurus of the New Wave, it also foregrounds some of the key themes in the film: the cinema, the world, the gaze, and desire. The first shot after the title opens in Bazinian deep focus onto "the world of the cinema" in the form of an Italian studio-lot – subsequently revealed as Cinecitta – as a small knot of human figures and a camera slowly progress toward us from the depths of the space. Although we tend to think of "the" camera, in fact of course there are **two** cameras, the one on the screen and the one filming the camera on the screen. As the visible "pro-filmic" camera approaches, the invisible pre-filmic camera reframes slightly to center the on-screen camera, then tilts up respectfully, while the visible camera tilts down, directly fixing the spectator with its rectangular Cinemascope lens. We see the famous cinematographer Raoul Coutard, the director of photography for such films as *Breathless* and *Jules and Jim*, checking the light meter.

The only completely honest film, Godard once said, would show a camera filming itself in a mirror. Although *Contempt* never achieves such an exacting standard of self-reflexivity, it approximates it by having the pro-filmic camera eye, which in conventional cinema slyly and surreptitiously equates itself with the gaze of the spectator – Bazin's "substitutes for our gaze" – focus on the spectators themselves. It is as if the apparatus itself were nodding at us, in an apparatical equivalent of Brechtian direct address to the audience. The same shot also features camera tracks, light meters, electrical equipment, booms. But, more importantly, we are made aware of the **look** of the camera. Instead of identifying unconsciously with the camera through which we see, here we are reminded that films are constituted by looks – the look of the camera; the spectator's recapitulation of that look; the looks between characters in the fiction; the programmed transfers of looks which carry us from shot to shot – without which the cinematic experience would not exist.

This opening camera-eye is also a camera-gun aimed at spectatorial voyeurism. Fiction films in the dramatic realist mode usually shelter us from the glance of the actors: we look at people on-screen who do not look back at us. But here Raoul Coutard and his camera return our glance. The aggressive designation of our voyeuristic position is reinforced in the subsequent shots of Michel Piccoli and Brigitte Bardot. And if the first shot of *Contempt* references the world, the next shots reference desire. The nude shots of Bardot, which Godard was reportedly pressured to include by the producers, and especially by Joseph Levine, presumably come to fulfill the "desires" first mentioned in the overture Bazin quotation. But in fact, Godard, while giving in to the producers on one level – indeed, the only case in his career where he accepted such pressures – does so in ways that ultimately undercut their intentions.[50] The three-shot "love-making" sequence is a typical Godardian exercise in defused titillation. A series of filters renders the image alternately red, white, and blue, reminding us of specifically cinematic mediations and transfiguring the image of Bardot's body into pure chromatic plasticity. (The colors are those of both the French and the American flags — another theme in this film about international co-productions.) The film renders Bardot's body as statuesque, comparable in eroticism to the perfectly respectable classical nudes seen recurrently throughout the film, a clear contrast with the perpetually moving sex-kitten Bardot of Vadim's *And God Created Woman* (1956). The two motionless lovers mingle shopping-list trivialities with oddly dispassionate declarations of love. Piccoli makes a verbal inventory of Bardot's body: "I love your feet . . . I love your legs . . . I love your thighs." This "Ezekiel's bones" approach to female allure sends a mocking message to both producer and spectator: "All right, if its nudity you want, here it is: in words!"

Equally important is the positioning of these shots within the text. Godard gives in to the producers' wishes but subverts their intentions; he vanquishes by submitting. He quickly dispenses the required shots as if acquitting himself of a disagreeable duty. In classically erotic films, moreover, love scenes usually come as a culmination to an inexorable crescendo of carefully nurtured desire, an explosion after a long repressed erotic chase. The "love scene" in *Contempt*, in contrast, occurs in advance of any real spectatorial involvement. Brigitte Bardot has not yet become Camille; she is just the icon BB. Since the processes of secondary identification by which we emotionally invest ourselves in the fiction have not yet taken place, the sequence is syntagmatically displaced, as if narrative orgasm were made to precede foreplay.[51]

Since casting constitutes one of the potential advantages of film, it is important to see this scene in the context of Bardot's career. In 1963, she was at the very height of her fame, having made not only *And God Created Woman* by Roger Vadim, but also Clouzots's *La Verité* (1960) and Louis Malle's *La Vie privée* (1961). The casting of Bardot comes in the wake of the relative commercial failure of a number of second and third films by New Wave directors. It was Godard's answer to the problem of the audience, part of his plan to make a relatively mainstream and successful film. Although the *Cahiers* director/critics had praised Bardot as an actress in their reviews, significantly they had rarely cast her in their films. She was not a "muse" figure like Bernadette Lafont or Ana Karina or Jeanne Moreau. At the same time, Brigitte Bardot very much symbolized the free and liberated "new woman" of postwar France, usually in its unmarried, sexually available version, but here in its married version. Godard capitalizes on what critics had admired in Bardot's performances — her naturalness and spontaneity — a form of acting that appeared not to be acting. Yet at the same time he plays against the "mythic" BB to emphasize the domestic, quotidian Bardot as Camille, who, unlike most of Bardot's characters, is defiantly not interested in sex. Nor is she a submissive wife. Unlike the Juliette of *Et dieu créa la femme*, who welcomes the husband's taming slap, Camille slaps back, and despises Paul even more when he becomes violent.

After the opening bedroom sequence, we meet an important new character – the producer Jeremiah Prokosch, played by Jack Palance, accompanied by the secretary/translator/lover Francesca. Even before we meet Prokosch, we have indications of crisis in the industry. Paul comments that the studio lot looks empty; "everyone's gone," Francesca tells us, since Prokosch fired everyone. And through much of the film we do not see an atmosphere of effervescent cinematic activity, but rather deserted streets and buildings, a clear contrast with Godard's other earlier films, which tend to be set in busy streets or noisy cafés. A long, lateral, right–left tracking shot takes us over to Prokosch. The producer is presented under the sign of theater, quite literally, since we read "Teatro 6" above his head. Godard characterizes him through the pomposity of his manner and diction; with a stentorian, theatrical voice, he declaims: "Once there were kings here." Here, too, Godard also plants references not only to classical tragedy but also to the poor state of Italian cinema. We have the sense of the end of the studio system à la Cinecitta and a crisis in cinema in general, where movie theaters are being replaced by supermarkets, all of which Francesca mistranslates as "it's the end of cinema."

Godard made *Contempt* at a time when he was still an *auteurist*, some five years before he moved into the militant anti-*auteurist* collectivism of the Dizga–Vertov period. But at the time of *Contempt*, Godard saw producers as obstacles in the path of talented directors, and here he heaps scorn on the figure of the Hollywood producer, portrayed as vulgar, crude, sexist, and ignorant. In the new version of the *Odyssey* schema, Prokosch is already in a negative position, since he reincarnates the unsympathetic suitors who court Penelope during Ulysses' absence. Just as Paul Laval represents a debased shadow not only of his epic prototype Ulysses but also of Hollywood actors like Dean Martin, so Jeremiah Prokosch, more profiteer than prophet, represents a grotesque parody of his Biblical namesake. Prokosch lacks even the aesthetic coherence of the classical Hollywood producers like Irving Thalberg and Daryl Zanuck. Unlike them, he has no love of cinema; he is just an investor, who might as well be financing a chain of supermarkets. His voice, his swagger, and his body language suggest vast stores of unwarranted arrogance. Prokosch is a caricature, the product of Godard's *auteurist ressentiment*. His opinions are generally stupid, as when he argues that *The Odyssey* needs a German director because it was a German, Schliemann, who discovered the ruins of Troy. Prokosch illustrates Marx's statements about the transforming power of money: a man may be quite stupid, yet money enables him to buy the intelligence of others.

The critique of Prokosch is continued in the projection room sequence, the first sequence which brings together the five major characters. The sequence reinforces Godard's *auteurist* cry of irritation against producers generally and against Carlo Ponti and Joseph Levine in particular. (Godard reportedly referred to Carlo Ponti as "Mussolini" and to Joseph Levine as "King Kong.") The casting of Jack Palance, an actor typically identified with *noir* gangsters, as the producer, also intimates something about Godard's view of the cultural role of producers as gangsters. Through an instance of the "definitive by chance," the name of the actress – Georgia Moll – plays into this portrait, since she is Prokosch's "moll." The reported tensions between Godard and Palance on the set – Palance apparently wanted to settle his own scores with producers – feed into the felt tension between Prokosch and his film collaborators. Godard also deploys a specific intertext to parodic purposes.[52] Many of the producers and actors in *Contempt* had some association with the "spaghetti epic" genre. Joseph Levine had produced *Cleopatra* (1963) and *Hercules* (1959); Jack Palance had played Attila the Hun in *Sign of the Pagans* (1954) and *The Barbarians* (1959); Brigitte Bardot had played Helen in *Helen of Troy* (1954) and acted in *Nero's Weekend* (1956).

The German director Rheingold, from the novel, who Moravia describes as "definitely not in the same class as the Pabsts and the Langs," becomes, in the Godard film, Fritz Lang himself. Lang forms part of a long series of director "characters" (Roger Leenhardt in *Une femme mariée* [1964], Samuel Fuller in *Pierrot le fou* [1965]), who play themselves in Godard's films. Unlike the novel, it is not the screenwriter's point of view that predominates but rather that of the director, or better, of the cinema itself, or even better the dignity of the cinema as incarnated by the historical Lang. An ideal image of cultivated pan-European identity, Lang is ultimately the only true epic hero of *Contempt*. Observing the scene with Olympian serenity, Lang exudes old-fashioned courtesy and grandeur. Only Lang is shown to know all of the four languages – English, French, German, and Italian – used in the film. His monocled gaze evokes the superior look of an impassive authorial eye/I and even, in a sense, the blind Homer, with whose bust he is juxtaposed.

Godard embroiders the film with references to the Lang career and persona. Lang aptly personifies the history of the cinema, having actively shaped it both through his work in silent film in Germany, through sound innovation in *M* (1931), on to his influential work in Hollywood as a precursor and participant in *film noir*. Lang is an "epic" director in both the Greek and Brechtian senses of that word. One of his early silent films – *Die Nibelungen* – treated a Germanic saga, the Nordic equivalent of Homer's Mediterranean epic. Lang's rigorous anti-naturalism and disinterest in characterological depth recall Brecht, and indeed Brecht and Lang collaborated in Hollywood on *Hangmen Also Die* (1943). Lang refers at one point to "our poor BB." Indeed, one way to read *Contempt* is as showing one BB (Brigitte Bardot) as seen by another BB (Bertolt Brecht). In the words of Paul's voice-over commentary, superimposed on a *Playboy*-like nude shot of Bardot, we now see her with "a cold, distanced eye."

Fritz Lang is both a real person and a character in *Contempt*. He is a real person in that he is called "Mr Lang" and in that the film refers to his actual career. On this level, Lang represents the potential dignity and high principle of a certain cinema, especially in his refusal to collaborate with the Nazis. At the same time, Lang is a character, in that he is speaking lines scripted for him by Godard, and in the sense that he is not "really" the director of the adaptation of *The Odyssey* shown in the film, since Godard really directed those scenes, and since Godard makes no effort to suggest that they are somehow filmed in a typical Lang style. Godard stages himself as the assistant director, waiting in the wings, as it were, to become the "real" director, much as the New Wave came to replace the classical directors they admired. (In later films, such as *Numéro deux* [1975], Godard would stage himself as the real director.)

The reflexive projection room sequence reveals the workaday processes of filmmaking. The projection room itself embodies what film theorists in the 1970s called "the cinematic apparatus" – the theater, the screen, the projector, and the desiring spectators. The sequence alternates the rushes from the film-within-the-film – presumably "Lang's version" of *The Odyssey* – with shots of the principal characters watching, and commenting on, the rushes. We see the process whereby the director chooses from the various "takes" of the same scene. It is here that Lang makes his ironic comment about Cinemascope, that it is "good for filming snakes and funerals." Ironically, Lang's and Paul's oral recitation of Dante communicates the epic feeling more effectively than the rushes of *The Odyssey* that we see. The shots seem dead. They feature the three principal colors of the film – the blue of the sea, the yellow/white of the sun, and the red of blood. The shots from the film-within-the-film differ from *Contempt* as a whole; they are more violent, less elegant, more contrasted.

Contempt constitutes an *auteurist* cry of resentment against producers generally and against Carlo Ponti and Joseph Levine in particular. Prokosch is portrayed as a kind of savage god. In fact, he claims a special relationship with the pantheon: "I like the gods," he tells Lang, "because I know how they feel." The thundering Jupiter of the cinematic Olympus, Prokosch wields lightning power through the electrifying force of megabucks. If Fritz Lang conveys the dignity and prestige of the cinema, Prokosch evokes the self-importance of its industrial managers. Prokosch's body language communicates domination. Prokosch deploys the look as an instrument of power. He arrogantly looks at those, like Camille, who prefer not to be looked at, yet with equal arrogance looks away from the interlocutors who solicit his attention. His discourse inclines to the imperative. He demands simple "yes" or "no" answers; nuance is not his forte. In a Brechtian **gestus**, Godard has him use others, for example his secretary, as literal props.[53] His populist anti-intellectualism goes hand in hand with an elitist scorn for the public that he presumably serves. Reacting lasciviously to some scenes of nude mermaids, he tells Lang: "This is fine for you and me, Fritz, but do you think the public will understand it?" A twentieth-century Polonius, he quotes maxims from his *vade mecum* (a little red book of vacuous aphorisms): "The wise man does not impress others with his own superiority." Prokosch, in sum, plays the barbarian to Lang's Greek.

Godard does not limit his critique to the personality of one producer: rather, he focuses, if somewhat crudely, on the structure of relations between the producer and the artists and technicians who actually make the film. It is this insight into the material and organizational infrastructure of cinema that saves *Le Mépris* from being merely an outburst of *auteurist* pique at uncomprehending producers. Prokosch represents the industrial "owners" of cinematic culture; he sees art as a commodity to be bought and sold. Lang quotes a friend and colleague, Brecht, who also had his share of problems with Hollywood producers, on the subject of the artist who is obliged to sell his own talent as if it were a commodity. More specifically, he quotes Brecht's Hollywood poem "The Ballad of our Poor BB:"

> Each morning to earn my bread
> I go to the market of lies
> And full of hope take my place
> Alongside the vendors.

This frank recognition of the artist as a hawker in the open market of lies deepens the critique in *Contempt*. Although the analysis of cinema's economic infrastructure remains superficial, *Contempt* does show the director as subject to the aesthetic whims and financial manipulation of producers. Godard even brings out certain fascist overtones in Prokosch's heavy-handed manipulations. Lang, as Paul points out, fled Nazi Germany immediately after Goebbels asked him to head the Reich's film industry. Prokosch interrupts Paul to say: "It isn't

1933 any more, it's 1963." The precise dating of the text is typical of Godard, who never pretends that his films are timeless or outside history. Indeed, Godard called *Contempt* a "documentary on filmmaking in Italy in 1963." But the juxta-position of the two dates also suggests that Godard sees Prokosch as reincar-nating fascism in a different form. This suggestion is reinforced on various registers. For Lang, Prokosch "isn't a producer; he's a dictator." Even locale points to the historical memory of fascism: Cinecitta, where *The Odyssey* is being filmed, was founded by the Italian fascists in 1937. When Paul mentions the word "culture," Prokosch responds: "Whenever I hear the word culture, I get out my checkbook," a variation on Goering's notorious and too-well-executed *diktat*: "Whenever I hear the word culture, I get out my revolver." A proleptic avatar of what later came to be called "globalization," Prokosch embodies the tyranny of money and its contempt for all non-monetary values. Goering-style Nazism literally murders the representatives of culture; Prokosch-style financial fascism buys them off. The former works through racist totalitarianism; the latter through the relentless commodification of art. While it would be a form of hyperbole to equate Nazism with neo-liberalism, the latter too has its dom-ineering and tyrannical dimension.[54]

Paul, meanwhile, is mimetic and insecure, uncertain about what kind of char-acter he wants to be. At a later point, he imitates movie heroes when he wears a certain kind of hat so as to look like "Dean Martin in *Some Came Running*." Very much the anti-hero, Paul is portrayed as a man of the theater who does films mainly for the money. Godard famously told Piccoli to think of Paul as a character from *Last Year at Marienbad* who would have preferred to be a char-acter in *Rio Bravo*, a *boutade* which we can roughly translate to mean that he is a character from a European art film who would have liked to be a hero in an American Western. In the case of Paul, too, casting plays a primordial role, subtly altering the dynamics of adaptation. The casting of Michel Piccoli as the screenwriter, for example, resonates ironically with the history of the New Wave. As an actor, Piccoli had already played in over thirty feature films, having worked with Renoir (*French Cancan*, 1955), Buñuel (*La Mort en ce jardin*, 1956), and also in the films of some of the "tradition of quality" directors like Jean Dellanoy and René Clement; he was therefore very much associated with the "tradition of quality" excoriated by Truffaut and Godard. In the film version, Paul incar-nates precisely that figure in the production hierarchy most demonized by New Wave rhetoric – the screenwriter. It is hardly an accident, in this sense, that the modicum of heroism displayed in the film is transferred to Fritz Lang, play-ing himself but also a surrogate for the real director – Godard. In the novel, ironically, the screenwriter Molteni complains that his profession of screenwriter

Figure 6.3 Paul, Prokosch, and Lang in *Contempt* (1963), produced by Compagnia Cinematografica Champion / Les Films Concordia / Rome Paris Films

is **under**valued (p. 39), while the New Wave had argued that the profession was **over**valued. The result is a dislocation in the target of the anger: while the novel gives voice to the screenwriter's **ressentiment** against directors, the film gives voice to the director's **ressentiment** against producers.

In film-intertextual terms, *Contempt* fits squarely into the tradition of films about filmmaking and even of Hollywood films about Hollywood. Indeed, in his book *Introduction à une veritable histoire du cinéma*, Godard links *Contempt* to two antecedent self-referential films: Vertov's *Man with the Movie Camera* (1928) and *Two Weeks in Another Town* (1962).[55] As an international co-production (French, Italian, and American) in an era of co-productions, when American money was being invested in European film production, *Contempt* also reflects on this internationalization of European cinema. Godard paints a world in which the camaraderie of a Renoir ensemble production, or even that of Hollywood-style studio collectivity, has given way to the ephemeral, artificial, and polyglot impersonality of transnational cinema. In this sense, Godard anticipates latter-day critiques of the overpowering of the "local" in the age of the "global."

If the first and final parts of *Contempt* focus on the filmmaking milieu, the long middle section focuses on the couple's personal relationship. In fact, the apartment sequence showing the tensions between Camille and Paul "grew" during the production to constitute roughly a third of the film as a whole.[56] In a major departure from the novel, the sequence occupies a disporportionate amount of time; the novel consisted of a long series of minor incidents; there was no long passage detailing a single quarrel. A conventional version of a couple's fight, especially in 1963, would have featured eloquent and dramatic confrontations and would have explicitly cued our feelings and attitudes through the use of a commentative music of crescendos and ominousness. Godard, in contrast, uses no "mood" music, no hyper-dramatic dialogue, but only the slow unfolding of tense exchanges within a vague and indefinable malaise. The George Delarue music, whose style is that of musical romanticism à la Brahms, seems to come into the film arbitrarily. The music's tragic, grand, morose tonalities contrast with the petty tensions displayed on the screen, which have nothing grand or romantic about them, but only bitterness and emptiness. The music does not dictate our emotional response to the events portrayed. It is not there to underscore the dramatic theme but rather mark off distance from it. It supplies just one more "track" for our consideration, one more element to absorb as part of a larger totality. The music especially marks transitions and breaks, serving more as punctuation than mood-setter. It is as if Godard were experimenting with cinematic duration. There is no dramatic confrontation, no eloquent lines or dramatic effects, but only the corrosive sarcasm of petty harassment and sniping around apparently trivial issues.

The sequence in general bears witness the death of a couple, the breakdown of communication. But, more importantly, Godard communicates this breakdown not just through the dialogue but also through the *mise-en-scène*. The apartment itself is in a state of disarray. As with the couple, it is not clear whether it is under construction or being taken apart. Will it become a home, or return to its status as an empty shell of an apartment? At times, Godard exploits what French film analysts call "*champs vides*," shots of walls or décor, devoid of human presence. The dialogue is fragmented, jagged, full of incomplete sentences, unanswered questions, and misfired communication, never reaching fruition. Camille's words are full of aggressive expressions of disgust, "I'm tired of . . . ," "I'm fed up . . . ," which are not specifically aimed at Paul, but which are easily transferred to him. Camille oscillates between hostility and mock affection. In spatial terms, the two rarely share a stable space of coupledom; often they speak to each other from different rooms. There are few of the eyeline matches that would normally communicate intense engagement between the characters because here everything seems awkward, tense, syncopated, jerky, abrupt. Godard also emphasizes their separation by the filmic means used to register the couple's conversation. The characters are relegated to the edges of the very wide-screen frame. The technique itself literalizes the concept of their distance and separation. What we have is the *mise-en-scène* of conjugal solitude and the staging of a breakup. Their movements are uncoordinated, not in harmony, as if they were living at different speeds, utilizing two distinct performance styles.

Godard is an anti-grammatical director; he works against the rules taught in film schools and filmmaking manuals. One way to look at Godard's work is as a relentless search for **alternative** ways of filming even the most banal situations – conversations, car rides, and so forth. Rather than use the conventional ping-pong of alternating over-the-shoulder shots, a technique which sutures the spectator into the subjective positions of both interlocutors, Godard at one point uses an unconventional real-time tracking shot – precisely the filmic technique which emphasizes the literal traversal of space – to record the dialogue. A lamp occupying a prominent place in the shot is turned on and off, as if triggering the back and forth tracking movements. It is as if Godard were saying: "Here is a tracking shot, like those you have seen before and will see again in the film, filmed on tracks like those you saw in the opening shot." In the sequence generally, Godard provokes discomfort in the spectator, as if we felt **their** discomfort through our own. We feel the discomfort not only because of what we see of their relationship on the screen, but also because we feel in our media-programmed viscera the unconventional approach to dialogue, to editing, and *mise-en-scène*.

The quarrel scene is intercut with Paul's distracted viewing of pictures and reproductions in art books. Here we find a frequent theme and technique in Godard, found in all the films from *Breathless* to *Histoire(s) du cinéma* (1998), a fondness for including apparently extraneous materials, often two-dimensional materials such as newspaper clippings, photos, and magazine illustrations. Ironically, Paul looks at images of erotic statues at a time when Eros in the flesh is not available to his marriage. He reads aloud a passage concerning the Judgment of Paris, here rudely summarized as an "ass contest" (**concours de fesses**). He also taps on a metallic modern version of a classical Greek statue, a parallel with the Moravia novel and the Godard film as "updates" of classical culture. At the same time, Godard seems to be highlighting the often-denied erotic element in classical culture itself.

The continuity of the apartment quarrel sequence is interrupted briefly through eleven lightning flashback memory shots. The shots form a parenthesis which is framed by Camille's sarcastic invitation to Paul to make love ("Let's go, and

Figure 6.4 Camille's ironic invitation: Bardot and Piccoli in *Contempt* (1963), produced by Compagnia Cinematografica Champion / Les Films Concordia / Rome Paris Films

make it quick!"). The flashes consists of three types of shots: (1) highly posed "achronic" *Playboy*-style shots of a nude Bardot (shots we have not seen before); (2) analeptic shots cited from earlier points in the film; and (3) anticipatory proleptic shots which anticipate later moments in the film (e.g. on Capri). Many of the flash-images are from Camille's point of view, which is significant in view of the fact that the novel was focalized entirely from Molteni's point of view. Indeed, these flashback shots are the only shots that could be said to be linked so clearly to the point of view of a particular character. Unlike the novel, the film offers Camille flashback voice-over reminiscences about happier days. While Molteni "speaks for" her in the novel, here she speaks, however briefly, through interior monologue, for herself. In this sense, the film upgrades the role and presence of Emilia/Camille vis-à-vis her role in the novel, perhaps because she is no longer seen through the narrator's neurotically masculinist filter. (Although some might argue that she is now seen through **Godard's** masculinist filter.)

Camille maintains an exasperatingly cool disdain toward Paul, yet the reasons for the disdain remain uninterpreted and therefore left up to our imagination. Reading the character through a feminist grid, we can regard her either as a victim of the director's sexism, or as victim of the character's sexism. If she is a victim of the **character's** sexism, she becomes an instrument of Godard's critical analysis, which is, in the end, more hostile to Paul and to Prokosch than it is to her.

Contempt represents a "metatextual" work, in Genette's sense, in that it critiques another uncited corpus of texts, in this case Hollywood cinema, not only through dialogue and theme but also through its very techniques. The audition sequence, for example, demonstrates an extremely unorthodox use of sound. We see performers auditioning for roles in the film, particularly an Italian actress dancing to the sound of Italian *yé-yé* music, while the major characters in the film – Prokosch, Lang, Paul, Camille – are seated in the audience. Each time one of the major characters speaks, all the sound, except that of the dialogue of the characters, is turned **off** completely. Through parodic exaggeration, Godard calls attention to the conventions of sound in the cinema. Usually, noises and music are conveniently toned down when characters speak, so that the dialogue will be comprehensible. Thus Godard foregrounds the "mediations" inherent in cinema, all the ways in which it is **not** like real life, where ambient noise is **not** turned down simply for our convenience, highlighting a taken-for-granted filmic device to which spectators had rarely paid any serious attention.

The penultimate sequence of the accident is strikingly economical in its use of sound and image. Rather than pursue the Hollywood illusionistic approach of staging an actual (and doubtless very expensive) car crash, Godard evokes the crash in the spectator's mind through a "library sound" recording of a crash, combined with a panoramic slide over Camille's farewell message, followed by a shot of Camille and Prokosch in his presumably wrecked convertible. The shot of the wreck is strikingly stylized and anti-realistic. Rather than the actual crash, we are given its highly artificial aftermath. The characters are painted with what is obviously paint rather than blood, and the car is barely damaged, although the rear-view mirror is bent a bit out of shape. The *mise-en-scène* emphasizes the scene's total improbability. The sports car is caught, pincer-like, between two tractor-trailers facing in **opposite** directions, an extremely unlikely situation. Furthermore, the dead Prokosch and Camille are shown as facing away from each other, when in reality any such accident would have impacted on them in identical ways; they would never have ended up facing in **opposite** directions. Godard's approach, in sum, is Brechtian and minimalist. Rather than stage an actual car crash, Godard arranges, like a painter, the signs and symptoms of an accident, indices sufficient to trigger the **idea** of an accident in the spectator's mind.

Contempt incorporates the Brechtian principle that art should reveal the principles of its own construction. The film documents all the stages of film production: scripting, location hunting, casting, rehearsals, rushes, and so on. Film texts are shown to be the end-result of innumerable practical and aesthetic choices, shaped by diverse collaborators before being "frozen" into a definitive sequence of signifiers. Like the Hölderlin poem of which Lang speaks, films too undergo successive "versions." The filmmakers debate alternative strategies of adaptation. Paul proposes a psychoanalytic reading closely reflecting his personal domestic crisis, while Lang hopes to transmit a sense of heroic grandeur and untarnished heroism. Prokosch, for his part, prefers a nicely packaged "artistic" spectacular. *Contempt* itself, we are reminded, resulted from the very creative processes that we have been observing. By showing the process of constitution of the text, Godard shows it to be a made thing, a laboriously constructed artifact which is not "natural" and therefore need not be "naturalistic." The style of *Contempt* illustrates what I described as the unstated aesthetic program of the left wing of the New Wave: a kind of "reflexive realism," which reconciles Bazinian respect for the spatio-temporal integrity of the event with a Brechtian concern for distancing the spectator. Here we can return to the opening shot of the film. By having the camera emerge from the deep space into a full close-up of the camera lens, the opening shot combines a Bazinian respect for the spatio-temporal integrity of the real world with the reflexive foregrounding of the camera. The Rosselini of Cinecitta gives way to the Vertov of *Man with the Movie Camera* (1928). And within a circular structure, the last shot "rhymes" with the first; once again we see tracks, and once again the camera, but this time less noticeably, nods in our direction. The same film that calls attention to its own artifice, in sum, also calls attention to the real processes of filmmaking in Italy in 1963. And just as *The Odyssey* looked backward to folk epic and forward to James Joyce, *Contempt* looks back to Lumière and forward to Haskell Wexler, who cites the initial shot of *Contempt* in the final shot of his film *Medium Cool* (1969).

─────────── *Don Quixote* and the New Wave ───────────

We noted in previous chapters that many of the novels central to the European tradition — *The Red and the Black, Madame Bovary, Notes from Underground*

– chart a Cervantic trajectory of disenchantment. Literature, like film, gives us a world "in accord with our desires." But the illusions fostered by adolescent reading are systematically undone by experience in the real world and mocked, in literary terms, by parody. Ancient epic and medieval romance, in these texts, are made to do battle with the contemporary world. But this dialectic is not alien to the French New Wave. Many New Wave films stage the Quixotism of protagonists who envision their everyday experience through deforming literary or cinematic lenses. The bookish pair in Truffaut's *Jules and Jim* is repeatedly compared to Don Quixote and Sancho Panza. Antoine, in Truffaut's *400 Blows* (1959), sees life through the novels of Balzac and the films of Bergman. The director played by Truffaut in *La Nuit Américaine* (1973) tells Guillaume (Jean-Pierre Leaud) that "life is more harmonious in the movies." The mentalism of Robbe-Grillet and Alain Resnais, in *Last Year at Marienbad*, is also Quixotic in its way: there mind triumphs over matter. Godard, for his part, constantly rings the changes on the Quixotic theme, hardly surprising in an artist who once claimed to have "learned everything from the cinema" much as Quixote learned everything from chivalric romances. Even Godard's counterpointing of styles can be seen as Cervantic, in that it pits Sancho-Panza-style Bazinian realism against Quixote-style montage fantasy.

Many Godard characters conceive life on the model of the movies they have seen. Paul in *Contempt*, as we have seen, wants to be a hero in *Rio Bravo*, but he is lost in the labyrinth of modernism. But we find this same Quixotic quality in other Godard characters. Angela in *Une femme est une femme* (1961) emulates, with awkward charm, the gracefully dancing heroines of MGM musicals. When Michel in *A bout de souffle* (1960) apes Bogart's tough-guy cool as he blows smoke across a Bogey poster, the American star comes to fill the accentual slot of Amadis de Gaul as textual exemplar. The lives of the ersatz Parisian hoods in Godard's *Band of Outsiders* (1964), as dedicated imitators of Hollywood and *serie noire* gangsters, are similarly Quixotic; their lives and imaginaries are mediated by the fictions thrown up by the pop culture intertext. The characters of *Band of Outsiders* confuse metaphorical accounts of modes of feeling with literal prescriptions for everyday behavior. In an imaginary shoot-out, Arthur does a gut-clutching mime of the death of Billy the Kid. Even their robberies are planned in conscious imitation of "second-rate thrillers." Their first theft, symptomatically, is not of money but of a text; Franz steals a paperback while watching himself in a mirror, in a gesture that neatly epitomizes Godardian cinema: law-breaking, bookish, self-conscious. It is hardly an accident that another postmodern maker of Quixotic fictions – Quentin Tarantino – named his production company *Band of Outsiders*.

The Cervantic interface of art and life also entails, at times, the promiscuous mingling of characters of diverse ontological status within the same fiction. Many New Wave films trigger what Robert Alter, in reference to *Don Quixote*, called the "ontological vertigo" that arises when Don Quixote converses with a character from the spurious continuation of *Don Quixote* by Alonso de Avellaneda, "a fictional character from a 'true' fictional chronicle confronting a character from a false one in order to establish beyond doubt his own exclusive authenticity."[57] Godard's *Weekend* (1968), for its part, arranges a threshold encounter between purely fictitious characters – Corinne Roland – and historical personages (Emily Brontë, St Juste). Other Godard films have "real people" play themselves in-character (Roger Leenhardt in *A Married Woman*, 1964; Francis Jeanson in *La Chinoise*, 1967), yet converse with fictional characters. One moment in *Pierrot le fou* points up the problematized ontology of many Godard films. Ferdinand (Jean-Paul Belmondo) goes to a cinema where *Le Grand escroc* is playing. As he enters the theater, Jean Seberg, on-screen in the film-within-the-film, asks: "at what moment had we abandoned the fictitious character to return to the real one . . . if in fact the real one ever existed?" The spectator presumably recalls that Jean Seberg played opposite Belmondo in *A bout de souffle* and thus another dimension is introduced. When an actor incarnates many roles, which is the "fictitious" character and which the "real?"

With other New Wave directors, the Quixotic theme is expressed in a sly, indirect, more subdued manner. Although one does not usually associate Eric Rohmer (né Maurice Scherer) with Miguel de Cervantes, the Quixotic theme is omnipresent in his work. Apart from the perhaps incidental fact that in 1965 Rohmer directed a TV program entitled Cervantes' *Don Quixote*, Rohmer's films and stories often allude to the Quixotic theme. Indeed, his film *Perceval Le Gallois* (1978) treats the same kind of chivalric materials as the Cervantes novel; Perceval goes to the court of King Arthur to become a knight. But, more generally, the Rohmerian hero, like a knight on horseback, is engaged in a quest not only for the heart of a woman, but also for the honor won by an almost heroic resistance to the temptation offered by the other woman, who is almost always refused in the end. The character Adrien, in the written version of *La Collectionneuse* (1966) says that he is reading Rousseau, but that he might as well be reading *Don Quixote*. In the preface to the published version of the *Contes moraux*, Rohmer writes: "My heroes, like Don Quixote, see themselves as heroes in a novel, but perhaps there is no novel."[58] Rohmer's "Cervantic" narratives also proceed by digression and interruption, through interpolated tales; they do not proceed smoothly toward their narrative *telos*. His bookish characters are constantly reading and quoting, and in this sense they too emerge from the same generative matrix of many European novels, i.e. the Cervantic formula of systematic disenchantment. At the same time, Rohmer is also Dostoevskyan, in that his narrators are slippery and unreliable; the challenge for spectators is to discern the contradictions in their discourse, the gap between what they say and what they do.

Rohmer's *Le Genou de Claire* (Claire's Knee, 1970) also makes explicit allusion to Cervantes. Rohmer has his novelist character, Aurora, say that "the heroes of stories always wear blinders. Without them they would do nothing, the action would stop." The reference is to an episode in the Second Book of *Don Quixote*, represented in a painting in the protagonist's (Jerome's) villa. The picture shows Quixote, who thinks he's flying but who in fact is only feeling the effect of bellows producing wind. The bellows evoke both the Duke and Duchess's simulacral machinations in *Don Quixote* and the apparatus of illusionism in the cinema. The painting as a whole suggests, by analogy, that the film's hero, Jerome, is also blinkered and deluded like Don Quixote. The film features a kind of *mise-en-abyme* of authors and narrators: the author (Rohmer) has the author-in-the-film (Aurora) prod another self-narrating Quixotic character (Jerome) to act in ways that will serve her written stories. And, again like *Don Quixote*, the film thematizes writing itself, as Jerome and Aurora reflexively ruminate on the nature of stories and storytelling. In Rohmer's *Ma nuit chez Maud* (1969) meanwhile, the bookishness is religious and philosophical, since the protagonist is a practicing Catholic and a reader of Pascal and the Jansenists. The protagonist, the film leads us to suspect, sees himself as a hero in a knight's tale, or more accurately a saint in hagiographic literature, as someone undergoing an ordeal, but in fact he is only another Quixotic character lost in a disenchanted world.[59]

These films, like *Don Quixote* itself, reflect the Janus-faced doubleness of what Borges calls the "partial magic" of self-conscious art, its simultaneous joy in both mystification and demystification. Within the artist a struggle takes place between the will to create an illusion and the conscious decision to destroy that illusion. The lucidity of the illusionist, the puppeteer, or the filmmaker does battle with the desire to create a believable and lifelike image. For the reader or spectator, meanwhile, all the reflexive devices in the world do not necessarily preclude affective participation. *Don Quixote* is a purely textual entity, a verbal artifact, yet his imaginary self has served as a pole of identification for readers for centuries.

In its search for a "new avant-garde," the New Wave navigated between reflective realism and reflexive fantasy, between *mise-en-scène* and montage, and between the formal provocations of the "historical avant-garde" and the pleasures of the mainstream commercial film. At its best, the New Wave mobilized spectatorial pleasure in order, paradoxically, to interrogate those very pleasures, while at the same time making that interrogation itself pleasurable. The New Wave films often adopt the Cervantic strategy of playing with fictions rather than doing away with them altogether. They follow the comic epic path traced both by Cervantes and by Brecht: to tell stories, but at the same time to step out of the story and question it. They articulate the play of mimetic desire and the pleasure principle **and** the obstacles to the realization of desire. The challenge for reflexive realism is to revel in the fabulating impulse and the joys of storytelling, while also maintaining a certain intellectual distance from the story. The pleasure generated by a Cervantes, a Brecht, or a Godard consists in telling stories while comically undermining their authority. The enemy to be done away with, the best of the New Wave films suggest, is not fiction but socially generated illusions, not stories but rather alienated dreams. The Latin American "magical realists" discussed in the next chapter, as we shall see, take both trends, the pleasure in magic and the awareness of fiction, to dizzying new heights.

Notes

1 See Michel Marie, *La Nouvelle vague: une école artistique* (Paris: Nathan, 1997), p. 27. For an English version, see Michel Marie, *The French New Wave: An Artistic School*, trans. Richard Neupert (Oxford: Blackwell, 2003).

2 Astruc's essay was first published in *Ecran Français* (no. 144, 1948) and is included in Peter Graham (ed.), *The New Wave* (London: Secker and Warburg, 1969), pp. 17–23.

3 Jean-Luc Godard, "Bergmanorama," *Cahiers du Cinéma* 85 (July 1958).

4 Cited in Jean-Claude Bernardet, *O autor no cinema* (São Paulo: Brasiliense, 1994), p. 14.

5 Eric Rohmer, *Le Gout de la beauté* (Paris: Cahiers du Cinéma, 1984).

6 André Bazin, *What is Cinema?*, vol. 1, trans. Hugh Gray (Berkeley, CA: University of California Press, 1967), p. 75.

7 André Bazin, "Adaptation, or the Cinema as Digest," in André Bazin, *Bazin at Work: Major Essays and Reviews from the Forties and Fifties*, trans. Alain Piette and Bert Cardullo (London: Routledge, 1997).

8 Ibid., pp. 48–9.

9 See Antoine de Baecque, *Histoire d'une revue*, vol. 1: *1951–1959* (Paris: Cahiers du Cinéma, 1991), pp. 107–9.

10 Bazin, "Adaptation, or the Cinema as Digest," p. 46.

11 Ibid.

12 The "Celluloid and Marble" essays were published in *Cahiers du Cinéma* in five parts: "Le Celluloid et le marbre: le bandit philosophique," no. 44 (February 1955); "Le Celluloid et le marbre: le siècle des peintres," no. 47 (July 1955); "Le Celluloid et

le marbre: de la metaphore," no. 51 (October 1955); "Le Celluloid et le marbre: beau comme la musique," no. 52 (November 1955); "Le Celluloid et le marbre: architecture d'apocalype," no. 53 (December 1955).

13   The roundtable concerning *Hiroshima* is included in Jim Hillier (ed.), *Cahiers du Cinéma: The 1950s, Neo-realism, Hollywood, New Wave* (Cambridge, MA: Harvard University Press, 1985).

14   See Bernard Dort, "Pour une critique Brechtienne du cinema," *Cahiers du Cinéma* 114 (December 1960).

15   Alain Robbe-Grillet as quoted in Jean-Louis Leutrat, *L'Année dernière à Marienbad* (London: British Film Institute, 2000), p. 52.

16   André Gaudreault, *Du littéraire au filmique: système du récit* (Quebec: Presse de l'Université Laval, 1988).

17   Alain Robbe-Grillet, "Temps et description dans le roman d'aujourd'hui," in *Pour un nouveau roman* (Paris: Gallimard/Idées, 1963), p. 161.

18   For a discussion of the theoretical limitations of Robbe-Grillet's view of the cinema as creating a "perpetual present," see my "Introduction: The Theory and Practice of Adaptation," in Robert Stam and Alessandra Raengo (eds), *Literature and Film: A Guide to the Theory and Practice of Film Adaptation* (Oxford: Blackwell, 2005), pp. 1–52.

19   Alain Robbe-Grillet, *Last Year at Marienbad* (New York: Grove Press, 1962). Subsequent page references in the text are to this edition.

20   Jean Ricardou, *Problèmes du nouveau roman* (Paris: Seuil, 1967).

21   Gilles Deleuze, *Cinema 2: The Time Image*, trans. Hugh Tomlinson and Roberta Galeta (Minneapolis, MN: University of Minnesota Press, 1989), p. 117.

22   In his very useful study, Freddy Sweet lists sixteen major interpretations that have been proposed. See *The Film Narratives of Alain Resnais* (Ann Arbor: University of Michigan Press, 1981), pp. 43–4.

23   Quoted in Kamilla Elliot, "Through the Looking Glass," unpublished thesis, English Department, University of California at Berkeley, 2000, ch. 1, p. 19.

24   See Deleuze, *Cinema 2*, p. 101.

25   Quoted in Leutrat, *L'Année dernière à Marienbad*, p. 7.

26   *Last Year at Marienbad*, screenplay, p. 68.

27   See Marguerite Duras, *Les yeux verts* (Paris: Cahiers du Cinéma, 1980), p. 131.

28   See ibid., p. 9.

29   *L'Express* (May 8, 1958).

30   Quoted in Laure Adler, *Marguerite Duras: A Life*, trans. Anne-Marie Glasheen (Chicago: University of Chicago Press, 2000), p. 221.

31   Gilles Deleuze, *Cinema 1: The Movement Image*, trans. Hugh Tomlinson and Barbara Habberjam (London: Athlone Press, 1986); Deleuze, *Cinema 2*.

32   For a related discussion of the fossil and film, but not in the context of *Hiroshima mon amour*, see Laura U. Marks, *The Skin of the Film: Intercultural Cinema,*

Embodiment, and the Senses (Durham, NC: Duke University Press, 2000), esp. ch. 2.

33 Michel Chion, *La voix au cinema* (Paris: Cahiers du Cinéma, 1982).

34 But not, ironically, in Japan itself. The Japanese translation of the title of *Hiroshima mon amour* was *24 Hour Love Affair*, a title which elides not only the reference to the Japanese city but also loses the title's oxymoronic thrust, while simultaneously creating expectations of a very different genre – the erotic comedy.

35 Quoted in Adler, *Marguerite Duras*, p. 225.

36 Duras, *Les yeux verts*, p. 41.

37 Duras recounts her own memory of that day in a succession of images that recall the linkages of *Hiroshima mon amour* itself. "I remember August 6, 1945. My husband and I were in a center for Deportees near the Annecy Lake. I read the headlines about the Hiroshima bomb. Then I left the pension and leaned against the wall next to the road, as if I had suddenly fainted. Bit by bit I came to my senses and I recognized the life around me, the road. Just as in 1946 during the discovery of the mass graves from the concentration camps." See *Les yeux verts*, p. 40.

38 Gerard Genette, *Narrative Discourse: An Essay in Method*, trans. Jane E. Lewin (Ithaca, NY: Cornell University Press, 1972).

39 Deleuze, *Cinema 1*; *Cinema 2*.

40 See the article by Jean-Andre Fieschi in *Cahiers du Cinéma* 146 (August 1963).

41 Quoted in Michel Marie, *Le Mépris* (Paris: Nathan, 1990), p. 26.

42 Ibid., p. 67.

43 Alberto Moravia, *Il disprezzo* (Milan: Bompiani, 1954). The book was translated into French as *Le Mépris*, trans. Claude Poncet (Paris: Flammarion, 1955) and in English as *Contempt*, trans. Angus Davidson (New York: New York Review of Books, 1999), p. 99. Henceforth, all references will be by page number in the body of the text.

44 Gérard Genette, *Palimpsestes: la littérature au second degré* (Paris: Seuil, 1982).

45 See *Godard on Godard*, ed. Jean Narboni; trans. Tom Milne (New York: Viking, 1972), p. 201.

46 See Georg Lukács, *The Theory of the Novel: A Historico-philosophical Essay on the Forms of Great Epic Literature*, trans. Anna Bostock (Cambridge, MA: MIT Press, 1975), p. 41.

47 See Fredric Jameson, *The Political Unconscious* (Ithaca, NY: Cornell University Press, 1981), p. 146.

48 Harold Bloom, *The Anxiety of Influence: A Theory of Poetry* (New York: Oxford, 1973), and *A Map of Misreading* (New York: Oxford University Press, 2003).

49 Bazin's phrase "a world in accord with our desires" is echoed later by Lang in his assertion that for the ancient Greeks the world existed in accord with "nature."

50 Marsha Kinder and Beverly Houston make similar points in *Close-up: A Critical Perspective on Film* (New York: Harcourt, Brace, Jovanovich, 1972).

51 Jacques Rozier's short film *Paparazzi*, which concerns the making of *Contempt*, depicts the real-life voyeurism of the *paparazzi* (and the readers of the tabloid magazines for which they work) who rent boats and scale rocks just to get a glimpse of Bardot.

52 Michel Marie delineates, with his usual precision, the intertextual influences on *Le Mépris* in his book, *Le Mépris*.

53 Prokosch is shown as constantly objectifying people, as when he uses Francesca's back as an impromptu desk to make out a check. He simply tells — he does not ask — Paul that he will rework the script of the film.

54 We find a further buried reference to Nazism, perhaps, in the fact that the Casa Malaparte, which is so beautifully filmed in *Contempt*, belonged to an Italian writer (whose pseudonym was Malaparte) who was a strong supporter of Mussolini.

55 Brian Fairlamb elaborates on the connections between *Contempt* and *Two Weeks in Another Town* as "international co-productions set at Cinecitta being directed by Hollywood veterans [with] neurotic or insecure male protagonists in a subservient position to both director and money-conscious producers." For Fairlamb, the film's Hollywood references are central. Unfortunately, the essay mingles valid insights with gratuitously snide and ungenerous comments about the work of earlier critics. See "Coping with Contempt: Godard's Rejected Male and his Hollywood Prototypes," in *Cineaction* 48 (1998).

56 See Marie, *Le Mépris*.

57 Robert Alter, *Partial Magic: The Novel as a Self-conscious Genre* (Berkeley, CA: University of California Press, 1975), p. 6.

58 Eric Rohmer, *Six contes moraux* (Paris: Cahiers du Cinéma, 1998), p. 10.

59 Pascal Bonitzer briefly points out this Cervantic theme in his book *Eric Rohmer* (Paris: Cahiers du Cinéma, 1999), pp. 17–18, 36.

Chapter 7

Full Circle: From Cervantes to Magic Realism

In the Introduction, I spoke of a desire to "deprovincialize" the study of literature and film by seeing both arts as part of a much longer transtextual span, millennial in temporal terms, and planetary in spatial terms, even if we have "covered" here only a small portion of that planet. The tradition of illusionistic realism, I have argued, is somewhat provincial as an ideal, even within "Europe" itself. Prodded by multiculturalist critique, literary and cinematic discourse has tried to break out of the narrow frame not only of the mimetic constraints of realism but also of the restrictive frame of Eurocentric and nation-state thinking. The Latin American modernisms evoked by terms like "anthropophagy" and "magic realism," in this sense, fashion the magical out of materials thrown up by the "real" of history and everyday life, and in this sense reconfigure the whole question of realism.

But this reconfiguration of realism, as we have repeatedly stressed, is itself rooted in ancient traditions going back to Cervantes and Rabelais and the Menippea. A writer like Rabelais wrote about grotesque monsters and improbable and magical events, but at the same time tells truths that the nobility were not eager to hear. *Don Quixote* itself too can be seen as proleptically "magical realist," in that it stages the dialectical interplay between the "magical" imagination of Don Quixote – which alchemizes the base metal of brute fact into the storied gold of legends and fairy tales – and the "realistic" and earthbound concerns of Sancho Panza. Nor are the Americas alien to the world of *Don Quixote*. The first part of Cervantes's novel was published just a little over a century after

Columbus's voyage, and the novel makes frequent allusion to the Americas. In chapter 42 of Book One, a judge is bound for Mexico and a brother of a character is in Peru, where he has become enormously rich. In chapter 48, the canon, as if anticipating the improbabilities of magic realism, complains about a comedy in which the first act is set in Europe, the second in Asia, the third in Africa, and "if there had been a fourth act, the scene would have been laid in America and thus they would have encompassed the four quarters of the globe." Even Quixote's "golden age" is simultaneously fashioned out of remote (Arcadian) times and "exotic" American spaces. The utopian imagination was fueled by rumors of New World paradises characterized by a generous nature and an egalitarian socius, the same kinds of utopian echoes that made their way into Shakespeare's roughly contemporaneous *Tempest*. The grand Renaissance humanists – Erasmus, Thomas More, Rabelais – were avid readers of travel literature about the Americas. Conversely, the Americas were aware of Spanish culture and chivalric romance. The vestiges of Iberian culture animate Latin American popular culture even today. A popular festivity in Brazil reenacts the battles of the Moors and the Christians of the time of the *Reconquista*; black and mestizo Brazilians commemorate the Christian victory over the Moors. The popular **literatura de cordel** (string literature), from the Brazilian northeast, the memory of which informs the work both of Glauber Rocha and Guimarães Rosa, goes back both in its thematics and its strophic structure to chivalric romance, to tales of Roland and Charlemagne.

In the long view, an aesthetic school like Magic Realism belongs to that perennial "other tradition," that other mode, variously called the Menippean, the carnivalesque, the Cervantic, and the "anatomic" (from "Anatomy"), a variegated tradition whose charismatic power has waxed and waned over millennia, but which now seems to be experiencing another period of ascendancy. While the transrealist aesthetics derive on one level from ancient literary traditions, on another they derive from the historical reality of the Americas, and especially the polyperspectivalism provoked by the trilateral clash, sometimes euphemized as the "encounter," between Europe, Africa, and indigenous America.

The invention of "America" was also an intertextual event shaped, like *Don Quixote*, by romances of chivalry and Renaissance epic poems. For Alejo Carpentier, this intertextual element informs Bernal Diaz del Castillo's *The True History of the Conquest of New Spain* (1632), which Carpentier calls the first "**real** chivalic romance."[1] When the conquistadores encountered Mexico and Tenochtitlan (now Mexico City) – which at the time was roughly eight times as large as the Paris of the time, and much more grand and imposing – for the first time, they compared all "these lands, temples, and lakes" to the "enchantments in the book of Amadis." When Cortez arrived on the coast of Mexico, he asked God for the kind of military victory granted the paladin Roldan, from the Charlemagne romances. What Don Quixote, living in a disenchanted seventeenth-century world, could find only in books, the conquistadores found (and often destroyed) in the Aztec grandeur of Mexico and the Inca splendors of Peru.[2] By noting that some of the books of chivalry mocked by Cervantes were themselves inspired by the conquistadores' amazement in the face of Tenochtitlan, Carpentier reverses the current of international artistic influence, audaciously suggesting that early European literature was itself indebted to the (misnamed) "New World."

The twentieth-century incarnations of the Menippea intermingled European and extra-European influences to mold indigenous movements like "magic realism." Yet most writing on modernism restricts its attention to movements in European and North American capitals like Paris, London, New York, and Zurich, while consigning to oblivion similar modernist movements in such places as São Paulo, Havana, Mexico City, and Buenos Aires. A single, local perspective has been presented as "universal," while the productions of what is patronizingly called "the rest of the world," when discussed at all, are assumed to be pale copies of European originals, mere latter-day echoes of pioneering European gestures. But, in fact, artistic modernism owed a clear debt to the arts and cultures of Africa, Asia, and indigenous America. Leger, Cendrars, and Milhaud based their staging of *La Creation du monde* on African cosmology. Bataille wrote about pre-Columbian art and Aztec sacrifices. Artaud fled France for the Mexico of the Tarahumara Indians. The European avant-garde cultivated the mystique of vodun and of African art. Breton himself saw Surrealism as "linked with colored people," not only because Surrealism identified with their struggle against imperialism, but also because of the profound affinities between so-called "primitive thinking and surrealistic thinking," in their common questioning of the "hegemony of consciousness."[3] Thus, while it may be true that it was the "impact of surrealism," as Roy Armes suggests, "that liberated the Caribbean and African poets of Negritude from the constraints of a borrowed language," it was also African and Asian and American indigenous art that liberated the European modernists by provoking them to question their own culture-bound aesthetic of realism.[4]

European modernist views of non-European cultures were often tinged with implicitly colonial "primitivist" attitudes. Europe was seen as simply absorbing "primitive art" and anonymous "folklore" as raw materials to be refined by European artists, a view which prolongs the trope which regarded colonized people as body rather than mind, much as colonized land was seen as a source of raw material rather than of manufacture. A kind of primitivist "slumming" was a common cultural feature of what historians of slavery first called "the Black Atlantic." It is hardly an accident that artistic avant-gardes and bohemian life styles in the 1920s were all involved in the consumption of what Joe Roach calls the "circum-Atlantic" performances of Afro-diasporic culture.[5] We need only recall the downtown white intellectuals (and gangsters) going to the Cotton Club in New York for an "uptown Saturday night," or the elite white Brazilians enjoying the samba school performances in the *favelas* of Rio de Janeiro, or French Surrealists in Paris waxing enthusiastic about Josephine Baker in the **La Revue nègre**. What all of these interactions have in common is a sincere appreciation, on the part of European or Europeanized elites, compromised by the social distortions of an asymmetrical power situation, where exoticized vitalities became a means of escape for spiritually exhausted Europeans and Euro-Americans. At the same time, this dynamic was lived, somewhat differently, at different sites around the black Atlantic. Whereas France practiced colonialism and slavery largely outside its borders, even though the benefits of colonialism and slavery accrued to its metropolitan elite, the settler colonies of the Americas lived both exploitation and colonial syncretism closer to home. For Cubans and Brazilians, and to some extent even for North Americans, blackness was a quotidian thing, part of centuries of tense coexistence and assymetrical interaction.

Latin America has often been a crucible for cultural "indigenization," whereby European concepts and narratives were given meanings quite distinct from what they originally meant within Europe. The exotic metaphors of the European avant-garde had a strange way of "taking flesh" in the Latin American context, resulting in an ironic echo-effect or feedback between European and Latin American modernisms. In Latin America, avant-garde tropes of the marvelous and the fantastic, of cannibalism and carnival, became weirdly concrete and literal. Thus Alfred Jarry's "too neglected branch of anthropophagy" came to refer in Brazil to the putatively "real" historically existing cannibalism of the Tupinambá. Surrealist "trance" writing evoked in Brazil the collective trance of Afro-Brazilian religion. Latin American and Caribbean familiarity with the "madness" of carnival, with African-derived trance religions, made it easy for them to assimilate artistic procedures which in Europe had represented a more dramatic rupture with ambient values and spiritual traditions.[6] What was remote and metaphoric for European modernists – magic, carnival, anthropophagy – became more familiar and quasi-literal within the "quotidian surrealism" of Latin American life. The heterogeneous cultures that made up Latin America engendered a new historical reality which subverted the conventional common sense of occidental rationalism. As a result, writes Brazilian critic Antonio Candido, the "provocations of a Picasso, a Brancusi, a Max Jacob, a Tristan Tzara, were, in the end, more coherent with **our** cultural heritage than with theirs."[7] Latin American modernist movements thus dialogued with and absorbed Western art movements but also critiqued them and in some ways went beyond them.

The admittedly problematic term "magic realism," in this chapter, serves as a kind of shorthand for **all** the alternative aesthetics rooted in the multicultures of Latin America. Indeed, Latin America and the Caribbean have been fecund in neologistic aesthetics, whether literary, painterly, or cinematic. Alongside "magic realism," we find "anthropophagy" (Oswald de Andrade), *lo real maravilloso americano* (Carpentier), "marvelous realism" (Jacques Stephen Alexis), "**diversalité**" (Eduardo Glissant), the "aesthetics of hunger" (Glauber Rocha), "Cine imperfecto" (Julio Garcia Espinosa), the "aesthetics of garbage" (Rogerio Sganzerla), "shaman cinema" (Raul Ruiz), "Tropicália" (Gilberto Gil and Caetano Veloso), the "salamander" (as opposed to the Hollywood dinosaur) aesthetic (Paul Leduc), "rasquachismo" (Tomas-Ibarra Frausto), and *santeria* aesthetics (Arturo Lindsay). Most of these alternative aesthetics revalorize by inversion what had formerly been seen as negative, especially within colonialist discourse. Thus ritual cannibalism, for centuries the very name of the savage, abject other, becomes with the Brazilian modernists an anti-colonialist trope and a term of value. (Even "magic realism" inverts the colonial hierarchy which contrasts "rational" science and "irrational" magic.) At the same time, these aesthetics share the ju-jitsu trait of turning strategic weakness into tactical strength. By appropriating an existing discourse for their own ends, they deploy the force of the dominant against domination.

In this final chapter, then, I will focus especially not only on "magic realism" and "the marvelous American real," but also on earlier precursor movements like 1920s' Brazilian modernism and "anthropophagy." Rather than offer an exhaustive historical account of magic realism and the cinema, I will focus on transrealist strategies as exemplified in novels (and their filmic adaptations) by the Brazilian modernist Mário de Andrade, by the Colombian Gabriel Garcia Márquez, and by the Cuban Alejo Carpentier.

The cinematic realization of innovative aesthetics like "magic realism" and the "marvelous American real," it is important to add, cannot be limited to **adaptations** per se. Some Latin American films incarnate the "marvelous American real" without referring directly to a novelistic source. *Terra em transe* (Land in Anguish, 1967), Glauber Rocha's baroque allegory about Brazilian politics, for example, is not based on any magic realist novel, yet it is thoroughly imbued with the same spirit. The film is set in an imaginary country called "Eldorado," which closely resembles Brazil. Rocha's original title – *Maldorado* – would have linked Brazil and Europe's avant-gardes through a quadruple pun playing on "Eldorado" (an instance of Europe's Quixotic imagining of the "New World"), "Maldoror" (as in Lautréamont's *Chants de Maldoror*), "Maldourado" (i.e. badly gilded), and "maladorado" (badly loved). Here I will focus only on one sequence, a fantasy sequence dreamed by the narrator/protagonist Paulo Martins. In that sequence, the right-wing figure of the film (named Porfirio Diaz after the Mexican dictator), arrives from the sea, in a scene suggesting a myth of origins. Much as Walter Benjamin spoke of "memories flashing up in a moment of danger," whereby repressed aspects of history take on fresh meaning in the light of contemporary crises, here Rocha, in the wake of the traumatic 1964 coup d'état, conjures up the memory of Pedro Cabral, the Portuguese "discoverer" of Brazil. The sequence conflates the right-wing *putschiste* Diaz with Cabral celebrating the famous "first mass" with the Indians in 1500. Within official Brazilian historiography, the first mass evokes the pacific Christianization of the Indians and the "cordial" relations between whites and Indians. But Rocha's film magically scrambles temporality by having the whole scene played out in an anachronistic manner which stresses the continuities between the conquest and **contemporary** oppression; the present-day right winger is portrayed as the latter-day heir of the conquistadores.

Rocha further destabilizes meaning by making Africa a textual presence. The very aesthetic of the sequence, first of all, draws heavily from the Africanized forms of Rio's yearly carnival and samba pageant, with its bricolage historicism, its sacred polyrhythms, and its delight in extravagant *allegorias* (floats) and *fantasias* (costumes); indeed, the actor who plays the conquistador is Clovis Bornay, a well-known **carnavalesco** specialized in carnival pageantry and well-researched "allegories." Secondly, the mass is accompanied not by Christian religious music, but by Yoruba religious chants, evoking the "trance" of the Portuguese title. Rocha's suggestive referencing of African music, as if Africans had been in Brazil prior to the arrival of Europeans, reminds us not only of the "continental drift" theory that sees South America and Africa as once having formed part of a single land mass, but also of the theories of Ivan van Sertima and others that Africans arrived in the New World "before Columbus."[8] Africans, the music suggests, as those who shaped and were shaped by the Americas over centuries, are in some uncanny sense **also** indigenous to the region. The sequence manifests a dazzling aesthetic originality, exemplifying what I would call a "**trance**-Brechtian" aesthetic, through which Rocha manages to Tropicalize, Africanize, and carnivalize the theories of Bertolt Brecht through the possession-trance of West African religions. While Brechtianism deploys contradiction and disjunction between image and sound, here Rocha goes farther by staging the

Figure 7.1 Glauber Rocha's *Terra em transe* (1967), produced by Mapa Filmes

historical contradictions between vast cultural complexes existing in relations of subordination and domination, where the "chalice" of Catholicism is superimposed on music which incarnates precisely the religion historically suppressed by Christianity. Here music represents not merely a factor of disjunction but also the return of the historically repressed. Instead of the austerity and minimalism which characterize a certain Brechtian tradition in the cinema, we find a multi-layered saturation of image and sound, an hysterical *trauerspiel* linked both to carnival and to *candomblé*. The scene's fractured and discontinuous aesthetic stages the drama of life in the colonial "contact zone," defined by Mary Louise Pratt as the space in which "subjects previously separated" encounter each other within "conditions of coercion, radical inequality, and intractable conflict."[9]

The final shot of the film exemplifies this process quite brilliantly. As we see the film's protagonist wielding a rifle in a Che Guevara-like gesture of Quixotic rebellion, we hear a soundtrack composed of Villa-Lobos music, **candomblé** chants, samba, and machine-gun fire. The mix, in this feverish *bricolage*, is fundamentally unstable; the Villa-Lobos music never really synchronizes with the **candomblé** or the gunfire. We are reminded of Carpentier's gentle mockery of the innocuous juxtapositions of the European avant-gardists – Lautréamont's "umbrella and a sewing machine" – which he contrasts with the explosive counterpoints of indigenous, African, and European cultures thrown up daily by Latin American life and art, counterpoints where the tensions are never completely resolved or harmonized, where the cultural dialogue is tense, transgressive, not easily assimilated. Rocha's neo-baroque Afro-avant-gardist aesthetic here figures the discontinuous, dissonant, fractured history of the multi-nation through equally dissonant images and sounds. Style here becomes not "an absolute way of seeing things" à la Flaubert, but rather a politics, a displaced form of national allegory.

--------------- "Magic Realism:" From Literature to Film ---------------

The term "magic realism" was first coined as "**magischer Realismus**" by the German art critic Franz Roh in 1925, just three years after the apotheosis of Brazilian modernism in the "Modern Art Week" held in São Paulo, but without apparent knowledge of that movement. Unlike other artistic movements like Futurism and Surrealism, characterized by manifestos and explicit position-taking, "magic realism" was an ad hoc term first coined by critics in the visual arts and then transferred to literature, alongside cognate terms like "the marvelous" and the "fantastic." Following the itinerary of this term has been compared to tracing a piece of lost baggage that has been mishandled over a long trip in three continents. In Roh's coinage, the term was meant to characterize a "post-Expressionist" style in painting. Translated into Spanish in the pages of Ortega y Gasset's prestigious journal *Revista de Occidente* two years later, it then made its way through Latin American cultural circles. In Buenos Aires, it came to refer to the work of writers like Cocteau, Kafka, and Borges. A programmatic 1932 essay by Borges was entitled "Narrative, Art, and Magic." Seymour Menton, in his *Historia verdadera del realismo magico*, details the ways the term was variously invoked by the Italian Massimo Bontempelli, the Peruvian Jose Carlos Mariategui, the Spaniard Juan Ramon Juminez, the Mexican Rodolfo Usigli, the Americans Alfred Barr and Newton Arvin (who applied the term to the work of Truman Capote!), the Venezuelan Arturo Uslar Pietri, the German Gerhart Pohl, the Frenchman Charles Plisnier, and the Austrian George Saiko.[10]

The contribution of Cuban writer Alejo Carpentier was to territorialize magic realism more firmly in the cultural soil of the Americas. Carpentier spoke in

1949 of **lo real maravilloso americano** (the marvelous [Latin] American real), which he contrasted with European Surrealism in terms of a specifically Latin American fantastic rooted in the cultural mixtures typical of Latin America. Unlike the cool, cerebral, and in some cases Europhile magic realism of a Borges or Cortazar, Carpentier saw "the marvelous American real" as based in popular cultural practices and collective beliefs typical of the subaltern populations of the "New World." For Carpentier, the "magic" does not refer to surreal effects or strategies but rather to the "archaic" yet still living myths of a continent. Rather than emerging from the juxtaposition of an umbrella and a sewing machine, the New World marvelous comes from the juxtaposition of incommensurable cultural paradigms. Popular culture, as Jean Franco argues, promised native regeneration and the new synthesis which "codified racial difference as magic and the marginalized indigenous both as remedy and poison."[11] Writers of the Americas "looked to re-enchant the fallen world by drawing on indigenous spirituality and forms of knowledge unknown to Europe."[12] (We will return to Carpentier below.)

In 1955, Angel Flores adopted the term "magic realism" to apply to writers like Borges, Cesares, and Asturias, thus resulting in what Jean Weisgerber calls a "terminological imbroglio."[13] The same period of the 1950s and 1960s also witnessed a remarkable "boom" in prose fiction, in a line going back to the work of two Argentinians – Adolfo Bioy Cesares's *La invencion de Morel* (The Invention of Morel, 1940) and Borges's *El jardin de los senderos que se bifurcan* (The Garden of Forking Paths, 1941) – and ramifying into the work of the Mexicans Juan Rulfo and Carlos Fuentes, the Guatemalan Miguel Asturias, and the Colombian Gabriel Garcia Márquez. The word "boom," with its echoes of financial and economic "booms," had the effect of retrospectively consecrating earlier, relatively unrecognized work (for example, that of Carpentier or Juan Rulfo or Juan Carlos Onetti) as "magical realist."

Since the boom coincided both with US neo-imperial military interventions in Latin America – Guatemala in 1954, Brazil in 1964, and so forth – and with the 1959 Cuban revolution and the ideological currents of third worldism and nationalism, the movement took on an ideological overlay of pan-Latin anti-imperialism. The common search for a decolonizing language linked the boom writers to the sister-movement known as "New Latin American cinema." After the boom, "magic realism" underwent further inflationary pressures, at times degenerating into a marketing device to sell superficially "magical" cultural products. At its most elastic, the term was stretched to apply to transrealist writers as diverse as Salman Rushdie, Chinua Achebe, Ishmael Reed, Wole Soyinka, Günter Grass, and Wilson Harris. (Woody Allen's *Zelig*, or Toni Morrison's

Beloved, in this broad definition, could easily qualify as "magical realist.") When Bloomingdale advertisements began to mention magical realism, as Jean Franco puts it, the term had "passed into the twilight zone of idées reçues."[14]

Magic realism is not an avant-garde movement, but rather, as Jean Weisgerber puts it, "a literary current linking various writers who practice an expanded notion of realism in the 20th century,"[15] and in this sense forms part of the larger trajectory traced in *Literature Through Film*. Unlike Surrealism or Expressionism, magic realism is not terribly interested in oneiric subjectivity or in a subjectively disfigured reality. With "magic realism," the word "realism" remains the substantive, "magic" only the qualifier. Thus Márquez refers in *One Hundred Years of Solitude* to "an immediate reality that came to be more fantastic than the vast universe of . . . imagination."[16] In a sense, magic realism turns Defoe-style documentary realism on its head; instead of Defoe's inventories of objects and animals, wielded as "reality effects," we find Márquez's strange mingling of fact and (apparent) fancy to generate what might be called "irreality effects." The Defoe-like precision of "four years, eleven months, and two days" of rain, for example, is made in the Márquez novel to generate magical flowers popping out of the "driest of machines" (pp. 291–2). Magic realism generates anomalies, like those in Isabel Allende's *House of the Spirits*, with its coastal town where it "rained fish" and where characters from books escape to live their adventures. In Carpentier's *The Lost Steps*, the mere smell of mushrooms induces hallucinations, and swarms of butterflies darken the sky.

Yet this magic is not so distant from the truth. In the world of magical realism, the marvelous often has a prosaic explanation. Some mushrooms are powerful hallucinogens and in the Brazilian pantanal butterflies do suddenly darken the sky. Carpentier gives us a host of examples of this real that is realer than real. In what he calls the "quotidian epic" of Latin America, Carpentier encountered illiterate black poets, distant descendants of the Yoruba, who recited octosyllabic verse telling the story of Charlemange from the *Chanson de Roland*. Carpentier encountered indigenous myths which more or less told the same story as that of the Nibelungen or of the Trojan War or of Noah and the Flood. And he encountered the story of Mackandal, the lame former slave who in 1750, in Haiti, led one of the most extraordinary slave rebellions in the history of the Americas.

Magic realism can also be defined in terms of its non-synchronous, palimpsestic notions of temporality. Carpentier's *The Lost Steps* was inspired by the Amazon and the Orinoco River as the materialization of past, present, and future time, where a tavern is called "Memories of the Future." *One Hundred Years of Solitude* concentrates "a century of daily episodes in such a way that they coexisted in one instant" (p. 382). Isabel Allende's *Eva Luna* tells us that "While you and I are speaking here, behind your back Christopher Columbus is inventing America, and the same Indians that welcome him in the stained-glass window are still naked in a jungle a few hours from this office, and will be there a hundred years from now."[17] Thus magic realism encodes the multiplicity, the malleability, and the superimposability of time.

Magic realism has been variously defined in terms both of its magical and marvelous themes and in terms of its polyperspectival forms of narration. Magic realism and other alternative aesthetics bypass the formal conventions of dramatic, illusionistic realism in favor of such alternative modes as the carnivalesque, the anthropophagic, the reflexive-modernist and the resistant postmodernist. These aesthetics are often rooted in non-realist, often non-Western cultural traditions featuring other historical rhythms, other narrative structures, other views of the body, sexuality, spirituality, and the collective life. Many incorporate non-modern traditions into clearly modernizing or postmodernizing aesthetics, and thus problematize facile dichotomies such as traditional and modern, realist and modernist, modernist and postmodernist.[18]

The authors/directors discussed in this chapter share a number of common features. Most emerge from the cultivated Latin American elite but have sympathies with the marginalized masses, variously called o povo, el pueblo, or the "people." And unlike the cosmopolitan anti-nationalist European avant-gardes, these movements are nationalist, not so much in the sense of local Brazilian or Venezuelan nationalism, but in the larger sense of pan-Latin American diasporic anti-imperialism. While deeply conversant with European culture and the avant-gardes, they also revitalize their art through contact with the popular and the oral, thus creating a new synthesis at once popular and erudite, native and European. In generic terms, they are affiliated with what we have variously called the Menippea and the carnivalesque, with Apuleius, Rabelais, and Cervantes. (Mário de Andrade, Alejo Carpentier, and Gabriel Garcia Márquez have all expressed their indebtedness to Rabelais, for example.) While usually white (Mário de Andrade being an exception), these figures are still **culturally** immersed in the racial heterogeneities (indigenous, African, European) typical of the "multi-nation states" of the Americas (including the United States).

Carnivalesque Anthropophagy

The conceptual categories devised by Russian cultural theorist Mikhail Bakhtin are highly relevant to these modernist cultural currents. Although Bakhtin himself rarely made reference to Latin America, many Latin American intellectuals have found in his notion of the carnivalesque the key to the specificity of Latin American cultural production.[19] Since Latin America has been economically, politically, and culturally marginalized, critics such as Emir Rodriguez Monegal and Haroldo de Campos argue, its best artists have made this marginalization, this ironic sense of belonging to two cultures – one's own and that of the metropolitan centers of power – absolutely central to their work.[20] As necessarily bicultural and often tri-cultural people, Latin American artists and intellectuals inhabit a peculiar realm of irony where words and images are seldom taken at face value, whence the paradigmatic importance of parody and carnivalization as "ambivalent" solutions within a situation of cultural asymmetry. Latin American art is necessarily parodic, caught in specular games of doubling and redoubling, an art for which, as René Menil said in a West Indian context, "naïveté is forbidden."[21]

Latin American "magical" traditions have broad affinities with Bakhtin's "Menippea." Deploying Bakhtinian categories, Latin American critics have found carnivalesque reminiscences and strategies in the Rabelaisian gigantism of Márquez's *One Hundred Years of Solitude* (1967) and in the parodic intertextuality of Guillermo Cabrera Infante's *Très tristes tigres* (1967), as well as in the less "obviously" carnivalesque works of a writer like Jorge Luis Borges. At first glance a most patrician and Europhile writer, Borges carnivalizes European literary classics, by turning Dante's *Divine Comedy*, for example, into a "trivial" love story in *El aleph* (1949), or by having his Pierre Menard rewrite *Don Quixote* (but without changing a word). Carpentier turns Descartes's *Discourse on Method* into *El recurso del metodo* (The Recourse of Method, 1978), spoofing Descartes's treatise chapter by chapter by showing its irrelevance to a bloody and slavery-ridden century in what Carpentier himself called "the least Cartesian continent imaginable." (Descartes's **cogito ergo sum**, I am tempted to pun, becomes the Cuban's **mojito ergo sum**.) The ironic sense of European or North American ideas re-encountered "*fora de lugar*" (out of place), in Roberto Schwartz's felicitous phrase, pervades much of Latin American literature. The novels of Manuel Puig allude to this out-of-placeness by reminding us of the ubiquitous presence of Hollywood films as cultural **lingua franca** in Latin America. Puig shows us a Latin America metaphorically "betrayed by Rita Hayworth" in that first-world cultural domination has engendered a feeling that real/reel life, to recycle a venerable pun, is somehow "elsewhere," to be found only in the cultural "centers" of Europe and North America, and not on the "periphery" of Argentina or Brazil.

While European anatomists of carnival tend to reduce it to a merely textual phenomenon, the Latin American or Caribbean artist is inevitably aware of carnival in its living, breathing, sweating reality. For while European carnivals have become pale memories of Rabelaisian frenzies of yore, carnival in Latin America – especially in those countries impregnated by the African culture brought by slaves – remains a vibrant and protean expression of a polyphonic culture. It was in part contact with popular festivals that led Carpentier to contrast Europe's labored attempts to resuscitate the marvelous with the quotidian magic of Latin American life.[22] The Latin American world, Carpentier suggests in *Concierto barroco*, seems like a fable to Europeans because "they've lost their sense of the fabulous."[23] The special relevance of Bakhtin's notion of the carnivalesque for Latin America goes beyond literary analysis and production, however, for in countries like Brazil or Trinidad carnival has formed an integral part of the very **theorization** of national identity and culture. Philosopher José Guilherme Merquior, in *Saudades do carnaval* (Nostalgia for Carnival, 1972), argues that the cultural substratum of Brazil is "orgiastic," since Brazil "entered into modern culture vaccinated against its anti-carnivalism."[24] Charles de Gaulle inadvertently echoed Merquior's judgment, but on a negative register, in his famous remark on visiting Brazil that *"ce n'est pas un pays serieux,"* to which many Brazilians responded "thank God." Oswald de Andrade, in his "Brazil-wood Manifesto" calls carnival the "religious ritual of the Brazil-wood race," where "Wagner is submerged by Carnival revelers."[25]

At the same time, this invocation of carnival is not meant to suggest a paradise of "happy natives:" carnival has both utopian and dystopian poles. The Latin American carnivalesque also inscribes the realities of genocide, imperialism, dictatorship, traced in key words of historical trauma like **genocídio**, **desaparecidos**, **golpe de estado**, **testimonios**, and **refugiados**. Just as carnival reaches its "highest level of madness" in Márquez's *One Hundred Years of Solitude*, for example, the "delicate balance" is broken, leaving "many dead and wounded lying on the square: nine clowns, four Columbines, seventeen playing-card kings, one devil, three minstrels, two peers of France, and three Japanese empresses" (pp. 191–2). The bloody celebration turns the public square into an Elizabethan stage littered, like a Shakespearean tragedy, with corpses.

The artistic audacity of the 1920s' modernist movement in Brazil, a movement which anticipated aspects of both postmodernity and postcoloniality, casts doubt on the diffusionist narrative whereby European modernism is seen, in a unidirectional manner, as inspiring Latin American modernism. The provincialism of the currently fashionable talk of "hybridity" and "syncretism," which is usually associated with Anglo-Indian "postcolonial" theory, forgets that artists/intellectuals in Latin America and the Caribbean were theorizing hybridity over half a century earlier. The "Modern Art Week" held in São Paulo in February

1922 was an attempt by Brazilian poets, novelists, musicians, and visual artists to break with the Europhile academicism of the time. The Brazilian movement not only called itself modernism (*Modernismo*), but also saw itself as allied to and conceptually parallel to European avant-garde movements like Futurism, Dada, and Surrealism. In two manifestos – "Manifesto of Brazil-wood Poetry" (1924) and "Cannibalist Manifesto" (1928) – Oswald de Andrade pointed the way to an artistic practice at once nationalist and cosmopolitan, nativist and modern. In the earlier text, de Andrade called for an "export-quality" art that would not borrow imported "canned" European models but would find its inspiration in everyday life and popular culture. Where colonialist discourse had posited the Carib as a ferocious cannibal, as diacritical token of Europe's moral superiority, Oswald called in the "Cannibalist Manifesto" for a revolution infinitely "greater than the French revolution," that is the "Carib revolution," without which "Europe wouldn't even have its meager declaration of the rights of man."[26] Nor was Brazil "behind" in the arts. Oswald de Andrade saluted Surrealism, in a self-mockingly patronizing and "stagist" manner, as the most successful "preanthropophagic" movement.

The "modernists" called for cultural "anthropophagy," a devouring of the techniques and information of the super-developed countries in order to better struggle against domination. Just as the aboriginal Tupinambá Indians of Brazil devoured their enemies in order to appropriate their force, the modernists argued, Brazilian artists and intellectuals should digest imported cultural products and exploit them as raw material for a new synthesis, thus turning the imposed culture back, transformed, against the colonizer. For the modernists, cannibalism was an authentic native tradition as well as a key metaphor for cultural independence. "Only cannibalism unites us," Oswald de Andrade proclaimed, "Tupi or not Tupi, that is the question." Oswald dated his Cannibal Manifesto 374 – "the year Bishop Sardinha was swallowed" – in reference to the historical deglutition by Brazilian Indians of their first Portuguese-supplied bishop. The metaphor of cannibalism, then, was not only a way for Brazilian "redskin" artists to thumb their noses at their own Europeanized literary "palefaces," but was also a carnivalized response to cultural colonialism. By comically underlining the cannibalistic nature of all processes of cultural assimilation, the modernists not only desacralized European models, they also desacralized their own cultural activities.[27] "Anthropophagy" assumes the inevitability of cultural interchange between Latin America and the metropolitan centers and the consequent impossibility of any nostalgic return to an originary purity. Since there can be no unproblematic recovery of national origins undefiled by alien influences, the artist in the dominated culture should not ignore the foreign presence but rather swallow it, carnivalize it, recycle it for national ends. "Anthropophagy," in this sense, can be seen as another name for Kristeva's "intertextuality" or Bakhtin's "dialogism" and "carnivalization," but this time recycled for the neo-colonial cultural context.

As we saw in our discussion of *Robinson Crusoe*, cannibalism as metaphor has a long history. In the Western tradition, it has often functioned as the very "name of the other," the ultimate marker of difference in a coded opposition of light/dark, rational/irrational, civilized/savage. But even within that tradition, some writers turned the cannibalist trope against Europe. The sixteenth-century philosopher Montaigne, in *Des cannibales* (based, ironically, on interviews with Brazilian Tupinambá Indians), argued that civilized Europeans were ultimately more barbarous than cannibals, since cannibals ate the flesh of the dead only to appropriate the strength of their enemies, while Europeans tortured and slaughtered in the name of a religion of love. The Montaigne example shows the reciprocity of cultural influence. The Tupinambá, visiting France in 1550, at a time when France was trying to found the colony of France Antartique in Rio de Janeiro bay, were brought back to France to perform in a kind of proto-Disneyworld in Rouen, where the Tupinambá staged their daily practices for the delectation of French observers, among them Montaigne, who then relays the critical comments of the Tupinambá on the class divisions of European life. As "deconstructors" *avant la lettre*, the Tupinambá exercised intellectual agency, interrogating through laughter Europe's class system and authoritarian monarchies.

A different kind of adaptation, Nelson Pereira dos Santos's *Como era gostoso meu Francês* (How Tasty Was My Little Frenchman, 1971), was based not on a novel but rather on sixteenth-century chronicles, to wit the sensationalist first-person travel accounts of the German Hans Staden and the French Huguenot Jean de Lery concerning their sixteenth-century voyages to Brazil. Dos Santos turns the German Hans Staden into the Frenchman Jean, and seeds the film with citations from the colonial archive (Abbé Thevet, Manoel da Nóbrega, Jose de Anchieta). *How Tasty* performs an "anthropophagic" critique of European colonialism. The Frenchman is captured by the Tupinambá and sentenced to death in response to massacres inflicted upon them by Europeans. Destined to be ritually executed and eaten, he is first given a wife, Sebiopepe (widow of one of the Tupinambá massacred by the Europeans), and is allowed to participate in the tribe's daily activities. As he is taken to his execution, the Frenchman refuses to follow the prepared ritual in Tupi, and instead says in French: "My people will avenge me, and no Indian will remain in the land." Shortly thereafter, the camera zooms into Sebiopepe's face as she devours

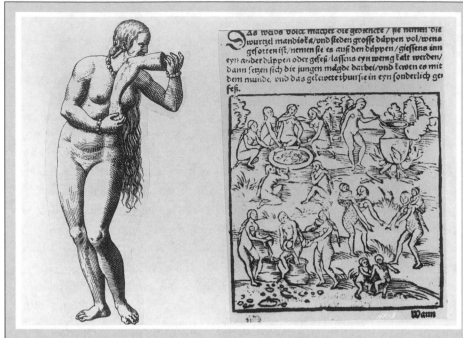

Figure 7.2 Nelson Pereira dos Santos's *How Tasty Was My Little Frenchman* (1971), produced by Condor Filmes / L.C. Produes Cinematograficas

her Frenchman, with no apparent regret despite her close relationship with him, an image which segues to a quotation from a report on genocide committed by Europeans.

In his deliciously unfaithful adaptation, Dos Santos subverts the conventional identification with the European protagonist of the captivity narrative. In the traditional narrative, the victim, usually a European, escaped to "tell the tale." But the film's title – *How Tasty Was My Little Frenchman* – implies an indigenous/anthropophagic perspective, while inverting the trope of ownership so that the European is now the slave. But, more generally, the film stages a didactic lesson in cultural relativism, indirectly posing Montaigne's question: "who are the real barbarians?" Ironically inverting the homogenizing convention by which Europeans perceive only generic Indians who "all look alike," here it is the Indians who cannot distinguish the French from the Portuguese. Relative nudity – relative because the Indian characters still wear ornaments, body paint, and tangas – becomes the cultural norm during the film. (Ironically, the film was rejected by the Festival in Cannes, the paradise of bikinis and semi-nude starlets, precisely because of its non-voyeuristic normalization of nudity, especially **male** nudity.) Throughout, the film systematically cuts off the conventional escape routes, maintaining an ironically neutral attitude toward the protagonist's deglutition. Here the European is the protagonist, but not the hero, and romantic love is less important than tribal loyalty.[28]

---------- The "Mother" of Magic Realism: *Macunaíma* ----------

Mário de Andrade's *Macunaíma*, written in 1928 and adapted for the cinema four decades later, formed the novelistic epitome of the modernist movement and a powerful (albeit rarely recognized) precursor of "magic realism."[29] Just as the European avant-garde became "advanced" by drawing on the "archaic" and "primitive," so Mário de Andrade drew on the "archaic" elements of indigenous Brazilian culture, elements less "pre-modern" (a term that embeds modernity as *telos*) than "para-modern." The distinction between archaic and modernist, in the case of *Macunaíma*, is non-pertinent as both modernism and indigenous narrative arts share a refusal of the conventions of mimetic realism. It is thus less a question of **juxtaposing** the archaic and the modern than of **deploying** the archaic in order, paradoxically, to modernize, in a dissonant temporality which combines a past imaginary communitas with an equally imaginary future utopia. *Macunaíma* is a brilliant example of what I would call "archaic (post)modernism," in that it uses the ancient myths of the Amazon within a proto-postmodernist collage aesthetic.

Although Mário de Andrade wrote *Macunaíma* in a week of jazz-like improvisation, the novel was the product of long and scrupulous preparation. An anthropologist and musicologist as well as composer, poet, and novelist, de Andrade compiled Amerindian, Luso-Brazilian and African legends to create *Macunaíma*. He called his text a "rhapsody" both in the musical sense of a free fantasy on an epic, heroic, or national theme and in the etymological sense of "stitcher" since the novel "stitches" tales to form a kind of artistic crazy-quilt. In what amounts to an anthology of Brazilian folklore, a miscegenated stew of mythologies, de Andrade combines oaths, nursery rhymes, proverbs, and elements of erudite literature with the indigenous legends collected by German anthropologist Theodor Koch-Grunberg in the headwaters of the Orinoco between 1911 and 1913 and published in his two-volume *Vom Roroima zum Orinoco: Ergebnisse einer Reise in Nord Bresilien und Venezuela in den Jahren 1911– 1913* in 1923.[30] The very language of the novel is syncretic, weaving African, indigenous, and Portuguese words; it is an imagined speech which carries the linguistic genes, as it were, of all the Indians, Africans, and European immigrants of Brazil.[31]

Macunaíma displays virtually all the Bakhtinian themes and devices – carnivalesque inversions, double-voiced parodic discourse, social and artistic heteroglossia, cultural and textual polyphony – to the point that the novel seems in retrospect almost to have been written expressly to elicit a Bakhtinian exegesis. Like *Gargantua* and *Pantagruel*, *Macunaíma* conflates two carnivalesque traditions: the erudite, literary tradition of the Menippea and the popular tradition of carnival as praxis. On the erudite side, *Macunaíma* is indebted to epic; indeed, critics called the novel a Brazilian *Odyssey*. More precisely, *Macunaíma* is affiliated both with the **comic** epic of Rabelais and with the indigenous romantic epic of Brazilian "Indianist" novelists such as Jose de Alencar. At the same time, the book is indebted to the European avant-garde and especially to the Surrealists, some of whom were the author's friends and whom he "invited" into the book as characters.

Mário de Andrade himself repeatedly claimed that he innovated nothing and that he was merely writing in the tradition of Apuleius, Petronius, Rabelais, and Lazarillo de Tormes, in short in the tradition of "Menippean satire." Indeed, Suzana Camargo has shown that *Macunaíma* features all of Bakhtin's "essential characteristics" of the Menippea.[32] To linger on just a few of those characteristics, the novel flaunts the freedom from historical limits and the liberty of philosophical invention typical of Menippean satire by having its "scene" bound improbably and without transition from the Amazon to the backlands of São Paulo in an impossible zigzag. The novel is also full of magical transformations, of characters changing color or dying and coming back to life, of animals metamorphosing into buildings or telephones and so forth. De Andrade also anachronistically mingles historical periods, facilitating what Bakhtin calls "the dialogue of the dead with the living," so that seventeenth-century characters, for example, rub elbows with contemporary ones. The novel also abounds in comic crownings and uncrownings, with sudden reversals of fortune which are in turn themselves reversed. This freedom of invention in the novel derives not only from the Menippea but also from the Amazonian legends themselves, with their heritage of totemic and animistic imagery. "Fish used to be people just like us," Macunaíma tells his brothers. A teeming rainforest of creativity, *Macunaíma* offers an "Amazonian" proliferation of narrative life forms. Indeed, in the world of this novel characters literally turn into stars, as they do in indigenous legends, becoming allegorical constellations to be deciphered by the amazed "readers" contemplating them from planet earth.

Rabelais's grotesque realism, for Bakhtin, evokes the collective voice of the people: "The material bodily principle is contained not in the biological individual, not in the bourgeois ego, but in the people, a people who are continually growing and renewed. This is why all that is bodily becomes grandiose, exaggerated, immeasurable."[33] Mário de Andrade's oxymoronic protagonist, by the same token, is a larger-than-life composite character, a summa of Brazil, who epitomizes the ethnic roots as well as the qualities and defects of an entire people. An amalgam of several heroes found in the American source-legends, his very name is oxymoronic, composed of the root "*maku*" (bad) and the suffix "*ima*" (great). Macunaíma," the hero without any character," as the novel's subtitle has it, lacks character not only in the conventional moral sense but also in lacking the psychological "coherence" of the autonomous ego and the sociological coherence of the verisimilar character. Ethnically, he is at once black, white, and Indian, and morally he is by turns selfish, generous, cruel, sensual, and tender. As a representative of "the grotesque body of the people" rather than a rounded personage, his character consists, as Mário de Andrade explained in a letter to Manuel Bandeira, in "not having any character and his logic . . . in not having any logic."[34]

Indeed, it is fascinating to note that just two years after the publication of *Macunaíma*, the Austrian novelist Robert Musil published an incomplete version of a novel – *The Man without Qualities* – whose title recalls the subtitle of *Macunaíma*. The Musil novel concerned a man lacking in any traits that would allow us to narrativize his life as a recognizable type, but in the Musil case there was no particular ethnic dimension to his quality-lessness, whereas *Macunaíma* stresses the ethnic/racial instability of its protagonist. Over fifty years later, Woody Allen produced his version of a "man without qualities" and a "hero without character" in his *Zelig*, a story about a bizarre chameleon man with an uncanny talent for taking on the accent and ethnicity of his interlocutors. Like *Macunaíma*, *Zelig* too revolves around a multi-ethnic protagonist who "condenses," as it were, the ambient ethnic polyphony. Both Zelig and Macunaíma undergo racial metamorphoses. Zelig is born white and Jewish but subsequently becomes Native American, black, Irish, Italian, Mexican, and Chinese. Anticipating the anti-essentialist critique of race, de Andrade's protagonist has no fixed racial identity. Born black to an Indian mother, he subsequently transforms himself into a white Portuguese prince and even into a French divorcée. Like Zelig, his oxymoronic character epitomizes ethnic interaction and hybridization. Both Macunaíma and Zelig play out all the three major positions within the racial triad typical of the Americas – red, black, and white. Their ethnic transformations underline the necessarily syncretic nature of the self within the context of the multi-ethnic metropolis. As walking polyphonies of cultural personalities, their metamorphoses render visible and palpable what usually remains invisible: the constant process of synchresis that occurs when ethnicities brush against and rub off on one another.

Both Mário de Andrade and Mikhail Bakhtin, without each other's knowledge, were elaborating theories of artistic "polyphony" in the 1920s. For Bakhtin, polyphony refers to the coexistence, in any textual or extra-textual situation, of a plurality of voices which do not fuse into a single consciousness but rather generate dialogical dynamism among themselves.[35] Mário de Andrade, in *A escrava que não e Isaura* (The Slave who is not Isaura, 1925) — the title's negative rejects the sentimental approach to slavery of Bernardo Guimarães's abolitionist novel *The Slave Isaura* — speaks of "*polifonismo*" as referring to the "theorization of certain procedures employed by certain modernist poets." "Poetic polyphony," for de Andrade, is "the simultaneous artistic union of two or more melodies whose temporary effects of sonorous conflict collaborate to create a total final effect," a definition not terribly distant from Bakhtin's.[36] And although neither Bakhtin nor de Andrade was thinking specifically of a polyphony of **ethnic** voices, an ethnic interpretation is in no way excluded by the term.[37]

The "autographed literature" of personal authorship, according to Bakhtin, is merely a drop in an ocean of anonymous folk literature. The novel *Macunaíma* exploits the anti-mimetic logic of folktales, which never pretend to be realist but rather tend to spatial and temporal indeterminacy. The characters of folktales, as Propp points out, lack psychological depth; they are "functions," instruments of action rather than interior revelation. *Macunaíma*, in a not insignificant coincidence, was published the same year as Propp's *Morphology of the Folk Tale*, in which Propp analyses Russian folktales into thirty-one "functions" or interchangeable incidents. In his *Morfologia de Macunaíma*, Brazilian poet-critic Haroldo de Campos applies the Proppian categories to the Mário de Andrade novel.[38] The logic of *Macunaíma*, he argues, is the logic of folktales, not the logic of individual tales but the logic of the processes by which the folk imagination constructs tales. Rather than mechanistically compile tales, de Andrade "interbreeds" them, so that characters from one body of legend (for example, Amerindian) perform actions taken from another body of legend (for example, African) so that the two traditions cross-fertilize each other. In *Macunaíma*, folktales become part of a productive *combinatoire* by which the collective language of the tribe is transformed into literary parole.[39]

The linguistic collage of *Macunaíma* constitutes what the author himself called a "veritable esperanto," a linguistic no-where borrowed from all regions of Brazil and ranging from the archaic to the neologistic. The novel exploits to the maximum the rich potentialities of Brazilian Portuguese. Weaving rhymed maxims ("Eat shit but never bet"), gnomic wisdom ("The whole marsh doesn't mourn when one crab dies"), and popular superstitions into a splendid verbal tapestry, *Macunaíma* taps the linguistic genius of the Brazilian people by fusing its jokes, legends, songs, nursery rhymes, and slang into a panfolkloric saga. By embracing what the modernists often called the "creative errors" of the people, the novel sounds a barbaric yawp of protest against a double colonization, first by colonizing Europe and second by the European-dominated cultural elite within Brazil. The novel captures the aphoristic cynicism of the people ("Every man for himself and God against everyone!), its sensitivity to injustice ("God gives nuts to people without teeth"), and its gift for nonsense ("Our hero closed his eyes so as not to see himself being eaten"). *Macunaíma* also carnivalizes language by comically exploiting linguistic incongruities: the author has his presumably illiterate protagonist learn Latin and Greek (in order to collect "dirty words") and compose a parodic letter in the chaste Portuguese of the epic poet Camões. In the world of *Macunaíma*, even monkeys speak Latin — "sic transit."

Carnivalesque art, since it sees its characters not as flesh and blood people but as abstract puppet-like figures, laughs at beatings, dismemberment, and even death. The cannibalism that pervades *Macunaíma* recalls that which pervades *Gargantua* and *Pantagruel*, where at one point Gargantua swallows six pilgrims with his salad, washing them down with a gulp of white wine. But it is all, ultimately, "*pour rire*" (to laugh). The Menippean comic tradition favors "ritual (cultic) indecency," in an atmosphere of "cheerful death . . . surrounded by food, drink, sexual indecencies and symbols of conception and fertility."[40] *Macunaíma* is full of macabre humor and comic mutilations. When Macunaíma becomes depressed over the loss of his lover Ci his brothers take him to a leper colony to "cheer him up." Just as Rabelais cherishes the image of the "cheerfully dying man" (for example, the poet Raminagrobis), and lists a series of "deaths from laughing," *Macunaíma* has its protagonist drop dead out of literal respect for the proverb "*caiu dente, é morte de parente*" (a tooth falls, a relative dies).

The carnivalesque transfers all that is spiritual, ideal, and abstract to the material level, to the sphere of earth and the body. By focusing on the shared physiological processes of bodily life — copulation, birth, eating, drinking, defecation — the carnivalesque aesthetic offers a temporary suspension of hierarchy and prohibition. Excrement, as a literal expression of the "lower bodily stratum," forms part of the fecund imagery of the grotesque. Old-time carnivals in

Europe featured the festive slinging of cow dung ("*le jeu de la merde*"), which was later sublimated into more refined forms of slapstick such as throwing talcum or water balloons and other amiable aggressions. Urine carries great dignity within the carnivalesque aesthetic. Gargantua urinates on the multitude, just as the child Macunaíma "pisses hot on his old mother, frightening the mosquitoes." Macunaíma is recurrently shat on by vultures and geese and all manner of fowl; within the novel's excremental vision feces enjoy auratic prestige.

The case of Mário de Andrade exemplifies some of the ambiguities of modernist attitudes toward race. Of mixed racial ancestry himself, the author culturally and phenotypically embodied the indigenous, African, and European inheritance. Conflicted about his identity in an age where "race men" were few and far between, Mário formed an unstable amalgam of black pride and "honorary" whiteness. Because of his position as a mixed-race Paulista from an artistic/intellectual milieu, the author was not always proud of his mixed identity.[41] Echoing another New World chameleon figure (and, like him, also gay) – Walt Whitman – Mário proclaimed that he contained multitudes: "I am three hundred, three hundred and fifty."[42] De Andrade had a proleptic intuition of what later was to be called "nomadic" and "palimpsestic" identity. In "Improvisations on the Sickness of America," written in 1928, the same year as *Macunaíma*, de Andrade spoke of the "red, black, and white strands" that wove his "harlequinade costume." His identity was self-declaredly multiple, at once indigenous, African, and European through ancestry, French through his schooling, and Italian because of his love of music.[43]

Mário de Andrade – and similar claims could be made about writers like Carpentier, Asturias, and Márquez – in some ways qualifies as one of James Clifford's "ethnographic surrealists,"[44] with the important difference that Mário was as much insider as outsider in relation to the cultures he studied and admired. His status as an anthropologist and musicologist became a way of probing his own roots as a mestizo Brazilian. Indeed, it was Mário de Andrade of all the modernists who demonstrated the greatest intimacy with African and Afro-Brazilian culture. *Macunaíma* is replete with references to African culture and legends, to Ogum and Exu, to Rei Nagô, to *babalaôs*, to Iemanjá, to Obatalá, to African dances like *Bamba Quere*, and to "Tia Ciata," the Bahian woman whose home was reportedly the site of the birth of Rio's samba. Indeed, one could argue that the poetic modalities of West African religion are themselves "magical realist," in that they combine the worlds of **orun** and **aiye**, of the spiritual and the terrestrial, linking the transcendent magic of trance and possession, whereby the spirit rides his or her "horse," with the mundane obligations

of color-coded dressing and spirit-oriented cuisine. Nor was de Andrade's intimacy with African culture merely bookish. De Andrade visited scores of *terreiros*
(*candomblé* temples) as part of his research on Afro-Brazilian music. And in *O
empalhador de passarinho*, he analyses the Northeastern *desafio* (rhymed poetic
challenge, which some see as a precursor of rap), insisting on the African as
well as the European (medieval) origins of the form.[45] In *Música de feitiçaria
no Brasil* (Witchcraft Music in Brazil), posthumously compiled from his notes,
de Andrade offers a global tour of music, both erudite and popular, European,
African, Asian, and Native American, insisting always on the dignity and complexity of non-European musical forms.

Macunaíma: The Film

Rarely has a film so brilliantly realized the artistic and political possibilities
of adaptation as the 1968 film adaptation of *Macunaíma* by Joaquim Pedro
de Andrade. Like the novel in its own period, the film crystallized for its historical moment a wide diversity of cultural energies. Just as the novel formed the
point of convergence of Brazilian popular culture and the European avant-gardes,
the adaptation condenses at least three major currents: the cinematic modernism
of Cinema Novo, the proleptic postmodernism of the pop movement called
"Tropicália," and the radical revolutionary politics of 1968 and tricontinental
Third Worldism, all mixed up with the international "counterculture" as
expressed within the harsh constraints of a US-supported Third World dictatorship. Made during the period of dictatorship that began with the coup d'état
in 1964, *Macunaíma* also constitutes a sterling example of adaptation as a trampoline for political critique within an extremely censorious situation.

 Of the two poles of the cannibalist metaphor – the positive pole of aboriginal
matriarchy and communalism and the negative pole of the exploitative Social
Darwinism implicit in savage capitalism – Joaquim Pedro de Andrade's 1968
adaptation of *Macunaíma* clearly emphasizes the negative pole.[46] Fusing the themes
of Oswald de Andrade's modernism with the theme of cannibalism that runs through
Macunaíma, the director turns cannibalism into the springboard for a critique
of repressive military rule and of the predatory capitalist model of the short-
lived Brazilian "economic miracle." In a preface written for the Venice Film
Festival, the director offered some basic background for the non-Brazilian spectator, providing a kind of cannibalistic hermeneutic to help viewers decode the
Rabelasian *paroles gelées* (frozen words) of the film:

Full Circle: From Cervantes to Magic Realism

Chapter 7

Figure 7.3 Grande Otelo in *Macunaíma* (1968), produced by Condor Filmes / Films do Serra / Grupu

Cannibalism is an exemplary mode of consumerism adopted by underdeveloped peoples. In particular, the Brazilian Indians, immediately after having been "discovered" by the first colonizers, had the rare opportunity of selecting their Portuguese-supplied bishop, Dom Pedro Fernandes Sardinha, whom they devoured in a memorable meal. It is not by accident that the revolutionary artists of the 1920s – the Modernists – dated their Cannibal Manifesto "the year Bishop Sardinha was swallowed." Today we can clearly note that nothing has changed. The traditionally dominant, conservative social classes continue their control of the power structure – and we rediscover cannibalism . . . The present work relationships, as well as the relationships between people – social, political and economic – are still, basically, cannibalistic. Those who can, "eat" others through their consumption of products, or even more directly in sexual relationships. Cannibalism has merely institutionalized and cleverly disguised itself . . . Meanwhile, voraciously, nations devour their people. *Macunaíma* . . . is the story of a Brazilian devoured by Brazil.

In *Macunaíma*, the cannibalist theme announced in the preamble is treated in all its variations: people so hungry they eat themselves; an ogre who treats Macunaíma to a piece of his leg; the urban guerrilla who devours him sexually;

the cannibal-giant-capitalist Pietro Pietra who cooks up an anthropophagous soup; the capitalist's wife who wants to eat him alive; and finally the man-eating siren who lures him to his death. The film shows the rich devouring the poor, and the poor, in desperation, devouring each other. The Left, meanwhile, while being devoured by the Right, purifies itself by eating itself, a practice which Joaquim Pedro de Andrade calls the "cannibalism of the weak."[47]

Like its source novel, *Macunaíma* offers many features associated with carnivalization and Menippean satire. The first narrated words (in both film and novel) – "In the depths of the virgin-forest was born Macunaíma, hero of his people" – signal entry into the carnivalized world of comic epic. The images convey what Bakhtin calls "the grotesque body of the people." An improbably old white woman (played by male actor Paulo José) stands and grunts until she/he deposits a wailing 50-year-old black "baby" (Grande Otelo) on the ground. The expression on the "mother's" face recalls Bakhtin's description of the grotesque body in Rabelais: "The gaping mouth, the protruding eyes, sweat, trembling, suffocation, the swollen face" have "the meaning of the act of birth."[48] Rather like Gargantua, born during a maternal bout of severe diarrhea, provoked by his mother's having eaten "too much tripe," the film's protagonist is virtually shat into existence. The film offers as well the "violent contrasts" of the Menippea: the man/woman "mother" (reminiscent of Bakhtin's "pregnant hag"), the adult "baby" or **puer rex**, the black/white "family. At once prodigious and grotesque, the birth itself encapsulates what Bakhtin sees as a privileged carnival image: the old, near death, giving bloody birth to the fresh and the new.

The overture sequence also performs the *mise-en-scène* of cultural miscegenation. The names of the family members – Macunaima, Jiguê, Manaape – are native Brazilian, but the family is at once black, Indian, and European. The decor and costumes, meanwhile, are syncretic, culturally miscegenated. The hut, which serves as maternity ward, is half backlander and half Indian, while the manner of giving birth, in a standing position to take advantage of the force of gravity, is Indian. At the same time, the institution of the family is desentimentalized and comically degraded through a Jarryesque *Ubu*-like approach. Instead of the customary exclamations at the newborn's "cuteness," the family reacts to the hero's birth with "How ugly!" and "He stinks!" The film further underlines the family's surreal kinship relations by having the same actor (Paulo José) play both the original "mother" of Macunaíma and Macunaíma himself (in his later white incarnation), while another actor (Grande Otelo) plays both the first and the second black Macunaímas. Thus the white Macunaíma gives birth to the black Macunaíma who is magically transformed into the white Macunaíma who marries Ci the guerrilla and thus fathers another black Macunaíma.

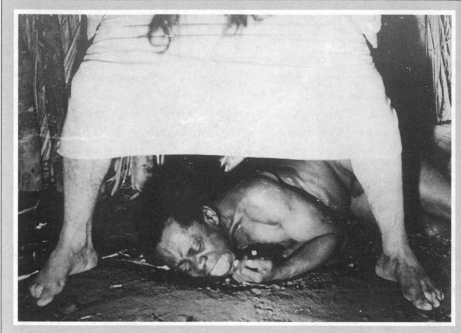

Figure 7.4   The birth of the hero in *Macunaíma* (1968), produced by Condor Filmes / Films do Serra / Grupu

The logic of carnival is that of the world turned upside down, in which the powerful are mocked and ridiculous kings are enthroned and then dethroned in an atmosphere of gay relativity. The most powerful figure in *Macunaíma* – the Ubuesque industrial magnate and people-eater Pietro Pietra – is repeatedly enthroned and dethroned. In his purple smoking jacket and with his green boxer shorts covering his padded buttocks, he looks very much like the burlesque Lord of the Revels, the *"Rei Momo"* who reigns over Brazil's carnival. Graced with multinational names and an Italian accent, the Pietro Pietra figure referred in the novel to the Italian *nouveaux riches* capitalists of the 1920s, but in the film he embodies the dependent national bourgeoisie with its second-hand American technology. In Pietro's kitsch palace, rococo clocks and breathing mannequins co-habit with Egyptian sphynxes. He wrestles with Macunaíma over an amulet whose traditional folkloric role was to guarantee fishing and hunting (i.e. prosperity). As a millionaire who wants to eat Macunaíma, the hero of his people, Pietro conjures up the "multinational" economic giants who devour Brazil and its resources. But even Macunaíma, despite his victory over Pietro, is also ultimately dethroned. After feeling the "immense satisfaction" of defeating the giant, he dissipates his advantage by returning to the jungle with the useless electronic bric-à-brac of consumer civilization. Thus the film's carnivalized critique also includes the "hero" as well, revealed, as Ismail Xavier points out, to be almost as selfish and individualist as his enemy Pietro Pietra, hardly a viable agent of progressive change.[49] Unlike the urban guerrilla Ci, who at least takes up arms against established power – the director called her "the most positive figure in the film" – Macunaíma is merely a hustler (**malandro**) without any coherent political project. In the final sequence, as Xavier points out, he incarnates the figure of the "Jeca Tatu," the toothless hillbilly created by Monteiro Lobato.[50]

Macunaíma draws on the broad, farcical performance in the vaudeville and **chanchada** traditions. Grande Otelo has the nasal whine of the spoiled child as he screams "**Mae**" into his mother's ears. Manaape is missing teeth so he pronounces every syllable. The Italo-Brazilian Pietro Pietra has the stentorian voice of opera at its most grandiloquent. Literally fat-assed, he seems to be carrying a suspicious load in his pants. Speaking more generally, the voices are larger and louder and more raucous than in life, often consisting of "paralinguistic" grunts and groans and shouts. The actors perform less with their faces – the privileged site of individual psychology – than with their entire bodies. The director gives them the space and time to "act out" by stretching the shots in duration and opening them up in terms of space. They act low to the ground, often with legs bent. Repeatedly, they get down on all fours like animals: Jiguê scampering through the mud of the magic fountain, Macunaíma prowling like a wild boar just as he is lying about a wild boar; Macunaíma speaking like a parrot as he speaks to a parrot. Here we have Bakhtin's self-transforming body, the body in the act of becoming.

Macunaíma was predictably censured by critics ignorant of the geneology of this Menippean tradition for its "bad taste," an irrelevant category for a carnivalesque aesthetic since it invokes exactly what is being derided.[51] The director himself described the film as intentionally in "execrable taste . . . innocently filthy like the jokes of children."[52] But however grotesque or fantastic, the carnivalesque aesthetic here retains a certain realism which addresses everyday life and contemporary events. In this sense, the film lampoons a host of satiric targets. These include the political repression triggered by the 1964 and 1968 "coups d'état" – "suspicious attitude," explains the plainclothes policeman as he arrests Macunaíma – as well as the rampant consumerism inherent in the dominant Brazilian economic model. The film also subtly critiques Brazilian racism, something about which the novel's mulatto author was doubtless personally aware.

When the white brother Manaape explains why his black brother Jiguê was singled out for arrest, he reminds Jiguê of the Brazilian proverb (reminiscent of the African-American "If you're black, stay back"): "a white man running is a champion; a black man running is a thief." And when the white Macunaíma speaks disparagingly of "that mulatto guy," Jiguê objects: "So now that you're white you've become a racist!" When Manaape and Jiguê, living in a *favela*, hint that Macunaíma should invite them into his spacious new home, Macunaíma responds with the proverb: "One is too few, two is great, but three is a mess." In social-allegorical terms, Macunaíma, "whitened" by money and class ascension, turns his back on his poorer *favelado* brothers. Yet even white Macunaíma cannot finally escape his originary blackness; the son born to him and to the equally white Ci, the urban guerrilla, is black (again, Grande Otelo), as if literalizing the proverbial trope of the "foot in the kitchen" (i.e. the presumed partial African ancestry of virtually all Brazilians).

The *umbanda* sequence in the film, based on the "macumba" chapter in the novel, weds the magic of trance religions to the magic of montage. A female medium "picks up" the cannibal giant's spirit; as Macunaíma beats her up, all the blows are transferred to the giant. In the novel Macunaíma goes to a Rio *terreiro* to ask for the protection of an *orixá*. He dances and is consecrated as a son of Exu, a perfectly appropriate *orixá* for a semiotic shape-shifter like Macunaíma. (For Henry Louis Gates in *The Signifying Monkey*, Exu figures the semiotic and translating process itself.) In the novel, Andrade invites a number of Brazilian modernists and European Surrealists (Manuel Bandeira, Blaise Cendrars, Raul Bopp) to the *terreiro*; in fact, he calls them all *macumbeiros* (practitioners of Afro-Brazilian trance religions), thus highlighting again the Brazilian literalization of European avant-garde metaphors.

The novel is replete with magical transformations: the hero variously transforms himself into a French prostitute, a leaf ant, a drop of water, and several varieties of fish. When Pietro Pietra chops up Macunaíma for his cannibalistic feijoada (black bean stew), the hero's brothers reassemble his scraps, wrap him in banana leaves and blow smoke on the ensemble to bring him back to life. But the film generally downplays these transformations, shifting the film's aesthetic in the direction of the social realism of Cinema Novo. (Only the animated cartoon, or some high-tech cybernetic morphing, might do justice to the magical metamorphoses of the novel.)

The film does feature two sequences of racial transformation, however; in both, the black Macunaíma (Grande Otelo) turns into the white Macunaíma (Paulo José). But the question of race almost inevitably plays itself out differently in the film as opposed to the novel. In the novel, Macunaíma is transformed into

Figure 7.5 The about-to-be-transformed Macunaíma in *Macunaíma* (1968), produced by Condor Filmes / Films do Serra / Grupu

a "**príncipe lindo**" (a comely prince); there is no racial specification. The film, in contrast, must choose actors to play roles, and actors come equipped with racial traits. Thus the fable-like, open-ended evocativeness of "comely prince" gives way in the film to the physical presence of two actors: the Euro-Brazilian Paulo José, and the Afro-Brazilian Grande Otelo.

In any case, in the first sequence of racial transformation, Macunaíma and Jiguê's girlfriend Sofará (Joanna Fomm) go into the woods to set a trap for a tapir. Sofará lights a marijuana joint and gives it to Macunaíma; one puff turns him into a handsome prince. (The joint led some non-Brazilian spectators to see *Macunaíma*, mistakenly, as a "psychedelic" film.) The pair romp in the woods as we hear an old carnival song ("Peri and Ceci") which references the characters from the Indianist novel *O Guarani*, where Peri is the noble savage Indian and Ceci the Euro-Brazilian woman with whom Peri is in love. As Randal Johnson points out in his illuminating study, the sequence, occasionally misread as racist by North American audiences, is in fact a satirical barb directed at the Brazilian "economic miracle" of the late 1960s.[53] Sofará, the European "Ceci" of the allegory, is dressed in an "Alliance for Progress" sack. Her magic cigarette, i.e. American intervention, has turned Macunaíma, hero of his people, into a papier-mâché prince, just as the "economic miracle" touted by the military junta supposedly turned Brazil into an apparently prosperous nation. In fact, the prosperity was short-lived, consisting largely of a brutal transfer of wealth from bottom to top, and soon gave way to a record national debt and widespread accusations of official corruption and giveaways to transnational (mainly North American) corporations.

The second sequence of racial transformation can best be read as a sardonic comment on Brazil's putative "racial democracy" and the "ideology of whitening." The sequence illustrates a common folktale about the origin of racial diversity, one in which everyone in the world is born black but where a step into the water filling a footprint left by Saint Thomas turns people white. (One of Joel Chandler Harris's Uncle Remus stories – "Why the Negro is Black" – tells a similar tale in a North American context.) In the novel, Macunaíma is born black but becomes white after touching the water, but he so muddies the water that Jiguê, who bathes second, becomes a red-skinned Indian; even less water is left for Manaape, who can only lighten his palms and the soles of his feet. The film eliminates the red Indian as intermediate stage. When the black Macunaíma enters a magic fountain that turns him white, the soundtrack plays the Portuguese version of "By a Waterfall," taken from the Lloyd Bacon musical *Footlight Parade* (1933), a film whose musical numbers were directed by Busby Berkeley. The choice seems uncannily apt when we recall that the original diegetic inspiration for the "By a Waterfall" number was the sight of black children playing with the water spurting from a Harlem hydrant, which suggests to the James Cagney character the spectacular possibilities of waterfalls splashing on **white** bodies. The allusion is richly suggestive, evoking not only a complex play of black and white but also the relation between the American musical comedy and Brazil's carnivalized musicals, called **chanchadas**, the genre in which Grande Otelo, the actor who plays Macunaíma, was the most famous star. Thus the adaptation not only updates the novel in terms of its sociopolitical context, but also "interbreeds" the novel with a whole series of other intertexts – from the **chanchada** and the Hollywood musical, to pop music and the counter-culture.

The case of *Macunaíma* illustrates some of the pitfalls inherent in cross-cultural readings of film adaptations. A reading oriented by a search for "positive" ethnic images, for example, would be disastrously inappropriate with *Macunaíma*. Like the novel, the film transforms the ultimate negative stereotype – cannibalism – into a positive artistic resource. Given *Macunaíma*'s raucously Rabelaisian aesthetic, it would be misguided to look to it for "positive images," or even for conventional realism. Virtually all the film's characters are two-dimensional grotesques rather than rounded three-dimensional characters, and the grotesquerie is democratically distributed among all the races, while the most archly grotesque characters are the white industrialist cannibal and his ghoulish spouse. *Macunaíma* provides an object lesson in the cultural relativity of spectatorship. In Brazil, a number of factors militate against a reading of the film as racist. First, Brazilians of all races tend to see Macunaíma as representing themselves and their national personality rather than some racial "other;" they see both the black and the white Macunaímas as a national rather than as a racial archetype. In Brazil, the film is not made to bear such a strong "burden of representation" as it might elsewhere. Second, Brazilians would likely be aware of the novel's status as a national classic (never accused of being racist) by a Brazilian of mixed race. Third, Brazilian viewers are likely to be more familiar with Grande Otelo as a performer who has played an enormous variety of roles.

Despite the grim underlying message of its allegory, in aesthetic terms the film *Macunaíma* renewed contact with carnival and the *chanchada*, the Rio-based musical comedies of the 1940s and 1950s. The chanchadas were literally linked to carnival, in that they featured carnival songs and were timed to be released at carnival, and figuratively linked to the cultural universe of the carnivalesque. The film proliferates in the sexual inversions common in carnival and in the *chanchadas*: Paulo José in drag giving birth to the protagonist, Macunaíma costumed as a French divorcée; and the giant himself bathing in a Hollywood bubblebath of the kind usually reserved for starlets. The renewed contact with the *chanchada* takes many forms, most notably through the casting of key *chanchada* actors like Grande Otelo and Zezé Macedo, but also through the inclusion of songs popular from the *chanchada* period. The socially conscious recycling of *chanchada*-style humor and irreverence enabled *Macunaíma* to realize a goal long unattained by Cinema Novo directors: the reconciliation of political and aesthetic modernism with popular box-office appeal. At the same time, the film rejected the implicitly rosy social vision of the *chanchada* by refusing the shallow utopianism of the *chanchada*'s conventional happy endings. In *Macunaíma*, the ideal of the hustler-trickster-hero typical of the *chanchada* is revealed to be a social dead-end.

The "cheerful death" of Menippean satire, claims Bakhtin, is "always surrounded by food, drink, sexual indecencies and symbols of conception and fertility."[54] Two sequences in *Macunaíma* brilliantly encapsulate this spirit. One is the sumptuous banquet-wake for Macunaíma's mother. As the family gorges itself and wails for the departed mother, Macunaíma is "consoled" by Sofara, his brother's girlfriend, whose ass the "child" begins to stroke lustily, thus illustrating what Bakhtin calls the "tight matrix of death with laughter, with food, with drink, with sexual indecency."[55] The other sequence features a party given by Pietro Pietra in celebration of his daughter's wedding, for which the cannibalistically inclined Pietra has devised a festive lottery in which the winners are thrown into a pool of fragmented bodies and (presumably) voracious fish. A close look at the pool reveals it to be an anthropophagic "*feijoada*" in which human limbs stand in for sausage. Macunaíma tricks Pietro into falling in, and as he is being devoured, the cheerfully dying giant shouts that the *feijoada* "needs more salt."

Adaptation sometimes becomes a way of dodging the constraints of censorship or even dictatorship. The film *Macunaíma*, in this sense, is an absolutely brilliant exercise in the political and aesthetic updating of a novelistic source. The filmmakers outwitted the regime's censors through a number of stratagems: (1) an appeal to the classic status of the novel, which was read in high schools all over Brazil; (2) the strategic garnering of prestigious prizes and favorable reviews in Europe and North America; and (3) the deployment of comic-allegorical strategies. The filmmakers also used decoy nudity, i.e. gratuitous sequences featuring female nudity which the censors, who were generally not very intelligent but who could at least recognize nudity when they saw it, could cut without compromising the larger project.[56] *Macunaíma* appealed to the anarchistic sentiments of the Brazilian people, nourishing feelings of revolt through outrageously satiric festivity even at the height of dictatorship. The film establishes a tangential relation with another innovative 1960s' cultural movement – "Tropicália" – through the anthropophagic theme and technique as well as in the emphasis on camp, on the lack of national character, and in the *mélange* of high-art tradition and mass-mediated culture. Yet its ultimate allegiance is with the allegorical strategies of Cinema Novo, with its desire to make a broadly symbolic critique of the Brazilian situation, but here performed with an oblique humor and cunning which caught even the regime's censors off-guard.

Magic Realism à la Brésilienne

Brazilian cinema since the 1960s has proliferated in moments that might be described as "magical realist." Glauber Rocha's *Idade da terra* (1978), for example, features four Christ figures, each of a different ethnicity. Other magical realist moments form part of adaptations of works that, while not part of the magic realist movement per se, nevertheless do share some of its features. The various adaptations based on the novels of Jorge Amado, for example, proliferate in magical or supernatural moments where the spirits of Afro-Brazilian religion descend into the narrative and transform it. In Nelson Pereira dos Santos's adaptation of Amado's *Tent of Miracles*, for example, the Afro-Brazilian cultural hero Pedro Arcanjo, a turn-of-the-century researcher into Afro-Brazilian culture, defends the black spiritual inheritance of **candomblé** against the then fashionable racist theories of Social Darwinist professors. Both the novel and the film, interestingly, show solidarity with **candomblé** by endorsing "magical" explanations of supernatural events, for example the incident where the spirits of the **orixás** disarm the police who try to repress African religious expression.

A number of Brazil's "magic realist" films adopt the work of the novelist Guimarães Rosa, whose complex, esoteric, and "baroque-modernist" texts led to his being called the "James Joyce of the backlands." Rosa's influence on the cinema sometimes took the form of adaptation – as with Roberto Santos's *A hora e a vez de Augusto Matraga* (The Time and Hour of Augusto Matraga, 1965), Pedro Bial's *Outras estorias* (Other Stories, 1999), and *Diadorim*, a TV series based on Rosa's *Grande sertão: veredas* (translated into English as *The Devil to Play in the Backlands*). Bial's version weaves together five stories from the collection *First Stories*, while also mixing genres (adventure story, erotic romance) and formats: computer graphics and digital images try to shape the cinematic correlatives of Rosa's innovative language and style. But at times Rosa's influence is more diffuse and subtle. For example, the spirit of Rosa's *Grande sertão: veredas*, a transposition of the Faust story into the Brazilian interior, informs the symbology and solemnity of Rocha's backlands epic *Black God White Devil*. Both Rosa and Rocha drew on Euclides da Cunha's classic text *Os sertões* (Rebellion in the Backlands) and its depiction of the historical confrontation between backlanders and government troops at Canudos at the turn of the century, but in Rocha the labyrinthine literary techniques of Rosa turn into winding camera movements and the exasperated sound track of *Black God White Devil*.

In his adaptation of Rosa's *A terceira margem do rio* (The Third Bank of the River, 1993), Nelson Pereira dos Santos ingeniously "stitches" diverse stories by its source author. Beginning with the story which provides the title for the film – the virtually wordless drama of a man who abandons his family to live on a boat in the middle of a river – dos Santos integrates four other stories. Liojorge (Ilya São Paulo), the son (in dos Santos's recreation) of the enigmatic boatman of the first story, follows an enchanted cow, and thus becomes the protagonist of another story (*Seqüência*) in which the cow leads him to the most beautiful woman in the world (Sonja Saurin). From their romance is born the miracle-working saint Nhinhinha (Barbara Brandt) from still another story (*A menina de lá*). But the family is then persecuted by an evil group of brothers evocative of corrupt policemen or "death squads" – the Dagobe brothers, one of whom desires Nhinhinha, from yet another story. To get rid of him, Liojorge calls the philosopher-assassin (Jofre Soares) from still another story (*Fatalidade*). Feeling threatened, the family flees to Brasilia. The postcard vision of the magnificent buildings of the city – concretizations of official baroque modernity – gives way to scenes of squalor reminiscent of the *favelas* of Rio. Apart from interweaving different source stories, *The Third Bank of the River* also mixes distinct styles and motifs from dos Santos's own oeuvre. As long as the film takes place in the interior of the country, the film remains close both to Rosa's mythic-rural literary universe and to the *sertão* of dos Santos's own *Vidas secas*. (The mother is played by Maria Ribeiro, the Vitoria of the earlier dos Santos film.) The communication between the son and the mysterious river-loving father, for example, is delicately evoked as an asymmetrical dialogue; we see that the father's plate has been emptied, but we never see the father. But when the family moves to the periphery of Brasilia, the spectator moves with them from rural fantasy into a version of urban squalor reminiscent of that portrayed in dos Santos's other films like *Rio 40 graus* (1954), *Rio zona norte* (1957), and *Amuleto de Ogum* (1974). Magical effects, not all of them effectively done, characterize both sections, however. Nhinhinha engenders many Márquez-style metamorphoses: she conjures up rain and frogs during a drought; candy moves out of the TV screen into the mouths of waiting spectators; a samba school materializes mysteriously. But the film reveals the limits of magical solutions: a close shot showing Nhinhinha giving out candy to children opens up to reveal an infinite line of desperately waiting children. A pessimistic undercurrent infiltrates the magic realism; no one seems safe anymore, whether in the city or in the *sertão*.

Márquezian Magic

Magic realism was linked to the cinema long before it was adapted in films. Many of the figures from "the boom" were involved with film – Borges's first exercises in fiction derived from von Sternberg's films, Manuel Puig studied filmmaking, Fuentes, Cabrera Infante, and Cortazar all wrote film scripts or film reviews. But the phrase "magic realism" has been especially linked to Colombian writer Gabriel Garcia Márquez. Márquez's life and work were always intimately linked to the cinema. Indeed, Márquez famously compared his relationship with

film to that of an ill-matched couple who "can't live with, or without" one another.
As a young journalist in the mid-1950s, Márquez was sent to Rome to do film criticism, but ended up studying filmmaking at the Centro Sperimentale, where he met Cesare Zavattini and Vitorio de Sica. Moved by de Sica's *Miracle in Milan* (1951), Márquez praised the film in terms anticipatory of his own magic realism: "The story of *Miracle in Milan* is a fairy tale, but one realized in a surprising milieu, mingling in a brilliant way the real and the fantastic, to the point that, in many cases, it is impossible to know where one ends and the other begins."[57]

In Mexico in the early 1960s, Márquez collaborated with Carlos Fuentes on *El gallo de oro*, based on a short story by Juan Rulfo. While working as a film critic for *El Espectador* in Bogota, Márquez wrote a script entitled *Tiempo de morir*, subsequently filmed by Mexican director Arturo Ripstein, a director who had begun his career as an assistant to Luis Buñuel. Márquez also wrote a short "cinematic" story – *El coronel no tiene quien le escriba* (No One Writes the Colonel) – also subsequently filmed by Ripstein. Márquez worked as well on three film scripts with Buñuel's screenwriter, Luis Alcoriza. But in 1966, Márquez dramatically abandoned the cinema, deciding to write the "unfilmable" novel which turned out to be *One Hundred Years of Solitude*. In a *Playboy* interview, Márquez declared that he would never allow the novel to be filmed.[58] His reasoning was apparently based on the venerable notion of the novel as uniquely verbal, virtual, and phantasmatic. Although producers had offered him two million dollars, he revealed, he preferred to let readers go on seeing the characters as they had imagined them.

Márquez ultimately returned to the cinema in 1986, founding, funding, and presiding over the Third World Film School in San Antonio de los Banos, Cuba. Within two years, a number of adaptations (mostly co-productions with Spain) based on Márquez's work (and with his collaboration) emerged: notably *Un senor muy viejo con alas enormes* (An Old Man with Enormous Wings), directed by Argentinian director Fernando Birri; *El verano feliz de la Senora Forbes*, directed by the Mexican Jaime Humberto Hermosillo; *Fabula de la bella palomera*, directed by Rui Guerra; *Cartas del parque*, directed by Tomas Gutierrez Alea; and *Milagro en Roma*, directed by Lisandro Duque Naranjo.

Here I will discuss just a few of these films. *An Old Man with Enormous Wings*, published by Márquez in 1972 and filmed by Fernando Birri (with Márquez as co-scriptwriter) in 1988, exploits the typical magic realist technique of "implanting" the extraordinary within the quotidian, here in the form of an earthbound, flesh-and-blood angel. Both the short story and the film tell the tale of a Caribbean every-couple, Pelayo and Elisana, who live in a rickety house by the sea. After brightly colored *faux naïf* cartoonish credits, the film begins with a wild storm that sends crabs crawling into the couple's house, while the titular "old man with enormous wings" and matted hair scrambles from the waves onto the rocks of their back yard. Not particularly surprised by this apparition – we are, after all, in the deadpan world of magical realism – the couple lodge him in their chicken coop, where villagers come to gawk at him. "Long Live the Angel!" the villagers cry, and add: "And Maradona too!" The local priest speaks to the old man in Latin but the old man remains mute. The priest immediately asks the Vatican for advice; the Vatican suggests that he check if the angel has a navel, and whether he speaks an ancient dialect of Aramaic. With commercial good sense, the couple decides to charge admission for a glimpse of the earth-bound angel. Some neighbors offer him camphor, "the favorite food of angels." The winged man provokes a wide range of reactions. To some he is an angel, to others a demon or an "albino vampire," and to still others he is Elvis Presley come back from the dead. Some speculate that he is an invading Martian from Miami preparing to invade Cuba – a clear allusion to right-wing Cuban exiles in the United States. The angel's appearance triggers a process of popular fabulation and exaggeration, a lower-class form of "magic realism," where a grain of truth is embroidered with magic and hyperbole and the supernatural, like the angel, is brought down to earth. The magic, in the Birri film, is conveyed not through the "magic" of editing but rather through the more domestic tactic of costume design – the man's enormous wings – resulting in a kind of domestication of the fantastic. We recall that Birri was the founder of the Santa Fe documentary film school in Argentina, and the style of the film is that of a documented dream.

Bit by bit a wild fairground develops around the winged man, where popular entertainments, such as the **nueva trova** singer Pablo Milanes, mingle with palm-reading, lotteries, and religious miracles, all in an atmosphere of popularesque hysteria. The Catholic Church is here portrayed as a relatively unpopular purveyor of obsolescent forms of entertainment. The priest is portrayed as a voyeur, who uses binoculars to spy on the shaking breasts of a local woman. But the winged man is ultimately upstaged by the arrival of a woman who has been transformed into a spider for having disobeyed her parents. Attracted to this new, more melodramatic spectacle, the public quickly loses interest in the old man. In his essay "For an Imperfect Cinema," Cuban filmmaker/theorist Julia Garcia Espinosa argued that the cinema should invigorate itself with the energies of just this kind of popular entertainment. At the same time, the fairground mixes cynical commodification with intimations of transcendence, serving a people desperate for miracles. The cinema, itself, we are reminded, grew up in the shadow of the sideshow, quite literally situated next to the fairground and the penny arcade, and offering the regressive pleasures of commercial carnivals.

Narrated in the third person but successively adopting the points of view of diverse characters, the Márquez story exploits the typically magic realist technique of inversion, whereby the marvelous and the everyday exchange places; the supernatural becomes banal and vice versa. The village doctor, for example, is amazed at the naturalness of the angel's wings, to the point that he wonders why all human beings were not born with wings. At the same time, the sudden but ephemeral commercial "successes" of the winged man and the spider woman, while on a literary level reminiscent of the transformations of the Menippea, on a more historical level, recall the "booms" and "busts" of Latin American economies, and even the sometimes commercialized "boom" of magical realism itself.

An admirer of the gigantism of Rabelais, Márquez saw Latin American reality as always already "out of proportion." In his writing, he concocted tales replete with magical events – flying carpets, telekinesis, living corpses, wild portents – in a new Adamic world where "things still lacked names." The novel *One Hundred Years of Solitude* relates a century in the history of one family, in whose lives the fantastic and the everyday intermingle promiscuously, where realities like Jose Arcadio's village of Macondo vanish into the thin air of illusion. When an insomnia epidemic invades Macondo, its residents lose the capacity to separate dream from reality. This blurring of the oneiric and the factual also has a political dimension. When a strike is repressed by the owners of a banana plantation, the powers-that-be impose their "dream" on the population, who are obliged to accept the fiction that the police never really fired on the demonstrators and that consequently the casualties they had witnessed did not actually take place.

Despite Márquez's original prohibition, there have been many adaptations of *One Hundred Years of Solitude*. Brazilian director Rui Guerra's *Erendira* (1983) provides a particularly effective example. A co-production funded from Brazilian, Mexican, and German sources, *Erendira* was originally written by Márquez as a screenplay. When the prospects for a film version began to fade, Márquez placed a mention of the story in *One Hundred Years of Solitude*, while also refashioning the materials of the screenplay into two works of prose fiction – a novella (*The Sad Story of Innocent Erendira and her Diabolical Grandmother*) and a short story (*Death Constant Beyond Love*). By the time Guerra was chosen to direct a film version, Márquez had lost the original screenplay and had to write a new script based on the existing works of fiction and on his memories of the screenplay.

Both Rui Guerra and Márquez come from rich, ethnically "polyphonic" cultural backgrounds. Born in Mozambique, Guerra studied filmmaking at the Institute des Hautes Etudes Cinematographique in Paris, but has always been identified with the Cinema Novo of his adopted country Brazil, while Márquez is associated with the mestizo culture of the Caribbean coast of Colombia. Like Márquez, Guerra too has always mobilized the fantastic in the service of an underlying realism. His tropicalist *The Gods and the Dead* (1970), for example, combines a realistic portrayal of the historical "Wars of the Colonels" in the backlands of Brazil with an allegorical style incorporating popular legends and theatrical exaggeration. With its gaudily painted rivers and exuberant artifice, that film might have easily been an adaptation of a Márquez novel – even though Guerra had not read Márquez at the time – with the Brazilian Northeast standing in for Márquez's legendary Macondo. As Claudia Cabezon Doty points out, *Erendira* touches on many of Márquez's favorite themes: the solitude of the tyrant, the power-hungry matriarch, the use of simulacral artifice as part of political demagoguery, all against a backdrop of Third World misery, here encapsulated by the niece Erendira.[59]

The lengthy title of the Márquez novella evokes eighteenth-century picaresque fiction, and the Guerra adaptation pursues the picaresque through the paratactic accumulation of incidents and the mixing of genres. When the film begins, Erendira (Claudia Ohana) is fourteen and living with her eccentric and autocratic grandmother (Irene Papas) in a lugubrious mansion, where the girl serves as maid, cook, and confidante. When Erendira forgets to extinguish the candelabra one night, the mansion catches fire and burns to the ground. "My poor dear," the matriarch tells Erendira without a trace of hostility, "your entire life will hardly be sufficient to repay me." After informing Erendira of the exact extent of her debt, she begins to set up the means of repayment – the prostitution of Erendira. The first customer, the local grocer, weighs Erendira and pays for her by the kilo. Thanks to Erendira's natural beauty and the grandmother's entrepreneurial skills, Erendira soon becomes the most sought-after courtesan in the region. As she services endless files of smugglers, deserters, and other marginals, the grandmother sits at the entrance, haggling over prices and checking coins with her teeth.

As their ambulatory bordello progresses from region to region, the matriarch and her ward, rather like the winged old man in the other story, become the focal point of a carnival of entertainments – snakecharmers, freaks, musicians. At one point, monks abduct Erendira, cut her hair and force her to work, but she escapes and returns to her ogre-like guardian. (That she prefers the ogre to the monks is a damning commentary on the latter.) The pair then begin to

Figure 7.6 Irene Papas as the matriarch in *Erendira* (1983), produced by Atlas Saskia Film / Austra / Cinequanon / Films A2 / Les Films de Triangles / Ministère de la Culture de la Republique Française

follow the electoral campaign of Senator Onesimo (Michel Lonsdale), in hopes of a letter of recommendation "certifying their morality." The senator makes populist speeches in front of a pasteboard luxury oceanliner backdrop; he promises rain and prosperity. In the source novel, the scene evokes the insubstantial pageant of the "revels now are ended" speech in Shakespeare's *Tempest*, where Prospero informs the spectators that the "baseless fabric of this vision" has faded, leaving "not a rack behind." In the Márquez story, the narrator designates the tricks behind the politician's artifice. In the Guerra film, in contrast, it is the grandmother who discerns the trickery, as she sees the senator's aides feverishly producing illusionistic smoke.

The senator ultimately sleeps with Erendira, telling her that they are both alone in the world. Their two professions, the liaison implies, have more than a little in common. (A scene in which the senator caresses Erendira, only to discover that she is wearing a chastity belt is directly lifted from Buñuel's *That Obscure Object of Desire*.) One day, a golden-haired boy named Ulysses sneaks into Erendira's tent and introduces her to a non-commercial love, one which transcends the cash nexus. He persuades Erendira to escape with him in a truck, but his father and her grandmother catch up with them after a desert chase. From that point on, the lovers conspire to take the matriarch's life. After a number of abortive attempts, they finally manage to kill her, but Erendira runs away from Ulysses as well, leaving footprints that mysteriously fill with blood. (A corollary theme in the film has to do with parental violence against children: Erendira abused by her grandmother, Ulysses whipped by his father, a woman [also seen in *An Old Man with Enormous Wings*] turned into an insect for filial disobedience.)

At times, Guerra comes up with particularly telling equivalents for the magical mango world of Márquez, where blood flows green and tastes like mint, and where the sun rises at night and sets at dawn. Guerra preserves the Márquez magic not through Spielbergian pyrotechnics but rather through minimalist evocation. Guerra showcases the words themselves by transforming the third-person narration of the story into the direct-voice dialogue of the film. The well-selected dialogue repeatedly evokes the nonchalant surreality of verbal non-sequiturs. "Waltzes are more expensive," a musician declares, "because they are sadder." The improbable names of the characters – "Amadis" with its reference to Don Quixote's literary exemplar; "Ulysses," with its epic ring – not only invoke the long Menippean traditions of which we have often spoken but also introduce us to a world where ordinary life participates in millennial grandeur and enchantment. The decor, meanwhile, co-mingles with anachronistic abandon turn-of-the-century cameras, World War II planes, and contemporary trucks, reinforcing the feeling of a transtemporal tropical nowhere land. While absurd on a literal level, the superimposition of temporalities speaks on a deeper level of the palimpsestic time of the Latin American experience, where the simultaneous coexistence of different historical strata – pre-Columbian (i.e. indigenous), colonial, and contemporary – is a fact of everyday life. The more obvious magical touches in the film – flakes that change color, love that lights candles, footprints that spring blood – evoke a **la vida es sueño** world where the borders between sleep and wakefulness have become blurred. It is hardly an accident that the film features two sleepwalkers – Erendira and her grandmother. The latter sleeps with her eyes open and rants while she dreams. The dreams share with magical realism their paradoxical nature as both oneiric and realistic. "What day was it in your dream," Erendira asks her grandmother, whose own dreams repeat themselves predictably like so many daily routines.

The images in *Erendira* are carefully crafted, with striking contrasting colors associated with specific characters – royal purple and black for the grandmother, white and blue for Ulysses. The film features perennial Guerra-style devices such as long, elegant tracking shots which advertise their own autonomy, along with some novelties such as the deployment of dissolves in which one of the images momentarily freezes. Guerra, an accomplished musician and composer, also exploits sound, orchestrating music, animal noises, and sound effects into a polyrhythmic montage. The film also plays on diverse generic registers. The attempts to murder the resilient grandmother, for example, are treated in modes ranging from broad farce to tragedy and opera. A poisoned cake lethal enough to kill three elephants provokes nothing more than a self-satisfied belch and a good night's sleep. An explosive device leaves the grandmother only mildly disoriented, rather like those momentarily dazed cartoon characters who rebound quickly after being bombarded by massive quantities of dynamite. Ulysses' interminable knifing of the old woman, meanwhile, not only recalls the ponderous, stylized agonies of tragic opera, but also the invincible, irrepressible monster figures of the contemporary horror film.

The Guerra adaptation interbreeds the intertexts of the novel with other intertexts drawn from other media. The near-indestructible grandmother in *Erendira* presents a grotesque yet queenly presence; she is the direct descendant of the queens of both Sophocles and Ionesco. Claudia Cabezon Doty points out that she recalls the cannibal giant Pietro Pietra in *Macunaíma*.[60] Her royal status is evoked by significant props (chair-throne, regal robes, scepter) as well as by the regal performance of Irene Papas, who as a classical actress comes to us already wrapped in the aura of Greek tragedy. While hugely villainous, the grandmother is not an unalloyed ogre. She is also an oracle who speaks truths, especially about men and love. In a bizarre way, she wants to protect Erendira. In her tyrannically retrograde "feminist" credo, wealth signifies freedom from manipulation by men. Erendira, meanwhile, partakes of the enigmatic. At the beginning, she passively submits to each outrage and humiliation with a mechanically obedient "Yes, Grandmother." In sociological terms, Erendira evokes a familiar reality within Latin America – that of young girls obliged to prostitute themselves to survive. Isolated in her grandmother's mansion, imprisoned within the ambient hypocrisy, Erendira has no critical distance toward her oppression. She evolves from innocence at fourteen – symbolized by her lack of palm lines – to experience at twenty. Ulysses introduces her to love, but she ultimately flees him as well. She remains the matriarch's daughter.

Evocative and suggestive rather than didactic, rooted in deep cultural values rather than in any obvious political agenda, *Erendira* deploys both allegory and realism. The grandmother on some levels forms an allegorical figure for capitalism at its most rapacious and predatory. Portrayed as an immense whale in the Márquez story, she is "embodied" in a more realistic manner in the Guerra film. A realistic subtext undergirds the film, furthermore, in that two central metaphors in the film – debt and prostitution – indirectly call attention to what Brecht called "the causal substratum of events."[61] In the present historical conjuncture, Erendira's situation inevitably calls to mind peripheral globalization and the IMF-sponsored "debt trap" plaguing Latin America. Erendira's debt is massive, cruel, and rooted in a past that weighs, as Marx said, like a nightmare on the brains of the living. The film also points allegorically to the criminal origins of wealth. The grandmother initially becomes wealthy through her association with a smuggler. Like the conquistadores, the grandmother exploits Indian labor, and she renews her wealth by pandering her granddaughter. Childhood prostitution here is both literal fact and social parable. Prostitution is shown not only as pervasive but also as intimately linked to the "respectable" worlds of religion, politics, and the media. The Church, meanwhile, abducts Erendira and exploits her even more brutally than the grandmother had. The politically powerful "man of weight," Sanchez, meanwhile, gives his blessing to the whole enterprise. The entertainment media, finally, are also linked to prostitution: the bordello stands at the hub of an array of commercialized entertainments. While the events of *Erendira* seem fantastic, then, they point to recognizable and familiar social realities. Márquez and Guerra use fantasy to expose the real, and the real to give fantasy a local habitation and a name, in a style at once historical and fabulous.

Carpentier: "The Marvelous American Real"

The Franco-Cuban novelist Alejo Carpentier first coined the phrase "the marvelous American real" in his preface to *El reino de este mundo* (in 1949) to evoke the mestizo magic of a continent, but over subsequent decades he revised and elaborated on its meaning. Although the precise meaning of the phrase is somewhat elusive, it points to a number of themes and leitmotifs: the botanical/meteorological sublime of rainforests, hurricanes, and volcanoes; the prodigious, uncanny qualities of Latin American social reality; the continent's syncretisms of indigenous, African, and European cultures; the tragic heroism of Latin American history as incarnated in figures like Montezuma in Mexico and King Henri Christophe in Haiti; murderous cross-cultural clashes such as Cortez's entrance into Tenochtitlan. Carpentier contrasts what he sees as the labored efforts of the European avant-gardists to **engineer** the marvelous, through techniques of dislocation, with the marvelous as it inheres in Latin American quotidian reality itself. For Carpentier, it is first a question of discerning this marvelous, and then translating it into art. Although the very phrase "marvelous American real" locates this aesthetic in the contemporary Americas, at times Carpentier finds its aesthetic antecedents in earlier times – in the pre-Columbian past of mythological texts like *Popol vuh* and *Chilam balam*, for example – or in distant locations, whether in Hindu and Persian literature or in the Europe of Ariosto, Rabelais, Cervantes, and Shakespeare.

While European modernism sought the fantastic and the marvelous in the exotic and the surprising, subverting conventional "realism" through improbable juxtapositions, "marvelous real" modernism incorporates the fantastic inherent in the ambient social world, where fabulous syncretisms were generated not by manifestos but by a complex and conflictual confluence of cultures. "Surrealism sought the marvelous," Carpentier writes, "but it rarely sought it in reality itself."[62] While for Surrealism the marvelous was little more than a "literary ruse," the marvelous real of Latin America was animated by a deep ritual and collective sense of magic. In fact, an annoyed sense of Latin American cultural superiority, a sense of fatigue with European condescension, informs many of Carpentier's observations. "Our nineteenth century," Carpentier writes, "offers characters who are much more interesting than a little Scottish king like Macbeth."[63] Carpentier mocks the Surrealist André Breton as a "tone deaf," slow learner who only belatedly acknowledged the cultural importance of Latin America.

The title of Carpentier's novella *Concierto barroco* (1974) gives expression to the common trope of the baroque as a cultural dominant in Latin American art and society.[64] The "baroque" has been defined in terms of a loose constellation of traits and concepts – the irregular, the asymmetrical, the excessive, the grotesque, the sensual, the melancholy, the frenetic, the transrealist – all of which have at various times been seen as integral to Latin American culture. By now, the term has become a baggy-monster, evoking such disparate phenomena as: voluptuous religiosity, labyrinthine structures, architectonic decentering, the cohabitation of contraries, the spectacularization of faith, the melding of the sacred and the profane, messianic aspiration, and the exaltation of the senses. For Carpentier, Latin America was baroque by definition because it was formed by "symbiosis, mutations, vibrations, **mestizaje**." Even the extravagant excesses of Aztec sculpture and the texts of the *Popol vuh,* for Carpentier, were "monuments to the baroque." And Carpentier racializes this aesthetic since it is miscegenation that generates the baroque: "The Latin America baroque joins with *criollidad,* with the consciousness whether of the son of a white man coming from Europe, or of a black man from Africa, or of an Indian born in the continent . . . of being something new, of being a new synthesis . . ."[65] Although Europe originated the term "baroque," for Carpentier the baroque was truly realized only in the curvaceous architecture, the teeming vegetation, the polychromatic luminosity, and the telluric vibrancy of Latin America.

A man of immense culture, Carpentier was deeply familiar both with Europe, where he spent much of his life, and with Latin America, where he also lived and which he studied passionately. *Concierto barroco* forms a pan-Latin American allegory which mingles a critique of the cruelty of the Spanish/Portuguese **conquista** with an exaltation of the miscegenated culture which formed the long-term cultural precipitate of conquest. Carpentier shares many traits with Mário de Andrade. Just as de Andrade drew in *Macunaíma* on the taproot of Amazonian legend, calling his hero a "son of the fear of the night," Carpentier in *The Lost Steps* roots the **logos** in the Amazonian forest: "And in the vast night jungle filled with night terrors, there arose the Word."[66] Like the Brazilian writer, Carpentier was a musicologist and musician as well as a novelist. The author of a book on Cuban music (*La musica en Cuba*), he wrote librettos for Cuban composers, along with scenarios for Afro-Cuban ballets. While in Paris, Carpentier became a close friend of Heitor Villa-Lobos, the Brazilian composer who infused Bach-style counterpoint with the variegated cultural energies of the music of Brazil's mestizo popular classes, a counterpoint evoked by titles like "Bachianas Brasilianas." For Carpentier as for de Andrade, musical/cultural counterpoint provides a royal road to the Latin American collective unconscious. And again like de Andrade, Carpentier defended black and Indian cultural values in a very racist period, a time when Carpentier's contemporary, the Cuban musicologist Fernando Ortiz was told that he should not "waste his time studying negroes."[67] (Orson Welles was told the same thing in 1942 when he made his film about Brazilian carnival.) Carpentier builds on Ortiz's notion of "transculturation" as reflecting a more egalitarian and reciprocal shaping of a new culture. Just as Mário de Andrade took his European artist friends to Afro-Brazilian **macumba** ceremonies, Carpentier took them to hear the **son** music of popular Afro-Cuban groups. The major differences between the two writers have to do with race – Carpentier was white, while de Andrade was of mixed race – and with worldly experience; Carpentier was a cosmopolitan world traveler, while Mário de Andrade never left Brazil.

Concierto barroco was first conceived when Carpentier learned, in 1936, that the Italian composer Vivaldi had written an opera on the conquest of the Americas, entitled *Montezuma*, with a libretto by Alvise Giusti. The opera premiered in

Venice in 1733. Further research led to the discovery of a meeting between Vivaldi, Handel, and Scarlatti in Venice during the Christmas carnival of 1709, a meeting referenced in the climactic scene of the novella. The plot line of the novella centers not on Vivaldi, however, but rather on a wealthy Mexican silver miner, named El Amo, and his servants, the Mexican Francisquillo and the Afro-Cuban Filomeno. The Latin American characters follow in the steps of Columbus's voyage, but in reverse motion. They travel to Europe, but only to discover their own misconceptions about Europe and European misconceptions about Latin America. Hoping to discover the wonders of the Old World, they encounter a frosty, disenchanted Europe, deeply in need of New World wonders. Like countless Latin American intellectuals before and after, the protagonist rediscovers his "Latin American-ness" only in Europe.

As the novella begins (in 1709), the wealthy Mexican mestizo El Amo spends his last night at his hacienda before departing on his adventure. Here is Carpentier's description of the hacienda:

> Of silver the slender knives, the delicate forks; of silver the salvers with silver trees chased in the silver of the hollows for collecting the gravy of roasts; of silver the triple-tiered fruit trays of three round dishes crowned by silver pomegranates; of silver the wine flagons hammered by craftsmen in silver; of silver the fish platters; a porgy of silver lying plumply on a seaweed lattice; of silver the saltcellars, of silver the nutcrackers, of silver the goblets, of silver the teaspoons engraved with initials ... (p. 33)

This passage reflects the artfully crafted, "baroque" style of the novella. The prose virtually swims in silver, as if to remind us of the material basis of New World wealth. The literary style, like the architectural decor, is ornate, full of parallelistic motifs and decoration. The long, labyrinthine sentences, meanwhile, remind us of the winding streets of the medinas of Moorish Spain. Instead of using direct description, Carpentier uses evocative metonymies to directly address the senses of the reader. Here the decorative – conveyed by nouns, verbs, and adjectives – is of the essence.

El Amo sets sail from Vera Cruz, but on the open waters his ship is beset by the contrary winds "that on allegorical maps puff out the cheeks of perverse genies, the enemies of seafaring people" (p. 45). Much as Columbus stopped for supplies in the Canary islands before continuing his voyage to the Americas, El Amo, after losing both ship and servant to a Caribbean storm, stops in Havana on his way to Europe. The Cuba El Amo encounters is plunged into mourning

Full Circle: From Cervantes to Magic Realism

Chapter 7

because of an epidemic brought by the conquistadores. In Cuba he hires Filomeno, a freed black Cuban and a singer of "irreverent ditties," as his servant and side-kick. After dressing Filomeno in a red jacket and white wig, El Amo and Filomeno together then set sail for Spain. Rather than being overwhelmed by the grandeur of Europe, in Madrid El Amo misses the "diaphanous mornings" and the "dark-hued sauces" of Mexico. Surprised to be followed by a crowd of beggars cursing the misery of the Spanish city, El Amo reflects that "to him, raised amidst the opulence of Mexican silver and red lava stone, the city appeared drab, gloomy, and mean" (p. 59). Reversing the customary Eurocentric hierarchies, Mexico is portrayed as materially and spiritually superior to Spain.

The episodes of the novel set in Spain make constant reference, quite logically, to Carpentier's adored Cervantes. Earlier, in *El arpa y la sombra*, Carpentier had anachronistically posited Cervantes as the inspiration for Columbus's voyages. In *Concierto barroco*, in an almost verbatim quotation from *Don Quixote*, a traveler interrupts one of Filomeno's stories with an abrupt: "Get on with your story in a straight line, boy . . . and don't be veering off on tangents and curves . . ." (p. 50). Like *Don Quixote*, Carpentier's own novel too constantly veers off on "tangents and curves." Invoking Quixote's destruction of Master Pedro's puppets, he declares: "Had I been Quixote of the *Retablo de Maese Pedro*, I would have thrown myself with spear and shield upon my own people . . ." (p. 122). At another point, El Amo diverts Filomeno with "tales of a mad **hidalgo** who had once roamed these regions" and on one occasion mistook some windmills for giants ("like the one you see there"). Sancho Panza-like, Filomeno protests that the windmills do not resemble giants, but then, with an Afrocentric twist, claims that Africa knew "giants so big and powerful that they played with lightning bolts and earthquakes" (p. 63). As a literary heir of Sancho Panza's proverbial wisdom, Filomeno also cites his proverbs, for example the Mexican aphorism: "Do not put off until tomorrow what you can put off until the day **after** tomorrow" (p. 63).

The duo then moves on to Italy and Christmas carnival in Rome, where "respectable women, disguising their voices, relieved themselves of all the salaciousness and dirty words held in for months" (p. 69). During carnival, only harlots plying their trades were "unmistakably, unimpeachably themselves" within a "universal dissimulation of personality, age, demeanor and shape" (p. 69). Unaccustomed to black people, the Italians pinch Filomeno's cheeks to see if he is wearing a mask. El Amo decides to dress up as the Aztec Montezuma, but the Italians mistake him for an Inca. "Good theme for an opera," one priest comments. Alluding to the spectacular musical entertainments of the time, the priest imagines prodigious feats of *mise-en-scène* (reminiscent of those performed in the Duke's palace in *Don Quixote*: "smoking mountains, apparitions of monsters, and earthquakes with collapsing buildings" and even a "live elephant [flying] through the air" (p. 71).

Carpentier sees "America" itself as a baroque concert, the fusion of European, African, and indigenous elements, at once classical and popular, a cut 'n' mix of highly elaborated melodies and complex African polyrhythms, set in a landscape whose lush vegetation hides the gold and silver which financed European capitalism and Latin American luxury. The title intimates the novella's structure: it is itself structured as a concert. Not only are many of the characters themselves musicians – Vivaldi, Scarlatti, Handel, Stravinsky clearly, but also Filomeno and Montezuma – but also the book's very structure is musical. The novel's orgy of musical **jouissance** climaxes in an astonishingly syncretic jazzistic romp at the Venetian festival, which Africanizes, as it were, the climactic finale to Vivaldi's *Montezuma*. When Priest Antonio implores George Friedrich Handel to "Hit it, you bloody Saxon," the German composer launches into "dazzling variations that violated all the rules of figured bass" (p. 79). Filomeno, meanwhile, runs to the kitchen to fetch a "battery of copper kettles of all sizes." Banging on the utensils with "spoons, skimmers, rolling pins, stirrers, feather duster handles and pokers," he produces "such prodigies of rhythm, syncopation, and complex patterns that he was given a thirty-two bar chorus all to himself" (p. 80). Filomeno then leads a procession which snakes through the concert hall. The conga line moves to a percussive Afro-Cuban chant – "Kalaba-son" – now rendered as a kabalistic "Kabala-sum-sum-sum." But this musical paroxysm divides the European observers along lines of taste and racial hierarchy. Handel calls the whole scene a "fantastic symphony," while Scarlatti complains that Filomeno is forcing him to play "cannibal music!" What Handel calls a "marmelade," Filomeno calls a "jam-session."[68]

In humorous terms, Carpentier's fantastic Venetian symphony calls anachronistic attention to the later-to-be realized Africanization of world music. It was this Africanization that led an erudite composer like Aaron Copeland to say that all American music came from black music, and that has allowed Afro-diasporic musics like salsa and samba and reggae and rap to dominate planetary popular culture. Filomeno's kitchen **batucada** calls attention to the specific modalities of Afro-diasporic music. Shorn in the New World of their freedom and of their African instruments, enslaved Africans managed to tease musical beauty out of the very guts of deprivation, turning discarded low-caste, cast-off materials such as oil drums and washboards into a proud musical resource. In aesthetic terms, this redemption of detritus approach embodies what I have elsewhere called an "art of discontinuity" and "an aesthetics of garbage." These trash-collage styles incorporate diverse idioms, time periods, and materials, whence their alignment with artistic modernism as an art of jazzistic "breaking" and discontinuity, with postmodernism as an art of recycling and pastiche.[69]

At the same time, *Concierto barroco* pinpoints the tendentious ignorance that dismissed non-European forms of music and art as mere "noise" and "barbarous din." Echoing the stereotypical view of blacks as born entertainers, tailor-made for minstrelsy, the novella's Handel protests that blacks should not be featured in opera but only in "masques and comic interludes" (p. 92). Relaying a common view that sees black sexuality as literally "obscene" in the context of "legitimate" theater, Priest Antonio claims that "love between a Negro and a Negress" would be "ludicrous," while love between a black man and a white woman, on the stage at least, would be "impossible" (p. 92). In a transparent reference to Shakespeare's *Othello*, however, Filomeno reminds Antonio that a certain Elizabethan playwright is rumored to have penned a play about a Moor in love with the daughter of a Venetian senator.

Concierto barroco reveals some of what is at stake in debates about representation. In Europe, El Amo and Filomeno become outraged by all the wildly inaccurate images – for example, the roaming elephants – which disfigure Vivaldi's portrayal of Mexico in *Montezuma*. The novella had touched on this theme of exoticizing misrepresentations earlier in its account of a European painting, part of El Amo's collection, that portrayed Montezuma "as part Roman and part Aztec – a Caesar with quetzal-feather headdress seated on a throne, its style a hybrid of Vitican and Tarascan Indian . . ." (p. 35). Historical representations, we see, can be highly problematic. For El Amo, the Vivaldi opera conveys a false message of harmony and optimism, prettifying what was in fact a genocidal confrontation by offering a fictitious reconciliation between the Aztecs (Montezuma) and the Spaniards (Cortez). What El Amo, more lucidly, saw as "a civilization of superior beings . . . imposed through the tragic agencies of reason and force" is transformed into an idyll and "the happiness of peace regained, the triumph of the True Religion, and marital bliss" (p. 114). As the curtain closes, El Amo decries the opera as "false, false, false!" and calls its finale "ridiculous." "There never was a Mexican empress," he adds, and "no daughter of Montezuma ever married a Spaniard." When El Amo protests about the mangling of Aztec names, Priest Antonio responds that "It's no fault of mine that you people have gods with tongue-twisting names – Iztlapalapa, Goazocoalco, Sixalango, and Tlaxcala – that nobody can pronounce" (p. 115). In America, the priest continues, "all is fable, Eldorado and Potosi, ghost cities, single-breasted Amazons and Jesuit-eating cannibals." El Amo also cites himself as an object lesson in the relativity of spectatorial positioning and investment. Taking in the

Vivaldi opera, he says: "I found myself perversely wishing Montezuma would punish the Spaniard for his arrogance . . . I realized all at once that I was on the [Latin] Americans' side" (p. 122).

At the end of the novella, El Amo returns to Mexico, while Filomeno, perhaps fatigued by the racism of the Americas (even though he was technically free in Cuba) opts to remain in Europe. Although Europe still exports colonialism and slavery, in Paris, at least, he would be known as "Monsieur Philomene," while in Havana he would just be "the Negro, Filomeno." But Filomeno also anticipates the future role of black music in Paris, noting that "Louis Armstrong's incomparable trumpet would be heard in a matter of moments" (p. 129). The future will be characterized by rhythms "at once elemental and Pythagorean," a coming together of the musics of various spheres. Filomeno's vision of universal syncretism offers a multichronotopic "threshold encounter," where the moon deities of Egypt, Sumer, and Babylonia meet the orixás of West Africa and the Caribbean, where the Bible becomes transformed into rhythm through "Ezekiel and the Wheel" leading into a Hallelujah chorus less reminiscent of Handel's *Messiah* than of the gospel music of the black church, where, as Yeats put it in another context, "soul claps its hands and sings."

In a final global apotheosis, an ecstasy of *jouissance*, the crowd deliriously follows the jazzistic pied piper Louis Armstrong in a glorious jamming of "I Can't Give You Anything but Love, Baby . . . ," all forming a "new baroque concerto in which, dropping through a skylight by marvelous fortuity, there blended the hours rung out by the Moors of Orologio Tower" (p. 131). (The Tower reference, again, is to Cervantes's *Don Quixote*.) But what is most interesting in *Concierto barroco* is its palimpsestically multitemporal aesthetic, its hosting of impossible encounters between historical figures not only from different centuries but also from different countries. With the multiplication of spaces and locations goes a scrambling of temporalities; more or less plausible dates – the meeting with Vivaldi and Handel on December 26, 1709 – are chronotopically grafted onto impossible encounters, as in the cemetery scene where the Latin American revelers, along with Handel, Vivaldi, and Scarlatti, stumble on the grave of Igor Stravinsky, another "modern" maestro who used jazz to reinvigorate European music. The narrative mimics, then, the polyrhythmic temporality of jazz itself.

For Carpentier, the "fantastic symphony" of Latin America also has a genetic/cultural dimension. Portraying the "marvelous American real" necessarily brings with it the variegated racial spectrum of "*nuestra America mestiza*." Like Mário de Andrade's multi-ethnic "hero without character," El Amo is part indigenous and part European, while Filomeno is epidermically black but culturally mixed. El Amo resembles Montezuma, but he is also a grandson of the conquistadores, while Filomeno is Afro-Caribbean. At the same time, class complicates these relationalities, since El Amo and Filomeno are also master and servant – indeed, El amo means "the master" (even while amo means "I love"), thus evoking the fraught specularity of Hegel's Master and Slave. Yet the hierarchical structure of their relationship does not prevent a Quixote–Sancho-like camaraderie, where the master is mestizo and benevolent, and the slave is mild and eager to be accepted, in a somewhat uncritical version of the Latin assimilationist model.

In an interview, Carpentier once defended the cinema, and adaptations, against the various high-literary attacks made against both. Against charges that the cinema had forced the novel to become more "speedy" and rapid, Carpentier answered that the point was invalid, since the great twentieth-century novels, those of Proust and Mann and Joyce, were extremely "slow." Paul Leduc's *Barroco* (1988), for its part, is less an adaptation of *Concierto barroco* than a kind of tone-poem "inspired" by the Carpentier novella. Rather than relay the plot and dialogue of the novel, the film tries to do a similar kind of aesthetic "work." As the "transatlantic" product of collaborating film companies from various countries, filmed in Mexico, Cuba, and Spain, *Barroco* is syncretic not only in its representations but also in its process of production. While retaining the broad outlines of Carpentier's novella, Leduc adds new scenes evoking the horrific toll of conquest, colonialism, and slavery. Yet at the same time, the film, like the novella, celebrates the hybrid artistic creations that are also the byproduct of conquest. But while *Concierto barroco* is told uniquely through the medium of language, *Barroco* eliminates the key "languaged" filmic track of the cinema – i.e. the synchronous speech track – or, more precisely, non-musical synchronous speech, as if in misplaced respect for the (mistaken) notion that cinema is a "purely visual" medium. This lack of speech would not necessarily be a problem, since Carpentier's novels generally feature relatively little dialogue. While El Amo and Filomeno on one level are more palpably present in the film, through embodied performances, on another they seem but insubstantial vestiges of their novelistic prototypes, precisely because they are deprived of speech. Since in a film we see the characters, their lack of speech seems more anomalous and shocking than in the novel. But, in another sense, the Leduc version simply brings to the fore the musicality that animates the Carpentier novella. Leduc sets each and every scene to music, turning the novella quite literally into a musical, although not of the kind to which Hollywood, or even Mexican commercial cinema for that matter, had accustomed us.

As a revisionist rewriting of an already revisionist source novel, the Leduc film respects the overall itinerary of the journey portrayed in the Carpentier novella, but also embellishes it for a new medium. Carpentier's ornate and "silvery" prose becomes literalized and architecturally "concretized" in the form of ornate decors, transected by majestic tracking shots that take us seamlessly from space to space, country to country, and epoch to epoch. Each locale calls up specific historical associations: the **conquista** in the Mexican sequences; slavery and insurrection in the Cuban sequences; the **Reconquista** and the Spanish Civil War in the Spanish sequences.

Barroco begins in Mexico, where we see a wealthy Mexican, presumably the El Amo of the novel, in his study in an ornate **hacienda**. Carpentier's argentine descriptions are literalized by a palace full of silvery objects. Trigger-happy conquistadores, looking bewildered, fire on everyone in sight, while Africans are rounded up to be sent to the Caribbean as slaves. Gold-obsessed conquistadores and sin-obsessed priests are amazed at the free and natural attitudes (including sexual attitudes) of the Indians. But the film draws a clear line between the spheres of art and politics. Despite conflict, the two peoples communicate through the medium of music, synchronizing their disparate sounds and musical systems.

The scene then moves to a besieged palace in what appears to be colonial Cuba. While the Mexican sequences relay the historical crime of anti-Indian genocide, the Cuban sequences tell the crime of transatlantic slavery. The smoldering embers of burning buildings suggest the aftershocks of a slave revolt. The narrative clock then jumps forward – and here the film dramatically changes Carpentier's equally transtemporal narrative – to the 1930s and the Spanish Civil War. After a musical demonstration of the Moorish influence on Spanish culture, El Amo and Filomeno metamorphose into Mexican and Cuban supporters of the Spanish Republican cause against Franco and fascism. Picking up on the common revolutionary trope of art as a weapon, the cases of the musical instruments are shown to hide ammunition. Silver can serve as ornament, or as revolutionary arm. In an homage to Cervantes and Quixote, Leduc gives us a shot in which a Spanish windmill features prominently. But El Amo also wanders through a wax museum featuring Groucho Marx and Louis Armstrong. The Latin Americans are then admitted to Vivaldi's chamber where a performance of his *Montezuma* is already underway. Leduc emphasizes the tacky anachronisms and mimetic gaffes of the Vivaldi opera.

The film also makes us aware of the subterranean affinities, the reciprocal feedback effect, between the erudite high culture of opera and the popular "low" culture of carnival, which share their extravagant costumes, their transvestism, and their syncretic portrayals. Deploying cinema's redoubled forms of narration and monstration, *Barroco* "performs" the critique about representation voiced verbally by El Amo in the Carpentier novella. The Latin Americans ultimately return home. El Amo, after rediscovering his "American-ness" in Europe, returns to Mexico, where he is serenaded in a cabaret by the same actress whom we had seen die in the Spanish Civil War. Filomeno, for his part, jets to Cuba where he helps animate a lavish salsa party at Havana's Tropicana nightclub. Francisco Rabal, as Vivaldi, delights in the new forms, now appearing as a progressive Spaniard who returns as ally and friend to Latin America. El Amo listens to music on a SONY Walkman; when he removes the ear device, the music stops and the film is over.

Adopting the musical structure of the novella, the Leduc film is structured like a baroque concert divided along classical lines into four musical (and thematic) movements: (1) **andante,** for the autonomy and freedom of indigenous peoples before the Conquista; (2) **contradanza** for the colonial period, as African drums and European minuets begin to fuse and blend; (3) **rondo:** Moorish and European musical currents mingling in Flamenco; (4) **finale:** a fantasy opera of social counterpoint and conflict, a musical summa of conflict and synthesis. Running through the film's sound track is the Caribbean rhythm known as **clave** (key), a 1–2–3, 1–2 staccato beat familiar from salsa and **son.** But the music syncretizes this Afro-Caribbean rhythm with a prestigious instrument rarely featured in salsa music – the cello – setting up a basis for the film's many musical styles, ranging from opera and flamenco to rumba, bolero, and danzon.

The characters in the film, unlike those of the Carpentier novella, remain both nameless and voiceless. At the same time, however, they clearly encapsulate historical/literary energies and typologies. Using a resource available **only** to the cinema – i.e. the distinction between character and performer – the film realizes the temporal condensations and displacements typical of magic realism by having the same players perform different (yet related) roles representing different historical periods. The characters played by Roberto Sosa, Francisco Rabal, and Angela Molina constantly mutate before our eyes, so that Rabal, for example, is both an oppressive conquistador and, later, a progressive friend to Latin America. Character, the technique suggests, is shaped by historical circumstance. Troupes of actors portray diverse characters representing different epochs in Mexico, Cuba, and Spain, as characters metamorphose into one another. An eighteenth-century Mexican señorita becomes a *criolla Cubana*, and a flamenco-dancing gypsy becomes a murdered Spanish *anarquista*, only to return as an international **roqueira.** At the same time, the characters encapsulate diverse cultural and even racial values. Although **mestizo** in appearance, El Amo is the culturally schizophrenic Indiano, the tremulous, mixed, in-between personage divided in loyalties between Europe and America, Spain and Mexico. The mixed-race Latin American man, who accompanies El Amo and Filomeno on their journey, ultimately comes to represent, in his way, the diasporic, syncretic, collective self

Figure 7.7 Musical performance in Paul Leduc's *Barroco* (1988), produced by Instituto Cubano del Arte e Industrias Cinematográficos (ICAIC) / Sociedad Estatal Quinto Centenario / Ópalo Films

of a continent. He confronts both the conquistador and the slaveowner (played by the same actor) and affirms his own indigenous spirit, but one now mixed with Afro-Cuban, gypsy, Moorish, and European culture. As a mestizo/mulatto he incarnates what Vasconcelos called **la raza cosmica**, yet his identity is also conflictual and conflicted. In Cuba, dressed in white pants and red headband, he is taunted by slaves when he discovers them practicing African religions and planning revolt. But his white master also rejects him when he catches him dancing in the master's house. In Mexico he is the Indian, in Spain the Republican.

Like the Carpentier novella, Leduc's *Barroco* orchestrates an encyclopedic orgy of musical citations, mingling the most diverse forms and figures: Bach, Vivaldi, Rossini, Mozart, Schubert, Moorish songs, French chanson ("*Plaisirs d'amour*"), liturgical chants, flamenco, salsa, boleros, mariachi, Spanish Civil War songs, and indigenous and African religious music. But film has the advantage of actual performance, and thus can offer a never-ending spectacle of music and dance, with a grande finale in Vivaldi's opera *Montezuma*. Various forms of music modulate into one another. The same theme is treated on a high and a low register: Rossini's *Barber of Seville* is overlaid with a rumba on the same topic ("*El barbero de Sevilla loco se volvio.*") Popular percussion instruments (maracas, cowbells, quijadas) add "salsa" to the European symphonic style. Festivals both European and African, sacred (santeria) and profane (carnival) energize the text, as various performance groups – the Grupo Xochipiltzahuatl, Grupo Andalusi, Pablo Milanez, Silvio Rodriguez – perform culture through corporal expression and movement. At the end of the film, most of the characters/groups come together at the Tropicana, Havana's 50s-style kitschy nightclub, for a kind of apotheosis.

As Suzana Pick points out, *Barroco* is less an adaptation per se than a thematic elaboration of the ideas of a source text, which operates alongside a diverse range of representations and practices.[70] In this sense, the film hyperbolizes the multiplication of registers and the amplification of intertexts that characterize adaptations in general. Culture, rather than character or plot, is Leduc's primary concern. The film also reproduces, unfortunately, the novella's reduction of women to passive objects of erotic contemplation. Within the film's, and the novel's, masculinist prism, women exist only as sights to be ogled, bodies to be abused, and pleasures to be enjoyed. We see always through the eyes of the male characters, and what we see are a bevy of beautiful women of various races, often naked. Even the scenes denouncing colonial violence against women are compromised by their masculinist politics of the gaze, which constantly offers up the naked beauty of women – and generally **only** of women – for male delectation. In one scene, a young, black woman is strapped naked, with legs spread, to a rack, as an aged white man, clearly identified as a grotesque and evil character, taunts her and probes her with his cutlass. We then cut to the white man's wife, relaxing in her bath; the implication is that the old white man has raped the slave and betrayed his wife. But the slave takes her revenge later; she confronts the white man in the halls of the palace, and kills him with a machete. But, as Tom Fast points out, it is not clear whether these scenes are meant as an indictment of the sexism and racism of white patriarchal society or "merely a sadomasochistic, fetishistic rape and death sequence" which promotes the "stereotype of the dangerous, sexual and exotic dark-skinned woman."[71]

Barroco also exploits another resource available to the cinema but not to literature: the real presence of actual historical decors and props and monuments. The film offers for our contemplation a wide variety of magnificent decors – Mayan ruins (Yucatan), Cuban colonial buildings, Moorish alcazars (Cordoba), plazas, churches, palaces, mosques, and Italian opera houses – rendered as stony, architectural embodiments of history. The Mexican sections are set against the backdrops of famous ruins like Uxmal, Chichen Itza, and Palenque, and the film's various concerts are held in diverse sites variously filled with artifacts from past epochs: pre-Columbian vestiges, colonial treasures of gold and silver, weapons and religious icons. But while the novella emphasizes a tense counterpoint **between** styles, *Barroco* homogenizes disparate cultures through a romantically baroque style which insists on the intense plastic beauty of all it touches. The spectator is assumed to have the requisite cultural baggage and critical faculties to intuit and analyze the relational tensions between and among cultures: indigenous fertility rituals, Afro-Caribbean carnivals, Andalusian Holy Week processions, Italian opera.

On one level, Leduc's *Barroco* develops an aesthetic based on what Nestor Garcia Canclini calls "multi-temporal heterogeneity."[72] It foregrounds the temporally palimpsestic identity of Latin America, criss-crossed by elements from the constellations of cultures which embroider a harlequinade mix of multicultural elements. European masked balls meet Latin American conga lines. Yet, on another level, there is something about *Barroco* that makes it at times feel leaden rather than silvery, aesthetically and culturally "correct" rather than spiritually and aesthetically scintillating. All the requisite elements are there, in every possible combination, and yet the film never takes off, rather like a **fiesta** that never reaches its critical mass of **alegria**. The problem, I suspect, lies in the occasional disconnection between the "pro-filmic" (i.e. what is shown in the shot) and its cinematic handling, especially in terms of camera movement and editing. Throughout the film, Leduc deploys long, inexorably rectilinear tracking shots, reminiscent of those typifying Resnais films such as *Last Year at Marienbad* or *Hiroshima mon amour*. The marvelously heterogeneous cultural materials are presented through a style which recalls the "art film" at its most brilliant, perhaps, but also at its most austere. What works in Resnais as an aestheticized version of European formality, becomes somewhat stilted in the context of Latin America. The impassive camera frames its "objects" – human and material – through a cool, glacial distance, in a style reminiscent of an art documentary made for Arte or Canal Plus.

Instead of the exuberance that pervades Carpentier's novella, an air of melancholy hangs over much of *Barroco*. The carnival is more Venetian than Trinidadian. The unexcited camera never veers from its track, never improvises like jazz, never goes off on digressive tangents like Carpentier's unpredictable narrative. The film thus never translates the exuberance of the marvelous American real. Although the film invokes trance-religions like **santeria**, the film never goes into what Jean Rouch called **cine-transe**; the camera never becomes "entranced" as it does in Rocha's *Terra em transe* (Land Entranced). Although Suzana Pick calls the film an extended music video, it lacks that genre's kinetic energy and sensuous fluidity. The film shows rhythm, but it does not **have** rhythm. There is no happy, drunken surrender to heterogeneity and sensation. It is as if the European art film came to form the cultural and aesthetic superego of the film, disciplining and taming the cultural heterogeneities to which Carpentier had given voice. On the other hand, it could be argued, as Margarita de la Vega-Hurtado does, that the film promotes a transculturated mix, where the film-maker's goal is to have the spectator absorb the music and the baroque visual excess, as if in a dream-like state outside time and historical space. The circular movements of the camera, in this sense, are designed to enclose the viewer in that space.[73]

While it has become a commonplace to speak of the end of innovation and the exhaustion of the avant-garde in a world where all the great works have already been written, in my view the carnivalized aesthetics of the Americas do offer something new. Their aesthetic innovation arises, not exclusively but importantly, from multicultural knowledges and practices. It emerges from the transnational encounter of a Picasso with African sculpture, for example, from the comings and goings between Europe and Latin America of an Alejo Carpentier, from the encounter of a Mário de Andrade with Surrealism, on the one hand, and Amazonian legend on the other, or from Villa-Lobos's simultaneous encounter both with European modernist music and with *sertaneja* melodies. "Newness enters the world," as Salman Rushdie puts it, through "hybridity, impurity, intermingling, the transformation that comes of new and unexpected combinations of human beings, ideas, politics, movies, songs [from] . . . Mélange, hotch-potch, a bit of this and a bit of that."[74] Novels and films like *Macunaíma* and *Erendira* and *Barroco*, each in their own way, offer glimpses of the artistic possibilities of archaic, syncretic postmodernism as expressed in polyperspectival and trance-realist works of art. Artistic innovation, as embodied in these "magic realist" and "cannibalistic" works, occurs on the transnational borders of cultures and communities and discourses.

Conclusion

We have now come full circle – from the "partial magic" of Cervantes to the "magic realism" of Márquez and Carpentier. Many of the works studied here, each in its own way, have used "magic" to go beyond the stale, flat, and unprofitable platitudes of conventional realism. Indeed, it is no accident that so many of the works and aesthetics discussed in *Literature Through Film: Realism,*

Magic, and the Art of Adaptation have strained against the limits of realism through active qualifiers: the **grotesque** realism of Bakhtin, the **magic** realism of Márquez, the **marvelous** realism of Carpentier, the **Sur-realismo** (South-realism) of Glauber Rocha. Carnivalesque realism, for example, turns conventional aesthetics on its head in order to locate a new kind of popular, convulsive beauty, one that dares to reveal the grotesquerie of the powerful and the latent beauty of the "vulgar." Within carnival's cosmic gaiety, laughter has deep philosophical meaning; it constitutes a special perspective on experience, one no less profound than seriousness and tears. Many of the texts we have examined here – *Don Quixote* and *Tom Jones* certainly, but also *Macunaíma* and *Barroco* – echo with the visceral guffaws and "gay relativity" of carnival laughter.

In this text, I have tried to call attention to the multifacetedness and protean variability of the relation between literature and film: films based directly on literature; films based indirectly on literature; novels based indirectly on films; films which are "literary" without being adaptations; novels which are "cinematic" quite apart from being adapted, along with all the sequels, prequels, rewrites, critiques, remakes, updates, and so forth. We have seen a spectrum of styles in the source writers – the reflexive play of Cervantes; the just-the-facts realism of Defoe; the mobilized perspective of Flaubert; the tortured self-consciousness of Dostoevsky; the neurotic narrative of Moravia; the polyperspectival transmutations of Carpentier. We have also seen a huge variety in approaches to adaptation: Welles's radical updating of *Don Quixote*; Jack Gold's revisionist rewriting of *Robinson Crusoe*; the literal fidelity of Chabrol's *Madame Bovary*; unrecognized adaptations like *The Purple Rose of Cairo*; politicized updates like *Macunaíma*; filmic tone-poems like *Barroco*. Time after time we have found that the notion of an originary source and a faithful copy withers away under close scrutiny. The original is never really original. The principle of the sequel was already written into the first renditions of *Don Quixote* and *Robinson Crusoe*. And the adaptation is never merely a copy; both source and adaptation are caught up in multiple repertoires and genres and intertextuality.

I have also tried to suggest some of the ways in which novels, and their adaptations, are "embedded" in their genre, in their tradition, in their culture, and in their historical moment. Bakhtin develops this notion of artistic "embeddedness" in his discussion of Shakespeare. The "semantic treasures Shakespeare embedded in his works," Bakhtin writes:

were created and collected through the centuries and even millennia: they lay hidden in the language, and not only in the literary language, but also in those strata

Full Circle: From Cervantes to Magic Realism

Chapter 7

of the popular language that before Shakespeare's time had not entered literature, in the diverse genres and forms of speech communication, in the forms of a mighty national culture (primarily carnival forms) that were shaped through millennia, in theatre-spectacle genres (mystery plays, farces, and so forth), in plots whose roots go back to prehistoric antiquity, and, finally, in forms of thinking.[75]

Both literature and the cinema, in this sense, inherit millennial traditions. The notion of embeddedness goes far beyond the literary-historical philological tradition of the tracing of "sources" and "influences" to embrace a more diffuse dissemination of ideas as they penetrate and interanimate all the "series," literary and non-literary, as generated by what Bakhtin calls the "powerful deep currents of culture." I have tried here to establish links between novel and film and the more general history of cultures, since adaptation, to paraphrase Bakhtin, "is an inseparable part of culture and it cannot be understood outside the total context of the entire culture of a given epoch."[76]

Intertextuality and "embeddedness," then, help us transcend the dead ends and pitfalls of "fidelity" and "realism." All of which reveals another fascinating facet of adaptation studies. Quite apart from the **quality** of the adaptations, I have tried to show that the adaptive twists and turns performed in the filmic adaptations of novels are fascinating in their own right because they reveal the constantly changing discursive **grids** – cultural, generic, ideological, industrial – through which source novels have been processed and reinterpreted. Filmic adaptations embody and "act out" these grids, rendering them palpable, substantial, visible, and "audible." Adaptations of novels often stage not only these grids but also the evolving critical orthodoxies about a book or a character. Most adaptations of *Don Quixote*, for example, instantiate the romantic, idealist view of Don Quixote as the defender of noble but lost causes, a view which was hardly the view of Cervantes's contemporaries and one which took centuries to develop. Each "take" on a novel thus unmasks a facet not only of the novel itself, but also of the historical time and the discursive culture of the adaptation. Each grid, in revealing aspects of the source text in question, also reveals something about the reigning ideologies in the moment of the reinterpretation. By revealing the prisms through which the novel has been reimagined, adaptations grant a kind of objective materiality to the prisms themselves.

For Bakhtin, entire genres, languages, and even cultures are susceptible to "mutual illumination." It is only in the eyes of another culture, Bakhtin writes, "that a foreign culture reveals itself fully and profoundly."[77] But we can extend this insight in relation to the various media. It is only in the eyes of another medium, one might add, that a **medium** reveals itself fully and profoundly. And this has profound implications for adaptation. Adaptation is potentially a way of one medium seeing another through a process of mutual illumination. It can potentially be an example of what Bakhtin calls "excess seeing," the process of reciprocal relativization and complementarity of perspectives whereby individuals and communities, and, I would add, media, learn from one another. Quite apart from generic shifts and ideological critiques, each medium has its "blindness" and "insight." The filmmaker sometimes sees what the novelist was blind to. Jack Gold "sees" the colonialist misogyny of *Robinson Crusoe*. Woody Allen sees the comic potential of *Madame Bovary*. And Joaquim Pedro de Andrade sees the potential critique of dictatorship to be found in *Macunaíma*. The filmmaker can flesh out and sound out the writer's vision. Adaptation can become another way of seeing, and hearing, and thinking the novel, showing that which cannot be represented **except by film**. The "excess seeing" of cinema at its best, I have tried to show, can illuminate the dark corners and dialogizing backdrops of the classics of world literature.

--------------- Notes ---------------

1   See Ramon Chao, *Conversaciones con Alejo Carpentier* (Madrid: Alianza, 1985), p. 52.
2   Cultural theorists such as Walter Benjamin, meanwhile, have noted the affinity between the baroque and the literary device of allegory. Fredric Jameson, in a different context, has argued that all Third World texts are "necessarily allegorical," In that "even those texts invested with an apparently private or libidinal dynamic ... necessarily project a political dimension in the form of national allegory; the story of the private individual destiny is always an allegory of the embattled situation of the public third-world culture and society;" see Fredric Jameson, "Third World Literature in the Era of Multinational Capitalism," *Social Text* 15 (Fall 1986). But Latin American intellectuals had been working with something like the concept of national allegory long before Jameson, at least since the debates revolving around "*la raza cosmica*" in Mexico or about "*indianismo*" and "*Tropicália*" in Brazil.
3   André Breton, *Entretiens* (Paris: Gallimard, 1969), pp. 237–8. Cited in Jean-Pierre Durix, *Mimesis, Genres and Post-colonial Discourse* (London: Macmillan, 1998), p. 109.
4   See Roy Armes, *Third World Filmmaking and the West* (Berkeley, CA: University of California Press, 1987).
5   Joseph Roach, *Cities of the Dead: Circum-Atlantic Performance* (New York: Columbia University Press, 1996).

6   In *The Formal Method in Literary Scholarship* (trans. Albert J. Wehrle [Baltimore, MD: The Johns Hopkins University Press, 1978]), Bakhtin and P. N. Medvedev note that Europe was liberated from the provincialism of its verism through contact with non-European cultures, a factor which contributed to the development of European modernism. Since these non-European cultural currents were even more present in Latin America, the eagerness with which some Latin American cultures "took" to modernism is quite comprehensible.

7   Quoted by Haroldo de Campos, "Ruptura dos gêneros na literatura Latino-Americana," in *America Latina em sua literatura* (São Paulo: Brasiliense, 1989) p. 293.

8   See Ivan van Sertima, *They Came Before Columbus* (New York: Random House, 1975).

9   See Mary Louise Pratt, *Imperial Eyes: Travel Writing and Transculturation* (London: Routledge, 1992), p. 6.

10 See Seymour Menton, *Historia verdadera del realismo magico* (Mexico City: Fondo de Cultura Economica, 1998), pp. 209–33.

11 See Jean Franco, *The Decline and Fall of the Lettered City: Latin America in the Cold War* (Cambridge, MA: Harvard University Press, 2002), p. 9.

12 Ibid., p. 166.

13 Jean Weisgerber (ed.), *Le Realisme magique: roman, peinture, et cinema* (Paris: Editions L'Age d'Homme, 1987).

14 Jean Franco, *The Decline and Fall of the Lettered City: Latin America in the Cold War* (Cambridge, MA: Harvard University Press, 2002), p. 160.

15 See Weisgerber, *Le Realisme magique*, p. 27.

16 Gabriel Garcia Márquez, *One Hundred Years of Solitude* (New York: Avon, 1971), p. 44.

17 Isabel Allende, *Eva Luna* (New York: Bantam, 1989), pp. 300–1.

18 For a comprehensive discussion of these alternative aesthetics, see Ella Shohat and Robert Stam, *Unthinking Eurocentrism: Multiculturalism and the Media* (London: Routledge, 1994), esp. chs 8 and 9.

19 Bakhtin's only reference to Latin American literature, to my knowledge, is, in *Rabelais and his World* (Cambridge, MA: MIT Press, 1968), to Pablo Neruda, in the context of "grotesque realism."

20 See Emir Rodriguez Monegal, "Carnaval/antropofagia/parodia," and Haroldo de Campos, "A escritura Mefistofélica," in *Tempo Brasileiro* 62 (July–September 1980).

21 See René Menil, *Tracées: identité, negritude, esthétique aux Antilles* (Paris: Robert Lafont, 1981).

22 See Alejo Carpentier, "De lo real maravilloso Americano," *Cine Cubano* 102 (1982), 12–14.

23 Alejo Carpentier, *Concierto barroco* (Havana and Mexico City: Instituto Cubano del Libro and Editorial Siglo XXI, 1975). All references in the text are to the English translation, *Concierto barroco*, trans. Asa Zats (Tulsa: Council Oakbooks, 1988); this quotation is p. 123.

24 See José Guilherme Merquior, *Saudades do carnaval* (Rio de Janeiro: Forense, 1972).

25 See Oswald de Andrade, "Manifesto da poesia Pau-Brasil," in *Do Pau-Brasil a antropofagia e as utopias* (Rio de Janeiro: Civilização Brasileira, 1972), p. 5.

26 For an English version of the "Cannibalist Manifesto," see Leslie Bary's excellent introduction to and translation of the poem in *Latin American Literary Review* 19: 38 (July–December 1991).

27 See Monegal, "Carnaval/antropofagia/parodia."

28 For an in-depth analysis of *How Tasty*, see Darlene Sadler, "The Politics of Adaptation: *How Tasty Was My Little Frenchman*," in James Naremore (ed.), *Film Adaptation* (New Brunswick: Rutgers University Press, 2000).

29 That Mário de Andrade is not recognized as a major literary figure like James Joyce or Marcel Proust, whose poetic universes are no richer than his own, is largely a matter of historical accident and of writing in the "wrong" language. As Mário de Andrade himself pointed out frequently in his writings, artistic prestige is often based on factors having little to do with artistic merit but rather with the power of a country's language, its currency, and even its army. For an illuminating discussion of the international mechanisms of literary prestige, see Pascale Casanova, *La République mondiale des lettres* (Paris: Seuil, 1999).

30 See Theodor Koch-Grunberg, *Vom Roroima Zum Orinoco: Ergebnisse einer Reise in Nord Brasilien und Venezuela in den Jahren 1911–1913*, vol. II: *Mythen und Legenden der Taulipang und Arekuna Indianer* (Stuttgart: Strocker and Schroder, 1924).

31 The basic text here is the critical edition by Tele Porto Ancona Lopez: Mário de Andrade, *Macunaíma: o herói sem nemhum caráter* (Rio de Janeiro: Livros Tecnico e Cientificos, 1978). The English translation by E. A. Goodland (New York: Random House, 1984). The English translation, unfortunately, is egregiously inadequate. While the Brazilian novel is linguistically polyphonic, taking advantage of words of African and indigenous as well as of latinate words, the translation tends to reduce the text to its lowest common denominator of denotation. Where Mário de Andrade uses "*cunha*," the indigenous Tupi word for "woman," the translator renders it simply as "woman," when the native American word "squaw" would have been more suggestive. A key exclamation in the novel – "*Ai, que preguiça!*," literally "What laziness!" but in fact evocative of a delicious stretch in a hammock, is rendered as "What a fucking life!," a phrase more evocative of Manhattan punks than of Brazil's Amazonian modernism. We still await an English translation which would transpose the culturally polyphonic prose-poetry of Mário de Andrade's novel into an equally polyphonic English which would draw on indigenous words, African-American slang, and immigrant speech. As a result, all the translations from *Macunaíma* are my own.

32 Brazilian critic Suzana Camargo explores *Macunaíma* in terms of the Menippea in her *Macunaíma: ruptura e tradição* (São Paulo: Massao Ohno/João Farkas, 1977).

33 Bakhtin, *Rabelais and his World*, p. 19.

34   Quoted in M. Cavalcanti Proença, *Roteiro de Macunaíma* (Rio de Janeiro: Civilização Brasileira, 1969), p. 17.

35   For more on the Bakhtinian conception of "polyphony," see Mikhail Bakhtin, *Problems of Dostoevsky's Poetics* (Minneapolis, MN: University of Minnesota Press, 1984).

36   See Mário de Andrade, *A escrava que não e Isaura*, in *Obra imatura* (São Paulo: Livraria Martins Editora, 1972), p. 268.

37   I further explore the analogies between São Paulo and New York, and between *Macunaíma* and *Zelig*, in "A Tale of Two Cities: Cultural Polyphony and Ethnic Transformation," *East-West Film Journal*, 3: 1 (December, 1988).

38   Haroldo de Campos, *Morfologia de Macunaíma* (São Paulo: Perspectiva, 1973).

39   Ibid.

40   M. M. Bakhtin, "Forms of Time and Chronotope in the Novel," in *The Dialogical Imagination,* trans. Caryl Emerson and Michael Holquist (Austin: University of Texas Press, 1981), p. 198.

41   Abdias do Nascimento, who met Mário de Andrade in the 1930s, describes him, somewhat harshly, as a "typical product of Brazilian racial ideology; one of those mulattos who spend their lives passing and would never admit to any African identity." See Abdias do Nascimento and Elisa Larkin Nascimento, *Africans in Brazil: A Pan-African Perspective* (Trenton: Africa World Press, 1992), p. 25.

42   See Mário de Andrade, *Poesias completas* (São Paulo: Martins, 1972), pp. 203–4.

43   See Mário de Andrade, *Obra imatura* (São Paulo: Martins, 1972), p. 266. For an excellent discussion of de Andrade's "harlequinade" identity, see David Haberly, *Three Sad Races: Racial Identity and National Consciousness in Brazilian Literature* (Cambridge: Cambridge University Press, 1983). For a discussion of the racial question within modernism, see Zita St Aubyn Nunes, *"Os males do Brasil": antropofagia e a questão da raça* (Rio: SIEC, 1989).

44   James Clifford, *The Predicament of Culture* (Cambridge: Cambridge University Press, 1989).

45   See Mário de Andrade, "O desafio Brasileiro," in *O empalhador de passarinho* (São Paulo: Martins, 1972).

46   Joaquim Pedro de Andrade made many films related to the modernist movement: *O poeta do castelo,* a short about the modernist poet Manuel Bandeira (with whom Mário de Andrade exchanged letters); the feature *O padre e a moça,* which adapts a poem by another modernist, Carlos Drummond de Andrade; and *O homem do Pau Brasil,* inspired by the other *monstre sacre* of *Modernismo,* Oswald de Andrade.

47   See Randal Johnson and Robert Stam (eds), *Brazilian Cinema* (New York: Columbia University Press, 1995), pp. 82–3.

48   See Bakhtin, *Rabelais and his World*, p. 308.

49   See Ismail Xavier, *Alegorias do subdesenvolvimento: cinema novo, tropicalismo, cinema marginal* (São Paulo: Brasiliense, 1993).

50   See Ismail Xavier, *Allegories of Underdevelopment* (Minneapolis, MN: University of Minnesota Press, 1997).

51 A well-known historian of Surrealism and the avant-garde, when I told him that *Macunaíma* was one of my favorite films, responded that "I guess the film does have a 'certain primitive charm.'" Thus the same Eurocentric critics who heap praise on Dada and Jarry fail to recognize the cognate brilliance of *Macunaíma*.

52 Quoted in Heloísa Buarque de Hollanda, *Macunaíma: da literatura ao cinema* (Rio: José Olympio/Embrafilme, 1978), p. 122.

53 For a thoroughly researched and closely observed textual analysis of *Macunaíma*, see Randal Johnson, "Cinema Novo and Cannibalism: *Macunaíma*," in Johnson and Stam (eds), *Brazilian Cinema*, pp. 178–90.

54 See M. M. Bakhtin, "Forms of Time and Chronotope in the Novel," in *The Dialogical Imagination*, p. 219.

55 Ibid., p. 198.

56 For an informed account of the workings of Brazilian film censorship during the dictatorship, see Inima Simões, *Roteiro da intolerância: a censura cinematográfica no Brasil* (São Paulo: Terceiro Nome, 1999). Simões emphasizes the stupidity of the censors, who actually looked for a "subversive" named Sophocles, author of a dangerous play called "Antigone."

57 Gabriel Garcia Márquez, *Entre Cachacos I* (Barcelona: Bruguera, 1982), p. 174 (my translation).

58 *Playboy* (December 1982), 174.

59 See Claudia Cabezon Doty, "Literatura y cinema Latino Americano en dialogo inter-medial," *Taller de Letras* 26 (1988), 29–54.

60 Ibid., p. 37.

61 Bertolt Brecht, *Brecht on Theatre* (New York: Hill and Wang, 1964).

62 See Chao, *Conversaciones con Alejo Carpentier*, p. 181.

63 Ibid., p. 183.

64 I worked with the Spanish edition: Alejo Carpentier, *Concierto barroco* (Havana and Mexico City: Instituto Cubano del Libro and Editorial Siglo XXI, 1975), though all references in the text are to the English translation by Asa Zats, *Concierto barroco* (Tulsa: Council Oakbooks, 1988).

65 Chao, *Conversaciones con Alejo Carpentier*, pp. 65–6.

66 Alejo Carpentier, *The Lost Steps*, trans. Harriet de Onis (New York: Longitude, 2001), pp. 162–3.

67 Ibid., p. 296.

68 An understudied phenomenon is the existence of black baroque composers and musicians in the Americas, the subject of Artur Omar's film *Música barroca mineira*, which treats of the free black composers of eighteenth-century Minas Gerais in Brazil.

69 See Robert Stam, "From Hybridity to the Aesthetics of Garbage," in May Joseph and Jennifer Fink (eds), *Performing Hybridity* (Minneapolis, MN: University of Minnesota Press, 1997), pp. 59–78.

70 Suzana M. Pick, "The Politics of Modernity in Latin America: Memory, Nostalgia and Desire in *Barroco*," *Cineaction* 34 (June 1994), 41–50.

71 Tom Fast, "*Concierto barroco o rapsodia canibal?* Defining Latin America's Cultural Identity in *Macunaíma* and *Barroco*," unpublished paper written as a master's project for Caribbean and Latin American Studies at New York University.

72 See Nestor Garcia Canclini, *Culturas hibridas* (Mexico: Grijalbo, 1990), p. 14.

73 Drawn from an e-mail conversation with Margarita de la Vega-Hurtado. Moreover, I would like to thank Margarita for insightful comments on this chapter.

74 See Salman Rushdie, "In Good Faith: A Pen against the Sword," *Newsweek* (February 12, 1990), 52. Interestingly, Europe itself has begun to recognize the artistic value of these hybrid cultures. It is no accident, in this sense, that Nobel Prizes in literature are now going to postcolonial and minority writers, or that the most recent Cannes Film Festival accorded special honors to the Egyptian Chahine and the Iranian Kiarostami.

75 M. M. Bakhtin, "Response to a Question from the *Novy Mir* editorial staff," in *Speech Genres and Other Late Essays*, trans. Vern W. McGee (Austin: University of Texas Press, 1986), p. 5.

76 Ibid., p. 2.

77 Ibid., p. 7.

Index

Index

Index